THE Geopolitics OF Super Power

THE
Geopolitics
OF
Super Power

COLIN S. GRAY

THE UNIVERSITY PRESS OF KENTUCKY

Scholarly publisher for the Commonwealth,
serving Bellarmine College, Berea College, Centre
College of Kentucky, Eastern Kentucky University,
The Filson Club, Georgetown College, Kentucky
Historical Society, Kentucky State University,
Morehead State University, Murray State University,
Northern Kentucky University, Transylvania University,
University of Kentucky, University of Louisville,
and Western Kentucky University.

Editorial and Sales Offices: Lexington, Kentucky 40506-0024

Library of Congress Cataloging-in-Publication Data

Gray, Colin S.
   The geopolitics of super power.

   Bibliography: p.
   Includes index.
   1. United States—National Security.   2. United
States—Military relations—Soviet Union.   3. Soviet
Union—Military relations—United States.   4. Geopolitics.
I. Title.
UA23.G7786   1988   355'.033073   87-25355
ISBN 0-8131-1627-9
ISBN 0-8131-0181-6 (pbk.)

For T.J.—*veritas prevalebit*

Contents

Maps

Acknowledgments

I wish to thank my typists, Kate Boschini, Beth Miller, and Evelyn Ranger, who worked so diligently on this manuscript at different stages. In addition, I am indebted to the skill of Larry Fink in the arcane business of computer mapmaking. Ken Cherry of the University Press of Kentucky is responsible for insisting that I find the time to turn a collection of chapters into a book; he knows my debt to his confidence and persistence.

Although this book is a personal product, it is also an expression of the ethos of the National Institute for Public Policy. That is, it is not an abstract text on geopolitical and strategic theory, and neither is it a global journalistic survey of U.S. security problems. Instead, at least by intent, *The Geopolitics of Super Power* shows the relevance of ideas to the real world of policy action. I am fortunate to have colleagues at the National Institute who combine so well a proper respect for ideas with suitable recognition of the discipline of feasibility.

Finally, I am grateful to my wife, Valerie, and my daughter, Tonia, who were magnificently tolerant—yet again—of what the process of book creation does to family sociability.

1

Introduction

This is an old-fashioned book about U.S. national security policy. Had the long-hallowed British verbal formula of "grand strategy" not been expropriated to such persuasive effect by Edward Luttwak,[1] this book might have been called *The Grand Strategy of the United States*.[2] Grand strategy, and indeed national security policy or strategy, is readily discernible in the words used by senior officials to put a gloss of verbal coherence on the multifarious activities of government with respect to external security.[3] The security objectives that American officials tend actually to pursue with some tenacity can be shown to reflect healthily a mix of inertia and perceived necessity. Those objectives contrast sharply with the more visionary goals of candidates for high office, the wish lists of the very recently elected, and the ritualistic citing of national purposes on occasions of significance for tribal solidarity (the idea that a nation should have "purposes" is a quaint and quintessentially American eccentricity).[4]

In its attitudes towards security, American political culture gives evidence time and again of domination by the seeming paradox of the problem-solving idealist. For the allies, not to mention the adversaries, of the United States, this paradox can be most unsettling when it assumes operational life. It is "the American way" first to identify a more perfect international order and then to identify policy intended to give reality to the ideal. Yet far more often than not the United States behaves very prudently day by day, notwithstanding its nominal adherence to millennial goals.

The broad and well-marked trail that unites every chapter in this book is what may be called "the Soviet problem" for the United States. However, it is more useful and more constructive to treat the Soviet Union as the principal variable element in the external security *condition* of the United States. Whatever coherence obtains in U.S. national security policy is provided by the perceived need to oppose Soviet power and influence. For as far into the future as can be claimed contemporarily relevant, the Soviet Union is going to remain *the* source of danger—narrowly to American national security, more broadly (and quite literally) to the exercise of the values of Western civilization. Furthermore, nothing is, or predictably for many decades will be, as great a source of peril to American lives as the nuclear dangers that pervade the Soviet-American strategic relationship.

U.S. security interests are engaged in the policy realms, *inter alia*, of nuclear proliferation, the international trade in conventional weaponry, poverty and hunger in the Third World, and the stability of the international economic system. But the immediate consequences for the physical security of Americans that lurk in these policy areas pale into insignificance—save insofar as they may be connected by "powder trails" to the superpower rivalry[5]—relative to the dangers inherent in the Soviet-American strategic nexus.

The global scope and complexity of U.S. security interests of varying intensity are more than casually reminiscent of the structure of erstwhile British strategic interests. Compare the contemporary U.S. security problem of the need to protect NATO-Europe while preserving a sufficiency of means to implement a global strategy of nautical maneuver with the problems of Great Britain in its imperial heyday. British statesmen had to cope simultaneously with problems of increasingly global imperial defense and of balancing power in Europe.[6] Without the benefit of much theoretical, let alone explicit defense-analytical, guidance, British statesmen and sailors learned by experience how to keep the country secure. The key to British security lay in proper understanding of the strategic meaning of geography. Despite the variable quality of performance by British statesmen and sailors, "it is no accident"—as Soviet commentators are wont to say—that Britain was not invaded in those centuries; nor was it for want of intention on the part of continental enemies.[7] Every would-be invader learned by more or less painful experience that—in the words of British naval historian and theorist Sir Julian Corbett—"invasion over an uncommanded sea" is not a practical operation of war.[8] Time after time over the course of a century and a half, the Royal Navy assumed the "interior lines" position by concentrating its Western Squadron off Ushant and denying enemy seapower the freedom of action it needed in order to assemble an invasion design, while avoiding strategic distraction that might yield a glittering, if temporary, opportunity to an invader.[9] The point is that although errors inevitably were committed, British national security was protected over a long period of time both by foreign policy and by military (largely naval) goals and methods that derived from extensive experience.

I do not suggest that the late twentieth-century United States could emulate closely the British development and practice of a strategic culture resting upon settled formulas for successful or generally tolerable performance. One must grant the volatility of weapons technology today, as well as the distinctive difficulties of conducting statecraft in a popular democracy. Nonetheless, this book argues that there is an identifiably superior national security policy and derivative strategy for the United States.

If there is to be consistency of purpose and suitability of method in U.S. national security policy, there can be no substitute for accurate appreciation of the character of the Soviet adversary. It would be difficult to improve on the following judgment by Robert Daniels: "Americans must face a basic fact: Russia is a mammoth power that will not disappear or cease to challenge the United States, regardless of the coloration of its government. The contest for world influence between the United States and Russia is grounded in history—indeed it was foreseen by writers in Europe and America more than a century ago. Russia will continue to be guided by the pride, ambitions, and interests that have carried over from prerevolutionary times—and no mere alteration in regime or ideology will quickly eliminate them."[10]

This book develops the thesis that the essential strategic relationship of antagonism between the United States and the Soviet Union constitutes a realm of necessity for U.S. policymakers. The United States is at liberty to choose among alternative policy goals and means, but it is not at liberty to choose a policy attitude of indifference toward Soviet power without expecting severely adverse consequences sooner or later. The United States can greatly influence the terms of strategic engagement with the Soviet Union but not the enduring fact of engagement. A U.S. president might decide to "fold American tents" abroad but should not harbor the illusion that such a retraction in the U.S. security perimeter would alter the nature of Soviet-American security relations.

This book is not about the totality of the rich tapestry of international relations, nor is it about U.S. foreign policy per se. Its purposes are, first, to explore and (where appropriate) explain the nature of the single strategic relationship that, if mismanaged, could kill most Americans in the span of a single day; and, second, to present the structure of the national security policy (and some detail as to methods and means of implementation) that addresses most effectively the most serious of the dangers that Americans face.

2

Sir Halford Mackinder and Geopolitics

The geopolitical ideas of the British geographer Sir Halford Mackinder have been accorded the first-echelon theoretical role in this book because they provide an intellectual architecture, far superior to rival conceptions, for understanding the principal international security issues. Geopolitics is about "the relation of international political power to the geographical setting."[1] It is about the "high politics" of security and international order; about the influence of enduring spatial relationships for the rise and decline of power centers; and about the implications of technological, political-organizational, and demographic trends for relations of relative influence. Mackinder was the intellectual father of U.S. containment policy after World War II. George Kennan may not acknowledge the debt, but the "Long Telegram" from Moscow on February 22, 1946, and the article by "X" in *Foreign Affairs* of July 1947 directly or indirectly bear the hallmark of Mackinder's worldview.[2]

Mackinder's geopolitical work is grand theory at its best. As one must expect of a holistic thinker, he was more concerned with the essential nature of phenomena than with the precise detail of their delimitation. However, skeptical readers are advised that Mackinder's interpretations of historically shifting power relationships in their geographical setting have stood the test of time much better than have the slings and arrows of his legion of critics.[3] What Mackinder provides is framework and perspective, organizing qualities that American foreign and defense policy debates most signally tend to lack.

The essence of Mackinder's theory, which lies in the "oppositions" at its core, has been usefully summarized by a recent intellectual biographer: despite the changes wrought by World War II, "the great geographical realities remained: land power versus sea power, heartland versus rimland, centre versus periphery, and individualistic Western philosophy versus a collective Eastern doctrine rooted in a communal past. Mackinder died but his ideas live on."[4] Writing in 1904, with subsequent revisions in 1919 and 1943,[5] Mackinder provided an intellectual frame-work for understanding recurring patterns in international power rela-tionships that was well founded in history and geography and that the events of the twentieth century have substantiated in most essentials. It was Mackinder's, though really the world's, misfortune that public recog-nition and some official comprehension of his central idea of the Heart-land did not occur until the fall of 1939—thirty-five years after he had first advanced his thesis.[6] Ironically, Mackinder's reputation, and certainly the reputation of geopolitics as a political and strategic expression of applied geography, suffered no little damage because his ideas were believed to be influential in Nazi Germany.[7] In common with the British military phi-losophers of armored warfare in the interwar period, Mackinder and his geographical philosophy of world power found more avid disciples abroad than at home. Britain was not ready in 1904, or 1938 for that matter,[8] to be told that the world was entering the post-Columbian era and that the future probably belonged to landpower in general and the great landpowers in particular. Admiral Alfred T. Mahan's gospel of command of the sea through decisive battle waged by line-of-battle ships was the authorized creed in Britain, as in many countries.

Prior to the Great War the rise of Japan and the United States as extra-European naval powers, though potentially deadly to the global strategic integrity of the maritime empire of Britain, did not pose an imminent threat. The Anglo-Japanese Alliance of 1902 was critical in allowing the homeward redeployment of force in answer to the growing German menace. The U.S. Navy, pre-1914, was becoming formidable in numbers, but it was short in strategic reach because it lacked overseas bases (and the Panama Canal was not open until 1914). The dilemmas and risks in Britain's centuries-long naval balancing act between the Mediterranean and home waters were eased mightily in 1904 and 1907 by the limited ententes with France and Russia, respectively. British statesmen in the decade after Mackinder's 1904 address to the Royal Geographical Society[9] were worried preeminently about the ability of a German *Drang nach Western*, not a *Drang nach Östen* to seize command of the Heartland. Not-withstanding the overseas imperial ventures of Japan and the United States at the turn of the century, British eyes were focused strategically on Europe—not on the world, and certainly not on theoretical constructs of shifting patterns in world power relations.

According to Mackinder, the history of Eurasia is a history of the competition between security communities preeminent in seapower and those preeminent in landpower. The history of Europe, he argued, was forged under the dual and sometimes directly competing pressures pro-vided by raiders from the sea and raiders from the steppelands of central Asia.

Mackinder's World

HEARTLAND

MARGINAL LANDS

DESERT

OR OUTER CONTINENTS

ISLANDS

Modern times—the "Columbian age," from the close of the Middle Ages until the time of Mackinder's initial theorizing in the early 1900s— saw the domination of the Atlantic-facing maritime empires of western Europe over much of the known world. This domination was possible because of the superior mobility and flexibility of maritime as opposed to land transportation. For example, the British and French navies could sustain expeditionary forces in the Crimea in 1854-56 with greater logistic ease than the Russian Empire could supply and reinforce its army there. In important part this was possible because allied maritime demonstrations in the Baltic compelled the Russians to prepare heavily against the possibility of raids or invasions in that crucial region.[10]

Although the littoral state-empires of peninsular Europe were in the ascendant from about 1500 to 1900, there was always a vast continental hinterland in Eurasia that was utterly inaccessible to direct pressure from the sea. This area, called by Mackinder "the geographical pivot of history" and also—the word that was to gain universal currency—the "Heartland,"[11] in mediaeval times was dominated by the succeeding empires of the steppes. The Heartland of a Eurasia-Africa that Mackinder called the "World Island" (and sometimes described geographically as a "promontory" because of the strategic impenetrability, inward or outward, of the northern coastal region)[12] has the potential to be the seat of a true world empire. In Mackinder's view the potential of the Heartland in its contiguity of territory, unmatched natural resources, and possibilities for promoting and sustaining demographic superiority has awaited suitable political organization, technological change in transportation, and perhaps sufficient folly in the statecraft of those peripheral communities who would fail to discern the threat to their independence that lurked on the steppes.

Mackinder predicted that the coming of railroads to the Heartland would dramatically alter the relative strategic advantage between the seapower of the maritime empires and the landpower of the great continental states, to the benefit of the latter.[13] Writing in 1904 and again in 1919—in the first case as a dispassionate applied geographer, in the second very much as a concerned citizen and devotee of the British Empire and indeed of the humane democratic values of the Western (maritime) world—he did not predict which polity would control the Heartland; it could be Russia or Germany or even, eventually, China in combination with Japan (or some mix of these). But he did warn that whoever became the Heartland power under modern political and economic conditions could make a plausible bid for a global imperium.

It must be added that Mackinder was not a determinist. Just as he did not predict, even in 1919,[14] that Russia would succeed in controlling the Heartland, neither did he predict that the peripheral maritime world— what he called the "Inner or Marginal Crescent" and what the American

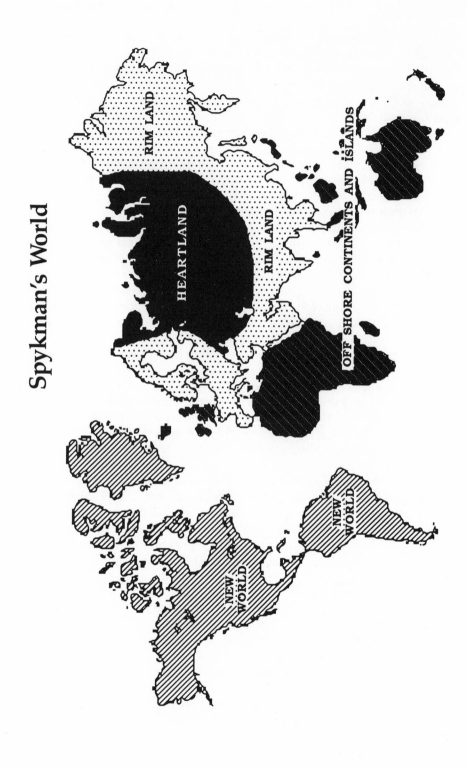

Spykman's World

geopolitical theorist Nicholas Spykman was to term the "Rimland"[15]—would be incapable of containing the outward pressure of the Heartland. Writing in 1919 in the hope of influencing the peace settlement of the Great War, Mackinder judged control of eastern Europe to be the key to command of the Heartland and of its resource potential as a necessary basis for a bid for World-Island (and eventually world) conquest:

> Who rules East Europe commands the Heartland:
> Who rules the Heartland commands the World Island:
> Who rules the World Island commands the world.[16]

Mackinder recommended creation of a *cordon sanitaire* of viable states in eastern Europe for the purpose of separating the German and Russian power centers and hindering—even precluding—the ability of either to gain or use the Heartland position for political and strategic unification of the World Island. The fate of east-central Europe in the later 1930s attests not so much to a lack of soundness in Mackinder's vision, though there are grounds for criticism there, as to the persisting blindness on the part of the 1914-18 victors to the strategic functions of the new "barrier" states, preeminently Czechoslovakia and Poland, that were licensed at Versailles.

Mackinder's conceptual opposition of seapower and landpower and the shifting relation of net advantage between them had reference to the struggle for power and space in Eurasia. Yet he always understood that either seapower or landpower, to be strategically effective, must be transmutable into the currency of the other. As a British patriot and imperialist[17] he was concerned not with the prospect of a superior continental landpower per se—be it Germany, Russia, or Germany-Russia (or Russia-Germany); except at the margins, landpower and seapower cannot wage a direct struggle for decision. Rather, he was alarmed at the possibility of a dominant Heartland power being so free from continental distraction that it could develop a strategic challenge to the maritime world in the natural geographical element of that world. In 1919 he wrote: "The surrender of the German fleet in the Firth of Forth is a dazzling event, but in all soberness, if we would take the long view, must we not still reckon with the possibility that a large part of the Great Continent might some day be united under a single sway, and then an invincible sea-power might be based upon it?"[18]

Thirty-nine years after presentation of his pathbreaking paper "The Geographical Pivot of History" on January 25, 1904, before the Royal Geographical Society, Mackinder, then eighty-two, was invited by the editor of *Foreign Affairs* to develop his geographical ideas further, particularly the contemporary relevance of his Heartland concept. The great man made it very plain in his article-in-response that the Heartland, defined in 1904 strictly with reference to the physical geography of continental or Arctic Ocean river drainage (that is, inaccessibility to seapower), should now be defined as approximately coterminous with the Soviet imperium (except for trans-Yenisei Siberia).[19] "All things considered, the conclusion is unavoidable that if the Soviet Union emerges from this war as conqueror of Germany, she must rank as the greatest land power on the globe. Moreover, she will be the power in the strategically strongest defensive position. The Heartland is the greatest natural fortress on earth. For the first time in history, it is manned by a garrison sufficient both in number and quality."[20]

Mackinder assumed that it was in the nature of a great power to seek such greater power as internal strength and external opposition would permit. In short, he did not claim that the Heartland U.S.S.R. would rule the World Island of Eurasia-Africa, let alone the world—including what he called the lands of the "Outer or Insular Crescent," the Americas and Australasia.[21] But he did believe that to be secure in its Eurasian holdings the Heartland power certainly would seek to dominate the marginal lands, or Rimlands, of peripheral Eurasia. The Heartland's motive would be to deny the insular maritime imperium of the United States and Great Britain continental access of a kind actually or potentially threatening to the Heartland-Soviet hegemony.

Mackinder's strategic vision was truly global. That fact sharply limited his influence until the very end of his life (he died in 1947), since his British official audience, notwithstanding its responsibility for a globe-girdling empire, was fixated narrowly and Eurocentrically upon dangers to the balance of power.[22] Two generations of British statesmen, worried about actual or impending German threats to Britain through the Low Countries and in the North Sea, were not easy to impress with the hypothetical notion of a Heartland superstate and its central Asian center of strategic gravity. By the time Anglo-American pragmatists recognized the shape of a very dangerous forthcoming world in Mackinder's "philosophical geography"—which is to say slowly after 1939 and with a great rush in 1943-44—it was too late to preclude the emergence of that world.

By far the most favorable opportunity for the maritime world to buy itself time would have been from late 1918 to early 1920. Briefly in 1919 Mackinder was British High Commissioner for South Russia: in effect he was British political adviser/pro-consul to General Anton Denikin and his White Army. Sadly, if inevitably, Denikin would not take his advice (in good part for excellent Russian patriotic reasons that were critical to the popular appeal of his cause: for example, his refusal to sanction territorial losses from what had been Imperial Russian territory). Neither would the British government. On January 29, 1920, Lloyd George's understandably war-shy cabinet flatly rejected Mackinder's plan to bring down or very severely fence in the new Soviet republic before it had consolidated its authority.[23]

In his 1943 article in *Foreign Affairs*, Mackinder sketched his design for an enduring association of Rimland and insular maritime states that should be capable of containing the Heartland power. It is noticeable that he wrote as though this power would still be Germany. (The Soviet flood tide had only just begun to flow back from the Volga and the Caucasus after the successive defeats of German arms in southern Russia in the winter of 1942-43;[24] Mackinder's article appeared simultaneously with the launching of the last, and ruinous, major German initiative on the Eastern Front, at Kursk, July 5-16, 1943.) He speculated on the creation of "unbreakable embankments of power" that would canalize a "cleansing counter-philosophy" to "sweep the German mind clear of its black magic." Those embankments would comprise both the "vast natural fortress [of the Heartland-Soviet Union, with]...a garrison adequate to deny entry to the German invader" and

my second geographical concept [the first was the Heartland], that of the Midland Ocean—the North Atlantic—and its dependent seas and river basins. Without laboring the details of that concept, let me picture it again in its three elements—a bridgehead in France, a moated aerodrome in Britain, and a reserve of trained manpower, agriculture, and industries in the Eastern United States and Canada. So far as war potential goes, both the United States and Canada are Atlantic countries, and since instant land warfare is in view, both the bridgehead and the moated aerodrome are essential to amphibious power.[25]

Mackinder had written in favor of an Atlantic alliance as early as 1905. In 1942, pursuing this theme, he said: "Such an association might have avoided this second World War, and ought to have done so if the triple alliance of the United States, Great Britain and France, negotiated after Versailles had not been abandoned before it became operative."[26] He was agnostic on the question of whether or not Rimland Eurasia-Africa would be kept free of domination by continental Heartland power. Whereas Mahan emphatically asserted and reasserted the ability of seapower to hold its own against new challenges from the land,[27] Mackinder was not in any sense partisan in his proposition that the half-millennium era of maritime dominance was ending. In keeping with the spirit of his theory, it is appropriate to notice that the empires of the steppes did not conquer peninsular Europe in the pre-Columbian era (though they had conquered much of maritime China in 1260), and that the maritime empires of Atlantic-facing Europe did not conquer Heartland Eurasia in the Columbian era. One should not read into Mackinder the proposition that the Heartland Soviet Union is "destined" to rule Eurasia, let alone the world.

In 1919 Mackinder warned that: "we have defeated the danger on this occasion [of a victory by land power, i.e., Germany, over sea power, i.e., the British Empire], but the facts of geography remain, and offer ever-increasing strategical opportunities to land-power as against sea-power."[28] The decades that have passed since he wrote those words have not borne out the worst of his anxieties. The seapower whose future most concerned him, Britain, has been replaced as principal security organizer for the Western world by a strategically insular power with a continental base of resources. Furthermore, the Second World War and the subsequent Soviet-American antagonism have demonstrated that the geostrategic unification of Eurasia is a task of heroic dimensions. Nevertheless, Mackinder provided a tolerably accurate framework for understanding contemporary Soviet-American relations; asked many of the right questions and identified plausible reasons for worry about the defense of Western values; but fortunately was overly pessimistic in his belief that the twentieth century would "offer ever-increasing strategical opportunities to land-power as against sea-power."[29]

3

The Problem of Security

Governments and their advisors seek security through such certainty as they can procure. Since few policy matters in time of peace, and even fewer in war, are truly certain, magic formulas have a way of substituting, de facto, for an unattainable predictability. Prior to the rise of Imperial Germany after the Treaty of Frankfurt (1871), Great Britain had, in its balance-of-power policy and its understanding of the utility of the "Ushant Position" for naval deployment, probably as close an approximation to a political-military formula to guarantee national security as any country could ask. But geostrategic conditions change, and old formulas must give way to new methods, if not always to new goals.[1]

For every historical example of a "Ushant Position" that worked well over a long period of time, one can locate several formulas that manifestly could not bear the political or military traffic required of them. In 1914 the French general staff had (long) identified the key to French security in the *élan vitale* of the *poilu*. Victory was believed to be certain because of the allegedly superior moral qualities of French citizen soldiers. France had learned, or mislearned, from its experience of defeat in 1870 that the *offensive à outrance* was the proper method of war for a country that had grave doubts about the reliability of its allies and about the material and numerical strengths of its army.[2] When war came to France on August 3, 1914, the French war plan solved the problem of uncertainty over enemy intentions by the simple device of ignoring the subject.[3] With words of quite breathtaking folly, Plan 17 declared: "*Whatever the circumstances*, it is the C.-in-C.'s intention to advance with all forces united to the attack of the German armies" (emphasis added).[4] While France sought certainty of victory in a revival on a strategic scale of the tactical offensive spirit of the armies of the first Napoleon, the German general staff believed it had found the security of certain success in the process of planning itself. Overimpressed with the potential of an outflanking movement on the grand scale and underimpressed (not for the last time in twentieth-century warfare) with command, logistic, intelligence, and plain human frailties, the Germans thought they had their formula for victory.[5]

More recently, the problem of security in a nuclear age has been re-solved for many people through what amounts to a happy assumption that deterrence is existential. From the writings of such scholars as Robert Jervis and such public figures as McGeorge Bundy,[6] one learns that the age of force-backed forward diplomacy between nuclear-armed super-powers has effectively been banished by the prospect of general nuclear catastrophe. Elsewhere on the range of contemporary attitudes toward national security, one finds those who seek certainty of control through the elaboration of fine-grained theories of limited war.[7] I am not at all unfriendly to the weaving of strategic theories for the control of escala-tion, but I am nervous lest the nominalist fallacy apply. Speculative theory has a way of capturing its authors and blinding them to the difference between named conceptions and prospective realities. For example, one can speculate, as Carl Builder has, that deployment of strategic non-nuclear weapons might create another and very useful ledge on the slope toward a general nuclear war.[8] But there are excellent reasons, having to do with friction in war and probable Soviet style and level of technical accomplishment, for being very modest in one's strategic claims for this new class of weapons. "The refined calculations of the nuclear games-men," in McGeorge Bundy's words,[9] constitute in one perspective a sensible and prudent approach to the problems of nuclear deterrence. Another perspective can see in those "refined calculations" and necessari-ly theoretical elaborations an attempt to seek enhanced security through the imposition of an essentially American intellectual order upon the chaos and uncertainty of hypothetical nuclear conflict.[10]

This book is concerned primarily not with the identification in detail of means and methods of forwarding the objectives of national security policy but rather with the identification of the longer-term objectives of that policy. It is an ancient truth, however, that inadequate means and faulty operational methods can reduce sound strategy and wise policy to the status of little more than vain ambition. Brilliance in strategy sub-sumes a prior appreciation of tactical feasibility.[11] Means and methods in the military sphere are not discussed at length until Chapter 14, but they are in my mind throughout the book.[12]

It is not the perennial quest for certainty or for the reduction of uncertainty that merits criticism but the fact that such a quest all too often degenerates into the hunt for a panacea. Such a hunt tends not to go unrewarded for very long. Two points are of particular importance here. First, much of the detail concerning means and methods for policy implementation is necessarily fraught with a major level of uncertainty. Second, the strategic meaning of the Soviet Union for U.S. national security policy should be made comprehensible.[13] U.S. defense commen-tators debate in great detail whether this or that basing mode for this or that number of intercontinental ballistic missiles (ICBMs) will provide an adequate war-fighting capability for deterrence. But there is too little debate about the enduring structure and evolving terms of the Soviet-American strategic relationship. If one poses the question addressed in an article to his readers by journalist Thomas Powers, "What Is It About?" ("it" being the Soviet-American rivalry),[14] one tends to meet with either a baffled silence or an ideological "bumper sticker" reply. Yet the nature of the rivalry influences mightily the scope for relatively safe innovation in U.S. national security policy. If one does not understand what the rivalry is about, one is unlikely to have a secure intellectual grip on the subject of how best to prosecute it or to have anything worthy of respect to contribute on the issue of its prospective duration and the terms, if any, for its possible conclusion.

Because it is rooted in geopolitical soil, the character of a country's national security policy—as contrasted with the strategy and means of implementation—tends to show great continuity over time, although there can be an apparently cyclical pattern of change.[15] But even if foreign or, more inclusively, national security policy remains unaltered in its essentials, major shifts in means and methods may be necessary. As circumstances alter, so may the weight of the burdens placed upon a defense establishment if strategy is changed.

A classic case is that of British strategy under Herbert Asquith's Liberal government prior to 1914. The port of Antwerp had long been regarded by Britain as "a dagger pointing at the heart of England." For the better part of three and a half centuries prior to the 1900s, British statesmen had endeavored, with more than fair success, to keep that dagger either sheathed or blunt through manipulation of a balance-of-power system, with Great Britain as the agile "balancer" (hence the sobriquet "perfidious Albion"). The British purpose was to deny continental hegemony to any state or coalition of states, because a hegemonic enemy, undistracted by the need to wage major conflict on land, would have been able to use all or most of western Europe as a base for developing a quantity and quality of seapower fatal to Britain's ability to command the narrow seas and hence to thwart invasion and protect its maritime commerce. As an insular and relatively affluent power, in no need of a large (and civil liberty–threatening) expensive army for homeland defense, Britain applied its weight very substantially through maritime power and the financial subsidization of continental allies.[16] Belatedly, this method was recognized as obsolete when the rise of a unified Germany removed much of the traditional balancing efficacy of a maritime peripheral strategy, diplomatic agility, and timely subsidies.

Maritime preponderance remained important, even essential, as Gen. Erich Ludendorff was to discover to his cost in 1917/18,[17] but Germany was not nearly so susceptible to pressure from maritime action as Britain's previous continental enemies had been—Spain, the Netherlands, and France. Like the Soviet Union today, Imperial Germany lacked overseas possessions of great strategic or economic worth to the metropolitan country. The German High Seas Fleet in 1914 (and the Soviet Navy in the 1980s) could venture into blue water only with the acquiescence of a Great Britain (the United States and NATO) which, geostrategically, guarded the exits to the open ocean. Notwithstanding Kaiser Wilhelm's dreams of *Weltpolitik*, Imperial Germany was not a maritime empire; hence the British Royal Navy could not provide compensation in the seizure of sugar islands for defeat or stalemate on the Western Front.[18]

British foreign policy objectives did not change in the 1900s, but there was a dramatic shift in British strategy as the identity of the "most probable enemy" shifted from the Franco-Russian alliance to Germany. For the first time in its history, the British Army organized and trained in peacetime to provide an expeditionary force intended (and more or less committed) to stand with a continental ally from the beginning of a future war.[19]

The example of Britain in the 1900s illustrates the fact that strategy can change in a major way even when foreign policy objectives do not. At a yet more elevated level of policy, an essential continuity of purpose is possible despite the appearance of a fundamental redirection. It could be argued that the very obvious changes in U.S. foreign policy behavior required for participation in the world wars of this century and, more particularly, in global political-military affairs after 1945 show a genuine change not so much in foreign policy objectives as in method, alterations mandated by dramatic shifts in the balance of power in Eurasia. Until the twentieth century the United States had scant need of an explicit, purposive foreign policy or, *ergo*, of an implementing strategy. Edward Luttwak has argued:

> Until the beginning of this century, the United States enjoyed the classic prerogatives of the great sea powers of history: it could take as much or as little of the world's affairs as it wanted. Neither a powerful navy nor broad oceanic borders assured this fortunate state. Rather was it the power of Great Britain, a nation then itself exquisitely strategical, that secured for the Americans all they really needed of the outside world...the Americans had the Great Powers balanced for them and kept from their door.... Until 1945 the Americans were merely called to war, and that briefly. It was the British who set the strategy and who chose our enemies for us.[20]

British statecraft in the nineteenth century was never as "exquisitely strategical" as Luttwak claims, but his main point is well taken. With the Royal Navy commanding the oceans and the maritime gateway from Europe, the United States was at liberty to devote itself to continental empire-building without let or hindrance from the great powers of the day. The uniquely American experience in nation-building left an enduring and distinctive stamp upon American political and, hence, strategic culture and its derivative national style.[21] The United States was far removed from the defense concerns endemic to societies that must coexist with predatory and powerful neighbors.

The pressures for continuity in policy tend to be as compelling as they are inevitable. Dramatic change, even the semblance of such change, is difficult to effect politically in the absence of appropriately dramatic, legitimizing changes in the external or internal circumstances of U.S. security. So long as a policy is working "well enough," which may mean no more than that it has yet to fail unambiguously, the certain costs of experimentation are likely to weigh more heavily in the balance of deliberation than the costs of managing a familiar structure of policy. Much of the NATO-European objection to President Ronald Reagan's Strategic Defense Initiative owes little to the outcome of careful strategic analysis but flows from a deeply ingrained conservatism, a strong disinclination to sanction what could lead to important changes in alliance strategy and in burden-sharing within the alliance.[22] Even if the European allies could be persuaded, on the evidence of analysis, that the SDI would promote greater security for all alliance partners, the risks associated with a "defensive transition" would still be accorded a large (perhaps unreasonable) measure of respect. Incentives are lacking for the voluntary assumption of new risks.

In Chapters 10-13 I offer objective characterizations of five central organizing concepts for U.S. national security policy, ranging from disengagement to a far more activist role in the world than that of today. Such an identification and review of different policy concepts may appear to be only an academic exercise, since basic orientation in national security policy, the identity of friends and actual or possible enemies, and the character of the international order favored by the United States rarely seem to be matters for choice by Americans. These important features on the landscape of external policy lend themselves to discussion almost in deterministic perspective, as being imposed by geopolitical circumstance. And indeed, it is essential that the geopolitical structure of U.S. security problems be identified and described before full play is given to concepts that differ radically from those familiar in the policy practice and rhetoric of the recent past.

There is, of course, no "hidden hand," no Iron Law of Geopolitics, that requires the United States to maintain what amounts to a client-state protection system for the containment of the Soviet Union as a landlocked continental superpower. States are entirely capable of failing to appreciate their own survival interests. Britain and France failed utterly to recognize the quality of their national interest in stopping the accelerating pace of

German political aggression in 1938. In retrospect the path of policy folly is generally plain enough, at least in the sense that the historian knows the path that did lead to disaster, even if the existence of available alternatives must forever remain a matter of conjecture. When approached geopolitically, the realm of necessity in policy tends to loom very large. With respect to understanding the great conflicts of history, however, the perils of determinism are probably less serious than is the temptation to stress the role of fortuitous elements. For examples very far apart in time, one can argue that the Punic Wars were triggered by an unintended process of rather casual escalation: the commercially minded Carthaginians did not understand the scale of risk they were running in provoking highly militaristic Republican Rome.[23] Similarly, one can demonstrate that the First World War need not have occurred when it did. But it is one thing to show that the First Punic War did not have to begin in 264 B.C. or the First World War in 1914; it is quite another to assert that Carthage and Rome could have avoided an armed struggle for supremacy or that the European balance-of-power system could have maintained order for long after 1914 without a general war.[24]

Albeit rarely, great debates on foreign policy do occur in the United States: for example, over expansion in the 1840s and the late 1890s; over involvement as a guarantor of international order in the context of the Versailles Treaty and the League of Nations in 1919; over military involvement in Europe in 1940-41; over the proper character of U.S. containment policy in the late 1940s;[25] (arguably) over the basic character of the United States as an "ordering power" in the late 1960s and early 1970s; and, most recently, over the proper mix of positive and negative sanctions in relations with the Soviet Union (the debate over detente that sputtered from 1975 until 1979).

What is apparent is that the terms of foreign policy debate on similar themes have varied markedly from era to era. The dawn of "the American Century" was announced by Henry Luce in 1942.[26] It was accepted so widely and deeply as a fact that the major demarches in policy of the 1940s, which signaled cumulatively a historic shift in American involvement in international security politics, were accompanied by more debate over means than over ends. Indeed, since the 1940s there has been a remarkable consistency as to national security objectives throughout American debates over foreign and defense policy. Rarely indeed has a commentator endeavored to call into fundamental question the "guardianship" mission of the United States as that mission emerged out of U.S. leadership in the Western Grand Alliance of World War II in 1943-45.[27] References to the "fragmentation" of the foreign policy consensus forged in the late 1940s are incorrect, whatever their superficial plausibility. Strategies and means have been challenged, but not ends. To a degree, this is unfortunate because it has led to unbalanced, even incompetently conducted, debates. Since defense policy must support foreign policy in a design for national security, logically and prudently there should be a constant dialogue between defense policy means and foreign policy ends. If the terms of military and economic relationships shift to a major degree, then the burdens that foreign policy places on the defense establishment should be altered.

In some important respects the quality of the public debate over national security in the United States is lower today than it was in the early 1960s. Ideas and important distinctions that were explained with admirable clarity a quarter-century ago have been lost or are simply ignored. For example, the central idea in U.S. defense policy is deterrence, as it has been since 1945, but opinion leaders today often confuse deterrence per se with a particular theory for its achievement. So-called "war-fighting" or "classical strategy" approaches to deterrence are misidentified as basic challenges to the concept of deterrence itself.[28] If ideas or policy assumptions pass unexamined for many years, the reasons why they were once found to be poor ideas may become increasingly elusive. Since 1949 every U.S. administration has affirmed and reaffirmed, as though it were an eternal Revealed Truth, that "NATO is the cornerstone of our security." That belief may be as well based in fact today as it was in 1949, but when policy becomes dogma, it tends to remove itself from discussion save at the level of ritual. I suspect that a responsible-sounding *though erroneous* argument could be made against the NATO connection today, such that senior U.S. officials would be hard pressed to defeat it both on its own terms and with reference to its assumptions. Worthy causes, and necessary strategies and weapons, can be lost if their intellectual defenses are not maintained in good repair.

National security professionals talk largely among themselves and typically have no day-by-day need to address basic questions of policy purpose, or even broad issues of policy means. As Edward Luttwak has observed, shared assumptions on statecraft are in scant need of public articulation.[29] Notwithstanding occasional idealistic urges, British statesmen in the nineteenth century understood that the guiding light for their policy activity had to be the maintenance of the balance of power. This was so self-evident that it was rarely explained. The British Foreign Office of the period was neither staffed to produce nor inclined to commission weighty scholarly treatises on doctrine for statecraft. A similar judgment applies to the Royal Navy of the period, which was told by Mahan in 1890 that for centuries it had been developing and exercising "Sea Power" for the purpose of maintaining "command of the seas." The Royal Navy had always been a hands-on operation, generally disdainful of theory and theorists: a collection of admirals and ships with no central organizing "brain," no naval general staff (an innovation of Churchill's first period at the Admiralty on the eve of World War I).

Similarly, it has been alleged that strategic thinking worthy of the name is alien to "the American way" of national security, that the distinctive national American experience has produced an enduring bias in favor of managerial and technical skills.[30] But that claim needs to be considered in the light of the pressures upon politicians and officials to go on doing what has been done before. In a nuclear-armed world in particular, the familiar course is typically judged to be the prudent course; adopting a superior policy design whatever its theoretical attraction, is bound to increase uncertainty and may produce novel and needless risks. The bold redesigner of American policy therefore has at least two major structural problems to overcome: first, the resistance of the policymaking system to strategic thought; second, the ingrained conservatism of the policy implementer, who is likely to equate suggestions for innovation with attempts to rock a boat felt to be none too seaworthy already. Policy change that is more than a change in slogans and general rhetoric is almost impossible to effect in a democracy unless the need for it is virtually self-evident or unless an opinion leader of extraordinary persuasiveness is willing to take unusual political risks on its behalf.

Barring some external security shock of a fairly unambiguous kind, the bureaucracy will always judge that the time is not right to rock the boat. Generally, but not invariably, the bureaucracy will be correct. Governments do not invite additional difficulties; it is in their nature to do only what they must, when they must. Security lies in freedom of action, and fundamental policy choice—if it is more than mere rhetoric—restricts future freedom of action. Also, no one can know just how fragile is the margin of stability in East-West relations. Academic theorists may play "alternative world order" games, treating the world as though it were a laboratory for their schemes, but responsible officials are aware that an international security structure that emerged out of world war and has been nurtured through many crises for more than forty years might not be easily reconstructed if some bold experiment for improvement failed to work well enough. History can be experienced only once. Major changes in international security arrangements tend not to be politically feasible until their necessity is demonstrated by events.

Satisfactory definitions of security are not in common currency.[32] In everyday usage, security is often discussed as though it were a commodity to be purchased directly with defense dollars. For good, though not very good, reasons, security tends to imply military security—at least insofar as the term is used by policymakers and commentators in the defense area.[32] Further, it is generally appreciated today (as it was then—outside France) that the interwar French notion of *sécurité totale* is a chimera.[33] Any quest for absolute security will be a self-defeating endeavor, invariably leading to overcommitment or (anti-)hegemonic war or both.[34]

George Kennan has advised: "In an age of nuclear striking power, national security can never be more than relative; and to the extent that it can be assured at all, it must find its sanction in the intentions of rival powers as well as in their capabilities."[35] Intentions are profoundly important in a strategic context where countries ultimately can be protected against the malign intentions of others only by the functioning of a deterrence system anchored on the threat of retaliation. Prior to the nuclear age the armed forces that could engage and prospectively defeat enemy fleets and armies could also, as a consequence of success in battle, directly protect their nations.[36] The security provided by the more or less credible threat to retaliate over long ranges with nuclear weapons is a security provided in good part by the ability and willingness of a potential enemy to be deterred.

It would be an error to believe that a condition of only relative security is unique to the nuclear age. Few, if any, states in history have experienced an absolute quality in their national security, nor could they have done so even had their statecraft been better conceived and conducted. The apparently near-absolute security enjoyed by the United States in the nineteenth and early twentieth centuries, for example, was relative to circumstances that it could influence and manipulate but by no means determine comprehensively. American security in the pre-nuclear age depended critically upon both the working of the European balance-of-power system and the preservation of the federal union. The logistic difficulty that would have attended any trans-oceanic operations against U.S. territory,[37] even with Canada as a forward base area, made disunity in the republic an essential precondition for any European military intervention of anything more than a raiding character. In practice, of course, the divisions within great-power Europe precluded the emergence of serious imperial designs upon U.S. territory; had nineteenth-century Europe, including Great Britain, constituted a hegemonial state or coalition, the protracted antagonism between North and South could have resulted in the kind of multinational insecurity in North America that John Jay predicted contingently in Federalist Paper No. 5.[38]

The endeavor to promote national security unilaterally by very high defense expenditure evokes a sense of insecurity abroad. Measures taken in the interest of an ill-defined concept of national security may be judged so excessive as to betoken a drive for hegemony through military preponderance, and are certain to fuel countervailing programs by others in self-defense. Yet an absolute security may plausibly be discerned to be the authoritative idea, though probably not the anticipated condition, in the Soviet Union. In practice, the Soviet Union accommodates when and where it must—for example, at Brest-Litovsk in March 1918—but the dynamics of empire, married to the Soviet view of the world, lead to a view of defense preparation that would seem to exclude the notion of mere adequacy.[39] For its full postural expression, the Soviet view requires a state of splendid superiority over the military power of all plausible adversaries in combination. Such a definition of the requirements of Soviet national security, or imperial forward defense, is plainly incompatible with the security—or tolerable insecurity—of other nations. In his study of Soviet grand strategy, Edward Luttwak has claimed that "the Soviet Union is no longer simply a Great Power but has now become a great continental military empire. As such it is engaged in the classic quest for total preclusive security."[40]

More disturbing still, in the tradition of the geopolitical analyses of Mackinder and Spykman, Luttwak predicts that Soviet capability and ambition could one day be in balance: "There is really nothing new about the fact that the Soviet Union is a classic, power-accumulating, expanding empire. What is new is that it is the first one with a real global potential in an era when other limits to empire have fallen away [geographical, logistic, ethnic]. Napoleon couldn't conquer the world. The Romans, even if they wanted to, couldn't conquer the world. Russia is the first one that can."[41] In principle at least, security is not a function of relative position in a weapons balance. Threat attends not upon a foreign weapons arsenal but upon the marriage of a weapons arsenal with perceived political intent. The Soviet tank and motor-rifle divisions deployed in central Europe are a threat to Western security only in the sense that Western countries, prudentially, are obliged to assume that they could serve inimical functions as instruments of Soviet foreign policy.

Full recognition of the importance of strategy is not quite the same as discovery of the philosopher's stone for national security.[42] No matter how well constructed and persuasive a strategy may seem in peacetime, its careful design and detailed elaboration should not obscure the fact that it rests upon guesses. One cannot be sure which objectives a president one day may wish to pursue, or which moves and countermoves an adversary may make. Defining the military needs of national security is an art, not a science. Officials appearing before congressional committees are obliged to speak as if they have discovered how much resource input, designed to produce a particular output in capability, will be sufficient for security. In fact, much of it is guesswork—but the process of defense budgetary debate inclines the participants to forget the indeterminate nature of their subject.

In his review of theories of alliance formation, Stephen Walt has provided a useful reminder that the size and strength of a coalition forged to oppose a particular state or states will reflect not only the mass of the threat but also perceptions of what may be termed its political velocity.[43]

The prudential rule in statecraft that inclines states to balance power must be modified to accommodate the proposition that perception of an extraordinary scope of hostile ambition can, and typically will, trigger a great overbalancing of material power against the potential menace.

At a high level of generality, NATO-Europe asks of the United States that it contribute in a major way to the containment of the Soviet military (and, *ab extensio*, political) threat; and, in addition, that it so conduct itself, nationally and as alliance leader, that the Soviet Union will discern no pressing policy reasons seriously to consider taking military action against NATO-Europe. In short, a structure of security is perceived wherein negative military sanctions play only one, albeit an essential, part. The United States should feel secure either if the Soviet Union lacks sufficient military means to take successful coercive action or if the prospective costs that must attend any coercive enterprise can be kept at what Moscow will likely assess as a prohibitive level. Failure to understand this elementary distinction between theories of deterrence through denial and through potential punishment continues to plague the American strategy debate.[44] Pure forms of either strategy are infeasible.

Security by positive sanctions points to the hopes for achievement of a condition of international life wherein crisis, war, or even seriously deteriorating relations would be assessed by decisionmakers as too costly. In a form of argument reminiscent of Richard Cobden, John Bright, and Norman Angell,[45] some Western theorists in the early 1970s appeared to hope that Soviet leaders, behaving like Rational Economic Man, would be unwilling to forgo the economic and political boons of detente.

Much of the detente-promotion literature of the early and mid-1970s was naively optimistic concerning the political feasibility of changing well-settled Soviet (and Russian) attitudes toward security; it greatly underestimated the price that the Soviet Union would demand for detente and generally neglected to dissect the character of the intended Eastern traveling companion on the great detente voyage. Furthermore, it was not appreciated widely that detente was a policy line that could be pursued safely and could work only if the Soviet Union perceived the United States to be leading from strength. Unfortunately, the disarray in American society in the 1960s, the U.S. failure in Vietnam, and the formal U.S. endorsement of strategic parity in SALT I all inclined the Soviet leadership to believe that the United States was attempting, through a detente policy, to cover a strategic retreat as best it could. As if this were not bad enough, the eruption of the Watergate scandal in 1973-74 and the consequent reduction in the authority of the executive branch of the U.S. government led the Soviet Union to believe that it could embark in unprecedented safety upon a series of opportunistic imperial ventures, in search and support of new security clients.[46]

It was not that detente—an easing of tensions through the functioning of a framework of political rules of limited cooperation—was fundamentally flawed in concept but that many Western opinion leaders did not see detente in the context of the ongoing geopolitical opposition of East and West. Also, the United States could not at that time manage to operate a prudent national security policy that mixed threats and bribes in a sophisticated way. Worst of all, the Soviet Union could not resist the temptation to seek imperial gains in Africa and the Arabian peninsula while U.S. capacity for effective action was impaired. In American eyes, Soviet behavior from the time of its backing of the Egyptian-Syrian surprise attack on Israel in October 1973 until the invasion of Afghanistan late in 1979 was the behavior not of a responsible partner in world order but rather—as Speaker of the House Sam Rayburn once put it—of a hotel burglar trying all the doorknobs and entering when he finds any unlocked.

Nonetheless, there were important truths underlying the wishful thinking of the Western promoters of detente: namely, that the driving fuel of international conflict is political, and that military rivalry is only a manifestation of political conflict. Had the United States and NATO-Europe been able to augment their military preparations through the 1970s to a more prudent level, had Western statesmen been able to pursue "carrot and stick" policies in a tactically flexible manner, and had officials been able to discipline the expectations (which, perhaps inadvertently, they encouraged) of more responsible Soviet behavior, then the detente theme of the early 1970s would have constituted an appropriate thread for the guidance of statecraft.

The sad story of an unduly public arms-control diplomacy in the 1980s supports the proposition that a formal process of East-West arms control cannot help being an instrument for political warfare. That process is unlikely to further the attainment of arms-control objectives if the backdrop to the negotiations is one of open political conflict.[47] The long history of arms-control arrangements between Western-democratic and totalitarian states is almost uniformly a cautionary tale of negative examples. In principle, U.S. security can be enhanced by arms control; U.S. political leaders tend persistently not to design, execute, and debate national security policy within a disciplining, accurate framework of settled geopolitical assumptions. Between theory and reality lies the fact of enduring weaknesses in U.S. statecraft, characterized later in this chapter as "missing or shaky pillars" of national security policy.

Soviet military posture and the tightness of Soviet imperial political organization is not simply a function of perceived threat, as is often assumed in the West. Lower levels of Western military preparedness and political cohesion serve not to reassure the Soviet Union and encourage a sympathetically parallel reduction in assessed defense requirements but rather to encourage more forward policies. Attempts at enhanced Soviet influence are pressed as far as circumstances permit.

Hypothetical future security systems are condemned to irrelevance if they fail to acknowledge the Soviet leadership's small degree of freedom for innovation in national security policy. The actual degree of fragility of Soviet political control over the multinational U.S.S.R. and the eastern European satellite-clients is unknowable. But the evidence of Hungary in 1956, of Czechoslovakia in 1968, of Soviet hostility to West German *Östpolitik* directed at eastern Europe, and of Polish events in the early 1980s suggests strongly that no Soviet leadership can be expected to believe that it can afford to take chances with its imperial inheritance.[48]

It must be presumed that the generic threat posed by Soviet power to Western security is unlikely to diminish. Early 1970s-style processes of East-West detente cannot enhance Western security significantly by diminishing the threat. The threat comprises components which, for practical purposes of strategic planning and foreign policy choices, realistically have to be viewed as permanent. Cynical though Soviet leaders and citizens may be about the validity of the state religion of Marxism-Leninism, the facts remain that that pseudoreligion provides the conceptual arsenal of Soviet leaders, orders their thought processes, and is a quite literal necessity for the legitimacy of Soviet rule.[49] Any measure of strategic flexibility or tactical expediency is permissible, but the Soviet ideological commitment to an essentially conflictual relationship with the West is thoroughly inalienable.

Paul Nitze, an elder statesman in the tradition of American pragmatic conservatism, has observed that "the Soviet concept of 'peace' (or *mir*) has come to mean a continuing struggle, rather than a state of equilibrium, as peace is often defined in the West. *Mir* takes as a given that there is a natural and irreconcilable conflict of interest between the socialist and non-socialist worlds."[50] This is neither to argue by ideological premise nor to denigrate the significance of ideologically neutral geostrategic considerations. Indeed, time and again I return to the proposition that there is a wholly compatible synergistic relationship between the power-political needs of Soviet imperial statecraft and the tenets of a gloriously permissive legitimizing ideology. For the attainment of peace between the superpowers, in the normative Western sense of the concept, the Soviet Union would have to renounce both the security lessons of Russian history and the revolution with the political system it spawned: in other words, it would have to renounce itself. If an important measure of success for U.S. national security policy is the achievement of a quality of security deriving from the absence or sharp diminution of Soviet incentives to encroach upon vital U.S. interests, then policy success is not possible.

The Soviet leadership cannot afford to relax the exercise of its authority, either at home or abroad, for fear that the total edifice of political control may slide beyond correction. Past experiments in liberalization have not proved encouraging. Furthermore, it should not be forgotten that great powers have difficulty placing bounds upon their interests, and hence upon the power that it might be useful to accumulate. They value power and reputation for genuinely defensive purposes in the achievement of ideological goals,[51] as well as for self-aggrandizement. Great imperial powers, be they maritime or continental, invariably concoct a legitimizing rationale for the character of their polity and their rule over nonnationals.[52]

Alone among the members of the Western Alliance the United States truly has global interests and responsibilities. Though relatively less powerful within the alliance than in the 1950s and 1960s, it remains the only Western country that can act unilaterally in support of general Western (as well as its own) security interests in regional stability. But the American nerve for unilateral action has not been fully restored, and the allied counselors of restraint cannot suggest, let alone provide, effective substitutes for American action.[53]

For the indefinite future the Soviet Union is going to pose a multifaceted but overwhelmingly military threat to U.S. interests in Europe, Asia, Africa, and the Americas, no matter how restrictively or expansively the scope and intensity of those interests are defined. The Soviet desire to acquire influence over countries beyond its current *glaçis* is best regarded as a constant. Soviet perceptions of the risks entailed are more likely to alter than is Soviet propensity to take risks.[54] Nothing can obviate the fact that there will be regional political-military "balances," constituting fractions of a global balance, that must be managed, mismanaged, or ignored by the United States. The degree to which the United States might, and should in its own interests, perform the management effort is a principal focus of this book.

Anyone closely attentive to the ebb and flow of public discussion and debate in the United States on subjects of national security will notice the dual phenomena of platitudinous assertion on broad issues of threat, purpose, and policy architecture, and of precipitate retreat into detail. What is lacking is, first, a sophisticated and reasonably settled understanding of the nature of the Soviet-American relationship and hence of the character of the most appropriate security policy; and, second, a strategy design that can sort the wheat from the chaff among the myriad details of defense proposals and contenders for adoption as arms-control policy.

Time after time, U.S. political leaders and senior officials indulge their hopes and fears in public rhetoric, projecting some very American attitudes as standards to which alien political cultures should aspire. This rhetoric is conducted at the expense of recognizing the bounds imposed by necessity. There is an evident lack of grasp of the essentials of statecraft. Tactical challenges are met with tactical responses generally uninformed either by strategic purpose or by a firm comprehension of the difference between problems that can be solved and conditions that can only be alleviated, circumvented, or accepted.

To perform adequately in providing for the national security, the U.S. government and American opinion leaders require a grip on the essentials of international politics—including the skills of adversary manipulation and alliance management—in no important way inferior to that displayed over centuries by the more successful great powers of the past. If anything, the nuclear fact demands a higher standard of policy performance than was tolerable for the governing elites of Athens, Rome, Byzantium, Venice, China, Spain, France, Germany, or Britain.

The organization of this book, tied with the thread of the Soviet-American strategic nexus, addresses the missing or shaky pillars of U.S. national security policy. In order, these are sufficient comprehension of
- the nature of international politics;
- the geopolitical basis of U.S. national security problems and opportunities;
- a mature self-knowledge of American political and strategic culture;
- the character and varying intensity of national interests;
- the terms and conditions of the Western Alliance;
- the (Russian) nature of the Soviet adversary;
- the range of choice, theoretical and prudent, in national security policy; and
- the proper relationship between policy means and policy goals.

To improve understanding of national security problems is not necessarily to register any genuine progress toward their alleviation or resolution. It may be that the United States, given its political culture, is incapable of doing other than wobbling between an inappropriate belligerence and an unwise accommodation in its Soviet policy. However, the stakes are so high and the benefits even of modest improvement in policy quality may be so critical that there is no responsible alternative to an attempt to improve understanding—in the hope that improved understanding may serve as a basis for more effective action.

4

Statecraft: Retrospect and Prospect

In the public debate over U.S. (and, more generally, Western) national security policy there are voices, reflecting what Michael Howard has generously called a "naive innocence," urging radical solutions to current problems.[1] Sundry physicians, psychologists, lawyers, and scholars of international relations urge the view that the United States could and should conduct its foreign relations and see to its security in ways fundamentally different from those practiced at present.

Millennarian visions have had a long history in the thought and social movements of Western civilization.[2] From Kant with his *Permanent Peace* and Lenin with his communist society bereft of states (which will have "withered away" somewhat mysteriously) to the authors of *One World or None*[3] and Jonathan Schell predicting that "the fate of the earth" is likely to be very grisly indeed unless international politics as practiced through all of recorded history are transformed by the growth of a true global community,[4] chiliastic fantasies have rarely been in short supply.

Details differ among the radical visionaries, but all tend to agree that a drastic change of policy course is essential if the long-standing "one world or none" prediction is not to be fulfilled in the pessimistic column. The sincerity of visionaries is not the issue. The case for radical action has been well expressed by Jonathan Schell: "If a busload of people is speeding down a mountainside toward a cliff, the passengers do not convene a seminar to investigate the nature of their predicament; they see to it that the driver applies the brakes."[4] But the analogy is a false one. Schell may be correct in his prediction of nuclear catastrophe, but insistence by the "passengers"—that is to say, the citizens of Western democracies, the only "passengers" who have genuine access to a driver—that the brakes be applied would be more likely to produce a fatal skid than to halt the perceived slide to Armageddon.

Vision can be useful when it is disciplined by appreciation of the realm of necessity. Politicians and officials may require occasional reminders of "better things that might be," lest they be unduly brutalized by the daily routine of *Realpolitik*. It may be necessary for our mental health and essential for the moral welfare of our civilization that the distinction between aspiration and contemporary achievement never be lost. Unfortunately, a thread that runs with depressing consistency through the radical visions of new world orders is an inability to prescribe in persuasive detail the political transformation from the *here* of permanent insecurity to the *there* of permanent peace. More often than not, the proponent of a new world order seems to believe that he has fulfilled his obligation by identifying the ills of today, describing the new order, and waxing lyrical on the blessings that will follow from its accomplishment.

Root-and-branch critics of U.S. national security policy, and of the nuclear deterrence system central to that policy, have much in common with some of the loudest voices speaking out for superpower arms control. The common elements include, first, a disdain for or neglect of the very character of "great" and "super" powers—particularly the geostrategic scope of their interests. To ask of a great power that it eschew an active interest in perhaps geographically distant security issues is to ask it to be other than it is. A great power or super power is by definition a vital player in the "game" that maintains the international order of the day. The national security of a great power, or any power, can be theatened by systemic disruption. One difference between great and lesser powers is that great powers both are able to influence the functioning of international order and must act or be prepared to act if the disordering behavior of other powers is to be disciplined.[6] Left-radical critiques of U.S. national security policy typically identify a uniquely wicked quality in U.S. interventionism abroad, but what they are really condemning is a historically close-to-universal principle. Specifically, if states are able to influence their external environments in ways judged to be benign, they are certain to be strongly motivated so to do, and it is far more likely than not that they will make the attempt. Non-interventionism may be held to be a virtue, but more accurately, it is a necessity for the less powerful players in international politics. The arms control community, in common with the more obviously radical critics of U.S. national security policy, is prone to ignore some of the political-military duties of super-powerhood for the United States. Those duties include the extension of protection over some of the peripheral, Soviet-blocking lands of Eurasia.[7]

Second, many of the staunchest, self-identified soldiers for arms control share with the radicals a practical indifference to the distinctiveness of the Soviet and American political and strategic cultures.[8] True to their histories, the Soviet/Russian and American political systems are, respectively, deeply pessimistic and deeply optimistic over the prospects for peace. The slogans of the radical—"freeze now," "end the arms race," "give peace a chance," and the like——are scarcely more idealist by way of inspiration than is the proposition that the arms-control process is likely to contribute importantly to U.S. national security.[9] The real historical Soviet adversary, as contrasted with an imaginary Soviet collaborator, cannot be a voluntary partner in a struggle for stability. The Soviet commitment to seek military advantage—that is to say, instability for the rest of humankind—is inalienable. Much Western sermonizing on the blessings of arms control suffers from the signal weakness that it has nothing of interest to say on the all-important subject of Soviet incentives to agree.

The backdrop to the discussion later in this study of different national security concepts for the United States is the enduring character of international politics. As a sovereign actor the United States in theory is at liberty to refuse any active role in the international politics of security. But exercise of such a choice would not mean that those politics would cease, or that the United States would not be affected by them, or that U.S. inactivity would not itself have an important influence upon the international system. In short, there is no alternative system of security available as a refuge for states that are too tired or consider themselves too virtuous to continue the game. States play actively and purposefully in the realm of the "high politics" of security for a variety of motives, but the most important and enduring of those motives is the prudent search for some measure of benign control over the external environment.

Much has been alleged concerning discontinuities in international politics deriving from the development of nuclear weapons.[10] The truth concerning "the nuclear revolution" is less dramatic than has often been claimed. It would be difficult to improve on Robert Gilpin's judgment that "international relations continue to be a recurring struggle for wealth and power among independent actors in a state of anarchy. The classic history of Thucydides is as meaningful a guide to the behavior of states today as when it was written in the fifth century B.C."[11]

The most important change wrought by nuclear weapons is that nuclear-armed states in political conflict are far more cautious in their mutual security dealings than are nonnuclear-armed states, or than great powers were prior to 1945. Moreover, this caution extends to the behavior of nuclear-armed states vis-à-vis nonnuclear-armed states that are allied to other nuclear powers. The anticipated costs of nuclear war are generally believed to be so high that the political threshold for war has risen quite markedly—or so it would appear. One cannot be sure, because there is no unambiguous historical evidence of the dissuasive effect of nuclear fears. One cannot know for certain which wars have not occurred because of the nuclear fact. Nonetheless, on the basis of plausible inference and some direct evidence in the calculations of (Western) politicians, one has to argue that nuclear weapons have served as a potent force for peace. It remains to be seen whether or not this highly probable fact turns out to have been a Faustian pact whose ultimate payment cannot be avoided.

An understandable cause of major confusion is the historical coincidence of the development of nuclear weapons with the emergence of the United States and the Soviet Union as superpowers. It is not widely appreciated that the shape of the post–World War II international security order was the product of geopolitics, not of nuclear weapons. The United States was the world's first atomic power because it was a superpower; it was not a superpower by virtue of being an atomic power.

Two circumstances often thought to have played causal roles in shaping the adversarial relationship between the United States and the Soviet Union are, first, their preeminence in nuclear ordnance capabilities and, second, their ideological differencs. Nuclear weapons have undoubtedly played a large role in the adversarial security nexus binding the two nations. But Soviet-American conflict probably should be viewed as foreordained by geopolitical reasoning; it did not flow from the facts and fears of nuclear weapons production. The circumstances and outcome of World War II guaranteed future conflict between the United States and the Soviet Union. Had the United States not been compelled to enter the war and had the Axis powers triumphed in Eurasia, then eventually there would have been a protracted conflict between the United States and a superpower Third Reich.[12]

The security pattern that has been the central feature of world politics since the late 1940s has been competition between an insular superpower leading a maritime alliance and a continental Heartland superpower and its imperial dependencies.[13] That pattern has been influenced greatly by nuclear risks, but its basic architecture has not been determined by those risks. The Cold War and the emergence of a substantially bipolar military standoff would have occurred even had nuclear weapons not been invented.

"Superpower" is a novel word but far from a novel phenomenon in international politics. Athens, Alexander's Hellenistic Empire, Rome, the Empire of Charlemagne, sixteenth-century Spain, Napoleonic France—to name but a few—were all superpowers, properly so-called. There is no authoritative definition of the term—certainly nothing as formal as the international legal recognition of great-power status that existed from the Congress of Vienna (1815) to the First World War—yet there is little historical dispute as to which states have merited the ascription and which have not. In the nineteenth century, "great powers" were distinguished from "secondary states" by the weight of their capacity for action. That weight, ultimately, was expressible in military terms or, in the British case, by a maritime preponderance and an economic ability to finance war waged in good part by others. The great powers of Europe's classical balance-of-power period were of approximately equivalent weight in their several abilities to play in the game of states.[14] Superpowers, like great powers, emerge as a consequence of a process of elimination—most typically by war, but also through the relative economic and perhaps demographic decline of previous rivals.[15]

Although the claim is historically true that every "great" or "super" security community either will carry within itself the seeds of its own eventual decline or must meet in due course an unmanageable external challenge (most often some blend of the two), there is no law of stable equilibrium through a balance of power in international politics. For example, when Rome established a territorial and hegemonic empire over all of the known world that was worth controlling (logistics, geography, and low incentives to further conquest determined what proved to be very stable boundaries)[16] it did so through a process of violent elimination of rivals. Whether Roman motives involved purposeful aggrandizement for gold and glory or a "defensive imperialism" for the protection of core-value security was a matter of little moment to its victims.[17]

In the last stages of World War II, the United States and the Great Russian Empire (in the new outer clothing of the Union of Soviet Socialist Republics) had become superpowers simply through their unmatched ability to wage war relative to all other state actors. It had long been a very approximate rule of thumb that a great power, to be so considered, should be able to hold its own, overall, against any other great power. By 1945 it was evident to most observers that, the United States and the Soviet Union were not as other states—although they had arrived at superpower status by different roads.

Strictly speaking, the Soviet Union in 1945 (and still today in important respects),[18] while more than a great power—by virtue of the removal through defeat or exhaustion of the other traditional European great powers from the column of leading active players—was not a superpower of the first rank. Much of its superpower quality derived not so much from Soviet strength assessed overall relative to American strength, as from the hostage status of western Europe to regional (not global, by way of contrast to the United States) Soviet power. The geostrategic contiguity of Soviet landpower to western Europe, married to a superior (to the U.S.) capacity to retain mobilized military power in peacetime and—after 1949—the unarguable reality of nuclear capability, served effectively to offset and even obscure the fundamentally second-class quality of the Soviet claim to superpower status. The Soviet Union remains a selectively, or semi-developed country whose enduring backwardness relative to the technological culture of the West places it in permanent danger of being left behind in the struggle for world power.

There is nothing in economic or military history to suggest that one or more states in competition cannot be permanently relegated to an inferior position. *If* high technology is the future key to military and economic competitiveness, then the Soviet system may be condemned to follow the path of demotion in international ranking already plainly marked by Turkey, the Netherlands, Sweden, Spain, France, Britain, and Germany. I am neither quite willing to concede so important a role to technology, given the offsetting strengths of the Soviet imperium, nor fully convinced that the Soviet Union will be unable to remain sufficiently in touch with useful techology. But it would be as foolish to discount the possibility that the Western world could impose a peaceful demotion of the Soviet threat as to discount the impact of predictions in Moscow of such a future upon nearer-term Soviet national security choices.

A sufficient basis for Soviet-American suspicion and therefore enmity was stated with exemplary clarity by Thucydides in the words of the Athenians as they explain the permanent realities of international politics to the unfortunate Melians (an ally and former colony of Sparta):

> You know as well as we do that, when these matters are discussed by practical people, the standard of justice depends on the equality of power to compel and that in fact the strong do what they have the power to do and the weak accept what they have to accept....Our opinion of the gods and our knowledge of men lead us to conclude that it is a general and necessary law of nature to rule wherever one can. This is not a law that we made ourselves, nor were we the first to act upon it when it was made. We found it already in existence, and we shall leave it to exist for ever among those who come after us.[19]

The capability of imposing a particular self-serving variant of justice is presumed to invite and encourage, even license, a like policy intention. National threat detection systems scan the outside world to discover who may be able to inflict major pain. In 1945 the United States and the Soviet Union could identify only each other as powers with the potential to thwart the securing of vital national interests.

The real discontinuity in the international "high politics" of the twentieth century resides in the reduction of the number of essential players in the international, now global, security system to two. This bipolar condition actually emerged in military reality in the 1960s, though it was discerned prematurely in the 1950s by commentators who were misled by Soviet acquision of the trappings of an intercontinental nuclear-weapons capability.[20] In the late 1940s and very early 1950s American military power was far more potential than it was realized in ready capability; then, following the rearmament surge of the Korean war era, the United States in the 1950s did not fully appreciate the measure of its own global preponderance.[21]

Europe-oriented international politics has seen a single universal state (not literally) but for all practical purposes in the Rome of the early empire. It has also seen several periods when one state was by far the most powerful player in the system—for example, sixteenth-century Spain, late seventeenth-century and early nineteenth-century France, and early and middle twentieth-century Germany—but in each of these cases three, four, or five other sufficiently important powers, acting in combination (albeit in unreliable combination) were able to balance and eventually defeat the preponderant power. The situation today is that the United States not only is an essential player in the international security system; it is the only essential player if Soviet power is to be contained.

I have accepted the risk of overstatement for the sake of clear exposition. Of course other players are important: the alignment of West Germany, France, and Great Britain is significant, as are the policy tilts of Beijing. Nonetheless, without the active participation of the United States, not only would the current structure of international security simply fail to work but it is not obvious that there would be any international security in a normative sense. The United States is both its own last line of defense and potentially the last line of defense of every other country that does not wish to join the extended socialist commonwealth of the Great Russian Empire. The character of the discontinuity from the genuinely multipolar, or oligopolistic, international security structures of past centuries clearly cannot be sidestepped if Americans wish to consider their choices in national security policy in a responsible matter.

To claim that the United States is the only truly essential player in the containment of Soviet power is not to argue that Americans are compelled by some nuclear-age "hidden-hand" mechanism of proper balancing either to contain Soviet power or to thwart it by particular means and methods. U.S. statesmen certainly could decide to seek a general political settlement with the Soviet Union, to accept whatever proved to be negotiable, and to fold American military tents abroad. This process could rest upon a wide range of possible suppositions of the nature of Soviet power and Soviet foreign policy purposes. The United States might decide that although Soviet statecraft was as predatory as ever, the risks of a forward containment perimeter in Eurasia were just too severe to American survival interests.[22]

The domestic preoccupations of the United States and the newly created Soviet Republic between 1919 and 1941 obscured the fact that the Great War had destroyed for all time the essential architecture of the European balance-of-power system. The reality was, first, that by 1914 the balance system, instead of serving to preserve order—at the cost of occasional armed conflict ("permissible war") to impose discipline upon a transgressor against the rules—had ceased to function. The European security system could not accommodate a united German Empire that had grown too powerful to permit its ambitions and fears to be contained by rules of international behavior tolerable to other major European powers. As it was, both in early September 1914 and again, in desperation, in March 1918, Germany came tantalizingly close to securing victory on the battlefield. Paradoxically perhaps, the German willingness, even eagerness, to go to war in 1914 owed more to German lack of confidence in its ability to compete in the years ahead than to any determination to affirm by action a claim to preeminence.[23]

Second, the First World War destroyed the exclusively European character of the balance-of-power system. American assistance was required in order to defeat regional-superpower Germany; and victory in Europe was succeeded by recognition in Britain and France of the geopolitical and economic necessity of accommodating American and Japanese security designs. The British Empire was viable militarily only so long as there were no extra-European maritime threats to its integrity. The Royal Navy could effectively close the oceans against transit by the naval power of any European country, but the "Ushant Position" had no relevance to the U.S. or Imperial Japanese fleets. The international security system had become a truly global one. The great powers, even the nominally victorious great powers of Europe, could neither sustain a balance of power in Europe without extra-European assistance nor protect their overseas holdings through action in and about Europe. The United States, without fully recognizing the fact, had replaced Britain as the necessary balancer in a European security system that had lost the flexibility it needed in order to function.

The marginal character of the Anglo-French ability to contain Germany's strength in 1914-18 had slipped dramatically by 1939-40—most precipitately in 1938-39[24]—at which point a Third Reich that was vastly undermobilized for total war dispatched the Western allies from live contention on the continent in less than six weeks.[25] The Soviet Union, with direct assistance at the margin from Britain and indirect assistance (through Britain) from the United States, *might* have defeated Nazi Germany (though I am skeptical); that must remain one of the "might have beens" of history. What was apparent to a few people as early as 1943, however, was that the defeat of Germany would *ipso facto* create a most urgent need for the balancing of a Soviet power base projecting far into central Europe.[26] The role of the United States as principal provider of security for those portions of peninsular Europe not liberated by Soviet arms derived from the destruction of Germany as an essential actor in the European balance-of-power system.

On reflection, it is surprising to discover just how few of the significant changes in the international politics of the last century are even half-plausibly attributable to the influence of nuclear weapons. One should not be so mesmerized by the prospective horrors of nuclear war that one neglects to appreciate the effect of the nonnuclear global wars of this century upon popular enthusiasm for future conflict. World Wars I and II demonstrated that rather evenly matched states in coalition have to do one another a very great deal of damage before the fine print of attrition determines the victor. And long prior to 1945, Western democratic societies had become heartily disenchanted with the prospectively minimal returns of employing the military instrument on a large scale. World War I, in particular, left a permanent mark on British and French political (and strategic) cultures.[27]

The ideological character of Soviet-American political hostility is a notable discontinuity in the succession of security systems from the Thirty Years' War (1618-48) until 1914. However, it is important to note that the ideological antipathy between the superpowers provides strictly redundant fuel for their rivalry. That rivalry is locked in place by the exclusivity of their strength. The variably messianic nature of the Soviet and American polities lends an additional rigidity to the competition; the distinctive ideologies that animate and decorate their political cultures provide fuel for irritation, misunderstanding, and locally legitimizing rationales for hostility. But these are not the root causes of the competition.

Nor is a Russian threat to Europe, the Near East and southern Asia, and the northern Pacific Rimland distinctive to the Soviet period of Russian history. The Great Game in central and southern Asia was being played well over a hundred years before President Jimmy Carter came to understand in December 1979 that Russian power abhors a vacuum on its borders. There is no such thing as a Marxist, let alone a Communist, kind of, or style in, foreign policy. Marxist theory predicted that the contradictions of capitalism would lead to imperialist wars for overseas markets *between the major capitalist countries,* and that these wars would be transformed into class-based civil wars. Marxism offers no advice for the conduct of foreign policy in a socialist state; indeed, the very idea of a situation wherein such a policy would be needed is close to ridiculous in Marxist terms.

Stalin explicitly reintroduced Russian national themes in state policy in 1934 and implicitly praised the *mission civilisatrice* of czarist imperialism. The Soviet Union of the late 1980s is very much the Soviet Union of Stalin's day with respect to national security policy. The drive for military preponderance launched with the First Five Year Plan in 1928 has continued into the nuclear era. Stalin's heirs and successors have not repudiated in deeds the quest for an ever-expanding imperium that Stalin found so praiseworthy in his imperial predecessors.

The world of the late twentieth century is a world to which the statecraft of ancient China and Greece is still relevant; the classic texts of Sun Tzu, Thucydides, and—from early modern times—Machiavelli generally apply today as they did when they were written. The means of production and their social relations (to employ the Marxist formulation) have altered dramatically, as has the technology of commerce, transport, and war, but political and military ideas seem to emerge and reemerge from an apparently fixed common stock of intellectual assets. Twentieth-century politicians, officials, and policy commentators are typically alert to the undoubted facts of change. But with respect to statecraft, remarkably little of consequence has changed since Nicias led the Athenian imperial expedition to Syracuse (415-413 B.C.) in order to waste the Spartan granary.

Security communities today, as then, compete politically, militarily, economically, and culturally. The range of international behavior of states is of an enduring character.[25] The RAF Bomber Command and the U.S. Army Air Force approached the achievement of a "Carthaginian peace" upon the urban areas of the Third Reich and of Japan;[29] Henry Morgenthau, a decent American, sought official adoption of a plan to deindustrialize Germany on a permanent basis. International standards of behavior are driven by technology and the tactical and strategic necessity, or expediency, that attaches to particular technologies.[30] For example, the United States entered World War I on the specific issue of unrestricted submarine warfare, yet itself, in the Pacific in World War II, waged a submarine campaign scarcely less ruthless than that for which Germany had been vilified a generation before.

Several factors have contributed to the partial discontinuity in the international security politics of the nuclear age. First, the Eurocentric international security system of recent centuries has been transformed into a global system dominated by the rival ordering activities of two extra-European powers (the Soviet Union is in but not wholly of Europe). Soviet-American rivalry is implicit in the lonely preeminence of the two powers, not traceable to the nuclear facts of this age. But an essentially bipolar security system is a novel phenomenon in modern history.

Second, the Eurocentric system of 1914 and 1939 has been displaced not only by an intercontinental rivalry between superstates but also by the rise in relative importance of new, or newly influential, regional states out of the demise of the great European colonial empires. Nationalism and, in some cases, religious fervor render the Third World in general a graveyard for the hopes of superpower statesmen seeking reliable clients. Nonetheless, the modest scale of the stakes means a modest scale of risks—always bearing in mind that Soviet and American leaders perpetually are condemned to worry about the "Balkan trigger" problem. As a maritime power which, in geostrategic terms, is laying siege to the Heartland Soviet Union, the United States deems it prudent both to secure strategic access to peripheral Eurasia and Africa and to deny strategic "breakout" opportunities that might be exploited by a prudently opportunistic Soviet statecraft.[31]

Third, there has been a decline in the value of military power as an instrument of decision in major war between nuclear-armed states.[32] In 1914 and 1939, war—even general war—was an instrument of policy in a Clausewitzian sense that has been eroded severely by the nuclear fact.[33] However, the superpowers believe and speak as if the details of balance or imbalance between nuclear-force postures do matter, as if deterrence is not simply an existential fact.

Fourth, increasingly rapid communications with global visual reach to individual homes has meant, *for the Western democracies,* that some of the more brutal (and televisual) aspects of statecraft-in-action are unprecedentedly difficult to effect and explain. The liberal conscience was alive and well in nineteenth-century and early twentieth-century America and Britain, but there were then no television news teams covering campaigns against the Indians or counterinsurgency against Filipino nationalists and Moro tribesmen.[34]

Unfortunately, it does not follow either that war has been functionally abolished between powers of the first rank or that public opinion provides much sanction against brute-force *Realpolitik.* Louis J. Halle did not exaggerate in any important way when he emphasized that "Thucydides, as he himself anticipated, wrote the history not only of the Peloponnesian War. He also wrote the history of the Napoleonic Wars, World War I, World War II, and the Cold War."[35] The consideration of basic choices for U.S. national security policy then, must be rooted in the understanding of an essentially unchanging field of international political behavior. Even should a United States defining itself as a uniquely virtuous "City on a Hill"[36] choose not to play international politics as others do, it must still cope with those security communities that lie, cheat, and steal what they can. Nuclear weapons have altered the immediate stakes in some potential military conflicts and have thus helped discourage risk-taking. But the game of "high politics" is the same game it always was. One may deplore the apparent frivolity of statesmen who seem unable to design political structures appropriate to the novel scale of danger in a nuclear age, but they are locked into the performance of the necessary duty of prudent system maintenance. U.S. policymakers have yet to be advised of a workable scheme for system transformation that would not carry unacceptable risks.

5

Geopolitics and Strategic Culture

Because of its geography the United States has an insular perspective on international politics. Serious external challenge to its integrity as a distinct polity was concluded by 1814, though admittedly this is a judgment easier to offer from twentieth than from early nineteenth-century perspective.[1] Geographical distance and the Royal Navy combined to leave the United States at liberty to solve continental problems and seize continental opportunities substantially without reference to the interests and preferences of the European powers. The accident or good fortune of an isolated geography understandably came to be confused in the minds of many Americans with a unique national virtue. Did the United States succeed in nation-building and in forcible nation-restoration because it was virtuous, or because it had Canadians and Mexicans as its neighbors rather than Russians and Germans and because the Royal Navy guarded the maritime gateway from Europe?

Notwithstanding the enduring "oppositions" of global geopolitics,[2] important changes in the U.S. role in international security are possible in the future. Indeed, there can be a very marked distinction between the role to which a state is committed and the operational role it is capable of assuming in time of great stress. It may be salutary to remember the case of France in the 1930s. In political-strategic reality, the France that bled so profusely between 1914 and 1918 was not the same France that was cast in the leading military role against German aggrandizement in 1936-40.[3] Although one can specify geopolitical realities that explain rationally why the United States should pursue a fundamentally steady course in national security policy from decade to decade,[4] American society and its political culture and derivative strategic culture may change over the years.[5] The United States may have explicit commitments in the late 1980s, inherited from the 1940s and 1950s, that pertain to U.S. national interests which in any objective assessment must be judged to be vital but for which American society would be unwilling to fight—or, perhaps, to fight very long without swift success.

Political circumstances, relative capabilities, and public mood change constantly. Simply because one may be able to demonstrate through geo-strategic analysis that a particular interest is vital and should be defended, it does not follow necessarily that the United States at a particular point in time either could defend it or would be persuaded that it should. In historical practice the identification of vital interests tends to shift with relative national capacity for collective action. Capability, or believed capability, has a way of begetting an escalation in commitments. In the context of exploring a radical retrenchment in U.S. overseas military commitments, this book examines the propositions that the United States is overextended in its foreign security connections (meaning connections wherein, overwhelmingly, the U.S. produces and others consume se-curity); that overseas interests defined publicly as vital are in many cases nothing of the kind; and that U.S. strategy and military posture should be adjusted accordingly.

A zero-base review of U.S. foreign policy might be needlessly disrup-tive of interallied confidence and trust; it would suggest inaccurately a degree of U.S. dissatisfaction with the status quo. Nonetheless, such a review could well prove educational to policymakers in Washington; they might discover many examples of the phenomenon that one is doing and saying what one does and says today for no better reason than that one did and said it yesterday. Furthermore, it would be healthy in the long run for some of America's closest allies in Europe and eastern Asia to be reminded that the United States recognizes the distinction between true survival interests and contingent vital interests, to amend somewhat a part of Donald Nuechterlein's valuable organizing scheme.[6] Denial of Soviet control, or security supervision, of Europe and Japan is not in and of itself a survival interest of the United States. More to the point perhaps, achievement of such denial is not an immediate U.S. survival interest. Indeed, critics of a forward global containment policy can argue that it is the practice of that denial which imperils U.S. national survival. In the words of Robert Tucker:

> The chief attraction of a policy of withdrawal to this hemisphere is that it would avoid the principal risk a policy of global involvement, with or without alliances, must incur. It would avoid the risk of war and, above all, of nuclear war...nuclear weapons give substance to the long-discredited isolationist dream. So long as it is clear that they will be employed only in the direct defense of the homeland, they confer a physical security that is virtually complete, and that the loss of allies cannot alter. Instead, alliances must *detract* from physical security, since it is the prospect of defending allies that may one day result in a war destructive of this security. [Original Emphasis][7]

Too often in domestic debate on American foreign policy there is an unhelpful polarization of attitudes between those who are resentful of NATO-European reluctance to be led and those who are unduly sensitive to the (real or imagined) local perspectives of essentially regional allies. There are rules of behavior for the United States and its allies in their mutual relationships, and the U.S. government should not hesitate to remind its domestic and foreign critics of their existence and content.

The geopolitically rooted bureaucratic despotism of the Soviet state is almost as likely a source of competitive weakness in international security matters as are the constraints and the temptation to take soft options that characterize the democratic polities of the West. The legitimacy of Soviet rule and public acquiescence in the sacrifices that it imposes rest heavily upon national pride in the foreign (and military)successes of the state. It follows that the possibility of undisguisable failure should help reinforce whatever other considerations argue for caution in Soviet policy. By way of contrast, it is a paradox that the popular democratic politics of the Western world that most contribute to the possibility of a national security disaster serve also to maximize the prospect of that world's weathering the storm without traumatic political convulsion at home.

It is commonplace to observe that dictatorships maintain systemic political strength only in the context of a public aura of success; that is, given that it is the lot of all governments to receive and be responsible for both good and bad news, a dictatorship dares not admit that it has failed. Clear evidence of failure is typically a cause of that loss of awe and respect for those in power which can lead to uncontrollable demands for political change. Of course, this fear of the people is not confined to authoritarian regimes, though the perceived individual risks for rulers tend to be higher there.

Western democracies also have seen evidence of official disinclination to tell what is believed to be the truth for fear of political consequences. For example, the governments of Stanley Baldwin and Neville Chamberlain believed they could not tell the British people the truth about German rearmament in the 1930s. Initially, those governments feared rejection at the polls by what they believed to be an overwhelmingly pacifist, or at least still war-weary, electorate; later, public recognition of the facts would show that they had either lied or been incompetent in past years. By 1938 the facts believed by the government were so bleak in their implications that effective action to discipline Hitler's ambitions was judged imprudent in the near term. Considering the 1930s as a whole, it is probably correct to argue that the British problem lay not so much in inadequate access to the details of the German rearmament program as in inadequate interpretation of the meaning of that program for Hitler's foreign policy. The truth most in need of divination was not precise numbers of first-line aircraft, reserve aircraft, and pilots; it was the strategic purposes toward which Hitler intended to apply those military means.[8]

Halford Mackinder had a great deal to say about the enduring opposition between empires founded on land and on sea mobility, and he was very sensitive indeed to the contrasting values and philosophies of East and West, but he said very little about rivalry in the "will to compete."[9] This book, while employing Mackinder's and Spykman's geopolitical framework of Heartland-Rimland, is very much concerned about the ability of Western security communities to sustain an adequacy in countervailing pressure against Soviet grand strategy.[10] Concepts for the direction of U.S. national security policy need to identify both security endeavors that are bearable over a long period for a coalition of democracies in time of peace, and a strategy for war that capitalizes upon Western strengths and exploits Soviet systemic vulnerabilities insofar as they can be discerned.

There is a very large and perceptive, if heavily anecdotal, literature on the academically unfashionable subject of national character.[11] It is the somewhat unhelpful thesis of this book that American national character and style in strategic behavior accommodate oscillations in policy emphasis that invite characterization as gross instability.[12] The methodological weaknesses in studies of character, culture, and style are all too obvious. The careful scholar of "the American way" must be aware, first, that American history has many threads: how is one to determine that one pattern of behavior is typically American and another is not? Second, American culture is recently derivative. A nation of immigrants may blend to produce a new culture, but the intellectual and emotional roots of some important American thinkers (and doers) in international politics have been continental-European in inspiration.[13]

Third, much of international political behavior is culture-neutral. Human beings under pressure have much in common, whatever their individual cultural affiliation may happen to be. Fourth, all countries exhibit apparently deviant behavior from time to time; some have been known to elect political leaders who are quite dramatically unrepresentative of the more dominant characteristics of their electorates. Fifth, given some degree of common circumstance and roots, a nation's style of behavior is shared, in part, with other polities. Any attempt to define an American political or strategic culture and style should anticipate well-founded claims that other countries also exhibit some of the traits identified.

Sixth, one must be alert to the fact that industrious and competent scholars generally are able to find what they seek. Given the rich tableau of the American historical experience from which to draw the kernel of a distinctive "American way," many theories should be supportable. Finally, culture is as far from immutable as are geographical realities, which can change in their security implications as new technologies evolve. The socially transmitted attitudes, habits, and skills that, *in toto*, constitute culture will change under the pressure of novel circumstances. [14]

Can anything of value for this analysis be said, then, on the subject of American political culture, strategic culture, national style? On the grounds that the difficult is merely difficult, rather than impossible, generalizations can and must be offered on the subject of "the American way." [15] Social science has developed no exact methodology for identifying distinctive national cultures and styles. If the cultural and stylistic proclivities of Americans were not so important for the consideration of basic national security policy, they would be excluded from discussion here. But those policy choices *are* considered by an American people distinctive in its strategic culture from other security communities. The American people are geopolitically conditioned as Americans to think and feel in a reasonably distinctive American way about those choices. The roots of American strategic culture lie in a frontier tradition, an experience and expectation of success in national endeavors, experience with an abundance of resources for defense, a dominant political philosophy of liberal idealism, and a sense of separateness—moral and geostrategic—from the evil doings of the Old World.

Geopolitics, in relating "international political power to the geographical setting," [16] embraces human and cultural factors as well as the statistics of territorial dimensions, landforms, economic assets, distances between political entities, and the like. The "cultural thoughtways" of a people or peoples who conceive of themselves as a nation[17] are very much the product of geography. The "geographical setting" is important for the forms of economic activity that are profitable; for the degree of vulnerability to alien penetration or invasion; for the identity, character, and proximity of neighbors and even for the range of forms of government that are consistent with national preferences. [18] The political behavior of a country is the reflection of that country's history; and that country's history is in great part (though certainly not entirely) the product of its geographical setting.

The unique geographical setting of the United States suggests possibilities rather than mandating particular choices. Properly employed, a geopolitical perspective upon foreign policy does not have major deterministic features. [19] But as Ken Booth has plausibly asserted, "strategy, society and culture cannot be divorced unless strategy is to be understood as a mere technique." [20] Even though the choices in national security policy theoretically available to Americans may be deduced from an acultural logic of geopolitics, American policy choices and actions are influenced by the kind of people that Americans both are and consider themselves to be.

Physical geography largely governs economic geography, which determines social geography, which in its turn is a major influence on the evolution of political forms. The quality of performance of a state over time in defense of national interests must always be influenced by the quantities of assets that may be mobilized in pursuit of national goals, and by the facts of physical and political geography; location (nature of terrain, latitudes, weather) and national territory; defensibility of frontiers; identity, size, and character of states in close proximity, and so forth. But statecraft is at least as much a matter of discovering and exploiting effective "work-arounds" for national weaknesses and vulnerabilities as it is of exploiting national strengths. Substantially, though not exclusively, the effectiveness of a particular security community in defense of its interests is a function of the quality of strategic guidance provided for sustained collective action.

Nazi Germany lost its brutal bid for Eurasian hegemony because it lacked physical assets on a scale to match the political ambitions of its leader.[21] Statecraft and strategy are about making choices among goals in the light of the means available and reliably obtainable.[22] The first duty of a statesman to the nation's generals is to give them a reasonable chance of success. German military skill, determination, and bravery could not overcome the sheer unfavorable weight of the quantitative imbalance. They could delay inevitable defeat and set a high price on victory for the grand alliance, but they could not compensate fully for incompetent statecraft. The same judgment applies to the German military experience of the previous generation. In the words of a British scholar: "For the four and a half years of the first World War, Germany, with no considerable assistance from her allies had held the world at bay, had beaten Russia, had driven France, the military colossus of Europe for more than two centuries, to the end of her tether, and, in 1917, had come within an ace of starving Britain into surrender."[23]

The moral for this book in the German military failures of 1914-18 and 1939-45 is that a national defense effort, no matter how impressive, must meet tests of external as well as internal logic. The internal logic of armed forces pertains to the efficiency with which national resources are transformed into military capability. The external logic of armed forces pertains to the adequacy of the military instrument to meet the tasks set for it by national security policy. As Trevor Dupuy and Martin van Creveld have demonstrated convincingly, German "fighting power," unit for unit, was manifestly superior to that developed by the armed forces of any of its opponents in both world wars.[24] Yet, superior though the Germans were, they were assigned missions beyond their absolute capability to perform. The United States should not have to seek compensation in the sacrifice of its soldiers for weaknesses in the terms, conditions, and structure of conflict that could have been alleviated or neutralized by more appropriate policy choices.

The United States is an insular power of continental size. Both psychologically and in terms of military logistics, its traditionally protective oceanic distances retain major strategic significance in the nuclear-missile age. One must hasten to add that although distance alone can be important, even decisive (combined with adverse climatic conditions) in shaping military practicalities,[25] it does not offer absolute protection. The oceanic isolation of the United States from Europe and Asia can be a source of security or insecurity, depending upon the balance of naval strength. The Japanese provided a classic negative example in World War II. The strategic value of the defense perimeter they constructed in the central Pacific was entirely dependent upon the feasibility of inflicting massive attrition on intruding naval forces and then of concentrating superior assets against the gravely weakened intruder. As was the German case in Russia, the sheer geographical scope of Japanese expansion was a source of strategic weakness, not of strength.[26]

So long as the U.S. Navy sustains a working command of strategically important sea lines of communication, oceanic isolation is a source of strength for U.S. security.[27] If the maritime areas where the U.S. Navy enjoys a preponderance of strength should contract dramatically from the Eurasian littoral, then the oceans would become more and more a means of access for the enemies of the United States. Physical geography alone, while providing important constraints and opportunities, is given specific strategic meaning only with reference to time, technology, relative national effort, and choices effected among strategies and tactics. In short, insularity is not an unmixed blessing, particularly with respect to the attitudes that it encourages in a power that has chosen to function in a global guardianship role for international security. Nonetheless, ICBM's and SLBMs (submarine-launched ballistic missiles) admitted, oceanic distance continues to have a net beneficial effect upon the American security condition. These benefits are the result of Western maritime superiority, which supports an array of allies on the Eurasian periphery that could block Soviet access to the open ocean.[28]

The continental insularity of the United States is not casually to be compared with the insularity of Great Britain. Britain never faced an immediate security threat even remotely comparable to that posed today by Soviet strategic nuclear forces. This is not to deny that the (vastly exaggerated) bomber threat in the middle and late 1930s certainly influenced British policy toward the Czech frontier issue in 1938.[29] Moreover, Britain did periodically face the danger of invasion; particularly in 1692, 1744, 1759, 1779, 1797, 1804-5, and, of course, 1940.[30] In the "age of fighting sail" the Royal Navy welcomed an attempt at invasion that forced the French fleet to put to sea, where it could be engaged and defeated. Alfred Mahan has described the British counterinvasion design:

> Holding the interior positions they did, before—and therefore between—the chief dockyards and detachments of the French navy, the latter could unite only by a concurrence of successful evasions, of which the failure of any one nullified the result. Linked together, as various British fleets were, by chains of smaller vessels, chance alone could secure Bonaparte's great combination, whch depended upon the covert concentration of several detachments upon a point practically within the enemy's lines. Thus, while bodily present before Brest, Rochefort, and Toulon, strategically the British squadrons lay in the Straits of Dover barring the way against the Army of Invasion.[31]

In the words of Sir Julian Corbett, invasion was rendered "an operation beyond the endurable risks of war"; an undefeated Royal Navy, by its concentrated presence in the western approaches to the English Channel, compelled an enemy's covering fleet to conform to the movements of the invasion transports.[32]

Several "what if..." pseudohistories of the summer of 1940 demonstrate that a German invasion of Britain in July of that year would have stood an excellent chance of succeeding,[33] but I have yet to see a plausible scenario for the Soviet invasion of the United States. Landpower and seapower cannot easily engage each other.[34] It is important to recognize the fundamental, geopolitically based divergence in Soviet and American strategic orientations. The preferred enemy of the United States, if one may be permitted the idea, would be a country which—like the Empire of Japan of 1941-45—is fatally vulnerable to pressure from the sea. Similarly, the preferred enemy of the Soviet Union would be one—resembling the Third Reich—whose national assets are all accessible to Soviet armies.

Geostrategically, the Soviet-American rivalry is a contest between states that have enormous difficulty exerting direct military pressure on each other except with reference to the nuclear war that neither wants to wage under any circumstances. Much of the contemporary debate in the United States over the maritime strategy adopted under President Reagan bears immediately upon this point.[35] What is the strategic utility of maritime preponderance against a foe that lacks seizable overseas assets of great value, is economically effectively self-sufficient, and has no coastlines easy of approach that offer ready access to vital national assets in the interior?[36] In its heyday British seapower could support peripheral continental distractions for Napoleon in the Baltic, in Iberia, in the Mediterranean, in Holland, and even on the coast of France itself. But what could the U.S. Navy do by way of useful distraction of Soviet landpower?

Strategic context, as always, would be critically important. Bearing in mind the nuclear shadow that would loom over all operations, it is very likely that a sound and effective peripheral strategy, *waged in conjunction with protracted continental campaigns* ("the British way in warfare," as it has been known), could be devised and implemented.[37] This subject is addressed in Chapter 14; it is important at this juncture to flag the geopolitical structure of Soviet-American rivalry, a rivalry that is very much a landpower-seapower contest. For the United States the long-term danger is that the Soviet Union might exploit success on land in order to build a potential preponderance at sea. For the Soviet Union the long-term danger is that the United States might exploit its maritime superiority in order to support a tricontinental coalition which could threaten the Soviet imperium on land.

American interests in Europe certainly can be characterized as vital. Indeed, twice in this century in action, and since 1949 by the promise of action (given physical effect in the form of more than 300,000 servicemen plus many dependents), the United States has declared that movements against the security of its interests in Europe constitute a *casus belli.* Unless one or the other of the superpowers elects to escalate out of a theater conflict, however, the immediate survival of the United States is not at risk to events in Europe. West Germany, France, Benelux, Great Britain, Sweden, and the rest have no choice other than to focus all but a small fraction of their mobilized and mobilizable defense resources upon the potential enemy at their gates in peninsular Europe.

It has always been true that continental powers have been more constrained by necessity in their choice of security policy than have insular powers who can establish command of the sea.[38] Because of the insular geopolitics of the U.S. homeland, respected American commentators can debate the rival attractions of a heavy continental-European focus, and a maritime orientation whereby a United States supreme at sea would apply its political-military weight after the classic fashion of an offshore sea power.[39] As Michael Vlahos (and indeed common sense) has suggested, these are not true alternatives.[40] Nonetheless, they do illustrate that Americans, as a free gift of geography and as the reward for prudent maritime effort, do have choices in security policy and strategy.

The base of U.S. maritime power could be an "American Heartland" embracing all of North and Central America and Venezuela and Colombia. This is a security concept that has considerable immediate, if not necessarily long-term, strategic and economic integrity. The survival values of Americans probably could be sustained for a while—adequately, though not generously—solely in the context of hemispheric (or even quarterspheric-plus) defense. But with respect to its prospects for long-term survival the United States would be ill advised to embrace the idea of a hemispheric security option as an alternative to the extant trans-oceanic alliance structures. Author George Ott has cited Nicholas Spykman accurately to the effect that the New World can balance the Old World, but only if the Old World is politically fragmented and the New World is not.[41] Should the United States disengage from security entanglements in the Old World, it is likely that virtually all the World Island of Eurasia would eventually come under the hegemonic sway of the Soviet Union. In Spykman's words: "If...the Old World can be united or organized in such a manner that large masses of unbalanced power can become available for action across the ocean, the New World will be encircled and, depending on its powers of resistance, may have to submit to the dictates of the Old. The possibility of encirclement depends, therefore, on the power potential of the Old and the New Worlds and the likelihood of their integration into single political units or coalitions."[42]

The continental insularity of the United States suggests mixed consequences for alliance management. On the one hand, with escalation possibilities not forgotten, a United States with a homeland very far removed from the potential scene of battle around Eurasia is more likely to behave resolutely than would countries fearful of immediate adverse military consequences for their home territories. On the other hand, a United States very far distant from the allies whose political integrity it is committed to support (possibly) à outrance has to be a United States potentially capable of disengagement under threat or under fire.[43] Its oceanic moats have generated anxieties among its forward-placed allies both that the United States might not really take ultimate risks on behalf of others[44] and that the United States might behave in a militarily reckless manner because its homeland would be so distant from the immediate zone of combat.

There is much to recommend the axiom that with sufficiently imaginative cartography one can prove, or at least illustrate the plausibility of, virtually any geopolitical proposition.[45] One can show, for example, that the maritime alliance led by the United States effectively encircles the Soviet Heartland superpower. One can cite the oceanic distances separating the United States from its security clients as the interior lines of a globe-girdling alliance system that poses threats to the Soviet imperium on very widely separated axes. As lines of communication, oceans can be advertised not as barriers to timely American intervention around the Rimlands of Eurasia-Africa but rather as safe highways. Such a judgment applies so long as the Western Alliance enjoys a clear maritime preponderance in most areas of strategic interest.

The geopolitical realities of Soviet-American rivalry include the geography of Soviet seapower: the fact that nowhere does the Soviet Navy enjoy easy access to the open ocean with the sole exception of Petropavlovsk in Kamchatka, and even there the utility of the naval facilities are constrained by seasonal ice and by their isolation from the center of Soviet strength in the European U.S.S.R. The Soviet Navy is impressive in size and quality, but the extent and character of Soviet physical geography limit its capability for mutual support among the different fleets. In addition, like France and Germany in past eras, the Soviet Union cannot afford to devote the proportion of scarce national resources to the development of its naval power that would be necessary in order to contest the command of the seas. Continental powers, for obvious and sound reasons of strategic logic as well as strategical-cultural conditioning, are essentially landpowers in orientation. To a degree, naval power is a luxury for a landpower. [46]

It should be noted that the Soviet Navy is all the more impressive a national acheivement for the fact that it may be a "luxury fleet." American strategists need to ask themselves how large a Soviet maritime challenge they might face were the Soviet Union no longer "distracted" by the prospect of major land conflict on two (or more) fronts in Eurasia. This point has relevance for the present discussion because some of the national security policy choices that the United States might exercise would entail U.S. military withdrawal from commitments to peripheral Eurasia. If local European and Asian security communities could function strategically as successor "containing" powers, then the Soviet Union would be no more at liberty to pursue extra-continental *Weltpolitik* than is the case at present. But it would be imprudent to assume that the United States could pass the containment baton to competent and reliable hands.

Some comfort can and should be drawn from geopolitical facts such as those cited above, but there is another side to the argument. It is true that the Soviet Union is at a severe disadvantage competing with the Western Alliance at sea. But it should never be forgotten that the Soviet Union has no strategic need of maritime command other than local control over closed-sea bastion areas for safe deployment of nuclear-powered ballistic missile-firing submarines (SSBNs). [47]

Corbett reminds us that "the object of naval warfare is to control maritime communications." [48] The Soviet need would not be to secure and exercise anything approximating a general command of the sea; for the foreseeable future the Soviet Union will have no strategically essential maritime lines of communications requiring control, beyond its coastal waters. Its object would be to deny the maritime alliance of the West a working command of the truly essential sea lines of communication, to harass the American exercise of seapower so that the United States could not effectively maintain and exploit a working command to and about Eurasia. Even if Soviet maritime assets were to be defeated comprehensively in a campaign at sea, that campaign might last long enough so that American ability to move men and material to Eurasia would be delayed fatally.

Some opponents of the U.S. maritime strategy of the 1980s contend that the new stress upon forward deployment and taking the battle to the enemy early in a war could result in blunting the U.S. Navy's strength and thereby facilitating a Soviet antishipping campaign later in the conflict.[49] If naval power constitutes the second collection of the crown jewels of national military strength (after the strategic nuclear forces), dare it be hazarded in any but the most advantageous of strategic circumstances? But if U.S. naval power is to be influential in the course of what may prove to be a conflict of only brief duration, what prudent choice is there other than ordering it to steam into harm's way? In reality, the alternatives are not nearly so stark as the somewhat overexcited debate of recent years could lead the unwary to believe. U.S. naval power must be strategically relevant whether a conflict be long or short—though not if the hostilities erupt rapidly into a massive nuclear "exchange." Regardless of how a campaign proceeded in Europe, both superpowers would be confronted with the question of what, if anything, to do next. A U.S. Navy that is substantially intact would enable the U.S. government to wage, and compel the Soviet government to fear, a protracted global conflict (always presuming that intrawar nuclear deterrence holds).[50]

For the Royal Navy of 1914, as for the U.S. Navy today, the sinking of the German/Soviet Navy was not essential to the command of the vital sea lines of communication. An enemy fleet confined in its bastions does not directly impede maritime communications. However, naval assets committed to a more or less distant blockade are themselves imprisoned, as jailers. Since the essence of maritime power is its mobility and geographical flexibility, that essence is diluted to the extent that a navy is tied to what amounts to guard duty. It should also be understood that just as no naval battle or campaign will be comprehensively decisive in the sense of driving the enemy totally from the sea, so no blockade effort can ever be totally impermeable.

In the late 1960s, Albert Wohlstetter argued that the traditional "loss-of-strength gradient," the proposition that effective power declines in proportion to distance, should not be applied simplemindedly to the logistic problems of the United States and the Soviet Union.[51] He was correct. The development and proliferation of strategically planned railroads in the Eurasian Heartland was suggested by Sir Halford Mackinder in 1904 as heralding a geopolitical revolution in favor of the continental Heartland power (Imperial Russia or Imperial Germany) and to the relative disadvantage of the maritime British Empire—with particular reference to the Near East and India.[52] Mackinder's prognosis has to be modified in light of the development of heavy-lift aircraft with transoceanic reach and of fast container ships, and in the context of fragile ground lines of communication in strategically important parts of Eurasia. For example, Soviet forces operating in the Far East remain dependent upon a single railroad track that hugs the border with the People's Republic of China (a problem only partially alleviated by construction of the Baikal-Amur mainline railroad), and combat in west-central Europe would have to be sustained logistically across Polish soil.[53] Still oceanic distances put the United States at an enduring strategic disadvantage relative to the Soviet Union with respect to military deployment in central Europe. The relation of net strategic advantage is arguable with reference to northern and southern Europe, the Near East, and South Asia. Soviet lines of communication to the Far East are vulnerable in theory, as already noted, but in practice the United States might lack the military means to make very good use of that theoretical condition.

An important reason for the relatively high "tail to teeth" ratio of American forces (of almost all kinds) is the geographical mandate that they would fight as expeditionary forces. However, as a burgeoning library of military reform literature reminds us,[54] the extraordinary reach required of U.S. forces does not sufficiently explain why the Army in particular, from the Civil War to the present time, has generated so much less effective combat power (relative to scale of effort) where it counts—at the sharp end—than have either U.S. enemies or allies.[55] Aside from the "tail" size attributable quite reasonably to the distance between the homeland mobilization base and the theaters of combat, one also has to acknowledge the pervasive influence of cultural factors, of national style. American soldiers have traditionally been much better fed and more abundantly—though not always better—equipped than their enemies.[56] Logistic affluence is nice to have, but it can translate into manpower poverty for the combat arms that take most of the casualties. Overall, American society, like other societies, wages war in accordance with its own way of doing things.[57] War is approached in the United States as if it were a very large corporate enterprise in need of efficient management. Unfortunately, that drive for efficiency tends to focus unheathily on the management of the military organization rather than the management of scarce assets for optimum effectiveness in combat.[58]

The influence of geopolitical setting upon choice in national security policy ultimately finds real-life expression in Americans in uniform performing according to American habits of mind and method. There is a sharp end to grand theory. Strategic culture—the socially transmitted attitudes, habits, and skills of a community in its approach to issues of national security—is very much the product of geopolitical factors as they are locally interpreted. There is an audit trail writ large from society to its armed forces. The contemporary military reform movement would do well to remember that a security community provides a reflection of itself in its armed guardians.[59] Technical fixes in defense organization, and even changes in military tactics and at the operational level of war, will be unlikely to have the desired effects if they affront important strands in American culture.[60]

Generations of British strategic thinkers of the maritime (as opposed to the continental) school stressed that the essential twin elements of a maritime strategy had to be mobility and surprise.[61] A United States committed seriously to a maritime centerpiece in its strategy[62] must be honest in its development of the prudently assessed requirements of strategic mobility. The enduring geopolitical advantages enjoyed by the United States at sea provide the basis, but only the basis, of the rationale for a Eurasian peripheral strategy against a continental landpower that enjoys some enduring and offsetting geopolitical advantages.

What has been lacking since the demise of U.S. strategic nuclear superiority in the late 1960s has been a combined arms strategy for the prospective guidance of war as a whole—for deterrence, in the first instance. The U.S. government—indeed, the U.S. defense community at large—offers scant evidence of careful thought on the subject of how the military requirements of its national security policy are to be met. Absent is some sense of overall design intended to integrate the separate stories of prospective space, air, land, and sea combat, each of which is too often approached in near-isolation.[63]

If the integrity of flexible response as a strategic concept is undermined further, by Soviet theater and strategic offensive nuclear deployments, by arms control, and perhaps by new Soviet strategic defensive weapons, how does a maritime alliance thwart or offset the potential for aggressive gain of Soviet landpower? The answers lie in denying prompt acquisition of important territorial "prizes"; supporting, reviving, or creating continental distractions; gaining leverage through seizing or threatening seizure of important assets; shifting the balance of forces progressively in the alliance's favor; developing flexibility and surprise in application of force from the sea; and eroding the enemy's confidence in the likelihood of victory. These are tall orders, but they speak to the historical record of seapower-landpower contests, and they encourage the United States to think broadly about armed conflict. Overall, they are not rigid requirements demanding detailed implementation but candidate markers for defense planning.

6

The American Way

Ken Booth has argued that to divorce strategic studies from area studies is largely to think in a void.[1] Obvious truth though that is, it is a fair indictment of the community of scholars and scholar-officials who have influenced and helped execute U.S. national security policy in recent decades. Cultural parochialism is far from unique to the United States, of course. The Soviet Union/Russia, long suspicious and fearful of foreign influence, is an order of magnitude less empathetic to alien perspectives than is the United States—notwithstanding the importation of the alien western European doctrine of Marxism, which V.I. Lenin promptly and bloodily Russified in practice.[2]

For its own unique reasons, however, the United States is a country not well equipped to deal effectively with other cultures on their own terms, or even on American terms, in ways that might neutralize unhelpfully distinctive foreign attitudes. As British historian Michael Howard perceptively observed:

> While the history of Europe certainly provides a perfect model of how not to conduct international relations, at least there has always been, among European governments and peoples, an awareness that there was a problem—that there were foreigners with whom we had constantly to interact, people who looked at matters in different ways and whose languages we had to learn if we were to cope with them effectively. Europeans have always been conscious of the pressures of a multi-cultural society, and of the skill and subtlety required to flourish in it. Diplomatic and linguistic abilities are still highly prized in Europe; foreign offices still attract the best of the élites. This was not so in the United States until half a century ago, and it is not fully so even today. American culture has been more concerned with emancipating itself from foreign influence than with assimilating it.[3]

Of concern here is not the quality of American attitudes, assessed omnisciently on some abstract universal scale, but rather the consequences of American attitudes for the effectiveness of the United States as a player in international politics.

American culture (political, civic, strategic) and the derivative "national style" necessarily reflect the unique American historical experience. To the profound annoyance of foreigners, the United States proclaimed itself from the outset to be a different sort of country from any other.[4] The concept of a uniquely virtuous republic of free men (apart from slaves, of course, who did not count) carving out some approximation (the vision has varied)[5] of God's purpose on earth from a continentwide wilderness (apart from the native Indians who, again, did not count) has had an understandably powerful impact on national self-evaluation. Whatever the merit, or otherwise, of that evaluation, the fact remains that the idea of American uniqueness—the notion that America is not an "ordinary country"—has not encouraged empathy or respect for local opinions, attitudes, or practices elsewhere. And however inevitable, such a lack of empathy for the worldviews of others serves greatly to hinder American efforts to exercise influence over them. (Needless to say, perhaps, American ignorance of alien perspectives has been fully reciprocated by foreigners' incomprehension of American psychological realities.)

The point is not to criticize Americans for being what they cannot help being—like everybody everywhere, the product of their local culture. Rather, the point is to suggest that there is a very great cultural distance between, on the one hand, the banner carriers for an American-style "free world" who typically command the U.S. ship of state and explain its course to the American public, and, on the other hand, the linear descendants of the village strongmen who command the police state of the Soviet empire.[6] It is a cultural distance between rivals much wider than has been usual in the great-power antagonisms of modern history.

Except for those rare periods when it is controlled by a foreign perspective on security (as in the Kissinger era, for example), the United States typically behaves in its external policy in ways that are distinctively American. Similarly, the Soviet Union functions by and large as the "village bully"—respectful of opposing power but quite unscrupulous in exploiting those who cannot resist effectively. Both countries, with their very strong local political and strategic cultures, have universalist ideologies. Their clash of ideologies reinforces their clash of security concerns and claims, which derives both from their historically unusual degree of preeminence among states and from the potential for global conflict that is permitted by the technologies of communication and transportation.

The leading pioneering scholar of ethnocentrism in strategic studies, Ken Booth, has observed that "strategists as a body are remarkably incurious about the character of their enemies and allies."[7] Prominent among the messages in Booth's analysis is the advice that even when Americans choose to behave or cannot help behaving, in a distinctively American way, it is still important that they understand a potential enemy on his own terms. Whatever doctrine may be selected as the organizing framework for U.S. national security policy in the future, to be effective as guidance for the defense of American interests it must not only be tolerable in its conception to American political culture and compatible in its action requirements with the national style; it must also be able to cope with Soviet behavior, no matter how alien that behavior and its probable motives may be in American terms.

Doctrine, as contrasted with strategy, is very much an American forte. As a country that is long on moral and political purpose but short on willingness to balance means and ends, the United States discovers new doctrines with singular frequency. Since World War II there have been the Truman Doctrine (proclaiming a global commitment to support "free peoples"), the Eisenhower Doctrine (for the Middle East), the Nixon Doctrine (announcing U.S. preparedness to support only those countries willing and able to make a major effort to defend themselves on the ground), the Carter Doctrine (declaring the Persian Gulf area a vital interest of the United States), and most recently the Reagan Doctrine (appearing to announce that the United States will endeavor to roll back Soviet influence in the Third World).

It is not difficult to criticize the scale and quality of U.S. defense preparation from a wide range of perspectives upon the desirable, but such criticism needs to be set against appropriate historical comparisons. Compared to performance in the years preceding its entry into both world wars, the national security record of every postwar administration (with the possible exception of Harry Truman's conduct of military affairs until mid-1950) has been of stellar quality.[8] Moreover, critics of U.S. national security policy on both the Left and the Right have tended to neglect the historically unique difficulties characterizing the strategic-military problems that are of most concern to American policymakers. Unlike the generality of British, French, German, or Russian statesmen in the nineteenth and much of the twentieth century, American postwar policymakers have discerned a necessity for a high quality of U.S. military-competitive performance in all the geographical dimensions of actual and potential warfare. Because of its insular geography, the United States as an actor in world security affairs has been primarily a maritime and air power. The U.S. Army has never enjoyed, or merited, the universal respect for combat effectiveness that has been accorded U.S. naval and air forces,[9] yet the weakness of the Western allies of the United States vis-à-vis first Germany and then the Soviet Union has driven the United States to become, and to remain, the largest military landpower in the non-Communist world. Traditional strategic culture and obvious military necessity dictated the particular geographical environments in which the British, French, Germans, and Russians would bid most consistently and persuasively for excellence. The breadth of the American commitment to excellence in military preparation after 1950 is historically unprecedented.

On balance, it is surprising that an effectively insular superpower, prone to wide-swinging mood changes in its popular assessment of foreign danger, has adhered to so steady a basic course in its grand strategy for so long. Political competition in a democracy thrives on promises of change. Candidates for high public office in the United States have an electoral need to achieve product differentiation for identity and recognition. This is a political culture that endemically is attracted—if only briefly in each instance—to the new. Furthermore, policy change or upset is a more marked feature of the American than of other Western political systems because of the extent of the diffusion of power in Washington. Any government can and will alter course under the pressure of perceived necessity, but very few administrations are in a condition of near-perpetual negotiation with their legislatures, after the American model.

The forces that have molded American political culture and given it a Janus-like quality of tension between isolationism and interventionism are substantially geopolitical in nature. Foreign policy commentators, particularly in the media, have a tendency to exaggerate the significance of the shifts and adjustments in policy that are promised or effected, and to neglect the major—less newsworthy—continuities.

The United States has not recently engaged in a great domestic debate over its role in the world. The basic American international role as global guardian of the Western end of international order which emerged gradually though unmistakably out of World War II, has come to be as widely understood an idea, as widely accepted as inevitable for policy design, as was the role of balancer to the small British foreign policy elite of the nineteenth century. Strategy has been challenged, as have the means selected and applied as instruments of the chosen strategy. But the legitimacy of and need for a global guardianship role apparently remain outside the realm of politically serious contention. Understandably sensitive allied leaders, not to mention editorial writers throughout the Western world, are attentive and even overattentive to the real and not-so-real shifts in American military doctrine.[10] But steadiness of course in U.S. national security policy *at the highest level with respect to essentials* has been the norm—despite the attitudes and characteristics discussed in this chapter, despite the oscillations in public mood, and despite the shakiness of the pillars of understanding on which U.S. grand strategy is founded.

Few close observers seem to have noticed the most remarkable feature of the postwar security system: a United States that as recently as 1941 was

locked into a legal condition of neutrality vis-à-vis a world conflict has—
by the late 1980s—accumulated a forty-year record of net security production for countries all around the Rimland of Eurasia.[11] This record is all
the more remarkable given the dramatic, cumulative objective shifts in
key factors bearing upon the terms of international security arrangements. Some of the more important U.S. security clients have so transformed their domestic economies that they pose major challenges to the
health of important American industries, while the Soviet Union has
constructed a convincing multilevel counterdeterrent to U.S. military
power. In short, while one should be sensitive to oscillations in American
mood,[12] one should also be aware of the quantity and quality of fuel that
has accumulated for feeding the fundamental American debate over the
wisdom of its basic policy course with respect to international security.
The debate has yet to occur.

The United States is, and prospectively will long remain, a giant in
world politics; its attitudes and behavior matter to the general quality of
international security. The attitudes and national behavioral traits, or
style, discussed here all have in common the feature that on balance they
are dysfunctional for a superpower seeking to pursue a tolerably steady
and prudent course in world affairs. By way of a somewhat halfhearted
caveat, it should be noted that negative factors can have positive results, at
least for a while. For example, important segments of American society
hold to an optimistic ideology concerning the future, an ideology that
reflects cultural "thoughtways" deriving from American domestic experience.[13] This optimism, or faith in progress, licenses excessive expectations and prepares the ground for excessive disillusion and a search for
scapegoats when the promise is not fulfilled. But faith in the future, naive
and ill-founded though it may be, can sustain a society through a severe
"time of troubles" that would see the political and social fabric of less
optimistic polities crumble. In addition, the attitudes examined here,
although deemed to have a net debilitating effect upon the ability of the
United States to design and execute effective long-range strategies for
national security, are by no means reprehensible in and of themselves. A
democracy cannot evade suffering from the vices of its virtues.

The kernel of truth in the following observation by Gregory Foster is
useful as a scene-setter for the discussion below: "The United States
...seems never quite to have made the psychological transition from the
societal values of truthfulness, fair play and the rules of the game to the
realities of international power politics."[14] The idea that U.S. foreign
policy in action is the story of "innocents abroad" can be overstated but
should not be totally disregarded. Semiseriously at least, a leading proponent of an SDI unconstrained by the legal impediments of arms-control
agreements has characterized the choice before the U.S. political system
as a question of whether to repose confidence in the competence of

American engineers or of American diplomats. On the record of demonstrated accomplishment to date, he argued, American engineers are far
more likely to protect the national security.[15] This anecdote is cited not as
evidence of U.S. incapacity in diplomacy but as a telling illustration of
popular American beliefs about the strengths and weaknesses of their
security community.

The remainder of this chapter considers five broad characteristics of
"the American way" of thought and method in national and international
security. These characteristics do not determine particular policy choices,
but they do provide a filter of attitudes and beliefs so deep and pervasive
that they are properly labeled as cultural.

First, the United States, as an insular power that developed very
substantially in isolation from the quarrels of balance-of-power Europe,
continues to harbor the belief that peace is the normal and universally
desired condition of mankind. This belief is no more untrue in the
American context than it is unworthy, but it can have unfortunate policy
consequences when it is projected upon very un-American polities
abroad.[16] The belief encompasses both the view that war is abnormal and
the notion that anticipation of, and hence preparation for, war is abnormal.[17] If it is true that war is an extraordinary event, occasioned only by
the machinations and ambitions of wicked people, then it follows that a
very substantial level of U.S. defense preparation in peacetime must be
intended to oppose wicked designs very specifically.

By contrast, traditional Russian geopolitical realism and Communist
ideology, in convenient combination, provide the Soviet defense establishment with a permanency of assumption of external threat; heavy
resource allocations for defense therefore meet no serious domestic bureaucratic challenge.[18] The entire history of Russia and the Soviet Union
reflects the perception of external danger. One authority has observed,
concerning the Russia that emerged from subjugation by the Mongols:
"The three centuries that followed Russia's proclamation of full sov-
ereignty were for her people a period of unremitting and relentless armed
struggle such as no other nation has had to endure in modern times, of
warfare that tied down all their energies and taxed their strength to the
utmost limits....The state of never-ending war gave their society its
distinctive form."[19]

Americans have difficulty believing that the Soviet state would consciously choose to take action that increases the risk of war. Peace is held to
be so obviously desirable that the risks of war must lie in misunderstanding, in misperception,[20] or in the wickedness of the Soviet political elite.
The United States finds it hard to design and execute a policy theme or
doctrine that mixes cooperation and competition. Just as peace and war
are viewed as discrete phases of international life, so conflict and accom-

modation are viewed as polar opposites. A U.S. administration knows that it must arm to parley, at least to parley to good effect. But it knows also that a process of parleying reduces the willingness of U.S. and NATO-European domestic constituencies to arm. Needless to say, Soviet leaders know it, too.

The fact of the matter is that the U.S. political system, notwithstanding its decades of experience, has yet to come to terms with its Soviet problem. In the Soviet Union the United States faces a country with which it cannot achieve peace by standard American definition yet with which it cannot afford war.[21] The United States has had no prior experience with a condition of permanent "war-in-peace." In the past, enemies presented themselves as immediate problems to be "solved" by victorious war, following which the country returned to its normal condition of peace. American policymakers today might reflect to their advantage upon the insecurity condition that confronted the later Roman Empire:

> The Romans did not face a single enemy, or even a fixed group of enemies, whose ultimate defeat would ensure permanent security. Regardless of the amplitude of Roman victories, the frontiers of the empire would always remain under attack, since they were barriers in the path of secular migration flows from north to south and from east to west. Hence Roman strategy could not usefully aim at total victory at any cost, for the threat was not temporary but endless. The only rational goal was the maintenance of a minimally adequate level of security at the lowest feasible cost.[22]

Similarly, the United States cannot afford to attempt to defeat the Soviet Union in a definitive manner: that is to say, the Soviet Union is not a security "problem" to be solved. Instead the United States has to design a grand strategy that will enable it to live with the fact of Soviet power, all the while protecting essential Western values for an indefinite period. The tunnel of Soviet-American political competition has no end identifiable at present.

Soviet strategic culture has no difficulty with this condition. "As long as capitalism and Socialism exist, we cannot live in peace," Lenin declared. "In the end, one or the other will triumph."[23] William E. Odom explains: "The Soviet definition of Peace is unique and incompatible with Western definitions. Defense, in this peculiar Soviet sense, means offense. Peace means the destruction of all non-socialist states....peaceful coexistence was a strategy for irreconcilable struggle, political and military, with capitalism. Peaceful coexistence remains Soviet policy today."[24]

A second characteristic of U.S. culture is an optimism about progress in human affairs which, when confronted with the intractability of international competition and conflict, translates easily into an oscillation of mood between hope resting upon illusion and the disenchantment that attends disillusion. Fluctuations between undue optimism and its inevitable sequel, undue pessimism, are perpetual sources of instability in U.S. foreign policy.

As the most prominent example, politicians and officials who should know better have repeatedly encouraged public expectations of progress in arms control that far exceed what the structure of East-West political relations and the asymmetry of Soviet and American political systems plausibly could permit. The inexorable result is that in an attempt to narrow the distance between original expectation and modest achievement, officials feel compelled to oversell whatever arms-control agreement eventually proves to be negotiable. Americans (and others) whose illusions are fractured become vulnerable to excessive pessimism concerning the present and potential achievements of arms control; they tend to seek scapegoats for its "failure." Hostile passions typically will be vented both against the Soviet Union, which will be judged not to have behaved as it should in the interests of peace and stability, and against the U.S. government for some mix of sins. Those sins include raising false hopes, not trying hard enough, not negotiating with sufficient competence, not competing with sufficent vigor in arms, or competing too vigorously.

Just as a fourth-century Roman emperor could not expect to solve the problems of barbarian pressure upon his frontiers, so a late twentieth-century American president cannot expect to solve the problem of political rivalry with the Soviet Union and the attendant risk of nuclear war. But it is very un-American to accept the need for competitive arms behavior as a regrettable necessity for the long haul. Traditionally, Americans have solved problems; they have not lived with them and redefined them as conditions. Hence, the United States is perpetually vulnerable to the proposition that "real peace" is just around the corner. Unused to the ambiguity of a protracted conflict that is neither war nor peace, Americans are prey to the illusion that some panacea of the moment—a "nuclear freeze," deep reductions in nuclear weapons, an ill-defined detente, or even some variant of strategic superiority—will deliver a marked improvement in the U.S. national security condition. Necessarily, no matter what fashionable panacea is adopted *briefly,* the Soviet Union behaves in "wickedly" un-American Soviet ways, and a mood of disillusionment fuels the search for a new panacea.

The oscillation in American attitudes between hope and despair or frustration flows from cultural conditioning and is a fact of life to be accepted and planned for. Probably it cannot be altered fundamentally by any program of public education, in large part because most of the prospective educators, politicians, senior officials, and media pundits share the predispositions of those whose attitudes they would be seeking to influence. These predispositions plainly do not provide optimum attitudes or methods for the management of long-term competition with a totalitarian rival that is not subject to any noteworthy domestic popular pressures. Americans can arm and fight in order to defeat a clear and present (and evil) danger; it is less certain that they can remain adequately armed decade after decade. It may be that U.S. politicians are wise to promise that there can be an end to the arms competition, or that the SDI may effect a defensive "transition" to some presumably happy plateau whereon nuclear weapons have been rendered "impotent and obsolete."[25] A democracy that is denied hope could seek to jump ship from the enterprise of endless competition altogether, or reject the bearers of bad tidings and clutch only at the straws of the ever-available panaceas.

Third, the American people are prone to personalize international relations. For *raison d'état*, states will lie, cheat, steal, and kill—but a government of the people, by the people, and for the people cannot afford to be caught doing those unpleasant things, no matter how worthy the motive or how important the policy goals. American society prefers to believe that all, or virtually all, problems—domestic and international— are susceptible to solution or major alleviation through direct person-to-person treatment. In summit conferences or simple tourism, personal contact is judged to be helpful. This widespread American belief, correct in principle, is often profoundly erroneous when put into practice— though as a general rule it is not the person-to-person meetings that are harmful but the expectations and political pressures that those meetings encourage in the United States and its allies.

The problem in U.S.-Soviet relations is not that the leaders of the two countries do not know or understand each other. Rather, it is that the Soviet and American polities are in pursuit of incompatible goals. World peace may be well served by meetings between the leaders of the United States and the Soviet Union in the sense that each man may glean insights into the other's probable future reactions to events. But a general secretary of the Soviet Communist Party is no more likely or, indeed, domestically able to change the main course of Soviet foreign policy as a result of a more or less cordial meeting with an American president than the Chinese People's Republic is likely to tilt definitively towards Washington as a consequence of the influx of tens of thousands of American tourists.

If personally amicable or at least cordially correct relations between key officials could alter the course of the Soviet ship of state in ways compatible with the American definition of international order and stability, then the early 1940s and even the early to middle 1970s would surely have effected such an alteration. But personal interaction can work both ways: what if the leaders take a strong personal dislike to each other? Moreover, for ever-optimistic Westerners, personal interaction can mask the incompatibility of the two states' interests and policies, and the very fact of such interaction can place dangerously different levels of constraint upon the leader of a Western democracy and the leader of the U.S.S.R.

Fourth, it has long been the American way to believe that persons of good will, attentive to the needs of their societies, can always reach agreement if they try hard enough. A willingness to compromise is the essence of the process of negotiation so widely familiar to Americans; it is assumed that one enters a negotiation both desiring agreement and, *ergo*, prepared to compromise in order to reach agreement. It is no exaggeration to say that the process is a cultural and political value in the United States.[26] To be unwilling to negotiate, save in very exceptional circumstances, is taken as virtual evidence of malfeasance.

Soviet ideology is almost infinitely flexible in its ability to rationalize new developments, but it is always dogmatic. Soviet policy, ritualistically legitimized as being guided by the timeless wisdom of Marxism-Leninism, is made and executed by a political culture antithetical to the principle of compromise. In the Russian tradition, to be unyielding is to be strong; to seek compromise is to be weak. In American culture, to be serious about arms control—a quality that U.S. leaders are required to affirm with a repetitiveness that is highly erosive of Soviet respect—is to be, and to claim publicly to be, willing to compromise. The American cultural attraction to compromise has the unfortunate consequence of encouraging Soviet leaders to be exceedingly self-serving in their initial positions, to protract negotiations while the U.S. government negotiates itself toward a more and more "reasonable" stance, and, overall, to despise their U.S. counterparts.

Of all the differences between the American domestic scene and international life, the rule of law in the former and its general absence in the latter is by far the most important.[27] The habits of mind of an American lawyer *qua* lawyer are substantially irrelevant not only to the security relations of East and West but also to the Soviet domestic scene; the rule of law in an American domestic sense applies generally neither between the superpowers in matters of national security nor within the Soviet Union. Soviet justice, like Imperial Russian justice before it, does not recognize in principle or in practice that citizens have rights that can be infringed by state power. *Raison d'état* has absolute value in the Soviet Union.

For reasons that transcend the scope of this inquiry, the United States values uniquely (among all countries) the skills of the lawyer, the manager, and the engineer. Much of the difficulty the United States finds today in competing effectively with the Soviet Union flows from the facts that there is no pertinent law to interpret and manipulate, there is no agreed system to manage, and the issues that lend themselves to ingenious assault by inspired engineers are of second-order importance. The skills of the lawyer, the manager, and the engineer are all logically subordinate to the skills of the largely missing elements in the U.S. defense community: the strategic thinker, planner, and doer. Without the strategic thinker's identification of goals, the strategic planner's design of paths compatible with different goals, and the strategists' orchestration of policy instruments, the lawyer has no framework of practical and authoritative desiderata within which to work, the manager cannot discover the purpose of the system he has to manage, and the engineer cannot know which technical problems need to be addressed.

It is a less than stunning revelation to recognize that Soviet leaders employ international negotiations as an instrument of grand strategy. Given that the Soviet Union has been in a state of perpetual war-in-peace with the capitalist West from the time of its birth in 1917, it is scarcely surprising that Soviet negotiators approach their task as a form of combat. In Soviet perspective, neither a negotiating process nor the fact of agreement has importance in and of itself. The same cannot be said of popular attitudes within the United Staes and its allies. In the very early 1980s, the Reagan administration came under politically intolerable pressure to demonstrate in policy action its willingness to negotiate. A little later, inevitably, the administration came under great domestic and NATO-allied pressure to demonstrate that it was truly serious about seeking an agreement in the negotiations then under way.[28] Again inevitably, the Soviet Union very understandably encouraged and exploited this popular pressure in and on the United States.

In spite of the value placed on compromise, however, the United States is constrained as a popular democracy by a public opinion that tends to think in terms of simple and stark alternatives. In the face of the particularly brutal Soviet imperial policing activity of late 1979 and 1980, the U.S. government was compelled by domestic politics to halt virtually all formal negotiations with the Soviet Union; the gates of discourse were closed. Yet by late 1981 and 1982 the sense of outrage had diminished, and it was back to business more or less as usual. Save for brief periods, such as those following the invasion of Afghanistan and the imposition of martial law in Poland, the U.S. government is not at domestic or allied political liberty to say publicly that it is not willing to enter negotiations. And once in a negotiating process, it is not free to say that it believes an acceptable outcome to be highly improbable; it comes under growing domestic and allied pressure to advance revised and more negotiable positions.[29]

The fifth characteristic of the American people as a political entity—though by no means in all individual cases—is to hoist order and stability as values to be promoted and defended internationally. At least in their current incarnations, the United States and its major allies and friends are among history's success stories. With few exceptions, the Western Alliance led by the United States is a rich person's club that seeks only to hold what it has and to protect the framework of international order that sustains prosperity. (This is not to deny the very real fragility of the international banking system, the energy vulnerability of some key members of the club, or the serious issues of relative prosperity that lurk within the imperfectly free trade system operating under the rules of the 1947 General Agreement on Tariffs and Trade.) In short, for reasons of plain self-interest the general political stance of the Western world is defensive.

It is difficult for the United States as a satisfied power to comprehend the attitudes of less-satisfied powers; nor is the United States educated by experience to comprehend a country whose quest after national security knows no natural limits. As an insular superpower that fulfilled its national dream by subduing a largely hostile, if lightly populated, continent and that has no fears for the domestic legitimacy of its political system, the United States is not well placed to understand the depth of the Soviet drive to achieve ever greater national security. Notwithstanding some similarities with respect to universalist pretensions in political ideology and cultural ambivalence toward (effete) Europe, Soviet Russia and the United States have comprehensively different political traditions and practices. The American Revolution had nothing in common with the Russian Revolution save the ascription; it warrants being called a revolution only by virtue of long usage. Writing Federalist Paper No. 9, Alexander Hamilton described a security condition that is inconceivable in Soviet perspective: "If we are wise enough to preserve the Union, we may for ages enjoy an advantage similar to that of an insulated situation. Europe is at a great distance from us. Her colonies in our vicinity, will be likely to continue too much disproportioned in strength, to be able to give us any dangerous annoyance."[30]

In maximum contrast, the Soviet Union is the uneasy suzerain of an inherently unstable empire.[31] While being careful not to raise to a dangerous level the risk of war with the United States, it has every good Soviet reason to seek to expand Soviet influence and, where feasible, control over countries that do not enjoy such guidance and protection at present. Developments in the strategic weapons "balance," or in the politics of western Europe or the Middle East, that American officials identify as contributing to disorder and instability are generally speaking, nothing of the kind in Soviet perspective.

Soviet leaders claim to seek only "equal security" with the United States, but geostrategic reasoning and supportive ideological rationalizations (to protect the legitimacy of the Soviet system) make a mockery of such a claim. In Soviet terms the Western Alliance led by the United States is a deadly enemy of the Soviet state and can be weakened if the order and stability that it sustains, and is sustained by, can be undermined. Stability, in Soviet perspective, is not an attribute of weapons or of political developments. Rather, stability is an attribute of weapon ownership (Soviet weapons are by definition stabilizing, since they strengthen Soviet national security—the ultimate value) and of the direction of political advantage (that is, whether or not Soviet interests are forwarded by a given event).

Notwithstanding the opposing attitudes registered above, there is a quite striking parallel between the United States and the U.S.S.R. in the Janus-like quality of their national political culture and behavior. Both countries harbor deep ambivalent feelings toward the outside world. In different degrees both countries feel threatened by pollution from abroad. Both countries have a conception of domestic nativist wholesomeness that is deemed at risk by contact with impure foreigners bearing the bacilli of alien ideas and methods.

A rigid geopolitical determinist should assert that the American international experience from December 1941 to the present day has committed the United States, *faute de mieux* and permanently, to the role of the principal and essential Western guardian of international security. But the United States has not assumed the eighteenth- and nineteenth-century role of Great Britain as the balancer of the international security system. Such a role requires a degree of diplomatic flexibility that has not been demonstrated since 1945. The U.S. role in the balance of power since 1945 has been closer to that of France in the 1900s and 1930s.

A United States true to its indigenous political culture could swing from global guardian of order to self-defined virtuous (though well-armed) recluse and still remain firmly within the American tradition. The allies of the United States would do well to look back to 1940-41 and reexamine just how and why the United States came to be precipitated into the role of leader of the free world. More to the point, perhaps, U.S. allies should worry lest many Americans come to question the wisdom of U.S. policy in 1940-41 and the sequence of events to which that policy quite inexorably led.[32]

7

Of National Interests

If the United States is overcommitted abroad to a column of allegedly vital interests and has fallen victim to uncritical universalist thinking, it is far from self-evident that the U.S. problem really reposes in the length of the list. When one considers the respective assets and vulnerabilities of the rival power centers, the U.S. problem tends to devolve upon issues of grand strategy and strategy. The more perceptive writers on the subject of means and ends—that is, strategy—in U.S. national security policy, do not appear to suggest that the United States should engage in a mere accountancy exercise.[1] They do not intend that U.S. policymakers should weigh the likely effectiveness of available military and other means in the balance against possible foreign policy draws against those means, and prune the latter until the scales achieve an approximate equilibrium.

It is probably helpful for the U.S. body politic to be reminded from time to time that if it attempts too much with too little, it will certainly fail; that some interests are considerably less vital than others; and that the strategic function in policymaking and execution entails the identification of priorities and probably some quite ruthless selectivity among competing courses of action in pursuit of alternative desirable goals. Nevertheless, given the respective strengths of the economies of East and West, the inescapably global geography of the competition between the insular United States and the Heartland U.S.S.R., and the strength of the U.S. interest in preventing Soviet hegemony throughout Eurasia-Africa, the case for "America overcommitted" is not an easy one to support.[2]

If Mackinder's geopolitical framework has enduring value—as I believe and as U.S. policymakers have tacitly affirmed over the past four decades[3]—although errors in strategy certainly will be committed, there is wisdom in the following assertion by John Jay in Federalist No. 3: "It is not a new observation that the people of any country (if like Americans intelligent and well informed) seldom adopt, and steadily persevere for many years in, an erroneous opinion respecting their interests."[4]

There are many traps for the unwary in the identification of national interests, in deciding which are vital—that is, worth fighting to defend or perhaps advance—and which are not. The logical precedence among interests that statesmen should assert is often confounded by the press of events. The fact that neither of America's two wars since 1945, in Korea and Vietnam, was waged in the immediate defense of interests that in and of themselves could be considered vital (let alone survival) in nature need not reflect imprudent statesmanship.[5] Strong critics of U.S. policy in Vietnam, for example, should recall that Britain and France went to war in September 1939 over the less than obviously vital interest of Poland's frontier. Why was Poland in September 1939 more vital than Czechoslovakia in September 1938—or in March 1939, when Hitler made a mockery of the Munich Agreement of September 1938? Clearly, the perceived importance of an interest can be substantially influenced by timing, as well as by prudential assessment of the costs and likely success of its military defense. Democracies have a habit of drawing a line that they mean to defend,[6] at a time and over an issue that is not confidently predictable by (mis)calculating foreign statesmen.

A country with global interests and commitments is always vulnerable to the charge that it is overcommitted. Indeed, strictly speaking, it *will* be overcommitted. As an analogy, consider the predicament of a bank that faces demands by all of its creditors for payment on the same day. Setting priorities among commitments is necessary and is reflected in the performance of military planners who endeavor to allocate scarce defense assets according to typically rather vague, high-level policy guidance. The armed services should not need to be reminded of the ancient military truth that the attempt to defend everything encourages a reality wherein nothing is defended adequately against an enemy who has or can seize the initiative. Vital interests may be interests worth fighting for, but assessment of the political and strategic contexts must determine both whether the interests in question can be protected and whether that protection should be extended by means of local or distant action.

Without benefit of an appropriate geopolitical framework, neither U.S. policymakers nor the general public can be well equipped conceptually to make sense of arguments about U.S. interests in particular cases. In the absence of such a framework, debate on the identity and intensity of U.S. interests has a way of being conducted unhelpfully at the level either of essentially ideological argument about universal opposition to Soviet influence (or, ludicrously, Marxist ideas)[7] or of disputation over the isolated merits of particular cases. The latter is reminiscent of the thinking of some elements in the British government in 1938 and 1939, who deemed it highly relevant to examine the worthiness of the German cases against Czechoslovakia and Poland. Considered pragmatically (a term of approval in American culture), remarkably few geostrategic interests around the world are worth the risk of a conflict that could escalate to nuclear holocaust. Indiscriminate globalism in the assertion of allegedly vital interests, and pragmatism without the guidance of principle—these anchor the two ends of debate over national security policy. Both are cases for treatment through geopolitical education.

A geopolitical perspective on U.S. national security policy and the interests protected and forwarded by that policy is not in any sense indifferent, let alone hostile, to the humane values of the American people. Halford Mackinder and his American successors did not teach a brutal *Realpolitik*. Indeed, the purpose of Mackinder's geopolitical writings was so to educate the statesmen and general public of the Western maritime civilization in the structure of their long-term security problems that through being forewarned they could be armed with the understanding necessary to formulate policies suitable to the defense of the democratic values that were their heritage and their trust. To argue that "for better or worse, international politics remains essentially power politics, and that the efficacy of military power in the conduct of foreign policy remains undiminished;"[8] is not to say anything of substance about the purposes for which power is accumulated.

As a general though not invariable rule, it is neither possible nor desirable for the United States to force American political values upon other societies (noteworthy historical exceptions include West Germany and Japan). Furthermore, again as a general rule, it is not possible for Americans to educate very different political cultures for American-style democracy. Yet even though the United States should not engage ethnocentrically in the hubristic and even grotesque exercise of "nation-building" abroad, there must be limits to the application of cultural relativism.[9]

Cultural relativism is healthy when it sensitizes Americans to the local integrity of alien values and methods. But it becomes dangerous when it advocates toleration, without U.S. response, of a "Soviet way" in defense preparation that is threatening to U.S. security and the values of U.S. society. Many participants in the transnational Western security debate have in effect come to assume and assert that there is a moral, or perhaps immoral, equivalence between the superpowers. The abstract proposition that armaments are a threat to peace, regardless of which country owns them, in practice means a distinct *lack* of equivalence in political pressure and effect. Halford Mackinder, with his forty year detestation for Germany, was not confused as to the contrasting merits of the political traditions of the maritime West and the continentalist East.

It is important to recognize that although both the United States and the Soviet Union dress their action policies in the clothing of domestically determined standards of "right conduct," neither superpower is in the *jihad* business. The Soviet-American rivalry is about ideas and values only in the sense that should one or the other side lose (in a physically survivable mode), its political culture would be massively at risk to reorganization from abroad. The detestable nature of the political systems of Imperial Germany, the Third Reich, and Stalin's Russia vastly eased the task of giving a morally purposive cast to American national security policy in 1917, 1941, and 1946-47. But Soviet-American hostility is not in essence about the clash of values between political cultures, any more than the United States went to war in order to bring down "Kaiserism" and Prussian militarism in Imperial Germany, or to thwart Hitler's threat to the values of the Western world.

There is, admittedly, a limited sense in which the absence of human rights in the Soviet Union constitutes a security issue for the United States. One cannot claim as a self-evident truth that democracies are inherently less "bellicist" than despotically governed polities,[10] but a government genuinely accountable to an electorate probably is more constrained from the exercise of brutal *Realpolitik* abroad than is a dictatorship. Nonetheless, there should be no confusion over the nature of the U.S. quarrel with the Soviet state. The quarrel bears upon the threat posed by the policy of the Soviet Union to American interests; it bears upon the domestic political arrangements of the Soviet state only insofar as the structure of those arrangements contributes to the generation and expression of that threat.

A quest for the identification of U.S. national interests must be sensitive to factors that are not easily demonstrable on any balance sheet of net U.S. advantage. Policy is guided not only by that which is believed to be materially advantageous to the state and its citizens but also by the moral and even sentimental impulses of the electorate. It could be argued that politically the least important of U.S. ties with Europe, for example, are those with the character of high-security politics (as embodied in NATO agreements and NATO practice).

Denial of Soviet conquest of, or hegemony over, western Europe may well be the first priority for U.S. national security policy in its continuing endeavor to keep the Heartland Soviet Union landlocked and distracted in Eurasia. But the proximate prize in a conflict need not itself be the decisive, or the only decisive, area for the concentration of military effort. In the eighteenth century, Britain upheld the balance of power in Europe by waging war against France very substantially beyond Europe and, through naval demonstrations in the Baltic in the 1850s, denied Russia the ability to concentrate single-mindedly upon the Crimea. One should recognize that threats to Soviet assets in the Far North, the South, and the Far East may contribute more to the deterrence of attack upon western Europe than would the addition of forces to the Central Front.

National interests may be expressed in the language of geopolitics. Geographical location and relationships continue to contain a logic that informs and helps direct national security policy. As an extension of the principle that guided British statecraft for four centuries, it is widely believed that the United States should oppose the hegemonic ambitions of the Soviet Union in Eurasia. The "main political objective" of the United States, said Nicholas Spykman in 1944, "both in peace and in war, must...be to prevent the unification of the Old World centers of power in coalition hostile to her own interests."[11] In so saying, he was reasoning geopolitically, defining the national interest of the United States with respect not to anti-German or anti-Soviet objectives but to managing a pattern of power relations, whatever the national identities of the key Eurasian state players. In 1942 Spykman foresaw the postwar world as "a world of power and politics in which the interests of the United States will continue to demand the preservation of a balance in Europe and Asia."[12]

In the geopolitical perspective of Mackinder and Spykman, then, although there are very important values at stake in the East-West, maritime-continental opposition, the threat to the United States is not the Soviet Union *qua* Soviet Union. Instead, the threat is the Soviet Union as the only plausible contemporary bidder for hegemonic control of the assets of Eurasia. The preeminent U.S. security interest, which is truly a survival interest, lies neither in opposing the ideas of Marxism-Leninism nor even in opposing Soviet totalitarianism and bureaucratic despotism. The U.S. interest lies in thwarting the potential uses of political intimidation or territorial conquest to which Soviet military power may be committed.

Pending some transformation in human nature, or in the dynamics of security relations among the distinctive tribes of humankind, the character of particular political systems in Eurasia is of far less importance for U.S. national security than is the preservation of some effective balance of power among them. Presciently, Spykman recognized that "the same conditions of political strategy that once led us to aid the Allies and that should guide our conduct of the war, will continue to demand our participation in the political life of the transoceanic zones in peace time."[13] He discerned that the complete destruction of the military power of Germany and Japan would likely diminish U.S. national security in the long term. For the United States, the world wars and the Cold War were necessary conflicts waged to preserve the balance of power in Eurasia—but the doctrine of unconditional surrender announced at Casablanca in January 1943, though admittedly unavoidable,[14] had the inexorable effect of subverting the geopolitical logic behind U.S. participation in World War II. To remove today's threat to the balance of power in Eurasia at the price of elevating the threat for tomorrow cannot be judged an act of high statesmanship. Geopolitical reasoning in the identification and assessment of national interests is rare today because modern technology is widely believed to have destroyed much of the significance of distance and spatial relationships.[15] Furthermore, few of today's leading policy scientists are very knowledgeable in geographical lore.[16]

The geographical situation of national life contains not a sufficient but certainly a necessary and usually obvious logic for the determination of national interests. The continental Heartland essence of the Soviet strategic situation is of the most profound importance for Soviet strategic culture, for Soviet identification of near-and far-term interests, and for an understanding of the strengths and weaknesses of Soviet military thinking. In a discussion of the origins and meaning of East-West antagonism, the structured realism of geopolitics directs attention away from the micro-detail of the business interests and individual psychological rigidities so beloved in revisionist literature, and toward the necessity—even the inevitability—of Soviet-American contention over the political future of east-central Europe.[17] It is strictly a matter of geostrategic context whether east-central Europe is a defensive *glaçis* for an insecure Soviet empire or a forward base for offensive action. The broad geopolitical functions of Soviet-controlled east-central Europe are not "essentially" of any particular kind. They depend upon the opportunities, or lack of them, provided by the quantity and quality of organized security resistance in the West. In geopolitical terms, Soviet control of western Europe would open the oceans to Soviet maritime power (the maritime defiles of the Turkish Straits, the Straits of Gibraltar, the Kattegat/Skagerrak and the NATO picket line between Greenland and Norway would no longer be garrisoned on shore by U.S. allies); it would facilitate Soviet hegemony in the Mediterranean and its littoral and the Middle East; and it would render the United States desperately short of advanced bases in the western Atlantic.

In a nuclear age, however, the threat that the Soviet Union poses to U.S. interests in Europe is not, preponderantly, a threat of territorial conquest. Danger lies rather in the shadow that may be cast by Soviet military power over the statecraft of the non-Soviet-aligned states of the region. A geopolitical view of U.S. interests should serve to remind U.S. policymakers that the security of the Soviet imperium "relies on concentric rings of domination."[18] Soviet military conquest of NATO-Europe is technically feasible in principle, though the uncertainties in such an enterprise and the probability of nuclear use and escalation would be daunting.[19] Less speculative than the prospects of military success without triggering a conflict that would both destroy much of the "prize" and cause major damage to the Soviet home power base would be the additional security problems posed by the Soviet Union's need to police its new holdings. Parker is probably substantially correct when he argues that:

the Heartland power, because of its economic self-sufficiency, based upon an abundant and almost complete range of mineral wealth, does not need the Rimland states for exploitation and trade in the same way as the United States.

From its point of view, a benevolent neutrality, such as Finland and India display, is ideal, for this prevents the United States from using their territories as part of its "perimeter of defense." It is infinitely preferable to incurring the cost and unpopularity of the relationship which it has perforce to thrust upon the countries of eastern Europe and Afghanistan for strategic reasons.[20]

The Soviet Union is not reliably self-sufficient in food production, may have to import oil before the end of the century, and is in very great need of high-technology transfer from western Europe. Nonetheless, Parker's strategic argument is plausible.

Edward Luttwak has made essentially the same point. He argues that the Soviet problem of imperial instability would best be resolved by a direct physical attack upon "the ultimate source of the problem, namely the power of the United States which guarantees Western Europe—if only it were not so dangerous! "The second-best solution is to erode and if possible break the security nexus between the United States and Western Europe. To do so would establish the strategic order that would already have emerged in 1945 had it not been for the intrusion of American power embodied in NATO. The countries of Western Europe, collectively an appendage of the Soviet-dominated Eurasian landmass, would then quite naturally come under Soviet influence, certainly to an extent sufficient to nullify all dissidence in Eastern Europe."[21]

The proper case for or against a U.S. security-system withdrawal from peripheral Eurasia has nothing to do with possible adverse effects upon the essentials of the American way of life. The survival-interest issue is the one identified so clearly by Spykman: the possibility that a hegemonic Eurasian power or coalition could develop a cumulatively fatal, multidimensional (economic, political, military, subversive) challenge to the United States closer and closer to the American homeland.

Notwithstanding the steadiness of general direction in U.S. national security policy since World War II, the "missing or shaky pillars" of that policy are a constant source of anxiety. The openness of the diverse U.S. bureaucracies that manage the instruments of grand strategy can mean that a great many politically appointed amateurs are insecurely in command of the ship of state. Even the professionalism of the permanent civil service can be called into serious question.[22] The problems of an unimpressive executive machine are compounded by the impact of a post-Vietnam Congress determined selectively, if unsystematically, to assert a micro-managerial authority—often according to what seems little more than the fashionable idea of the moment or with a view to pending elections.

Of course, other countries have had their amateur hours in the formulation and execution of national security policy. One need only recall the almost casually created disaster for international order that followed Kaiser Wilhelm II's abandonment in 1890 of the center of gravity of Imperial German statecraft—the maintenance of friendly relations, even quasi-alliance ties, with Russia—which catalyzed a hostile defensive alliance between Paris and St. Petersburg.[23] Or one can cite the personal (mis)conduct of British foreign policy by Neville Chamberlain in 1938.[24]

The reasons why there are missing or shaky pillars in U.S. policy at the level of profound comprehension of the nature of the "game of nations" do not lie in the fact of culpably ignorant officials, politicians, and other opinion leaders. The reasons flow from that American political, and by extension strategic, culture which is the product of the U.S. experience (and lack of experience). Speaking in March 1936, Winston Churchill said:

For four hundred years the foreign policy of England has been to oppose the strongest, most aggressive, most dominating Power on the continent, and particularly to prevent the Low countries falling into the hands of such a Power. ...Here is the wonderful *unconscious tradition* of British Foreign Policy....

Observe that the policy of England takes no account of which nation it is that seeks the overlordship of Europe. The question is not whether it is Spain, or the French Monarchy, or the French Empire, or the German Empire, or the Hitler regime. It has nothing to do with rulers or nations; it is concerned solely with whoever is the strongest or the potentially dominating tyrant....It is a law of public policy which we are following, and not a mere expedient dictated by accidental circumstances, or likes and dislikes, or any other sentiment. [Emphasis added][25]

The United States of the late twentieth century is a more important player in the game of nations than Great Britain ever was. What, if anything, constitutes the American equivalent of that "unconscious tradition of British Foreign policy"? Where is the body of principles for policy guidance, the conceptual center of gravity for political leaders as they endeavor to cope with the particular issues of the moment? The American tradition—if one can talk of tradition in a country that has no deep reverence for the lessons of historical experience, even its own—is one of moralism and of making a virtue out of the bequest of geographical distance from the amoral squabbles of the Old World.

An American political culture that remains very ambivalent about the role and legitimacy of the threat and use of force in international relations provides fertile soil for the superficially pragmatic proposition that there is an absolute necessity for arms control. In the heat of propagation and with repetition, this proposition translates into the assertion that arms control is a moral imperative—a holy cause, if you will. Absolute necessities and moral imperatives have a way of blinding their horse-holders to unwelcome facts. Development of a sound, geopolitically rooted U.S. national security policy is imperiled by an unruly arms-control debate that has the character of a gladiatorial contest between rival belief systems. To simplify, though not oversimplify, the belief systems of the Left and the Right both merit ascription as idealist rather than realist. The former seeks safety and perhaps even "real peace" through arms control; the latter seeks security through military strength. In their distinctive ways, both Left and Right seek an unattainable quality of security, decline to recognize the geopolitical structure of U.S. national (in)security, and hence fail to appreciate the goals that should be sought and might be achieved.

Lest there be any misunderstanding, though I see the malady of idealism on both the Left and the Right, I find it more prevalent on the Left and more dangerous to national security in its Leftist form. Specifically, while overarmament by the superpower that is the principal organizer and provider of security for the extant international order may be undesirable, it would not imperil the structure of international security. But underarmament inevitably must invite political pressure that could endanger the international order. History shows that a margin of safety—overarmament perhaps—on the side of the party of stability is an error on the side of prudence.

The identity of U.S. survival and vital interests has not been challenged in recent decades; that is, there has been no great American debate over the basic wisdom of the alliance framework for a multilateralist containment. But the U.S. survival interests in deterring nuclear war, in being able to recover from a nuclear war should it not be deterred, and in preventing an erosion in the correlation of forces that denies Soviet hegemonic control over Eurasia are perpetually at risk to the existential or minimum deterrers and to those who believe that the Soviet Union has finite security goals.

8

Organizing the Rimland

A defense community perpetually immersed in the taxing effort to maintain a multilateral alliance structure typically finds little leisure and less incentive to reflect upon the purpose of the coalition enterprise. To an important and generally healthy degree, U.S. policy toward its alliance partners in peripheral Eurasia is on automatic pilot. Its practical day-by-day purpose is system maintenance. Gregory Treverton's choice of title for his recent study of NATO was exactly correct: *Making the Alliance Work.*[1]

A potential problem for a policy that is fueled more by inertia than by explicit and careful understanding of U.S. security interests is that U.S. officials and policy commentators may fail to appreciate the importance of particular issues relative to the significance of the alliance connection as a whole. Furthermore, a defense community unschooled in geopolitical analysis is unlikely to be suitably equipped to debate intelligently those who would question the policy of security through coalition; hence, U.S. policy course for the containment of Soviet power could be at risk to the political potential of the views of Right-isolationists and Left-isolationists, as well as of Right-unilateralists and Left-unilateralists. These four somewhat imprecisely detectable tendencies agree at least on one proposition: that the United States should cease to depend upon allies in a multilateral framework in its pursuit of the national interest.[2]

The purpose of this chapter is to anchor the subsequent discussion of alternative policy courses (in Chapters 10-13) to an understanding of the alliance structure of the West as it has developed and as it functions today. It can be no easy matter to maintain perspective in face of the frustrations that attend (by way of analogy) assembly of the alliance convoy over particular issues, discouragement of independent policy sailings, choice of course for the convoy, its protection against highly selective assault by Soviet "wolf packs," and prevention of policy straggling.

One should not undervalue the quality of past performance. Notwithstanding the persistence of national particularisms, war among the states of west-central Europe is unthinkable today. The Soviet Union has a massive geostrategic incentive to coerce individual western European countries into a neutralist—preferably a Soviet-leaning neutralist—stance. But since the formal founding of NATO on April 4, 1949, no country has left the alliance, no neutral or neutralist European country has joined the Soviet security system, and the Soviet Union has not used force directly in any East-West dispute in the European region.

The extent to which the pacific interstate history of post-1945 Europe should be attributed to the creation of the first peacetime "entangling alliance" in U.S. history must remain a matter for speculation.[3] The U.S. security connection may have been less important for the political independence of western Europe than was either the devastation wrought by World War II upon the economies of all the European belligerents, or Stalin's reluctance to assume security responsibility for an empire so expanded as to include societies with very alien political traditions and cultures.[4] Nonetheless, the evidence of history unmistakably says that the NATO alliance, if not essential, has certainly been compatible with the maintenance of vital U.S. and western European security interests.

The Eurasian Rimland allies perform several important and arguably essential security functions for the United States. Above all else, geopolitically, the independence from Soviet control of important countries around the periphery of Eurasia keeps the Soviet Union landlocked and distracted from pursuing *Weltpolitik* from a secure dual-continent power base. The Soviet armed forces of today have the structure one would expect of a continentally minded landpower that faces a very serious prospect of ground war on two fronts.[5] However, if Moscow were to seize a position of preponderance in Europe by conquest or by intimidation, then the United States would be desperately short of regional access points on which to anchor a defense perimeter in the western Atlantic. It would not be sufficient for the Soviet Union to be denied control of the economic assets of western Europe; in addition, U.S. security requires that Soviet military power be denied uncontested egress from the "choke points" that could be used to confine its maritime power in the Barents Sea, the Baltic, and the Black Sea/Mediterranean.

In keeping with an axiom of balance-of-power politics—that one seeks alliance with the next state but one, geographically—the Chinese People's Republic is functionally in security alliance with NATO in Europe. The regional balance of power in northeast Asia depends upon the maintenance of a regional balance of power in Europe. Soviet hegemony in Europe would imperil the political independence of China and Japan.

The many strategic advantages relative to Soviet power that the United States as *the* global maritime power has enjoyed since 1945 have reflected not so much the nature of the Soviet and American polities, or even strategic geography, as the balance of power in Eurasia. There is a synergistic relationship between landpower and seapower.[6] Soviet distraction on land has prevented development of a global Soviet seapower, which could have negatively affected U.S. freedom of action in Korea, southeast Asia, and elsewhere. In its turn, U.S. command of the sea has sustained favorable regional balances on land.

One should not be confused, however, by the mere number of countries in strategic question. Crude arithmetic of the regional military balance in Europe could mislead if it counts half-trained, ill-equipped, and malpositioned Italian and Turkish infantrymen as the equivalent of Soviet soldiers in central or northern Europe. Similarly, strategic access is far more a matter of the quality, including quality of geostrategic location, than of the quantity of territory. To cite just one example, it is not self-evident that the continental security of NATO in Europe would be militarily viable were Great Britain to join the Warsaw Pact or even to slip into a position of Soviet-leaning neutralism.[7] Military issues aside, it is a reasonable prediction that were Britain to leave the alliance, the U.S. political constituency for the NATO connection would be fundamentally undermined.

A formal alliance nexus with peripheral Eurasia is not strictly essential to American security—provided the landlocking and continental distraction of Soviet power could be performed adequately by whatever peripheral-Eurasian security coalition(s) would become the successor(s) to NATO and to the mutual security treaty with Japan. Less plausibly, the formal alliance nexus would not be so necessary to American security should developments within the Soviet empire render an assertive Soviet foreign policy highly improbable. Unfortunately, increased Soviet anxiety over the internal stability of its territorial and hegemonic patrimony would be as likely to promote a militant course abroad as to promote a prolonged period of quiescence in foreign policy.

In the last decade of the twentieth century, as in the early years of the American Republic, U.S. national security policy cannot afford to be indifferent to the evolution of the balance of power in Eurasia. Consistent with due respect for the political-supportive needs of a global alliance architecture that to date has worked well enough, American policymakers should retain an open mind as to the methods and means that might continue to insure the necessary containment of Soviet power and influence.

A structural advantage enjoyed by the United States in the long-term competition with the Soviet Union is the fact that its friends and allies are friends and allies by choice. Geopolitically, NATO-European countries really have no interesting alternatives to the transatlantic security nexus, but they are at liberty to pursue novel paths for their national security should they so choose. Steven Kime argues that there is a strange paradox in the alliance architectures of East and West.[8] Save in extraordinary circumstances (which seem to occur roughly once in each decade: Hungary, 1956; Czechosolovakia, 1968; Poland, 1980), it is the western Alliance that appears near-perpetually on the brink of terminal fission, whereas the Warsaw Pact parades in near-lockstep on orders from its Soviet drill-master.[9] Yet the NATO Alliance, which looks so fragile in peacetime, would likely be staunch for the common enterprise in time of war, while the alliance that is generally so obedient to central direction in peacetime would likely fracture under the pressure and with the unique opportunities of war.

Kime is probably too optimistic concerning the reliability of allies and friends, and not sufficiently sensitive to the fissile effect of their separately perceived national survival interests. Geopolitical factors and cultural preferences suffice to insure that different national perspectives will clash from time to time. Nonetheless, there is an important truth in Kime's analysis. The NATO Alliance does rest upon a firm basis of common interests among its members. At the most basic of levels the alliance helps prevent the expansion of Soviet influence in (and ultimately beyond) Europe, helps retain active U.S. participation in a system of security for Europe, helps keep the still-unresolved "German problem" quiescent and helps sustain a framework of international order within which peaceful commerce can be conducted.[10]

It is possible, even probable, that in extremely stressful circumstances NATO and the security tie with Japan might fracture and local partners scurry for unilateral salvation. But unlike the members of the Warsaw Pact, none of the allies of the United States harbor such antipathy toward their alliance leader that they would be motivated to seize any opportunity, created by the military distraction elsewhere of their major partner, to work directly and deliberately against the interests of that partner. The eastern European security "partners" of the U.S.S.R. are, with the exception of Bulgaria, the more or less obedient but unwilling instruments of Soviet (really Great Russian) interests only for so long as they discern no viable alternative policy course. Soviet interests are either irrelevant or actually antipathetic to the essential concerns of Pact allies' societies, though not always of their ruling elites.

The United States has to be concerned lest the military situation of its forward-deployed forces be compromised by any spirit of *sauve qui peut* among NATO-Europeans under dire threat (one may recall the situation of the British Expeditionary Force in Belgium in May 1940), but it has no reason to question the depth of allied commitment to the common security enterprise. NATO-Europeans are prone to state, accurately enough, that the United States is a player in the security politics of Europe for its own selfish interests. But they know that the external security functions of NATO are of more importance to them than they are to the United States. The small and medium-sized allies of both superpowers

Percentage of GNP Committed to Defense

	1971	1984
Belgium	2.9	3.2
Britain	4.9	5.3
Canada	2.2	2.2
Denmark	2.4	2.3
France	4.0	4.1
Germany	3.4	3.3
Greece	4.7	7.2
Italy	2.7	2.7
Luxembourg	0.8	1.2
Netherlands	3.4	3.2
Norway	3.4	2.8
Portugal	7.4	3.3
Spain	—	2.9
Turkey	4.5	4.4
United States	7.1	6.5
Japan	0.8	1.0

Source: Casper W. Weinberger, *Report on Allied Contributions to the Common Defense* (Washington, D.C.: Department of Defense, 1986), p. 89.

might cave under duress, but only the allies of the Soviet Union have major security grudges against their alliance principal, and to some degree against other alliance partners. Soviet domination of eastern Europe has not so much resolved the irredentist politics of the region as frozen them. Every east European member of the Warsaw Pact has a set of more or less major irredentist claims against other pact members.

Defense debate within the United States is typically well larded with references to persisting deficiencies in the defense efforts of NATO-European allies. The claim has some basis in fact, but the popular American image of "free-riding" allies is a considerable exaggeration. Americans do have grounds for complaint about the absolute levels of the defense burdens carried by NATO-European countries, but the trend over the past decade is no worse than should have been expected. One should not forget the enduring factors that shape the scale of military contribution by the small and medium-sized members of a coalition led by a much larger power.

Although it is not clear whether a meaningful comparison can be made, on the basis of percentage of gross national product (GNP), between the defense budgets of regional powers and a superpower that has a global strategy in defense of worldwide interests, the accompanying table captures the trend of the 1970s and early 1980s. Some recent American estimates have identified 56-58 percent as the NATO share of the U.S. defense effort. Given this admittedly dubious calculation, it would appear that the United States has been devoting approximately 3.7 percent of its GNP to the defense of NATO—a figure noteworthy, if not suspiciously noteworthy, for its fit in the middle range of allied efforts.[11] Any such comparisons must be regarded with a skeptical eye, however. The more geostrategically exposed of the NATO allies argue that they are contributing (albeit of necessity, not by choice) the initial battlefield for the common defense. Moreover, there is something distinctly unpersuasive about the very concept of a NATO share in the U.S. national defense effort. The Soviet Union is not deterred from military action in Europe by that NATO share alone, for it cannot assume that it would have to fight only those U.S. forces explicitly assigned to the defense of Europe. Given that a war involving the superpowers easily could be global, on what analytical basis should some U.S. forces be identified as not relevant to the deterrence of aggression in the NATO area?[12]

Some American commentators have sought to quantify the "free-riding" sins of NATO-Europe by estimating what Europeans, bereft of U.S. military assistance, would have to spend in order to make up for their U.S. loss. Since there is a marked absence of plausible, let alone authoritative, alternative budgets and defense postures for a United States and a western Europe proceeding down separate security paths, these arguments lack persuasive substance.[13]

Protagonists for one or another position on the question have a way of selecting the figures that best support their argument. For example, those in the United States who seek to demonstrate NATO's unjust burden on the American taxpayer have a strong preference for citing per capita defense expenditures. By this measure it can be shown that in 1983 the United States, at $1,023 per capita, spent more than twice as much as Britain, three times as much as West Germany, and so on.[14] In common with the East-West strategic balance, comparative burden-sharing within NATO is an enormously complex subject that lends itself to political exploitation by sometimes remarkably amateurish analysts determined to make a particular case.

American opinion leaders who tend to think in simple bipolar terms are often surprised to discover just how substantial are the national forces maintained by the NATO allies. These are of uneven quality, are deployed substantially in accordance with national preferences, and in many cases are only very contingently available for centralized NATO disposition; nonetheless, the absolute levels of non-U.S. NATO forces are impressive. Laurence Martin, a noted British authority on NATO strategy, has observed: "In terms of output, the balance between the United States and the Europeans is not nearly so unfavourable to the latter as often supposed. In the European theater and surrounding oceans European members of NATO provide 90% of the ground forces, 90% of the armoured division[s], 80% of the tanks, 80% of combat aircraft and 70% of combat naval vessels. Europe's military manpower numbers some 3 million active forces and 3 million reservists; the corresponding figure for the United States is 2 million active and 1 million reserve."[15] Whether or not the NATO-Europeans are doing as much as they could or should, and allowing for the inflation of numbers caused by including almost strategically irrelevant Turkish and Italian forces, it is quite evident that the European allies of the United States are not just lightly armed; neither have they downgraded their defense establishments in recent years.

As recently as 1977-78 the United States, emphasizing its continental European commitment, secured formal NATO-wide adherence to a long-term defense program (LTDP) that required a steady 3 percent annual increase in real defense expenditure. The fall of the Shah of Iran and the Soviet invasion of Afghanistan seemed to redirect U.S. geopolitical focus upon the military implications of instability in the Persian Gulf region and to place at some risk the absolute priority to which NATO-European countries believed they were entitled in U.S. military planning. In practice, the European emphasis in U.S. military policy in 1977-78 was as shallow in its roots as the Indian Ocean–Persian Gulf focus of 1979-80. The former reflected the calculation that the defense of Europe was domestically the least controversial of the distant missions of the armed forces; the latter was an instrument of diplomatic signaling.[16]

Since 1979-80, NATO-Europe has witnessed a U.S. policy shift from the changing regional emphases of the Carter years to a far more global perspective, reflected in a major reemphasis upon maritime power. The 1980s have seen the demise of SALT II and the abrupt reemergence of U.S. official commitment to strategic defense. Closer to home for Europeans, the U.S. Army has formally adopted (1981-82) in its new AirLand Battle doctrine an approach to warfare that revives long-standing anxieties over both the quality of U.S. commitment to defend West German territory far forward and U.S. willingness to expand promptly the geographical scope of a conflict in central Europe.[17] Europeans are nervous about the proclaimed emphasis of AirLand Battle on "elastic" defense-in-depth, operational maneuver, and offensive action. The associated, though distinctive, strategic preference of SHAPE (Supreme Headquarters, Allied Powers, Europe) for follow-on forces attack (FOFA)—adopted in November 1984—raises many of the same anxieties in NATO-European minds.[18]

The merit of shifts in U.S. military policy over the past several years is not the issue here. The point is that a NATO-Europe perennially concerned about change in the political-military architecture of its regional security has had to accommodate major changes (and essentially unilateral ones: Alliance consultation has ranged from none on the SDI to close and continuous in INF negotiations), changes in U.S. foreign policy rhetoric; the regional battle doctrine of the U.S. Army; the strategy of the U.S. Navy; U.S. strategic-forces doctrine (the implications of the SDI for an "SDIskiy" and hence for the U.S. strategic-nuclear extended deterrent); and U.S. policy on strategic arms control.

The reasons for western European and Japanese adherence to their American security connection are as robust and enduring as is the geopolitical basis for the hostility between the United States and Soviet Union. Americans determined to recast the political and military postures of the non-Communist world are frequently frustrated by the skepticism or even frank disinclination of their allies. But the general commitment of so large a fraction of "the global product" to the American side of the scales of international order is a massive and enduring (short of upset by Soviet intimidation or conquest) source of strength in support of the principal Western guardian of international security.

There is, however, a persisting tension within the NATO Alliance caused by the growing number of "out of (NATO) area" security duties accepted by the United States in its role as global superpower, as opposed to its more narrow role as alliance-principal. There is no little irony in this situation. Through the late 1940s, the 1950s, and even the early 1960s, it was the out-of-area security and prestige responsibilities of Britain and France that were major sources of tension within the alliance. Whatever may or may not be desirable geopolitically for the West in the littoral area announced by Zbigniew Brzezinski to constitute an "arc of crisis" (from the Horn of Africa to the Indian subcontinent),[19] this is a region of which American policymakers are exceptionally ignorant. Given that the American way in strategy has always—generally of geographical necessity— been about logistics, and that "space [distance] determined the American way in war, space and the means to conquer space,"[20] observers need no general staff training to appreciate that U.S. strategic reach into the Persian Gulf area is exceptionally tenuous. The U.S. Navy of 1979-80 could not simultaneously have held NATO's northern and western flanks, supported its southern flank in the Mediterranean, defended Japan and encouraged China, and also projected power into and from the Arabian Sea. There are grounds for wondering whether the more global strategy of the last Carter year and of the Reagan administration has military integrity, even with the expansion of the U.S. Navy that has been funded in the 1980s.[21] But there is no doubt that the violent dismantling of the U.S.-blessed 1970s order in the Gulf has revealed a severe problem for American military power, either of strategy or of means.

In principle, the NATO-European allies have not been unsympathetic to the out-of-area problems of their superpower ally.[22] Indeed, France and Britain have both retained some supervisory roles in particular regions of traditional interest and political competence: France in west-central Africa and Britain in the littoral states of the Gulf. But NATO-Europe does not wish to be demoted in American geopolitical textbooks and strategic plans to the status of just one region among many that may need U.S. military assistance, or to see the United States husbanding its military power in North American geostrategic reserve to be available flexibly for application as circumstances evolve or erupt around Eurasia-Africa. The NATO allies understand that the U.S. continental commitment in Europe, once abandoned, could be very difficult to restore. (Their view is reminiscent of French statecraft vis-à-vis the British in 1938-40.)[23]

In global perspective for the United States, the NATO Alliance is a strong net plus, but one should not neglect the "net" while appreciating the "plus." Notwithstanding their demographic and economic strength with respect to the United States and the Soviet Union,[24] the NATO-Europeans persist purposively in providing local defense capability at a level sufficiently low that a major U.S. regional contribution remains essential for the balance of power. That contribution severely inhibits the American ability to design and fund the strategy and forces most suitable for a truly global security system. In addition to the possible "skewing" effect of the preponderant European commitment upon the balance of U.S. armed forces,[25] the NATO allies typically function as a policy brake upon what they regard as prospective U.S. adventures out of the NATO area. NATO-Europe has been less than empathetic to American concerns about Central America (a region about which NATO-Europeans tend to be as abysmally ignorant as are Americans of the southern and central Asian areas where British and Russian agents used to play the Great Game). Moreover, NATO-Europe remains generically uneasy about the ability of the United States to perform with minimal policy competence (with respect to European perceptions of European interests) in the Middle East, given the political nexus that binds Washington to Jerusalem. And NATO-Europe is always anxious lest the United States imperil the quiet security life enjoyed generally in postwar Europe, either by withdrawing much of the transatlantic military underpinning of that life in order to pursue more pressing global security duties elsewhere, or by generating tensions out of area that would spill over to the heavily political structure of security in Europe.

The Free World Alliance, as an earlier generation of political commentators termed it, is in no serious danger of jumping ship, provided the United States behaves internationally in a manner that European and Asian allies consider compatible with their survival and vital interests. The Asian allies know that for many years to come the structure of their security problems allows no attractive alternative to ultimate dependence upon the United States. NATO-Europe and Japan know that they probably cannot improve their security condition by seeking to build strictly regional security structures for the balancing of Soviet power, at least in the short run (and history is a series of short runs).[26] They know also that strictly national-unilateral security courses would entice Soviet regional hegemony by installments: the degree of political freedom enjoyed by Finland, constrained though it is, is the product of the weight of NATO-allied or NATO-leaning countries behind Finland.

The true source of the perennial complaint by Americans that their allies are not pulling their weight in the common military enterprise is geopolitical. The political cohesion, and hence the combined deterrent effect, of the NATO Alliance is constantly weakened by American dissatisfaction with the military performance of its allies.[27] This dissatisfaction is founded upon legitimate concerns. Americans have difficulty understanding why they should shoulder what appears to be a disproportionately large share of the common defense burden, given a general agreement on the military threat and no great asymmetries in economic ability among the allies to bear defense costs.[28] Yet all the allies of the United States are net consumers of security produced by the United States. In vain, many Americans look for tangible expressions of gratitude.

It is a political fact of life that a small country in an alliance among countries of very different size will contribute to the common defense to a disproportionately modest degree. The highly unofficial terms of the Western Alliance hold that the medium-sized smaller members must expend enough effort to satisfy U.S. domestic opinion.[29] In European perspective, enough must be done to soften the impact of American complaints that the allies are enjoying a free ride in security. At the same time, NATO-Europeans have always been aware that their likely reward, should they achieve a first-class local defense capability, would be a belief in the United States that Europe no longer needed substantial forward deployment of American forces. In short, NATO-Europe knows it must do enough, but not too much.

It is exceedingly unlikely that NATO-Europe will ever satisfy American desiderata for ideal security partners. A relatively small country in peacetime alliance with a very large country will rarely find persuasive reasons to expend more as opposed to less effort upon military preparation. The only exceptions pertain to political assessment of what is needed to keep the larger country tolerably satisfied, and to threats quite aside from the business of the alliance. Americans should know this as a perpetual historical truth, but they still have difficulty understanding the perspectives of much smaller countries. For example, if Denmark were to double the percentage of its GNP devoted to defense functions, from 2.3 to 4.6 percent, would Denmark be any more secure? It is virtually impossible for small countries in a greatly unequal alliance to relate even very substantial changes in levels of defense effort to their security. In recent centuries small countries such as Denmark and the Netherlands have not endeavored to build national military deterrents to aggression; their security has had to rest upon the protection offered by the balance-of-power system as a whole.[30] Security is a "collective good" that the United States cannot either generally withhold or reduce in a finely calibrated fashion in the event of underperformance by smaller allies.

The medium-sized powers of NATO—West Germany, Great Britain, Italy, and France—each has unique historical parameters guiding the kind and scale of its military preparations. Apart from being constrained by the terms of its accession to the Western European Union in 1954, West Germany is all too well aware of the genuine sensitivities both west and east concerning its military capabilities. Politically speaking, the West German military contribution to NATO could be increased very markedly only in the context of a general increase in all NATO defenses—meaning that the relative scale of the German military effort would not alter very noticeably. Readers should recall that former West German Chancellor Helmut Schmidt insisted in 1979 that his country's acceptance of new intermediate-range nuclear missiles was contingent upon their acceptance also by two other NATO-European countries, one of which had to be continental.[31]

The size of the British defense effort, trending upward from 5 toward 6 percent of GNP, is sufficiently close to American practice as to invite no adverse notice. The Italian defense effort is modest by medium-power NATO standards, though readily understandable in terms of Italian geopolitics. The Italian Army has had long-standing problems of unbalanced manpower-to-equipment budgets and uncertain political reliability. Even if Italian land and tactical air forces were greatly increased, their potential utility to NATO as a whole would be severely constrained. Indirectly at least, a larger and more competent Italian maritime and maritime-air capability could be of considerable value to NATO by reducing the U.S. Navy's need to maintain so substantial a presence in the Mediterranean with the Sixth Fleet. However, neither the countries of NATO's southern flank nor America's security clients in the Middle East would be at all enthusiastic over any noteworthy substitution of Italian for American military presence.

French defense policy has been directed for twenty years by the explicit, limited concern to protect the frontiers of France. Anything else is forward defense of those frontiers or, with the *force d'intervention*, protection of traditional French political, commercial, and cultural interests in Africa (largely). The character and scale of the French defense effort is related implicitly to French assessment of the freedom of action accorded by the NATO shield; French governments understand very well indeed that the quality of French security cannot be determined unilaterally. But France has endeavored to provide itself with a distinctive military—particularly nuclear-military—profile intended to permit the country a distinctive role in European security matters; the aspiration persists that even in war the Soviet Union might just treat France in a uniquely cautious fashion. By removing itself in 1966 from the unified military command structure of NATO, though not from the alliance in a political sense, France took itself out of the column of comparative defense effort.[32] It should be recalled that the long-standing French rationale for military disengagement from NATO has been the judgment that NATO unduly constricted France with respect to its ability both to play a uniquely French role in international security and to provide prudently for the protection of its distinctive vital and survival interests.[33]

NATO-European countries will never voluntarily sanction, or develop the necessary forces for an alliance strategy projecting the plausible defeat of a Warsaw Pact military offensive strictly within the European theater of operations.[34] NATO-Europeans are variably, though residually, nervous about formal and implicit American commitments to the employment of homeland-based U.S. strategic nuclear forces on behalf of distant allies, but they are even more disquieted by U.S.-authored plans to improve NATO's ability to impose a regional defeat on pact forces. The allies of the United States do not want to be defended successfully; even less do they take a comfort from distant and highly implausible prospects of liberation. Rather, they want war of any kind to be deterred. The new operational maneuver doctrine of the U.S. Army (AirLand Battle), SHAPE's preferred FOFA design, U.S. official interest in an antitactical missile component for a weaponized SDI, and the whole thrust of the U.S. defense community toward new smart technologies for battlefield application and for deep-strike interdiction of Soviet second-echelon armies are all of deep concern to a NATO-Europe worried that new defense capability may undermine the familiar if incredible structure of deterrence.[35]

This is to deny neither the national variations in doctrinal preference among the European allies nor the salience of the factor of affordability. Gen. Bernard Rogers has claimed that the FOFA option can be purchased by NATO if the 1978 LTDP guideline of 3 percent per annum in real growth in defense expenditure is increased to 4 percent. Since even 3 percent has proved beyond reach of sustained achievement,[36] the prospects are not glittering for a NATO-European 4 percent real-growth rate in support of an unpopular doctrine.

In political fact, the European allies of the United States favor a multilateral defense structure that commits the United States to local combat in the field from the outset[37]—which at every hypothetical level of violence opens up more and more plausible visions of explosive escalation, and which would not likely be able to contain a Pact theater-operational offensive à outrance. The seemingly perpetual irritation within NATO on the subjects of strategy in general and fair levels of defense effort and the roles of nuclear weapons in particular pertain at root to the geopolitics of the alliance. As observed earlier, the United States has a vital but not a strictly survival quality of interest in Europe—at least not an *immediate* survival quality. This means that a U.S. government responsible for its society, and at the same time seeking to devise and sustain a workable national security policy, cannot credibly promise *survival*-level military action on behalf of only *vital* interests. Armageddon may ensue from armed conflict in Europe, but the United States credibly and prudently cannot and should not commit itself to a course of military action that must, if ever executed, produce such an outcome. To state the matter with brutal frankness, the stakes are not high enough; Europe is not worth "Apocalypse Now" for the United States.[38]

The inevitable tension within a strategy simultaneously believed to be most efficacious for the deterrence of war yet nationally intolerable if ever implemented has been alleviated by what might be called creative ambiguity. Ambiguity over the use of nuclear weapons certainly should generate a healthy uncertainty in the minds of Soviet defense planners. However, that ambiguity also expresses both a quite genuine confusion and a psychological process of denial in Western minds. In short, one lives with a potentially intolerable contradiction—a strategy for deterrence that one could not face in action—by the familiar device of choosing not to admit the contradiction. Indeed, NATO has elevated confusion and contradiction to the status of valued principle, dignified by the terms "ambiguity" and "uncertainty."[39]

NATO's authoritative strategic concept of flexible response reflects both the diversity of locally identified survival interests within the alliance and the inevitable imprint of the "free-rider" phenomenon. Moreover, the evolution of U.S. strategic nuclear policy since the design of the first fully integrated strategic war plan in 1960[40] shows a sensible appreciation of U.S. self-interest in escalation control; a prudent regard for the necessity of providing for early war termination; and at least some regard for the adverse trends in the multilevel East-West military balance. The persistent refusal of NATO-European countries to accept a scale of conventional, chemical, and battlefield/theater-nuclear defense burdens that could greatly diminish the deterrent, counterdeterrent, and deterrence-restoration (or compellent) functions of U.S. strategic nuclear forces means that a noticeable element in the evolution of NATO-wide defense policy has been a refinement in the publicly advertised character of the "backstopping" U.S. strategic nuclear threat.[41]

On many different grounds there is a strong case for a strategic targeting policy that provides for considerable discrimination.[42] However, it is paradoxical that the thrust toward greater flexibility has fed latent European fears of dangerous American behavior—even though that thrust has been driven in good part by the American desire to sustain the value of strategic forces as compensation for theater deficiencies. During the 1980s, U.S. policymakers have shifted increasingly toward an explicit "war-fighting" theory. This shift expresses recognition of the incredibility of heavily punitive threats as a means of effective extended deterrence in a context of rough strategic parity.[43] On the one hand, it is attractive to NATO-Europeans not to have to pay the economic price that would enable them to answer for their own security in the last resort. On the other hand, the European dependence inherent in the contemporary military arrangements of NATO puts the security destiny of western Europe in the hands of an American president an ocean away.

Rights and duties obtain on both sides of the Atlantic. From time to time NATO-Europeans complain about the absence of American leadership, clarity of purpose, and firmness of policy application, but—understandably—NATO-Europe favors U.S. leadership, clarity, and firmness only with respect to the policy directions that it prefers. Europeans want to be led only where they wish to go. As the net security producer vis-à-vis all other members of the alliance, the United States has the right to insist that it should have the largest say, and certainly the initiative function, in alliancewide military policy. However, the duty that attends the leadership role—a tacit condition for European acquiescence in decisions that European countries view with less than wholehearted enthusiasm—is that the United States should not expose the alliance as a whole to needless military dangers (in the judgment, accurate or otherwise, of Europeans).

The unique style of the United States in its approach to international relations combines with the trans-oceanic geography of the alliance, the enduring major differences in military power among members, and the immediate eastward concern of Bonn,[44] to produce serious and permanent problems of system maintenance for NATO. If governed with tolerable competence, the Soviet Union will always be able to play upon NATO-European fear that the United States cannot be trusted not to behave in a manner reckless of security and peace in Europe. In addition, Soviet leaders can invoke the theme of "we Europeans" among countries sensitive both to the fact that the United States is not a European power and to the proposition that U.S. defense commitments to forward-placed allies would count for little if the American homeland were believed to be "on the line."[45]

This book is not pessimistic about the future of NATO. Nor does it suggest that basic choices in U.S. national security policy should be greatly influenced by the possibility that allies and peacetime friends will serve themselves first in moments of crisis, should they believe they have that choice. To notice that many allies cannot fully be trusted to adhere to the common cause under all circumstances is merely to notice the obvious. All alliances are alliances of convenience. The strength of the alliance structure led by the United States is that it rests upon a secure foundation of common interests. Those common geostrategic interests are sufficient to permit NATO to weather storms over a Soviet gas pipeline, over unfair trading practices, over deployment of intermediate-range land-based missiles,[46] and—looking to the future—even over the shaping of a weaponized SDI.[47] But should individual allies ever come to believe that strategic disassociation from the alliance would offer a real chance to evade nuclear damage that would otherwise seem inevitable (as opposed to merely possible) then all predictions of comradely staunchness would have to be revised.

George Washington's advice—that the "great rule of conduct for us, in regard to foreign Nations is in extending our commercial relations to have with them as little *political* connection as possible"[48]—was as practical for the nineteenth century as it has been impractical for the very different geostrategic circumstances of the twentieth. Moreover, as Selig Adler has pointed out: "The isolationism of the Revolutionary Era possessed a dynamic quality that men of the future failed to perceive. The earliest Presidents guided the destiny of a weak and untried republic, striving to make its mark in a warring, unfriendly, and monarchical world....The Founding Fathers would have been startled to learn that later generations, speaking in their name, would use non-intervention and neutrality to escape the grim realities of *Machtpolitik*. Strategies formulated by the Fathers as the means of statecraft became in time the final goals of American diplomacy."[49]

Adler was writing at the floodtide of national confidence in the American Century, in the mid-1950s (but pre-Sputnik). Thoughtful conservatives and liberals in the 1980s, chastened though no longer overwhelmed by the U.S. adventure in Vietnam, are not as dismissive of the policy sense in all variants of "the isolationist impulse" as was fashionable among national security sophisticates in the 1950s and most of the 1960s. Very much a sign of the times is an article titled "Do We Still Need Europe?" written by Eliot Cohen, a well-respected young conservative scholar. In keeping with the more globalist and maritime focus of contemporary U.S. military policy, Cohen argues that "broadly speaking, three changes have occurred over the history of the Atlantic alliance": he cites, or alleges, "Europe's relative decline as a strategic stake and asset in the competition with the Soviet Union"; he claims "that Europe has become more of a strategic liability to the United States, less for reasons intrinsic to Europe than because of transformations elsewhere"; and he asserts that "from the point of view of strategic geography it is the flanks of NATO that are becoming increasingly important."[50]

Cohen's argument is carefully reasoned and nonpolemical; it eschews oversimplified strategy choices (maritime versus continental, Atlantic versus Pacific). Rather, it promotes the increasingly popular view that the military arrangements of the alliance have failed to evolve in response to a changing security environment.[51] The U.S. ability to behave appropriately as a global power, Cohen alleges, is needlessly constrained by the biasing effect upon force posture of a European Central Front focus that is no longer warranted, given the economic and political recovery of western Europe, the evolution of the Soviet threat, and the emergence of new threats to Western security far outside the NATO region.[52]

There is a significant emergence on the American Right of explicitly strategic, pragmatic critiques that doubt the security sense for the United States of the long-traditional allocation of defense burdens among NATO members. Many of the critics are not obviously persons suffering from any delayed form of a Vietnam syndrome, are not nostalgic (neo)isolationists, and are not romantic unilateralists. In their view the "don't rock the boat" sentiment that is the standard response of American and European "Atlanticists" to proposals—however constructive—for change in NATO strategy, command organization, or distribution of burdens will no longer suffice: "Military logic suggests the peculiarity (at the very least) of a strategy which relies heavily on the appearance within a week of massive armies from a power thousands of miles distant from the main battle front. Such a dependence is as politically unhealthy as it is militarily tenuous. The primary responsibility for Europe's defense on the ground must rest with Europeans."[53]

One must also recognize the possibility that novel dangers, as yet unforeseen, may emerge. Readers might consider as a cautionary tale the history of European diplomacy following the Peace of Westphalia of 1648. *In retrospect*, as always, it is plain that the Hapsburg menace to the balance of power was very much a spent force by the 1650s.[54] However, to Britain and the Dutch Republic, the rising maritime powers of the time, this truth was not so plain. Hence, history records Cromwell's England joining France in alliance against Spain in 1657 and thus contributing usefully to the promotion of France as an overly great power.[55] It is possible that a century from now the balance-of-power problem for the United States will be not the Soviet Union but a Sino-Japanese alliance.[56] Halford Mackinder wrote of this possibility,[57] and Nicholas Spykman believed in the superior power of the Rimland over the Heartland.[58]

A weak China and a weak Japan are not desirable for the United States within the current framework of security relations. Ideally, China and Japan, separately or together, should pose a second-front problem—of dimensions arguing strongly against military boldness in Europe or the Middle East—for Soviet military planners. But a newly powerful China and/or Japan would be certain to have significant impact upon the very structure of the current international order.

Near-term Soviet purpose is capable of almost infinite variation as security circumstances alter. A Soviet Union that could sign the Brest-Litovsk (1918) and Molotov-Ribbentrop (1939) treaties is certainly capable under duress, of finding tactical common cause with the United States—yet again. Nevertheless, the principal thesis of this book, that the United States has a permanent security problem or condition with the Soviet empire, is not weakened noticeably by this brief consideration of the threat that one day might be posed by China and Japan. Because it is rooted in a conflictual worldview, the character of Soviet power and purpose is most unlikely to alter in a benign direction.

U.S. policymakers need to ask themselves whether or not the terms and conditions of the NATO Alliance are altering to so great an extent that muddling through may be the most prudent course to adopt. It is possible that the putative benefits of a restructuring of responsibilities within the alliance could be of less significance than would the risks that must attend such a venture. What benign consequences for U.S. security should follow a restructuring that would free U.S. ground forces from anything approximating their current European continental commitment? The United States should be able to plan for peripheral expeditionary warfare on a far more substantial and reliable basis than is possible at present—but that increased flexibility in force employment would have to be considered in its full geopolitical context. If greater U.S. freedom to pursue a maritime-peripheral strategy were purchased, albeit unwittingly, at the price of the collapse of the Western Alliance structure, then the maritime strategy would not offer satisfactory security.[59] To realize anything approximating its potential in threat and in action, maritime power requires that the principal enemy should not be securely preponderant on land. Furthermore, the use—not just the denial of use to the Soviet Union—of Rimland territory is, and will long remain, critical to the neutralization of Soviet maritime power.

U.S. policymakers have recurring difficulty reconciling the frequently divergent needs of the internal political management with the external security function of the alliance. European allies whose domestic politics reflect and express a fear of Soviet military power that is not matched in an insular United States an ocean away (albeit only minutes by ballistic missile) tend to be willing to sacrifice the military integrity of NATO's full strategy and defense posture in the interest of controlling actual or predicted political tensions with the East. The strategic purpose of NATO is to deny the Soviet Union hegemony over all of Europe. But satisfactory pursuit of that high purpose requires some degree of political solidarity within the alliance. The European members of NATO are concerned to shift as much of the burden of the common defense to the United States as the political traffic will bear—a universal motive in alliance politics—but are also determined that the United States should not press a strategy or posture upon the alliance which, no matter how intelligent in strictly military terms, might increase the Soviet political incentive to attack. Conceivably, a point could come when, in official American estimation, the European need for reassurance against war would threaten to undermine fatally the ability of the alliance to fulfill its overriding, antihegemonic strategic purpose of balancing Soviet military power.

Plainly, allies are a mixed blessing. Geopolitical argument is important both to discipline NATO critics who assert falsely that the United States as alliance leader is foolishly engaged in a dangerous and protracted act of charity, and to bring down to earth NATO advocates who are enamored of the alliance for reasons no more solid than those of sentiment or habit.

9

The Course of Soviet Empire

In common with its systemic complement, balance-of-power analysis,[1] geopolitical analysis is impartial as between one or another political system or philosophy. This book is decidedly partial in that I am interested in advancing the security interests of the Western world in general and the United States in particular.

The Soviet Union is identified overwhelmingly as the principal direct and indirect source of security problems for the West at the present time. However, it should be understood that this focus upon the Soviet adversary is entirely a matter of historical circumstance. Viewed in historical perspective, the Soviet state is not uniquely wicked in its political practices; indeed, neither the despotic character of the Soviet state nor the unlovable nature of Russian political culture merit particular Western security attention. The Soviet state and Russian political culture dominate the adversary column in this analysis strictly because the growth of Soviet imperial power happens to threaten the balance-of-power system that protects Western and U.S. interests. Had this book been written fifty or eighty years ago, the focus of concern would have been upon Germany. Fifty or a hundred years from now the focus may need to be upon China and Japan.

A systemic level of analysis should not incline a commentator to be indifferent to the strategic cultures of particular states, just as prescriptive analysis should not be confused with descriptive analysis.[2] Balance-of-power theory yields persuasive propositions concerning what states should do in order to maintain their independence. It is a theory of stability for the independence of states in an essentially anarchic world. Furthermore, the prescriptive theory of the balance of power rests upon an impressive empirical record of actual balancing behavior. Nonetheless, states do not always do what they should do, at least not in good time.[3] History is replete with examples of states and empires that balanced too little and too late—or even too much: by creating intolerable insecurity problems for others, states can fall victim to the consequences of malperformance in their response to the classical security dilemma.

It is not the physical geography per se of the world's landforms and oceans that demands attention in geopolitical analysis. To return to the definition of geopolitics preferred in this book, it is the relation of international political power to the geographical setting. The physical geography of Eurasia is a potential source of menace to the United States not because of some inherent threat but because of the use to which that physical geography might be put by a dominant power or coalition. This point is so basic yet so far removed from the policy debates that convulse Washington day by day that it is easily neglected. Competently conducted, geopolitical analysis is policy science; it addresses the structure of the problems of U.S. national security.

Given the time and place of its writing, this book cannot help having Soviet-American security relations as its central thread. A historical awareness warns that states, even superstates, rise and fall and that behavioral habits and habits of mind of proven efficacy for a workable balancing policy yesterday and today may well undermine what could be the basis of a robust balance of power tomorrow. For today, however, as Mackinder predicted on January 25, 1904, "Russia replaces the Mongol Empire. Her pressure on Finland, on Scandinavia, on Poland, on Turkey, on Persia, on India, and on China replaces the certrifugal raids of the steppemen. In the world at large she occupies the central strategical position held by Germany in Europe. She can strike on all sides and be struck on all sides, save the north. The full development of her modern railway mobility is merely a matter of time. Nor is it likely that any possible social revolution will alter her essential relations to the great geographical limits of her existence."[4] The purpose of this chapter is to assemble, develop, and interpret the diverse elements of commentary on the Soviet Union already presented as preparation for the subsequent discussion of different concepts for U.S. national security policy. If the sustaining roots and the purposes of Soviet military power are misassessed, the United States cannot—unless by accident—design and execute a national security policy suitable to the need.

There is sufficient evidence in Russian and Soviet history and in the more general history of international politics on which to base conclusions concerning the worldview of Soviet leaders and the purposes to which unbalanced Soviet military power most probably would be devoted. Ideas different from mine are not difficult to locate. For example, the vice-president of the British campaign for nuclear disarmament, Frank Allaun (M.P.), has said: "Russia wants detente so that the country can devote its resources to raising living standards. What's wrong with that?"[5] What is wrong is that Allaun demonstrably misreads the nature and purposes of Soviet power as defined in action by Lenin and his successors. It matters little in practice whether beneath the surface of a contemporary Soviet leader there lurks a Great Russian imperialist or a

Marxist-Leninist ideologue. In the Byzantine tradition either religion or an ideology functioning as a quasi-religious creed is integral to the power of the state.[6] In authoritative local belief and practice in Moscow, the interests of the ideology and the interests of the Soviet state are utterly indistinguishable.

American statesmen are at some liberty to decide how they will attempt to cope with Soviet power, but they are not at liberty to invent a fictitious Soviet Union that serves the policy-explanation needs of the moment. It is essential, then, to delineate the nature of the Soviet-American competition with great precision and to appreciate explicitly the most probable character of Soviet policy objectives, near- and far-term.

There is nothing the United States can do that would markedly alter the Soviet will to compete with the Western Alliance. Notwithstanding the differences between them, Nazi Germany and the U.S.S.R. have had in common both an inalienable desire to seek to expand influence at the expense of others, and a global ambition for their desired domain. The United States cannot change the basic official Soviet view of its proper relationship with the West.

An important element in Mackinder's geopolitical theory of power was recognition of the emerging fact that the world was rapidly becoming a closed political system. Unlike the situation in the so-called Columbian era, there were no longer any open oceanic frontiers for exploration and exploitation by the maritime powers.[7] Mackinder was proved correct within fifteen years of his first substantial venture into geopolitical theory. The course and outcome of the Great War were influenced significantly, probably decisively, by the entry of the extra-European weight of the United States on the side of the Western allies.

The Soviet Union today cannot seek security narrowly in Europe or even broadly in Eurasia without having a truly global framework for its grand strategy. The Soviet security position in Eurasia is imperiled by a resistance around the periphery that is organized, underwritten, and even substantially provided by an effectively insular superpower of continental proportions. In order to resolve or alleviate its problems of external security in Eurasia, the Soviet Union must first resolve or alleviate the problems posed by the capability of the United States to balance power in Eurasia. In the long run there can be no purely Eurasian solution to the Soviet problems of insecure empire. So powerful are the U.S. and Japanese economies that the Soviet Union cannot feel really secure until its hegemony is effectively global. Aaron Wildavsky has expressed the essentials with admirable directness: "By its very existence, whether it wishes to or not, therefore, America is and must remain the shield of the West. America is the only global power able to resist the Soviet Union. America's fault is that it exists. Therefore, it threatens the vital principle of

Soviet rule—no independent centers of power. So long as there is a global alternative, therefore, the Soviet system cannot fully consolidate its rule either inside or outside the USSR."[8]

For pressing reasons of tactical or strategic advantage, or to avoid or reduce disadvantage, the Soviet Union will enter into agreements with the United States. Moreover, so long as the United States insists upon treaty compliance and so long as Soviet leaders judge compliance to be to the net Soviet advantage,[9] the Soviet Union will abide by those agreements. But fundamentally, the Soviet Union is in a condition of political struggle with important centers of political decision that it does not control. By Soviet definition, the United States is a deadly enemy because of its geopolitical power-balancing role as the principal security organizer for Eurasia in opposition to the extravagant needs of Soviet security. Further, the United States is the most powerful example of a kind of society which, by its very independent existence, poses a potentially fatal challenge to the political legitimacy of the Soviet state.

Many commentators in the West, especially those innocent of much historical training, look to the particular in their endeavors to identify the causes of Soviet-American political hostility. The particular—be it a trade agreement or a SALT II treaty not ratified or undiplomatic language employed by leaders—can be important for the texture of Soviet-American relations day by day. But the adversary relationship rooted in geopolitics and Soviet ideology transcends and provides a higher meaning to any and all transitory phases.

Soviet strategic culture is not beyond influence in the long term by extra-Soviet factors; that is, the distinctively Soviet (Great Russian) attitudes and beliefs relevant to the definition and solution or alleviation of security problems cannot be totally sealed against influence from abroad.[10] But for the foreseeable future it is prudent to assume that Soviet culture and style are what Russian geography and history have made them. Russian historical experience and interpretation interweave malignantly both with a condition of uneasy empire and with an ideology that mandates permanent struggle against whatever forces are defined as hostile. Neither friendly gestures nor even substantive U.S. accommodation of claimed Soviet interests would encourage a Soviet leader to redirect the nature of Soviet-American relations along a nonconflictual path.[11]

Much has been written on the subject of possible Soviet anxieties over the legitimacy of their system of authority.[12] One can argue that a handful of adventurers staged a coup on November 6-7, 1917, seizing control of a social revolution that had previously escaped firm direction by any person, group, or party.[13] One might proceed to argue that the sole basis for the legitimacy of the Soviet regime, established so precariously at first, was the claim of the Bolsheviks to be the interpreters and executive agents of the correct theory of historical change. In this view, whether they believe it or not, present-day Soviet leaders have no choice but to wage perpetual struggle against all nonsocialist systems: such is their formal duty to history. Indeed, if they do not endeavor to hasten the historical process, they forfeit their right to rule in Russia.

The truth is a little different. Although the Bolsheviks did contribute to the instability of Alexander Kerensky's provisional government, it is still true to say that the tenuous authority of that government collapsed rather than was overcome by any bold purposive action on the part of Lenin and his supporters. The ideological legitimacy of the revolution was, conveniently, provided by the writings and rewritings of the leading revolutionary himself. The tight discipline and conspiratorial form of organization of an elite party was the product of the Russian nineteenth-century revolutionary tradition, of the police-state circumstances of the day, and of Lenin's preferences; they derived not from Marxist theory but from Lenin's comprehensive revision of Marxism and his subsequent practice for the Russian setting.[14] Indeed, because Imperial Russia was hardly ready for the social transformation judged by Karl Marx to follow of necessity from advanced economic development, the Bolsheviks' only practical alternative was to consolidate power through terror and to control ideological debate.

Marxism-Leninism had to be, and remains, a "living doctrine" subject to continuous revelation because there never was a plausible fit between Marxist theory, the Russian condition, and Lenin's practice. But the Soviet state cannot forswear its formal comitment to liberate all of mankind from the toils of capitalist exploitation. Explicit belief in the universalist, ever-flexible ideology of Marxism-Leninism is required if the Soviet state is not to suffer a profound and entropic crisis of legitimacy.[15] For *raison d'état* the theory cannot be admitted to be incorrect or repudiated publicly.

In reality, the Soviet Union today is the bearer of a state ideology with universal pretensions that can accommodate creative interpretation in the face of virtually any change in domestic or international circumstances. Marxism-Leninism (plus the theorizing of a battery of lesser prophets) comprises a body of writings, speeches, and sayings so vast that literally any twist or even U-turn in policy can be supported by quotations from more or less sacred texts. A Soviet Union capable of explaining the necessity of its pact with the Third Reich in August 1939 is a Soviet Union more than capable of explaining any relationship of temporary convenience with the United States. The sacred texts, particularly given the apparent legitimacy of the practice of continuous revelation by their contemporary guardians, do not specify when or precisely how the forces of reaction are to be overcome.

Marxism itself is conveniently vague on the actual mechanisms and instruments of historical change. Marx provided unremarkable economic analysis, some inspired rhetoric, some penetrating journalism, shoddy sociology, and an overambitious grand theory of historical change. He never satisfactorily analyzed the key concepts of class and class consciousness. Moreover, he had nothing worth reading to say on the all-important mechanics of revolutionary action and of the transformation of a proletarian dictatorship into a just, communistic global society. Leninist and subsequent practice entailed dictatorship by the leader over the Party, and dictatorship by the Party over the proletariat.

In practice, it is impossible and unnecessary for Western commentators to separate ideological drive from geostrategic motives in Soviet state behavior. In principle, it should be possible for the United States to achieve a limited *modus vivendi* with a great-power Russia, as Britain did in the Anglo-Russian Convention of August 31, 1907, whereas the state ideology of the Soviet Union would preclude anything more substantial than a mutual accommodation for transitory tactical advantage. However, this is probably a distinction without a difference. Had the Great War not occurred in 1914, it is probable that the Anglo-Russian Convention— which entailed a settlement of outstanding differences in south-central Asia[16]—would not have long endured.

In 1907 Russia was preoccupied with the need to rebuild domestic confidence after the disastrous events of 1905—defeat by Japan and revolution at home—and was in the market for limited accommodations with *all* potential external adversaries.[17] As events were to unfold after 1908, Imperial Russia could not tolerate Austria-Hungary's fearful and defensive bid for hegemony in the Balkans. But the policy of Foreign Minister Count Alexander Izvolsky was complicated by the fact that Russia's internal weakness provided St. Petersburg with a strong motive to develop the bonds of monarchical solidarity with Berlin and Vienna, a strong interest in maintaining the existing order in Europe, and a necessarily strong disinclination to any foreign military adventure. It was a paradox of the balance-of-power system that considerations of *Realpolitik* ranged absolutist Russia in alliance with democratic republican France and (after 1907) generally friendly association with democratic Britain, in opposition to the empires of Germany and Austria-Hungary.

Anyone considering continuities and discontinuities in Russian policy must attempt to distinguish the influence of an ideology of implacable basic hostility toward other social systems from the particular constraints and opportunities of an effectively bipolar distribution of power. The legitimizing historical mission of the Soviet state has encouraged policy decisions for the short term within a framework of long-term purpose or even principle; nonetheless, the international political system does not safely permit a *Soviet* foreign or national security policy that is ideologically distinguishable from the generality of states' practices. From 1921 to the present day, neither the successes nor the failures in Soviet policy would seem plainly attributable to the character of the state ideology. Similarly, it is difficult to detect the hand of ideology in the purposes of the Soviet state as laid down by Lenin and Stalin to rationalize a revolution that should not have occurred if Karl Marx truly was the authority on the march of history.

The state ideology since 1917 has rationalized the identification of enemies, mandated struggle unto predicted ultimate victory, and denied the legitimacy of the values of security communities that hinder the onward march of scientific socialism. I incline to the view that Soviet officials approach their legitimizing ideology with approximately the same respect that many Western politicians accord the Christian religion. The faiths, secular and sacramental, have in common the feature that neither provides a manual for statecraft.[18] The basic nineteenth-century texts of Marxism made no provision for a socialist superpower or great power conducting international politics more or less as usual. The revolution was to be transnational and, among industrial societies, universal. Of necessity, a socialist revolution limited to one country was justified after the fact. Soviet state ideology certainly is an unhelpful element in the international security order, providing as it does a framework of conflict-dominated assumptions for the guidance of long-range policy. But it would be wrong to assert that the Soviet Union is the principal foreign policy problem for the United States because Soviet *ideology* mandates enmity. Furthermore, it would be an error to draw a strong distinction between the assumptions behind Soviet statecraft and the assumptions behind classical balance-of-power policy. There is a novel rigidity of long-term purpose about Soviet policy but its day-by-day practice is plainly in the historical mold of balance-of-power statecraft—constrained by the circumstances of bipolarity and the fact of nuclear danger.

Enmity or friendship between states can rest only upon an opposition or complementarity of interests.[19] Sentiments of affection, cultural affiliation, or respect can play their part in the affairs of state, as can their absence. U.S.-Soviet political competition is fueled by Soviet recognition of the United States as the single most significant opposing force (and organizer of opposing force) in its external security environment, and by American behavior in response to the enmity demonstrated by the U.S.S.R. Whether one elects to explain the long-range character of superpower competition strictly in terms of *Realpolitik*, or of ideology, or of some sophisticated-seeming blend of the two, a basic appreciation that the character of the relationship essentially is one of conflict will remain the same (and valid). The explanations that lean most heavily upon geopolitics and the traditional *Realpolitik* of balance-of-power assumptions can point to sources of Soviet policy inspiration that are at least as enduring as are explanations that define Soviet policy chiefly in ideological terms.

Sometimes, American observers see what they interpret as evidence of Soviet ideology in action when what they are really seeing is the method and rigor typical of a good professional general staff.[20] Soviet military science certainly advertises itself as applied scientific socialism, but the obligatory references to Marx and Lenin[21] have all the directing authority of the extravagant illumination in the manuscripts of the medieval church. Up to a point at least, the references are certainly sincere. Karl Marx is revered as the Newton of social-historical physics, and Lenin—much like George Washington—as the father of his state. However, Lenin has no influence upon Soviet military policy today beyond the (very important) degree to which his aphorisms, his style of government, and the state structure he created dominate the attitudes and approaches of the people who must operate the system. He set an example of high-minded, ends-oriented brutality which, as a role model, is about as far removed as one could imagine from that of the *philosophes* who sought to realize the Enlightenment in an empire of reason in the new American republic.[22]

Notwithstanding the many grievous weaknesses of the Soviet system, the quality of its grand strategy—its degree of "integration," in Barry Posen's terminology[23]—tends to be higher than is that of U.S. strategy. The absence of popular pressures, the longevity of key policymakers in office, the obedience of Warsaw Pact "allies," the respect for and popularity of the military profession, historical memories of just how serious a business actual war can be, and what might be called an imperial mind-set—all these combine to facilitate purposive long-range planning and an opportunism based on principle.[24] Great Russian statecraft has been in the empire-building business since at least the reign of Ivan IV ("the Terrible," 1547-84). The imperial mind-set has long-term concerns; it is trained in methods of control over nonnationals;[25] it is multiregional (if not truly global) in its orientation; it is pragmatic as befits a system that must cope with great complexity; and it tends to seek security through an expanding hegemony.

Unlike their counterparts in the United States, Soviet officials who initiate projects can expect to remain in office through and beyond project completion. The coordination and political and military planning at the highest level in the Defense Council and the penetration by the Party of all levels of governmental activity mean that the scope for bureaucratically autonomous foreign, defense, and arms-control policies is virtually nonexistent. Unlike the U.S. political system, the Soviet system does not reward people who can appeal most successfully to popular opinion, or who succeed in displaying leadership qualities in the amicable management of relations with fractious allies. When need be, unsatisfactory allied leaders are subjected to socialist discipline, sometimes of the most vigorous and even terminal kind (witness Hungary in 1956 and Afghanistan in 1979).

It might be argued that praise for the efficiency of Soviet grand strategy should be qualified by recognition that Soviet policy has contributed in no small measure to the virtual encirclement of the state by foreign enemies. On balance, this argument is not persuasive—given the nature of international politics in a balance-of-power world, the basic character of the Soviet state, and the Russian legacy of that state—but it is certainly the case that Soviet leaders must compete for security today in a context where most of the gross world product is formally aligned against them.

Soviet allies (as contrasted with satellites) in Europe comprise one country, Bulgaria, plus Poland and Czechoslovakia with reference to German questions. Beyond Europe, the Soviet allies are preeminently Cuba and Vietnam (countries that have major geostrategic-distractive value *vis-à-vis* a maritime enemy), North Korea, and—in a much less reliable column—Libya, Syria, South Yemen, Ethiopia, Angola, Mozambique, and possibly Nicaragua. By any system of material accounting, the alliance or security-dependent system created by Moscow over the past quarter-century is of trivial worth; by a geostrategic accounting, however, its value is much higher. Cuba lies immediately on the flank of the North American end of the transatlantic sea lines of communication (SLOC), further, it has strategic value as a complication for the assured American use of the Caribbean and the Panama Canal. Vietnam flanks U.S. and Japanese SLOCs from the Pacific to the Indian Ocean and is classically located to divert Chinese attention to its southern frontier.[26]

The strategic value of distant and isolated though geographically key-sited allies in the Caribbean, Central America, southern Africa, the Red Sea, and southeast Asia has to be assessed with reference both to their effect on superpower competition day by day and to their prospective utility in war. The Soviet Union is not exempt from application of the general rule that all voluntary, if variably dependent, allies are allies of (mutual) convenience. For the course of a brief *attaque brusquée*, Moscow can be as certain as it need be that the Warsaw Pact allies in Europe will do what is required of them. Cuba or Vietnam, however, might well deem it profoundly inconvenient to attract prompt U.S. military attention on behalf of the Soviet Union.

True to its Russian historical character and legacy and without very notable exceptions, the Soviet Union has chosen the relative certainty of the kind of security that accompanies the pursuit of territorial and hegemonic possession goals, rather than the far less certain kind of security that might be obtained through the encouragement of cooperative attitudes on the part of others. Whatever else may have changed in the Soviet Union since World War II, it is evident that Moscow's view in the 1980s of what constitutes a sufficiently friendly government in Afghanistan differs not at all from Stalin's view in 1944-45 of a sufficiently friendly government in Poland. Moreover, Soviet methods have not changed over four decades—as Prime Minister Hafizullah Amin of Afghanistan learned to his terminal cost in 1979.

To praise the integration of military policy and political goals in Soviet grand strategy is to do so in plain recognition that the Soviet Union cannot help being what it is. It is attractive to consider the idea of a Soviet Union that could be far more secure than today, were it only to rewrite the goals and methods of its grand strategy for the purpose of playing a role preponderantly supportive of the existing international order. Speculation along that trail, however, involves the invention of a Soviet Union quite different from that which exists. Those who find little to applaud in a Soviet grand strategy that seems to insure the continued beleaguerment of a Soviet Heartland garrison fail to recognize the discipline of necessity that governs the Great Russian imperium of the Soviet state. Soviet leaders must play the cards they are dealt in obedience to long-standing rules of self-regarding prudence in international politics.

The heroic scale of the political-cultural mismatch between the United States and the Soviet Union is not conducive to accurate, judicious, and mutually empathetic assessment. The Soviet general staff has sought responsibly to effect in defense preparation the best attainable expression of a war-fighting/war-winning strategy.[27] That strategy is an operational expression of the military doctrine which emerged out of the protracted and intense debate on "the revolution in military affairs" in the late 1950s. Soviet *political*-military doctrine, or grand strategy, mandates public commitment to ultimate victory in the historical struggle between antagonistic social systems. But Soviet military science knows that either victory or defeat is militarily possible. Soviet military analysts know that had the Third Reich not held Slavs in racial contempt, thereby forfeiting a vast fund of potential local support, and had Hitler been a competent war leader capable of insuring that his Japanese allies tied down Soviet forces in the Far East, then the Siberian divisions could not have saved Moscow (and possibly the Soviet state) in December 1941.[28] In the long run the geopolitical ambitions of the Third Reich would have precluded any security relationship with other societies that the latter could deem tolerable. However, Hitler's early implementation of what should have been postwar policies of German-directed reconstruction was fatal to the prospect of military success.[29]

The United States and the Soviet Union are locked in a relationship of enmity for the predictable future, but only the Soviet Union seems capable of appreciating fully and acting steadily upon the implications of that fact. Soviet leaders, like American leaders, are the captives of their unique historical-cultural perspective. American leaders wish their country to function as the "city on a hill," but that wish—as policy rhetoric or as policy action— is a potentially deadly threat to the Soviet empire. American values are a fundamental challenge to the legitimacy of the Soviet state as well as to the stability of its hegemony in eastern Europe.

It must be emphasized that the principal American adversary is the Soviet state and its power, not the arcane nonsense of Marxist or socialist ideology. Lenin effected a ruthless Russification of Marxism. Soviet political practice is at least as far removed from the humane spirit of the early writings on alienation of Karl Marx as American presidential campaigns are from the theory and practice of popular democracy in a Greek city-state. The force and fraud that characterize Soviet practice are products of local Russian circumstances. Richard Pipes is very much to the point when he writes:

The very same socialist ideology that in Russia has come to be identified with totalitarianism has had no such result in the West, which suggests that the decisive factors are not the ideas but the soil on which they happen to fall....
Lenin's Bolsheviks were from the outset an elitist body of middle class intellectuals who appointed themselves to speak and act on behalf of the working class. In their internal organization, they followed a strictly authoritarian model; the Party's administration and theoretical authority were concentrated in the person of Lenin, the infallible *vozhd' (Führer)*, who claimed to embody the historic mission of the proletariat. This is Marxism-Leninism—that is, Marxism divested of its democratic component and adapted to Russian political conditions.[30]

Western commentators need to appreciate the sources of legitimacy of the Soviet state. From the perspective of the Communist Party of the Soviet Union (CPSU), the alleged correctness of the ideology is the *sine qua non* of the asserted "right to rule and obedience." In practice, the CPSU has legitimacy because it functions in so traditionally Russian a manner (providing a substitute czar, an authority or father figure, and meriting respect because of its demonstrated will to power); because it has sustained its effective authority for seven decades (few living Soviet citizens have firsthand experience of any alternative political authority);[31] because it can claim a decisive role in saving the Motherland from the foreign invader in the Great Patriotic War; and because it gives every appearance of serving distinctively Russian interests. Most features of the Soviet policy that distress American policymakers are quite as much Russian as they are Soviet. The Soviet Union maintains the largest standing army in Europe today, but the same was said of the Imperial Russia of Alexander I.[32] Soviet illiberality at home today epitomizes a fundamentally antipathetic political system, but British and French governments made similar observations of Russia throughout the nineteenth century. The secrecy and secretiveness that is the Soviet way today has always been characteristic of Russian political culture.

Throughout most of the nineteenth century the potential for irritation in Russo-American relations that their contrasting domestic political values could have engendered was more than offset by a rough working community of geostrategic interests. John Lewis Gaddis says of this "heritage of harmony," that "since Russia had fewer bases for conflict with the United States than any other European power, Americans saw it throughout the nineteenth century as a country worth cultivating good relations with, to the end that Britain and France not become too powerful in Europe and hence capable of threatening the balance of power in the New World."[33] But the functional geostrategic amity between Washington and St. Petersburg, which achieved its high plateau in the 1850s and 1860s and peaked in 1867 with the sale of Alaska, was eroded by changes in the European balance of power and by the domestic malpractices of czarist rule (a theme for frequent American political homilies) in the early years of the twentieth century. The illiberal character of Imperial Russia was a significant impediment to those in the United States who favored early American participation in the Great War.

The Soviet Union may evolve to a point where there will be truly major domestic constraints upon official freedom of action in foreign policy, but at present those constraints are almost as far in the future as they seemed in 1948, when U.S. policy advisors rejected defensive variants of the containment concept.[34] The United States must manage relations with a Soviet Union whose despotism is more oriental than European, whose statecraft (and much else) is in the Byzantine tradition, whose ideology eschews any notion of international order that requires stabilization of the existing distribution of power.

Soviet leaders are licensed to adhere rigidly to geostrategic principle, while behaving with great tactical flexibility (even though Russian/Soviet culture tends to disdain flexibility as a mark of weakness), by the absence of electoral pressures and the presence of an ideology that encourages a long-range perspective upon security problems.

Marxist-Leninist ideology says that the class-conscious workers of mature industrialized countries will (or should) throw off their chains. The economic disadvantages of "the socialist camp" are, of course, somewhat bizarre features of the historical process that Soviet leaders find difficult to explain. In effect Josef Stalin wrote *finis* to Marxist theory as a guide to practice when he invented the doctrine of "socialism in one country" to rationalize so isolated a revolution (as well as to serve as an ideological weapon against Leon Trotsky). Theoretically, the Soviet Union should not have occurred. As an arrogant urban intellectual, Karl Marx emphasized "the idiocy of rural life," yet his self-proclaimed disciples seized power in a country that was economically and socially dominated by rural life. The idea of an isolated bastion of socialism, let alone an isolated bastion dominated economically by agriculture, should be heresy to anyone at all faithful to the writings of Marx.[35] The shotgun marriage, effected in 1917 and consolidated in the "culture of War Communism,"[36] between the most backward of the industrializing countries and socialist theory necessarily resulted in a political system that was far more Russian than it was socialist.

Nevertheless, in the universalistic terms of formal Soviet ideology, the Soviet Union is still the vanguard of the transnational worldwide proletariat, assisting the world-historical process of change from feudalism to bourgeois capitalism to imperialism to socialism.[37] As such, by reason both of ideological necessity for domestic legitimacy and of geopolitical assessment, the Soviet Union is committed to the waging of political warfare against the United States. Whatever the true blend of ideology and *Realpolitik*, the objectives of Soviet security policy can be described in specific geopolitical terms with some confidence.

Soviet leaders may well believe that they will have to fight the United States one day. The principal reason, in likely Soviet assessment, is that the United States will come to recognize that it is losing the protracted struggle for power and influence; in that context some American government may be tempted to "roll the dice" to see whether a bold, adventurist military stroke can snatch rapid victory from the jaws of slowly unfolding defeat. If this assessment of Soviet reasoning has any merit, one may be certain that the Soviet Union will bend every effort to achieve political— and if not political, then strategic—warning of an American attack. Moscow should be presumed willing to attack first in the last resort— preventively or, at worst, preemptively.

Or, given a prospectively fatal erosion in the ever-more-important high-technology basis of the Soviet claim to super power and extensive empire, Soviet leaders could come to believe that they face an impossible *and intolerable* power-balancing problem. In this scenario, Soviet leaders would find no effective nonviolent competitive responses to the high-technology challenges posed by the United States and its allies. Should the Soviet Union be unable to offset an emerging multilevel military disadvantage through alliance; should it discern no convincing strategic, operational, or tactical responses and see no prospects for an effective internal arms-balancing reply, then a decision could be made to effect a violent ambush of an intolerable trend in the correlation of forces.

I am not predicting here that war will occur, but I am reminding readers of twin historical principles: that every security system is transformed over time by the effects of the dynamic interaction of many forces; and that such transformations are frequently accompanied, hastened, or

retarded by violent conflict.[38] Nuclear weapons probably provide a historically unusual degree of tolerance of change in the material detail of the
balance of power, while a substantially bipolar security system generally
works for efficiency in power balancing by minimizing opportunities for
buck passing among key actors. Nonetheless, essential equivalence and
equilibrium are Western conceptual desiderata; they do not constitute a
descriptive empirical theory of the security relations of the superpowers.

A crucial qualification to this argument is that incentive would need to
be matched by opportunity—a point frequently neglected by critics of the
SDI.[39] By way of historical illustration, what would seem to have made the
period 1912-14 so dangerous was not just the fact of a large German incentive to wage what was conceived as a preventive war against the be-
sieging forces of the Franco-Russian Alliance. It was also the belief of the
Germans (*inter alia*) that they had at hand the rapidly wasting asset of an
offensive military instrument of decision for (defensively motivated) victory.[40]

Very knowledgeable though a few senior Soviet officials are concerning the United States, it should never be forgotten that deep down
they probably hold some variant of the following presumptions: that
Western democracy is a sham, a facade for the profit of an exploitative
entrepreneurial class that rents or buys political parties to serve its objective interests; that bourgeois society must inevitably give way to socialism
but has nuclear-armed guardians who, in that society's death throes
would fight even in a hopeless cause if so ordered; and that there will be
some men of steel in the United States who, unlike the "useful idiots" and
"deaf-mutes" that typically weaken the ability of the capitalist democracies to compete with Soviet power,[41] will understand that their system
faces a truly mortal foe in the Soviet Union.

Soviet leaders have good reason to delay a Soviet-American clash of
arms for as long as may prove feasible. The Soviet Union is as sensibly
fearful of war as it is sensible of the advantage of constant defense
semimobilization—both as a rationale for political discipline for domestic
stability and as a means of cumulative improvement in its international
security position. This is not to deny that defense investment imposes
massive opportunity costs upon the Soviet system; however, one's view
of costs may be dominated by one's values. "The Soviet Union...found
itself in the 1970s much more powerful and also distinctly poorer than its
leaders could reasonably have predicted even a mere decade before,"
writes Edward Luttwak. "It was thus only natural that the goal of economic supremacy, which had become utterly unrealistic, should have given
way to the pursuit of imperial power as the new dominant aim of Soviet
national strategy."[42] The foregoing argument posits a double hypothesis:
first, that the Soviet security condition relative to the United States and
other external foes will likely improve over the decades ahead; second,

that Soviet leaders will believe in the prospect of such an improvement. If these hypotheses are not well founded, then the character of Soviet external policy could be very different indeed from what is cited here as the dominant case.

To identify a character of Soviet external policy which rests upon the assumption of prognoses that are optimistic in Soviet perspective is to invite some familiar critical charges. One may be accused of ignorance of the fragility of the Soviet empire;[43] of taking apparently at face value the doctrinal pabulum that the Soviet government feeds its people (which is probably not generally believed either by the issuing officials or by the public—who know from firsthand experience the degree to which the Soviet system does not work); of exaggerating the Soviet commitment to win internationally; and of harboring a dangerously defeatist perspective.

In fact, it may be fortunate for the prospects for peace that Soviet leaders do have some grounds for optimism. Few circumstances would be more dangerous than a condition wherein Soviet leaders confronted a highly plausible prospect of catastrophic failure for their system in the context of a favorable yet transient imbalance of military power. Soviet ideology could not accommodate such a prospect; the idea would have to be denied as heresy or treason. To do otherwise woud be either to confess the fallibility of that doctrine which is the *sine qua non* of Soviet legitimacy or to admit massive and protracted misconduct of Soviet affairs of state. As Robert Daniels has put it: "In the hands of strong leaders who could make ideology mean whatever was convenient for them without fear of contradiction, Marxism-Leninism became largely a system of self-justi-fication and legitimization for the Soviet regime, with incidental value as propaganda directed toward the gullible at home and abroad. Ideology is still reflected in policy only where it dovetails with the power-conscious concerns of the leadership. . . . Ideology functions in the Soviet system as a sort of nontheistic religion, couched in the language of science but de-manding faith in its infallibility from all its loyal communicants"[44]

Although Soviet ideology is and must remain a formal political neces-sity, an enduring framework providing settled habits of thought, Soviet leaders are as capable as any others of identifying what looks to be a very adverse trend in the correlation of forces—regardless of the requirement for optimism that is mandated by the official theory of historical change. There is every reason to believe that Mikhail Gorbachev's bid to reform the Soviet system in the interest of promoting its international competi-tiveness is motivated by just such a fear of future Soviet decline.

Western analysts have the habit of discovering the Soviet Union that best serves their policy-recommending purposes. On the one hand, the inability of the West to realize in peacetime anything approximating its true capacity for effective competition provides a solid objective basis for the depiction of a Soviet adversary that one day could be close to unmanageable from the standpoint of Western military security.[45] On the other hand, one can portray the Soviet Union as a stumbling and fumbling giant with an inalienable state ideology devoid of vitality, an economy that for structural reasons is heroically inefficient, a society plagued with severe social problems, a foreign imperium that can be held only by repression, and potential enemies on all sides.

This book recommends an agnostic stance toward the prospects for survival of the Soviet system. The Imperial Russia of the czars withstood the most fearsome test of protracted war before it collapsed in 1917;[46] the Soviet system has survived military crises of the most serious kind at the hands of White counterrevolutionaries and German invaders. Moreover, the future of Soviet power may be substantially contingent upon the quality of U.S. national security policy. If mobilized and managed for the prudent and effective defense of Western interests, the assets of the globe-girdling alliance led by the United States are so formidable that the Soviet Union could face a growing political crisis. It is just possible that such a crisis in competitiveness might lead Moscow into some novel channels of policy that could prove benign for international peace and security.

In designing the basic architecture of its national security policy for the next several decades, however, the United States must assume that the Soviet Union is unlikely to collapse by reason of its internal contradictions. A combination of cynicism and apathy appears to serve well enough to defuse the potential for political unrest in the contradiction between the official version of life in the "workers' paradise" and the reality of shortages and corruption. The contradiction between the transnational political promise of equality of opportunity in Soviet life and the reality of Great Russian domestic imperialism is managed, again well enough, by the trusty tools of police-state repression. For the Soviet empire to come unraveled from within, the Party would need to lose its will to power, and there is no empirical base upon which to predict such a development. I believe that Soviet leaders would attempt external military adventure before they would accept the necessity of domestic change so fundamental as to place in question the authority and capacity to rule of the CPSU. While remaining ever alert to the possibility of sharp discontinuities in Soviet policy, American policymakers should be properly impressed by the continuity that habits of obedience and techniques of control facilitate within the Soviet Union.[47]

The political survival of Soviet power in Russia is something of a historical oddity. The classical model of the dynamics of revolution has the Jacobins (Bolsheviks) themselves repudiated and consumed in their turn by the revolution, as the country in question seeks to restore some measure of normalcy for a new equilibrium.[48] Lenin and his co-conspirators performed their Jacobin function but then confounded the dominant model by retaining control of the postrevolutionary settlement. The "Bonapartist restoration" was effected by Stalin at least formally in the name of the Party. In the "great terror" of the mid-1930s the revolution, or Stalin's new quasi-czarism, consumed its children as Stalin institutionalized terror as an instrument of political control.[49]

Scarcely more surprising than the ability of the Bolsheviks to retain power through the protracted crisis period of "war communism" from 1918 to March 1921 was the resilience of Soviet authority in the face of Hitler's invasion in 1941. The insufficiency of the material and manpower base of the *Wehrmacht* for its military task is not really in question, any more than is the confusion of German command arrangements or the folly of German campaign strategy.[50] But so great had been the crimes committed against the Soviet peoples by Stalin's rule that the prospect that war would again be the mother of revolution in Russia had to be judged to be excellent. Lenin was saved by the incompetence and number of his enemies; Stalin was saved by "general winter," Nazi racialism, and Hitler's incompetent statecraft and generalship.

In geopolitical terms, the Soviet Union is seeking to expel American power and influence from, and deny the United States access to the assets of, the Rimlands of the World Island of Eurasia-Africa.[51] A Soviet security system that formally or informally embraced the entirety of Europe and Asia should be a security system substantially immune to American pressure. To achieve it, the Soviet Union need not acquire new territory or even, in many cases, new explicit treaty commitments; effective benign neutralization would suffice. Soviet leaders do not want to fight for western Europe; they want western European countries to behave in a manner independent of the United States in their foreign policies and in ways compatible with Soviet security interests. The politically effective expulsion of American power and influence from Europe, the preclusion of a western European superstate, and the prevention of Sino-American or Sino-Japanese alliances would set the stage for the final—if possibly very protracted—phase of Soviet-American competition. If the Soviet Union were effectively in security command of Eurasia, it would enjoy locally unrestricted access to the open ocean and could draw upon the industrial, scientific, and agricultural resources of western Europe, or at least deny those resources to the United States. Given such a hegemony, the Soviet Union would be far better placed than today either to press steadily against a much contracted U.S. perimeter or, if need be, to wage war against the United States.

In at least one critical respect, however, a Soviet imperium thus expanded could face a cumulative crisis of awesome dimensions: in theory and probably in practice, U.S. seapower would be able to blockade Eurasia against shipment of food from the Americas or Australia and New Zealand. Some American neo-isolationists are tempted by the hope that a

Soviet Union truly dominant as a landpower throughout Eurasia would be content to treat the extra-Eurasian world as an area of preponderant American interest. Such people should consider carefully both the implications for the stability of the Soviet empire of dependence upon *overseas* trade for food and the implications of that dependence for the Soviet incentive to challenge U.S. seapower in its natural environment.

I do not mean to imply that establishment of a Soviet world empire, hegemonic if not territorial in general character, will ever be a practical enterprise, but I do claim that the logic of the course of Soviet empire will likely require that Soviet leaders attempt to achieve the impossible dream: the total security implicit in the vision of a truly universal Great Russian Empire. The founding father of the Soviet Union was quite explicit: "We aim at the firm union and full fusion of the workers and peasants of all nations of the world into a single, worldwide Soviet Republic."[52] Yet national assets are hardly sufficient in scale or quality for secure command even of the Soviet and Soviet-allied system as currently delimited. It is entirely possible, then, that Soviet leaders would be almost as fearful for the authority of the CPSU in their own global security system as they are in the balance-of-power system of today.

How could a Soviet global hegemon enforce political discipline upon a formally friendly China, Japan, western Europe, United States, and Moslem Middle East? To pose the question in this admittedly extreme form virtually precludes the need for a detailed answer. In a narrow military sense one can envisage, though certainly one should not predict, a long trail of success for Soviet power and influence. But even if the Soviet empire should win battles and campaigns, as well as awe potential foes into a condition that Charles Krauthammer has infelicitously termed "Eurocowardice,"[53] how could power be consolidated, hegemony rendered politically truly secure?

Geopolitically, the two-step grand design—Eurasia first, then the Americas—carries plausibility as a Soviet long-term vision. First, isolate the United States in the Western Hemisphere and thereby alter radically the correlation of forces in the Soviet favor. Second, defeat the newly isolated United States either slowly by political means or—if feasible— rapidly by military force. Soviet leaders cannot help recognizing how few are their genuine friends and voluntary allies, but they require obedience and respect, not affection. The nominal strength of the U.S.-led column of Western (or Western-inclined) states is awesome in scale, but Soviet leaders know that they enjoy some structural advantages in the contest.

On balance, the fact of geographical propinquity operates in the Soviet favor. For reasons of geography, Soviet power is a permanent reality in Europe and Asia and is proximate to the Middle East, whereas American power is in and about those regions solely for reasons of American policy choice. It should be noted that Soviet geopolitical location is judged to be only a net advantage. Geographical propinquity works in two directions. The land borders of the Soviet Union in Europe facilitate threat projection on a scale that could not readily be balanced without the addition of the strategic weight of the United States. But those land borders also place Soviet territory and society at risk from abroad, and—as Stephen Walt reminds us—generating the perception of threat has the universal consequence of motivating those who feel threatened to consider the feasibility of balancing that threat.[54] The central position in Eurasia of the Heartland Soviet Union *ipso facto* promotes the encirclement and potential multifront war problems that weaken Soviet power.

Military intimidation functions to the Soviet advantage in a context where Western spokesmen lack easy access to the Soviet public and where that public lacks the ability to insist that its govenment accommodate its fear of nuclear holocaust. A condition of mutual deterrence that rests upon essentially equivalent military capabilities is a condition that must lead to the erosion of the Western capacity for collective action. U.S. defense and arms-control planners have long been obsessed with the technical aspects of the strategic balance. They have neglected to notice that although net military prowess is very important, the name of the dominant game is the war-in-peace that the Soviet Union is waging by nuclear intimidation in its several forms. Because of the differences between open and closed societies, rough parity in forces does not translate into rough parity in ability to withstand (nuclear) threats. As a matter of strategic logic, though not of political practicality, the West requires military compensation for the political vulnerability of a democratic society. U.S. strategic and arms-control planning should endeavor to take account of the asymmetry in superpower political systems. Half a million people can demonstrate in Central Park for a nuclear freeze, while eleven members of a week-old Soviet independent peace movement are harassed, arrested for "hooliganism," and have their leader dispatched to a psychiatric hospital. Formally equal military circumstances could have very unequal political results.

Soviet influence, like water, will flow along the lines of least resistance. In some cases the Soviet Union will promise and then deliver victory to new security dependents (as in Angola and Ethiopia). In other cases, where there are clear lines of demarcation between Soviet and American preponderance of interest, the Soviet Union will appeal to fear of nuclear war and to anti-American sentiment. In western Europe, for example, "useful idiots" can be persuaded that their survival interests are threatened not so much by a Soviet military power that needs to be balanced as by the extant system of international security itself, by nuclear weapons per se, and above all else by the alliance entanglement with a United States that is portrayed as unsteady in its policy and willing to contemplate the waging of nuclear war at the expense of Europeans.

Soviet military power is real and must be addressed on its own terms. But that military power is only an essential backdrop to the proximate contest. The real contest is for influence over the minds and emotions of understandably fearful people around the Eurasian Rimlands, and over the political willingness of geographically very distant Americans to accept risks of nuclear catastrophe on behalf of allies whom many Americans judge to be ungrateful, undisciplined, and unreliable.

10

Containment

The range of prudent choice open to statesmen is typically far more restricted than they would like. Politicians running for public office often proclaim, assuming a historically illiterate audience, that their objective is to "end the nuclear arms race" or to achieve "lasting peace." The nuclear arms race can be ended—or perhaps interrupted—by war, but a unilateral decision by the United States to stop competing would not halt the miscalled arms race. In the absence of an active American competitor, the U.S.S.R. could be trusted to press on to secure a more and more splendid degree of military superiority. Similarly, the United States cannot have a peace policy per se; peace is not a policy but a condition that may be achieved by policy. If it is to have a national security policy worthy of the name, the United States needs a coherent vision of its policy objectives, designed with close attention to means for implementation and a clear-eyed understanding of its own political-strategic culture.[1]

In public debate, complex architectures of ideas are simplified into summary concepts that function more as symbols for affiliation or enmity than as conveyers of accurate information. The recent past has seen "detente" and its supposed obverse, "cold war," solemnly discussed as though their meaning were self-evident. In the defense realm more narrowly, the 1980s have witnessed debates over "Star Wars" and over the respective merits of allegedly distinguishable maritime and continental-coalition strategies. Ever hungry for controversies that can be portrayed in very simple terms, the mass media persist in contrasting arms-control endeavors with arms-race behavior.

Summary concepts are employed in this and the succeeding three chapters—as labels for clusters of ideas that express a clear orientation at their core. Familiar though these concepts are, their meaning, feasibility, and implications for U.S. national security may be seen in a fresh perspective when they are set against the backcloth of the preceding discussion of geopolitical relationships, political and strategic culture, interests, alliance structures, and the character and purpose of Soviet power. It should be understood that the concepts identified and developed here are intended to guide the organization of national security policy or grand strategy, not of defense policy alone.

The five national security concepts selected for consideration are labeled as follows: *containment; dynamic containment; rollback; devolution;* and *fortress America.* To the extent possible, readers are requested to ignore the historical and theoretical baggage that these labels carry. This discussion is forward-looking and is not concerned to refight or revisit, for example, the debate over John Foster Dulles's colorful language on rollback in 1952.[2] The possible costs of inherited meaning are accepted here as a price worth paying for the ease of communication that attends the employment of familiar terms.

To choose a guiding concept for U.S. national security policy, one intended to be more than a mere public relations label for transient political needs, is not necessarily to select a strategy; still less is it to quiet disagreement over the means of implementation. Indeed, it is not sensible to fix upon an overall national security concept unless one has also identified an appropriate strategy and has good reason to believe that the instruments necessary for policy execution will be to hand. As George Kennan has illustrated in his many writings since 1946, the identification and selection of an attractive-sounding idea such as "containment" is to invite rather than to foreclose debate over the means.[3]

No general historical truths define strictly necessary consequences of ill-fitting tactics and strategy or of mismatches between strategy and policy. Superior competence in tactics and operational art can provide substantial compensation for even abysmally faulty strategy and policy, as the German Army demonstrated time and again in World War II. But, scarcely less often, tactical incompetence or plain impossibility can deny superior generalship sufficient scope for the exercise of its skill.[4] As noted already, grand strategy or national security policy may be held to constitute a "means-ends chain."[5] That chain can disintegrate if the ends selected are inappropriate either to the external security environment or to the tolerence of the domestic political culture, or if the means fail to achieve a balance with the scope and difficulty of the tasks assigned them. Nonetheless, this book is concerned primarily with the design of policy structure—while paying attention always to the complex issues of feasibility.

Strictly speaking, the United States and its European and Asian allies have the economic base from which they could construct and enforce virtually any terms of security relations with the Soviet Union that they might choose. Fortunately for the Soviet Union, the maritime alliance between Halford Mackinder's Inner Crescent (Nicholas Spykman's Rimland) and the Outer Crescent or the New World is far from functioning as though it were a military actor determined to secure a permanent relation of major security advantage over the Soviet imperium. The United States seeks as quiet an international life as its apparently inalienable (and generally overseas) security interests and its enduring national mission for human improvement will permit. The allies of the United States typically seek as quiet a life in security affairs as the politics of the alliance will tolerate. Given that local or even regional irritations in Soviet-American relations tend to affect immediately very few of the nominal state legionaries of the alliance, it is a general rule that the allies function as a restraint or brake on U.S. policy.

It is the purpose of these chapters to identify and analyze distinctive concepts for the guidance of policy. But I recognize that it may be far easier to build a working consensus in favor of any given guiding concept than to secure widespread agreement on just what the preferred concept implies in terms of strategies and means. For example, if containment remains the directing idea for U.S. national security policy vis-à-vis the Soviet Union, should that idea be expressed in action overwhelmingly within the framework of multilateral alliance ties, through an increasing focus upon bilateral alliance connections, or more and more by the United States acting unilaterally?[6]

So familiar and compelling is the concept of containment that any attempt to invent a new descriptive term would appear as a straining after novelty for its own sake. For reasons of geopolitical logic and internal dynamics, I believe that both Soviet power and the influence that flows from the shadow cast by that power will expand if they are not contained, and that U.S. survival interests are at stake in the containment enterprise. Since there is no practical alternative available that carries a promise of security superior to the policy variants of the concept of containment, this book will not shy away from broad-gauged endorsement of the familiar. The security concept preferred here, dynamic containment (see Chapter 11) might usefully be thickened with the apposition "a strategy for the long haul."

With the exception of fortress America, the concepts discussed here all rest upon the assumption that the United States has a vital interest in the containment of Soviet power roughly within its current Eurasian perimeter. Strategies may differ, but the principal purpose of U.S. national security policy should be to prevent the Soviet Union from achieving effective hegemony over Eurasia. The survival interest of the United States in avoiding catastrophic war with the Soviet Union is in a condition of some practical tension with that purpose: if the United States is too strongly attentive to the danger of war, it may limit its ability to compete effectively with Soviet power in the interest of preserving a tolerable balance of influence in Eurasia. The apparent logic of strategic geography poses at least the semblance of a dilemma between the risk of entanglement in foreign wars and what may be the illusion of relative safety at home—a dilemma that is summarized in the question, "Where are the strategic frontiers of the United States?"

U.S. strategic policy over the years has addressed the tension between the risks to American survival that attend security commitments around the littoral of Eurasia and the less than immediate survival quality of U.S. interests that are the explicit objects of those commitments. Many Europeans have judged American strategic thinking since the late 1950s to be more than a little fanciful, overintellectualized in fact, with its emphasis upon flexibility in response, thresholds, and other policy tools intended to promote the feasibility of escalation control.[7] Fanciful, or not, U.S. policy guidance for its strategic forces since the early 1970s has been informed by the intellectual Siamese twins of a concern to sustain sufficient credibility for extended deterrence threats in the context of a dramatically deteriorating strategic balance,[8] and a determination to minimize U.S. liability to damage in wars that begin abroad.

The distinction between containment and dynamic containment is both real and artificial. It is real in that containment policy as it has been practiced and explained differs markedly from containment policy as it could and (I believe) should be practiced and explained. It is artificial in that the basic concepts and the objectives in view are identical. The differences are at the levels of policy declaration and execution, not policy inspiration. Containment is the typical American practice; it refers to the way in which relations with Soviet power are managed and mismanaged by an insular democracy that either never quite believes, or believes only for brief periods, that its major adversary is conducting war-in-peace. If Demosthenes the orator is to be believed (which he should not be without considerable qualification),[9] Philip of Macedon behaved toward the squabbling Greek city-states much as Mikhail Gorbachev and the other heirs of Lenin have behaved toward the Western world. In his Third Philippic of 341 B.C., Demosthenes said:

But, in heaven's name, is there any intelligent man who would let words rather than deeds decide the question of who is at peace and who is at war with him?...For he [Philip] says that he is not at war, but for my part, so far from admitting that in acting thus he is observing the peace with you, I assert that when he lays hands on Megara, sets up tyrannies in Euboea, makes his way, as now, into Thrace, hatches plots in the Peloponnese, and carries out all these operations with his armed force, he is breaking the peace and making war upon you—unless you are prepared to say that the men who bring up the siege-engines are keeping the peace until they actually bring them to bear on the walls.[10]

Whether or not containment is the best that the United States can manage, given its cultural proclivities and the sheer weight and complexity of its security problems, must be a matter for judgment. In both the theory and the practice of the U.S.-led maritime alliance, containment has been the post-1945 policy expression of the key geopolitical concept of strategic opposition between Heartland and Inner Crescent/Rimland that was advanced and much revised in detail by Sir Halford Mackinder and Nicholas Spykman.[11] Containment is the plain linear descendant of the geopolitical premise central to British statecraft—the idea of balancing power *on*, not *with*, the continent of Europe. Britain allied with, and subsidized or bribed, the *second-strongest* state in Europe, successively and always (ultimately) successfully, to oppose Spanish, French, and German bids for hegemony.[12] The rise of superstates and the absence of balancing weight vis-à-vis the Soviet Union within Europe after 1945 propelled the United States into a new variant of the counterhegemonic organizing role formerly played by Britain—though the United States virtually became one side of the balance rather than the balancer.

In practice, the concept of containment has encouraged somewhat uncritical linear perimeter thinking. Similarly, the concept has defensive and static implications. The dangers of passive perimeter thinking were recognized as early as March 1948 in a draft policy document: "In view of the nature of Soviet-directed world communism, the successes which it has already achieved, and the threat of further advances in the immediate future, a defensive policy cannot be considered an effectual means of checking the momentum of communist expansion and inducing the Kremlin to relinquish its aggressive designs. A defensive policy by attempting to be strong everywhere runs the risk of being weak everywhere."[13] The policy document that President Harry S. Truman subsequently approved (in November 1948) provided a vision of a very dynamic containment. The "general objectives" of the United States in its security relationship with the Soviet Union were defined as follows: "(a) to reduce the power and influence of the USSR to limits which no longer constitute a threat to the peace, national independence and stability of the world family of nations; (b) to bring about a basic change in the conduct of international relations by the government in power in Russia, to conform with the purposes and principles set forth in the UN charter."[14]

Soviet leaders have long recognized that as a general rule the socialist commonwealth can expand and then be sustained only at the point of the (Soviet and Soviet-proxy) bayonet; to rework a familiar axiom, "Socialism follows the tank." However, they have also recognized that the Soviet Union, at first as a very beleaguered island of socialism and even much later as a superpower, was greatly inferior in resources to the sum total of those of its potential enemies. The essentially political character of the Soviet challenge has changed in detail but not in kind since the heady days when the first Peoples' Commissar for Foreign Affairs, Leon Trotsky, believed that all that the Bolshevik republic needed by way of a foreign policy was a declamatory summons to the workers of the world to revolt.

The original vision was that the capitalist and imperialist powers would crumble from within once Russian socialism functioned as a political spark to ignite the "prairie fire." The Soviet political challenge today and for the future has nothing whatsoever to do with Western workers' affirmation of ideological or class solidarity with the U.S.S.R. as a nominal workers' state. Instead, the challenge reposes in the potential of Soviet military power so to intimidate Western publics that their governments will be incapable of effectively mobilizing their theoretically available assets for collective anti-Soviet action. In the words of the former SACEUR, General Bernard Rogers: "I believe the major menace here in Europe is not a Soviet attack. The Soviets don't want war. I believe the real danger is that, with or without SDI, continued Soviet conventional growth will lead eventually to the Soviets achieving their objective of intimidating Western Europe without firing a shot."[15]

In practice, the containment concept has tended to encourage the United States and its allies to neglect the essential character of the Soviet threat. That threat is military in form but political in kind. It is true to claim both that Soviet ideology has no attractive value of security significance abroad and that the Soviet Union is exceedingly unwilling to accelerate the process of historical change by direct military action. The idea of containment has been given an all too simplemindedly military definition of requirements at the expense of the political underpinning needed to provide the stability of adequate public resolution in the Western democracies.[16] NATO's defense problem is, of course, in (essential) part military, but the Soviet Union recognizes that the most important of NATO's defense problems are the will to bear social costs for security in peacetime and the will to fight.

The NATO Alliance has sustained itself generally by taking what appeared to be the line of least domestic resistance.[17] The Soviet Union is contained in Europe by a heavily armed NATO that believes, perhaps correctly, that it cannot afford to face probable military-operational realities. Western governments have chosen to adopt a theory of supposedly controlled escalation—termed flexible response—rather than a doctrine of defense by denial, apparently believing that their publics would repudiate them if they prepared for war rather than for galloping holocaust as their approach to deterrence.[18] The problem with this practice of evasion is that NATO governments virtually invite an erosion of public will and confidence as a consequence of Soviet political warfare aimed at intimidation.

Much of the perennial NATO defense debate addresses second-order questions. It is increasingly important that NATO adopt the strategy and tactics, and develop the forces, most likely to defeat a Soviet invasion. But both the details of military plans and force posture and the public will to resist that gives them meaning are undermined by the way in which containment policy has been conducted. The contingent threat of nuclear punishment as the keystone in U.S. and NATO defense policies has undoubtedly helped contain Soviet power, yet in the long term that threat probably does more to weaken the will of NATO publics to defend themselves than to discourage Soviet military pressure.

In part for reason of the nuclear-related anxieties encouraged (though certainly not created) by Western defense doctrine, the concept of containment has lacked a robust supporting consensus on policy guidance beyond the agreed necessity to prevent the expansion of Soviet power and influence. Geopolitically, the heart of the containment concept is the prevention of Soviet hegemony in Eurasia. To date, the United States has not been able to develop a sustainable theory of political engagement, or even of selective engagement or nonengagement, to complement the austere balance-of-power proposition. The dominant characteristic of American containment policy has been change, or at least the appearance of change. Successively, the American public and political elite seem to expect first too much and then too little of their own country and of the Soviet Union.

It may well be that "God looks after children, drunkards, and the United States."[1] For whatever blend of reasons, U.S. national security policy since 1945 has worked well enough with regard to the essentials. Before lavishing praise on the designers and agents of that policy, however, one must recognize that the absolute weight of American power— mobilized for defense as well as latent for defense in economic strength— has provided considerable latitude for folly in policy and strategy, and that U.S. policy has more closely approximated a passive than a dynamic endeavor at containment. Furthermore, the great simplicity of the postwar international security condition, with its essential opposition between two superstates, has served greatly to reduce the quality of statecraft required to make policy minimally adequate in performance. Intense and controversial issues of alliance ties, contingent promises, and the like, which typically absorbed the small and highly professional foreign policy elites of pre-1914 Europe, have their functional parallel today in the domestic (and from time to time interallied) debates over defense policy and programs. While maintenance of a Eurasian onshore alliance structure is very important for the containment of Soviet power in a landlocked condition, containment policy is far more heavily focused on the deterring functions of one nation's armed forces than has generally been the case for great powers.

The structural simplicity of the East-West military opposition, the vast disproportion in security production between the United States and its individual allies, and the importance of technology in the arms competition have seemed to alleviate the problems for U.S. statecraft that flow from American political and strategic culture. Edward Luttwak makes the point that "superpowers, like other institutions known to us, are in the protection business."[20] For the cultural reasons discussed in Chapters 5 and 6, the United States does not have, and is unlikely to be able to acquire, an imperial mind-set. The Western Alliance persists more because of the absence of prudent alternatives for U.S. security clients than because of U.S. skill in the management of clients. The makers and agents of U.S. national security policy typically are ethnocentric to a fault,[21] prone to confuse persisting conditions with problems that can be solved, attracted to the restriction of policy debate to binary choices,[22] overimpressed with the security value of new technologies,[23] impatient for near-term results, and unschooled in the rules of the game of international politics (recall the list of missing or shaky pillars provided at the end of Chapter 3). The major variants of containment policy cannot help putting a strain upon the U.S. political system, given the enduring characteristics of American political and strategic culture.

The challenge of World War II could scarcely have been a better fit with American culture. Notwithstanding the difficulties of fighting on the the side of Britain while not seeming to fight on behalf of British imperialism,[24] and of being allied to Stalin's Russia while not endorsing Stalin's political methods or his emerging and predictable goals, the United States could indulge its strategic-cultural preferences. Wearing the cloak of guardianship of world civilizaton and order, it was able to wage a material war of annihilation for the goal of complete victory (unconditional surrender of the enemy) over demonic foes (Nazism and Japanese imperialism).[25] This is to imply not that most American policymakers of the World War II era were naive but only that they were able to defer facing inconvenient facts about a principal ally, and possibly future enemy, in the interest of achieving the immediate military task.

When one compares the close fit between American culture and strengths and the needs of leadership in global war with the gap between the policy needs of a prospectively permanent containment policy and American political and strategic culture, one realizes just how much worse the United States performance might have been since 1945. Changes in the content or the appearance of Soviet policy always have the potential to influence the policy fashion or climate in Washingon. There is a significant shift every few years in official U.S. definitions of what it is that is being contained, and how that containment can best be effected.

The U.S. government is in the unenviable position of having to recognize some very unwelcome, politically unpalatable, facts. First, the United States must balance power through arms competition for an indefinite period.[26] Second, the measure of American success will lie almost totally in the range of unpleasant events that do not occur, the reasons for the nonoccurrence of which the government will not be able to demonstrate beyond a reasonable doubt.[27] Third, should war occur, there is little prospect of achieving any approximation of the traditional concept of victory as the reward both for a seemingly endless high level of peacetime defense preparation and a historically unprecedented level of casualties.[25]

The United States has no interest in defeating the Soviet state in any definitive military and political sense except in a last-ditch defense of its survival interests. Even if the containment idea were to work so well that the U.S.S.R. evolved into a very different polity, geopolitical logic suggests that a successor—presumably Great Russian—state would pose many of the same problems for the balance of power in Eurasia and, by extension, for the Americas.

It may not be a very fruitful task but is certainly a relevant one to speculate on the kind of Soviet Union/Russia that might emerge if the current Soviet course of empire were to be arrested definitively by the factors that function to contain its energies and ambitions, factors such as purposeful U.S.-organized and -led countervailing action, the power of nationalism, the growth of religious fundamentalism in the Moslem world, and Soviet loss of economic and political vitality at home. Among many possibilities, two are of outstanding interest. First, one can postulate a Soviet Union weary of *Weltpolitik,* which—if not quite becoming a peace-loving member of the world community of nations, eager to replace Machiavellian and Leninist precepts for statecraft with the benign aspirations of the U.N. charter—would at least no longer seek imperium beyond its extant holdings. Second, one can harbor the hope that a very much older Russia, more amenable to the politics of accommodation and order, lurks beneath the surface of the present Stalinist state. Without predicting that this "other Russia" would necessarily be a more constructive player in world politics or would even require the wholesale dismantling of Soviet forms in order to emerge, Adda Bozeman has advised that the United States should affirm "Russia's timeless culture, more particularly…that heritage which is kin to ours but was driven underground with the installation of Marxism-Leninism. The accent here should be on Byzantine-Roman jurisprudence; Russian customary law; such medieval constitutions as that of the Hanseatic city of Novgorod; Greek-Orthodox Christianity, and the great ideas which sparked the nineteenth and early twentieth-century reforms."[29] (Bozeman is not merely indulging in wishful thinking; her first precept for U.S. policy toward the Soviet Union is "acceptance of the U.S./Soviet relationship as a war of nerves and of ideas, somewhat on the order of the great historic precedent for modern cold wars, the *guerra fria* for the minds of men in which Muslims and Christians engaged for centuries in embattled medieval Spain."[30] Although her war of nerves analogy is inapt, it is evident that she is not dressing up in respectable clothes what would amount to a soft option for the West.)

I am not persuaded of the plausibility of either of those Soviet-Russian futures; nonetheless, some speculation of this kind—disciplined, of course, by historically educated geopolitical reasoning—is badly needed to stretch the imagination beyond familiar, surprise-free projections of the future. U.S. policymakers confront a tunnel of military competition with no identifiable end, yet democratic societies are able to effect prudent defense preparation only when they discern danger. A good deal of the threat analysis that American liberals find so abhorrent stems not from the unbalanced judgment of parochial officials or paranoid conservative commentators but from the very structure of defense politics in a democracy. Repetition of threat analysis fuels a serious danger that familiarity will breed contempt. Furthermore, there is a success-entropic cycle in the defense politics of a democracy.

The defense build-up of the Reagan administration is a classic case in point. That build-up, traceable in its origins to the last year of the Carter administration,[31] was launched on the general argument that the defense budgetary trend of the late 1970s had promoted a dangerous reduction of respect in Moscow for U.S. definition of its vital interests.[32] By Reagan's second term, Soviet respect for the United States as a security competitor would seem to have risen markedly. New Soviet positions on strategic arms control in 1986 and 1987 seemed to indicate Soviet anxiety over some negative trends in the correlation of forces. The probable success of Reagan's defense policy in Moscow contrasted sharply, however, with an erosion in political support in the United States for staying the course with the build-up. Without defending the overall design or particular implementation of defense programs in the 1980s, one cannot help noticing that much of the Congress chooses not to distinguish between external security and domestic well-being in their relative importance as functions of government. The Congress moved to reverse a pattern of defense budgetary increase just as, and in part because, appreciation of that pattern in Moscow had had its intended and predicted effect.[33]

In short, the defense budget does not have a settled claim to a generally well-established fraction of the U.S. national product—even though the United States has not significantly reduced the geographical definition of its vital foreign interests since the late 1940s and early 1950s. On the contrary, U.S. foreign security commitments have grown in scale and in difficulty of potential fulfillment under stress, particularly in the Middle East and southern Asia, as British and French power has retreated to European bases and as Soviet military capabilities have increased.

When confronted with a seriously unfavorable means-ends mismatch, a country has four options: it can increase its means, reduce its ends, change the strategy that connects ends and means, or effect some mix of all three. Unsurprisingly, the present U.S. debate over national security policy has participants advocating each of the four. The relationship between military means and policy ends is probed in detail in a later chapter. Suffice it to say here that a geopolitically, as opposed to an ideologically, focused policy concept of containment is sound and should be retained; the Soviet Union is not going to evolve politically in the foreseeable future in such a way that the overall military burden of a containment policy will be reduced; U.S. and U.S.-allied defense efforts will not increase in real terms; and new "emerging technologies" (ET) for theater and strategic conflict will not themselves resolve the means-ends problem.[34]

For the first time in the twentieth century, the United States will not be able to resolve its means-ends national security problems by surging the production of military goods, by fielding superior technologies, or by allocating first-line defense duties to allies who have no practicable alternative. Instead, the means-ends problems that beset the variants of the policy of a forward, global containment can be treated effectively only through the agency of strategy and the exercise of strategic choice.[35] The U.S. defense community pays formal obeisance to the importance of strategy but, in practice tends to take flight with the military promise of ET, or to abandon strategic reasoning in the quintessentially astrategic politics of the annual defense budetary process, or to substitute Thomas Schelling's concept of a "diplomacy of violence" (with the emphasis on diplomacy)[36] for a more classical approach to strategy. Irregularly, the United States surges its national defense effort in response to a security shock, or series of security shocks, and then counts on the investment legacy of the surge for ten years or more until the next period of alarm produces a new short-term surge in effort. The American public does not realize that it is permanently in a state of war with the Soviet Union—at least by Soviet definition.

As the home-based U.S. backstop to theater conflict, to be invoked if needed in desperate defense of vulnerable forward positions, the central striking power of the Strategic Air Command (SAC) had more reality in the 1950s and early 1960s than many contemporary theorists allowed in their critiques of the strategic policy of the day.[37] U.S. strategic forces as an extended deterrent have been substantially neutralized by the Soviet acquisition of s strategic-nuclear force posture that should function, in all strategic logic, as an effective *counter*deterrent. U.S. strategic nuclear forces are required by policy logic to provide "top cover" to control escalation of military action at much lower levels of destructiveness, but their value as out-of-theater compensation for local military deficiencies has become severely restricted in scope.[38]

In part because of the vices of its virtues as a democracy, though rather more because of its lack of a tradition of strategic thinking, the United States has in the enduring concept of containment an idea that as policy-in-action could easily translate into defeat in war. In the apt words of the command manual of the *Wehrmacht* in 1936 (borrowing sensibly from Frederick the Great): "One cannot be strong enough at the decisive point. Whoever disperses his forces or employs them on secondary missions sins against the rule."[39] In World War II the *Wehrmacht* provided instruction by fatal negative example in the truth of this principle;[40] the Imperial Japanese Navy committed the strategic sin of dispersion of effort even more egregiously. The United States with a forward defense perimeter stretching (except for the southern Asia break) around the Rimland of Eurasia from the 38th Parallel in Korea to the North Cape of Norway, clearly cannot be strong everywhere. But where is the decisive point? The United States has encouraged the growth of strong indigenous military forces for forward cover of the major "stakes" in Eurasia, western Europe and Japan. However, save very briefly in 1952-53,[41] the United States and its allies have never really committed themselves to the construction of locally deployed military power capable of more than enforcing very large-scale combat upon (as opposed to the prospective defeat of) invading forces. The continuing authority of the concept of forward containment in Eurasia mandates in practice that compellent nuclear threats be a more or less prominent feature standing behind U.S. security commitments to politically close, if geographically distant, allies.

Given the difference between the superpowers in ease of geostrategic reach to Rimland Eurasia, the United States confronts a strategy challenge on a scale unprecedented in its history. It is tempting to argue that as a stark matter of geopolitics the United States could not wage a nonnuclear conflict in and around Eurasia with any plausible prospect of success. This argument would be a negative reflection upon the kind of defense preparation that the United States and the Soviet Union, respectively, are best able to sustain year in and year out, and upon the defense mobilization and reinforcement bases that the superpowers have respectively prepared.[42] Pessimistic geopolitical analysis might hold that the United States could not prevail in a protracted conventional war in Eurasia for roughly the same generic reasons of strategic geography that would preclude the Soviet Union from prevailing in a nonnuclear conflict anywhere in the Americas and, possibly, in central-southern Africa.

If the foregoing reasoning is found to be persuasive, it must follow that a national security concept of containment rests upon a dangerous bluff, while a concept of a more dynamic containment would virtually amount to an invitation to the Soviet Union to call the bluff. In its essentials the pessimistic argument summarized here amounts to claiming that the Western Alliance could not prevail in a short conventional war, could not prevail in a protracted conventional war, and could not prevail in a short nuclear war. The strategy bluff of the alliance lies in the extraordinary, not to say bizarre, proposition that it would choose to engage in hostilities that could not lead to a tolerable outcome. Western policy squares the circle with the calculation that Soviet leaders must fear that the most probable outcome for the U.S.S.R. would be intolerable also.[43] NATO rests its security upon what is known as the defender's advantage: if national survival is at stake, the most terrible risks might be run against only a very modest prospect of success, but for the prospective aggressor even a very high prospect of success tends to be offset by only a very modest risk of an intolerable outcome.

In fact, the military-strategic outlook for forward containment in and around Eurasia is not nearly so black as the arguments cited above might lead the unwary to suppose. The Soviet Union (to anticipate the military discussion in Chapter 14) cannot be at all certain of short-war victory in Europe;[44] would be strongly motivated not to escalate to a central war in quest of a victory that proved elusive on the ground in Europe; would be fighting beside some very unwilling allies or clients; would have strategically important vulnerabilities on its northern and southern flanks in Europe vis-à-vis a Western Alliance dominant in maritime power; might have an increasingly restive population at home in the non–Great Russian parts of the Soviet territorial empire; could not help becoming more and more sensitive to the security of its Siberian holdings in view of the active or latent Chinese threat; and, overall, might well find itself locked into a protracted war with the world's greatest economic powers.[45]

Too often, strongly pessimistic *or* optimistic assessments of the military context for the containment concept function as legitimizing cover for special pleading on behalf of parochial interests or cultural proclivities. For example, the isolationist impulse can seem truly respectable and responsible (if not very heroic) if it is expressed with carefully argued reference to unwise military risks. Similarly, it is rare to discover analysis of national military policy that is not doctrinally captive to the competing credos of one or another of the schools of thought on security policy that channel and focus the contemporary debate.

In some future acute crisis, political leaders might have to decide whether or not to fight (that is, they would be asking themselves whether or not they were deterred from fighting) the war *as a whole* that would be unleashed. But the U.S. defense community typically does not study war. Instead it studies defense issues. There is a burgeoning literature on the implications of strategic defense for stability (variously defined), on the value of new nonnuclear technologies for the defense of NATO's Central Front, on the utility of maritime preponderence in particular regions, and so on. What is lacking is a sustained endeavor to study war as a whole and to explore the connections among goals, methods, and means. Holistic perspectives have fallen victim to the expertise that is the benefit of specialization.[46]

The geostrategic opposition between landpower and seapower is a major thread running through the analyses of influential geopolitical theorists—certainly through the works of Mahan, Mackinder, and Spyk-man—but the opposition has never been a pure one. British seapower could not defeat Napoleon at sea; Britain had to finance continental landpower allies and itself sustain a large landpower commitment (after 1808 in Spain and Portugal) before Napoleon was beaten in the field. The British blockade triggered Napoleon's countervailing continental system which, in its turn, played a healthy part in aggravating Franco-Russian relations and led in due course to the demise of the Grande Armée in the invasion of Russia in 1812. British, and later Anglo-American, seapower was critical in laying the basis for the defeat twice in this century of the German bid for hegemony, though again, seapower had to be married to power on land before the aspiring continental hegemon could be cast down.[47] During the 1950s, although the United States and its allies were very comfortably superior at sea, the security of littoral Eurasia in the face of potential Soviet aggression rested overwhelmingly upon the very large and sharp sword of U.S. (and British) nuclear air power.

As U.S. policymakers today consider the military implications of global containment, they cannot with assurance seek safety in a heavily nuclear architecture of pre- and intrawar deterrence. Neither the Soviet Union nor NATO can contemplate without alarm the prospect of a possibly explosive process of nuclear escalation. The formal structure of NATO strategy, with its emphases upon flexible response, forward defense, and a seamless web of deterrence (in some tension with concern to control escalation by recognition of geographical or technological thresholds of violence), has not altered since the 1960s, but indications of what probably amounts to a cumulative sea change are there for those prepared to recognize them; they include the new AirLand Battle doctrine of the U.S. Army,[48] the FOFA (follow-on forces attack) design of SHAPE, and the U.S. Navy's new maritime strategy.[49] Looking to the end of the century, one need not be a latter-day Jean de Bloch[50] to discern the negative implications of the SDI (particularly of "SDIskiy") for extended deterrence by so-called central nuclear systems. Developments in Soviet ground, tactical air, and air defense forces—as explained in the writings, *inter alia*, of Nikolay Ogarkov and M.A. Gareyev,[51] strongly suggest that East and West may be entering a new era in the terms of prospective military engagement.

The practice of containment in a world where nuclear weapons dampen the urge to adventure but do not preclude a drive (perhaps defensively motivated) for eventual universal empire requires that the geopolitical structure of East-West antagonism be accorded careful treatment. Some of the critics of the U.S. Navy's maritime strategy argue in a vein reminiscent of the claims of the "Westerners" vs. "Easterners" in the First World War.[52] A few American maritime theorists have appeared unwisely dismissive of the geopolitical significance and military potential for effective regional defense of NATO-Europe. But it is no less true that some American Central Front–firsters (and -lasters) have concocted a travesty of maritime strategy in order to demonstrate the inutility of preponderant seapower against continental landpower.

The concept of containment raises the question of whether or not every Soviet penetration beyond its former sphere is of equal significance. The U.S. government understands that Soviet military power bearing upon western Europe must be countered, and that the intimidating effect on European publics of Soviet-encouraged fears of nuclear devastation needs to be offset. But once one looks beyond the European region, it is not so obvious what a containment policy means and requires. The Soviet threat to U.S. security stems not only from the specific political advantages that may be secured with reference to one or another strategically located country but also from the growth of the Soviet Union as a world power, as a player in world politics with a license to be heard on security matters pertaining to countries and regions far from the Soviet Heartland. From time to time occasions do and will arise when the superpowers, for their separate purposes, have converging interests in resolving a local conflict in a particular way; however, given its nature and intentions, the U.S.S.R. cannot as a general rule function as a responsible (by American definition) co-guardian or co-guarantor of international or particular regional security. Unfortunately for ease of American handling, aside from the recurrent important struggle for steady coalition will among NATO-Europeans, the real action in containment tends to lie in countries that score low in the democracy ratings, in countries where local grievance and subversion from abroad are not easily separable and where the kinds of American action most likely to prove efficient—that is, what has come to be called "low-intensity warfare"—tend to affront fashionable American ethical or political susceptibilities.

Despite a persisting discomfort with its negative defensive ethos, however, containment has passed very largely unchallenged as the guiding light for U.S. Soviet-oriented national security policy since 1947. Few if any official analysts have questioned the need for the containment of Soviet power and influence. But given the strategic geography of the East-West competition, the concept is truly global in its possible relevance and has thus been accused of licensing or encouraging an indiscriminate anti-Communist, even anti-socialist, policy thrust, as contrasted with a carefully focused endeavor to thwart Soviet power. It is true that U.S. policy explanations have often drawn heavily upon the inferred and explicit ideological drive of the Soviet Union. On the one hand, U.S. policymakers cannot know to what extent Soviet leaders are motivated by a sense of messianic mission to hasten the course of historical development or progress on behalf of the theory that supports their domestic legitimacy. On the other hand, U.S. policymakers can only guess at the extent to which Moscow is moved by a traditional Great Russian imperialist impulse to control, or exercise *contrôle* over,[53] whatever is accessible for domination abroad. However, one suspects that a convenient fusion has been effected in the minds of Soviet leaders between the requirements of ideology and those of *Realpolitik,* in much the same way and for the same reasons that medieval political leaders managed to reconcile feudal propriety, Christian duty, and self-interest.

The Soviet threat is the threat posed by Soviet imperialism; it is not the threat posed by Marxist-Leninist ideology. State socialism on the Soviet model has few foreign adherents beyond those who anticipate personal benefit as its potential administrators. The concept of containment is weakened when the U.S. government defines its policy as one of opposition to a vague Marxism-Leninism—which slips all too easily into opposition to a variously practiced socialism. The United States has rarely spoken clearly on the subject of exactly what it was that was to be contained or why. Paying due respect to local political cultures, U.S. policymakers have an interest in opposing only those political forces abroad that either are or plausibly may be stalking-horses for an extension of the Soviet imperium and those that are inimical to U.S. vital interests for other reasons.

While it is correct to say that the West can win the war of ideas with the Soviet Union, it does not follow that forceful propagation of an American-authored (and variably practiced) ideology is the appropriate response to the Soviet challenge. Soviet leaders talk of waging ideological struggle because they have no choice. The CPSU does not claim legitimacy by right of *coup d'état,* longevity in effective authority, or consistency with Great Russian traditions of rule and statecraft; instead, it claims legitimacy by right of the asserted authority of the laws of historical development as allegedly revealed in Marxism-Leninism. Nevertheless, the true adversary is not Soviet state ideology; it is Soviet imperialist behavior. The United States cannot and should not attempt to contain socialism; rather should it seek to contain the expansion of Soviet power and influence.

Just as the United States has had ideological, perhaps political-cultural, difficulty in distinguishing between communists and democratic socialists, so also it has had no small problem recognizing the functional value to the containment of Soviet power of nationalists both inside and outside the Soviet imperium. The Marxist proposition that "the working class has no country" has been belied by the events of the twentieth century. By far the most pervasive and effective support for the containment concept has been provided, however, nonpurposefully, by the nationalist sentiments of the former subjects of European colonial rule in Africa and Asia, not to mention the nationalist impulses of revisionist China.

Like all countries, the United States has understandable problems suppressing its most deep-felt, really cultural, national inclinations. As a country established, justified, and endlessly reaffirmed in ideological terms, it has considerable difficulty meeting the Soviet geostrategic challenge at the proper level for effective contest. From the outset of its appearance on the field as principal champion of anti-Soviet interests, the United States has presented a confused front of mixed geopolitical and ideological rationales for containment. No matter how sincere, American ideological rhetoric has often been misinterpreted as cover for narrow American self-interest or—scarcely less damaging—has been viewed as evidence of naiveté and inexperience, since the allied audience has known that the Soviet threat is geopolitical and not ideological.

U.S. policymakers should be aware of the fact that history provides many models of imperial style. In a most important sense, the United States does have a weak form of imperium (though not of empire):[54] it has a global set of security dependents who, within some variable bounds, acknowledge the U.S. right to determine what should and should not be done for the common defense. These dependents are neither constituent parts of an empire nor vassal states, but for reason of survival interests they are all more or less attentive to American definitions of the needs of international security. Foreign allies and friends of the United States do not relate at all comfortably, however, to homespun America rhetoric inappropriately projected for the intended betterment of very different political cultures.

The rhetoric of domestic American politics is appropriate for just that—domestic American politics. There is value in an American endeavor to contrast Soviet words and ideas with Soviet practice[55] and to portray an accurate picture of political life in the United States. But Soviet ideological pretensions can and should be defeated easily with reference to Soviet facts. Giving an ideological cast to American national security policy tends to be self-defeating. In stressing the ideals of American democracy, American officials permit Soviet propagandists to score points by pointing, in their turn, to the gap between American rhetoric and American domestic (and U.S.-allied) reality.

Although the United States has generally behaved in its international power-balancing activity as necessity required, the American national style is evident not only in the rhetoric of its foreign policy but in an obvious discomfort with certain distasteful realities of international politics.[56] The Klingberg-Holmes proposition concerning the persistence of "a fundamental conflict between the moods manifested in the liberal American ideology and the dictates of United States politico-military interests"[57] points to a potential unsteadiness of performance in national security policy which is a source of both hope and anxiety for the enemies of the United States.

For the best fit between external policy and domestic political culture, the United States would be able to seek the ends of *Realpolitik* with the means as well as the language of *Moralpolitik*. The "evil empire" of Soviet tyranny would be opposed by a free-world coalition led by a United States the justness of whose cause would be self-evident to all peoples with access to the facts. The United States would oppose evil by organizing and leading the just in an enterprise which by definition (since its purpose would be the opposing of evil) must be a noble cause. Unfortunately, reality diverges from the ideal: for example, Americans generally do not care very much about planting, let alone defending, the seeds of democracy in possibly very infertile foreign soil; and considerations of geopolitical convenience and advantage, or disadvantage denied, have caused the United States to embrace some distinctly unsavory political systems around the periphery of Eurasia, as well as in the Americas.

A problem with rhetorical idealism in policy is that there will always be people at home and abroad eager to contrast the performance of politicians with their own professed standards. An American public which is not particularly worldly-wise or generally cynical about the perfectibility of humankind, and which would like to hold its government to standards of foreign policy behavior not grossly dissimilar from domestic norms, is always likely to be shocked and to demand that the guilty be punished when Washington assumes abroad some of the brutal habits of its enemies (and friends).[58]

The design and attempt at steady implementation of a policy of containment is not a task for the strategist alone. To be sustainable, American responses to the geopolitical challenge posed by the Heartland Soviet Union must not offend the dominant values of American political culture. It is of no use for a commentator to advise merely the right way to contain Soviet power and influence; what is needed is "the right American way."[59]

Multilateral containment, or containment by coalition, speaks very much to contemporary American popular and indeed civic values. That judgment holds notwithstanding the problems of alliance diplomacy and, as practiced to date, of close-to-immediate nuclear risks on behalf of foreigners. It is always possible that very profound irritation with seemingly feckless or ungrateful allies might precipitate a move to "bring the boys home"; however, there can be no doubt that Americans do care about the possible extension of Soviet influence in the world, do conceive of themselves as the primary (though certainly not the only) guardian of the non-Soviet-organized world, and in general have no quarrel with the concept of containment.

For all the deficiencies that reflect fairly accurately the weaknesses of American democracy as a foreign policy actor, the United States generally has been successful in containing Soviet power and influence. The maritime coalition essential for the frustration of Soviet geopolitical objectives has been constructed and sustained. While the United States might have done better than it has, the score to date in the East-West competition is by no means unfavorable to the West. Nonetheless, it may be accurate to claim that the Soviet Union itself has contributed more to its containment than has the maritime alliance of the West. For example, it is evident that the Soviet Union has in China a permanent enemy, or at least a non-benevolent neutral. Furthermore, it is scarely less evident that forty- plus years of imperium have not served to consolidate Soviet power and influence in eastern Europe.

The only area of solid competitive success for Soviet imperialism over the past several decades is the military. In an era when territorial aggrandizement has gone out of style and the balance of power is substantially bipolar, the hegemonic impulse expressed in action appears most heavily in the field of national armaments. The Soviet empire may look scarcely more impressive on the map today than it did in the late 1940s, but such a perspective would fail to understand the character of hegemonic and antihegemonic power in the contemporary world. Because Soviet imperialism may break out of its landlocked condition by the intimidation of nominally sovereign states, or may acquire the military means to effect the forcible demise of the onshore containment structure organized by the United States, we must seek ways by which American national security policy might perform better.

11

Dynamic Containment

The worth of an ideal lies not in the number of people who achieve it but in its value as a standard for performance. Dynamic containment is presented less as an identifiable discrete option for national security policy than as a standard against which policy performance in the practice of containment should be measured.[1]

Like the generally passive containment policy practiced historically, a policy of dynamic containment would endeavor to compete with Soviet power and influence by means of the organization and, where necessary, the arming of actual and potential resistance around the Rimlands of Eurasia and in the extended Soviet imperium in Africa, the Caribbean, and Central America. Dynamic containment differs somewhat in method and perspective, though not in objectives or in the definition of which U.S. foreign interests truly are survival or vital in quality.

The adjective "dynamic," if taken seriously by policymakers, analysts, and commentators, points to the fact that change and potential change are permanent features of the international struggle for security. Soviet thinking on national and international security is sensitive to a dynamism in that struggle, a dynamism that is preordained as a law of international existence and that Soviet officials express in terms of an evolving correlation of forces.[2]

The American security problem at the level of fundamental concepts is twofold. On the one hand, for reasons of American political culture, the ideas of order, stability, and (nonviolent) management have value status as highly desirable norms. On the other hand, Soviet security concepts translate in American perspective as disorder, instability, and even consciously directed mismanagement vis-à-vis Western interests and values. Americans need to recognize the local roots of their own preferred security ideas, the local roots of the ideas of others, and the interests that those ideas represent.

Dynamic containment maintains, as does containment generically, that the Soviet Union seeks, first, effective hegemony over Eurasia and, second, the eventual subjugation of the United States.[3] Following the precepts of dynamic containment, a U.S. government would risk telling the American public more than it might wish to hear. It would tell the public that the danger of nuclear war reposes in the facts that the secret of atomic fission has been exploded long since (that is, nuclear weapons cannot be disinvented) and that Soviet leaders are the cautious legatees of an imperial system that cannot, at least *pro tem*, reach a genuine accommodation with other powers. The U.S. government would explain that the Soviet Union, from 1917 to the present day, has been committed to the waging of political warfare against non-Soviet-controlled political entities and that U.S. policy designs and actions have to be calibrated in full cognizance of that enduring fact. The public would be told that although many Western politicians and commentators have found it convenient to periodicize modern history between eras of cold war and detente, such periods have had only tactical meaning in Soviet perspective. It would be told that Soviet-American political rivalry is both permanent and transient, as were the Christian-Moslem and Protestant-Catholic antagonisms. In other words, it is long-lived but, in historical perspective, only another phase that certainly will pass.

The concept of containment, variably applied as a policy guide to date, either has failed to address the issue of whither the United States is tending or has implied that the dark tunnel of competition may have some relatively near-term conclusion. Dynamic containment, by contrast, can offer a dual vision of the future. First, by accepting the prospective permanence of competition, it can (and should) point to the probability of an important and relatively near-term shift of emphasis in military technology from offense toward defense. This should translate into improved prospects for successful deterrence and even into a reasonable basis of hope for personal and societal survival.[4] Second, dynamic containment points to the possibility of political evolution within a Soviet imperium that is denied opportunities for external hegemonic growth.

A Soviet empire with a structurally diseased economy and an ideology as nominal as was that of the later stages of pre-Christian imperial Rome may proceed into a lingering and increasingly self-absorbed old age. Still, the ability of the Soviet Union to provide brute-force compensation for deficiencies in technological competence should not be disparaged. In addition, the scope and scale of the Soviet problem in coping with the Western high-technology challenge to its security policy will depend in large part upon the political, economic, and strategic choices that Western governments make.

Americans should not neglect the very strong probability that the bureaucratic tyranny that is the Soviet state is at least as genuinely Russian as are any alternative Russias of which one might conceive. In short, it is not particularly persuasive to argue that a Soviet empire duly contained by prudent U.S. policy, among other factors, would be likely to evolve out of its post-1917 Soviet aberration into a modern variant of an eternal Russia that would be relatively benign as an international actor.[5] While the future will undoubtedly provide surprises, we would be unwise to build hope for the future on the basis of a very substantially mythical past.

It is essential to dynamic containment that the U.S. government explain to the American people the structure of their security condition. Virtually all the deficiencies in the competitive performance of the United States and NATO-Europe stem from a lack of public appreciation of the character of the Soviet threat and from an official inability (or unwillingness to attempt) to define a defense strategy that could be a source of realistic hope. The inevitable consequence is that the United States shifts political gears erratically between undue optimism and undue pessimism.

It is not certain that the Western democracies are capable of performing steadily in their competition with the Soviet Union. The American public could be persuaded by the interpretation placed upon events (though not by alarmist rhetoric alone) that the Russians are coming and would then undoubtedly mobilize with appropriate energy. But it remains to be seen whether a Western democracy can effect a very modest form of semimobilization in order to counter a long-term, indeed effectively permanent, threat.[6] The rearmament program of the Reagan administration has foundered on the fact that the American public and their elected representatives do not see a clear and present danger of Soviet aggression against vital American overseas interests. Moreover, and of no less relevance, the Reagan administration has thus far failed to provide an architecture of strategic argument that is even close to being self-evidently persuasive to Congressmen whose focus is typically upon domestic issues.[7] The question of how much is enough has not been related convincingly to the defense of particular vital interests. The geopolitical and geostrategic reasoning that should back military strategy has not played the part it could play, both in discouraging astrategically directed budget reductions and in guiding responsible officials to cut some programs rather than others.[8] It may be—in the face of domestic alarm over federal deficits and an absence of alarm over Russians who might be coming—that a Congress determined to reduce defense expenditure drastically cannot be deflected from its course by any quality of purely strategic reasoning.

It is beyond the scope of this book to take a position on the current issue of defense reform, but this issue will be one factor influencing the size of the defense budget. Analysis of geopolitics, national security policy, and military strategy can become very academic matters indeed if the Congress declines to authorize and fund the military means for the preferred kinds of global containment strategy and policy. In its list of "specific indicators of organizational deficiencies" in the U.S. defense system, an influential 1985 staff report for the Senate Armed Services Committee included the following item: *"Lack of strategic direction*—the strategies and long-range policies of the Department of Defense do not appear to be well formulated and are apparently only loosely connected to subsequent resource allocations."[9] But although American political and strategic culture will likely frustrate the more ambitious designs of some defense reformers, one should not be overly pessimistic concerning the ability of the United States to raise its game in order to perform well enough in national security policy over the long term. What is needed is not root-and-branch reform, or revolution, in policy and strategy but rather the sound construction or strengthening of those missing and shaky pillars of national security policy (see Chapter 3).

By way of a special case in dynamic containment, I see a need for the U.S. government to explain to its domestic and overseas constituencies just what the problems are and what potential security advantages might be secured, in the East-West arms-control process. The (mal)practice of arms control has descended to the pass where it can be characterized, not caricatured, as a plausible threat to Western security. This is a strong claim, but it is justified by the strategic history of the 1970s and 1980s. Arms control has both provided an important drive and served as a powerful excuse for the United States to settle for the geopolitically inappropriate concept of (rough) parity as the limit of its ambition for the strategic-forces relationship with Moscow.[10] In geopolitical terms, the forward containment policy of the United States requires either that American strategic forces enjoy a condition of important military advantage over the strategic forces of the Soviet Union, or that U.S. and U.S.-allied forces for regional defense be at least as strong in prospective defensive action as are their Soviet counterparts in prospective offensive action (though even that is unlikely to be good enough, considering the historical fragility of conventional deterrence).[11]

Arms-control negotiations in general tend to be invested by democracies with a symbolic value that augments the already astrategic tendencies of those polities. Given a totalitarian Soviet Union as a partner the Western democracies can proceed in reasonable safety with arms control only if important military safeguards and a quite rigorous sanctions policy for noncompliance are in place.[12] Twentieth-century Western democracies have not demonstrated the ability to negotiate prudently or to cope adequately with the all but invariable Imperial Japanese, Nazi German, and now Soviet practice of selective noncompliance.

If Western publics were informed that the Soviet Union basically views the arms-control process as an instrument for the prosecution of political warfare but that some agreements of mutual value are nevertheless possible, then much of the stress that arms control promotes for national strategic planning could be removed.[13] The contemporary difficulty in strategic-force planning and execution stems in part from the fact that the U.S. government has chosen to attempt to outbid the Left in its formal commitment to arms control and disarmament. A moment's reflection will reveal that this is a losing proposition.[14] If the truth of the matter is that *substantive* arms-control agreement of real strategic merit is not attainable, a U.S. government that chooses knowingly to encourage the view that very substantive and worthwhile agreement *is* possible invites eventual criticism for not having tried hard enough.

The recurrent campaigning between liberals and conservatives over arms-control issues tends, at its best, to be a debate between schemes for a world that might be or should be and schemes for a world that is extant. Conservative-minded strategic thinkers and defense planners do not distrust the Soviet Union because it is "the focus of evil in the modern world"; rather, they distrust the Soviet Union because the detailed history of Soviet behavior under arms-control agreements discloses a persisting pattern of noncompliance and because geopolitical analysis of the history of Russian and Soviet imperialism makes clear the motives behind Soviet military policy.

The American public should also be made aware that as the conceptual guide to national security policy, dynamic containment would seek to show respect for and to work with local political cultures. While parochial apologias for accommodation to Soviet intimidation would be opposed, considerable empathy would be shown for political practices and rhetoric that differ even markedly from the American model. The focus of U.S. policy would be on the essentials of its security needs, not on the attractiveness or otherwise to Americans of the local political game. In a much quoted passage, Bernard Brodie wrote: "Whether with respect to arms control or otherwise, good strategy presumes good anthropology and sociology. Some of the greatest blunders of all time have resulted from juvenile evaluations in this department."[15] His advice was far from original with him. Around 600 A.D., Byzantine Emperor Maurice devoted Book XI of his *Strategikon* to the "characteristics and tactics of various peoples"; his purpose, he said, was "to enable those who intend to wage war against these peoples [Persians, Scythians, Franks, Slavs] to prepare themselves properly. For all nations do not fight in a single formation or in the same way."[16]

Scarcely less important than American respect for local political culture is the need for U.S. allies to respect the facts of American political culture. If U.S. policy is to avoid domestic challenge of a fundamental kind—for example, challenge on the grounds that foreign allies and friends are no longer worth defending—those allies must meet their end of the requirements of "the trans-Atlantic bargain."[17] Moreover, those requirements will probably have to be adjusted in a cumulatively major way over the decades immediately ahead. The point was made in a previous chapter that the small allies of a very large ally tend to contribute less than proportionately to the common defense. There are reasons why this should be so; nevertheless, the United States has the right, and indeed the duty to its own citizens, to insist that its interests be reflected with tolerable accuracy in the terms of the security partnership.

Richard Pipes has summarized the conservative American's view of what ails the alliance: "The unwillingness of a fully reconstructed and prosperous Europe to join the United States in a policy of global defense, its political and military parochialism, have been the principal cause of the discords troubling the alliance during the past twenty years....The thing that is wrong...is not the United States commitment to defend Europe but the inequitable distribution of responsibilities....Economically, Europe and Japan have long been capable of ensuring their own defense in all but nuclear weapons." Noticing that "the ratio of social allocations to defense allocations is thus less than 2-1 in the United States and nearly 9-1 in Western Europe," Pipes concludes:

The United States has contributed to these financial inequities by its willingness to bear disproportionate burdens long after this has ceased to be necessary. As a result, the Allies have the best of both worlds: they maintain their military establishments at a minimum level acceptable to the senior partner, restrict their defense obligations to the European continent and adjoining waters, deposit the money thus saved in the pot for distribution among the voters, and rely on the United States to rescue them should Russia attack Europe.

Such a situation cannot go on forever, because the American electorate will not forever tolerate it. [Emphasis added][18]

There is sufficient truth in this argument, not to mention great potential political appeal in the United States, to warrant careful notice by people of all persuasions on U.S. national security policy. In asserting that the Soviet Union has a global rather than a narrow continental strategy, Pipes does exaggerate the degree to which Soviet power has managed to circumvent the defense perimeter erected by U.S. containment policy in its endeavor—still largely successful—to keep the Soviet empire land-locked: "Containment had postulated the existence of a territorially definable Communist Bloc, but the lines which in the 1940s and 1950s had separated the Communist realm from the rest of the world subsequently dissolved. Today, Soviet and Soviet supported forces are scattered in all parts of the globe. Moscow has client states in Asia, the Middle East, Africa and Central America. There is no longer a line to hold, even if the military capability to do so were available, which it is not."[19] Pipes is here stating as an established fact what is still only in a fairly early stage of becoming.

The preponderance at sea that the maritime alliance of the West continues to enjoy sustains the strategic meaning of the geography of insular-continental and East-West conflict that has been familiar for centuries. Soviet security clients in Asia, the Middle East, Africa, and Central America, and the deep-water naval squadrons supporting and exploiting these clients, provide a familiar strategic aspect to anyone who recalls the extra-European dimension of the nominally global threat posed by Imperial Germany in the years leading up to 1914.[20]

There is a Soviet global threat to the sea lines of communication of the Western Alliance, and Soviet clients in regions distant from the Soviet territorial empire do pose a problem of strategic distraction for U.S. military power. Nevertheless, the novelty of Soviet military outposts far from home (and of highly uncertain value in time of war) should not incline U.S. policymakers to underestimate the degree to which Soviet power and influence remain continentally landlocked. With the new emphasis in its maritime strategy upon a forward deployment of naval power in time of crisis and war,[21] the United States is in the process of strengthening the contemporary relevance of Arnold Toynbee's description of Britain's achievement in the nineteenth century: "The United Kingdom has managed to corral all the wolves formerly infesting her sheep-run in one pen with a single entrance."[22] The emergence of Japanese and U.S. naval power eroded and then negated this happy condition for Britain, but the contemporary Western Alliance—embracing U.S., British, and (barely) Japanese naval power in support of an onshore defense perimeter in Eurasia—has revived the strategic salience of Toynbee's metaphor.

Dynamic containment does not require that the United States seriously reconsider its existing alliance connections in Eurasia. For the reasons already explained, I believe that those connections are sound at the level of geopolitical desiderata—but geopolitical desiderata are by no means the only factors that matter. A U.S. government that honors its absolute trust to safeguard the survival interests of the American people is obliged to consider very rigorously the military risks that attend foreign security commitments. It is probably to the credit of the American people that they have not urged their government to reconsider the military obligations accepted for them by way of NATO strategy. Indeed, there is some irony in the fact that outside narrow defense-professional circles Americans continue to be relaxed concerning the risks they are running on behalf of the defense of Europe. The American proponents of a nuclear freeze have not elevated their sights from the alleged dangers of the nuclear arms race per se to the perils of the policy that broadly determines the character of U.S. arms-competitive effort.

Whether or not the U.S. government comes to feel domestic political pressure to reconsider the merit of its foreign security connections, it should be motivated to question whether the military strategy of the alliance exposes the United States to undue or needless long-term risks. In addition, it should ask whether NATO's strategy imposes unacceptable opportunity costs on a nation whose security concerns have a global domain. The deterrence of war must be given overriding priority, but the U.S. government can and should question the theory and policy of deterrence that underpin the concept of flexible response. NATO's defense posture and doctrine are more than adequate for day-to-day peacetime needs, but they would pose a terrible dilemma for U.S. policymakers were they ever to be tested in action.[23] NATO's authoritative theory of flexible and controlled escalation for the restoration of deterrence would have considerable merit if either the United States were to enjoy strategic nuclear superiority (a concept that must accommodate a U.S. capability to limit damage to the American homeland in a major way) or NATO forces were plausibly capable of halting any manner of Warsaw Pact offensive locally in its tracks.[24] As matters stand now, there is a prospectively short fuse between armed conflict in central Europe and a superpower central war concerning which the United States lacks a persuasive theory of national survival.[25]

I am skeptical, though not dismissive, of the defensive promise of new conventional tactics and technologies for NATO.[26] Nonetheless, the United States should insist that the alliance look very carefully at any and all promising ideas that enhance the prospects of success for in-theater defense. It is one thing to take grave risks on behalf of others; it is quite another to acquiesce in plans for alliancewide defense that virtually guarantee a U.S. position as deterree rather than deterrer. In other words, the United States is more likely than the Soviet Union to feel the stronger incentive to lead a process of escalation. Lack of political will, rather than the geography of East-West conflict in Europe, currently renders the prospects of a successful defense less than glittering.[27]

NATO-European lack of interest in and distrust of truly strong denial strategies is well understood and has some local validity for NATO-Europeans; however, the United States has the politically prior and superior duty to lessen the danger to American survival as best it can—always consistent with not increasing the risk of war in and about Europe by weakening deterrence significantly. Admittedly, there is some tension between these goals,[28] and there is probably a limit to NATO-European willingness to move toward a defense posture of denial, at least for so long as the major European members of NATO believe they have a choice. Should NATO-Europe come to believe that the U.S. extended nuclear deterrent is losing all credibility, its preferred policy response would

more likely be to seek augmented independent European nuclear deterrents, with an explicitly punitive threat, than to attempt the construction
of a solid conventional defense.

The policy quest suggested here would be a search for improvement,
not for perfection. The long-term U.S. need for risk reduction will have to
be met in large part by its own actions rather than by adjustments in
NATO strategy. No matter how immaculate a defense NATO might construct in Europe, a United States that chooses to forgo homeland defense
is going to be a United States acutely and possibly asymmetrically vulnerable to nuclear intimidation. It is greatly encouraging that with SDI the
U.S. government has recognized that its ability to look suitably deterring,
let alone to live responsibly with the consequences should deterrence fail,
is affected negatively by the (historically extraordinary) contemporary
dominance of offensive weapons. Somewhat less encouraging are the
prospects of NATO's coping prudently with a strategic context wherein
U.S., British, and French long-range nuclear offensive forces would increasingly lack deterrent clout. The nuclear reliance in NATO policy and
strategy is both a curse and blessing.

I do not suggest that a strategic defense "astrodome" will be constructed over the United States. Even proponents of the "high frontier"
space defense concept have not made such an extravagant claim.[29] I do
suggest that the military basis for the forward containment concept has
been eroded severely by the massive shift in the terms of the multilevel
East-West military balance over the past twenty years and that at present
the United States is posing implausible nuclear threats in ultimate defense
of vital foreign interests.

The military requirements of dynamic containment should not involve dramatic near-term changes in contemporary defense policy practice. Dynamic containment postulates direct connections between improved in-theater military stopping power, a major (though far short of
perfect) domestic damage-limitation capability, and the political viability
of current foreign security commitments in Europe and Asia. A militarily
convincing nonnuclear defense posture in Europe should greatly facilitate
the emergence of an intelligent theater-nuclear defense posture,[30] but
such a posture certainly could be trumped by interdiction of the Atlantic
sea lines of communication or by direct assault upon the U.S. homeland.

For reasons of the fog of war, Soviet style in war,[31] "friction,"[32] and
the probable military logic of events, I am not persuaded that "the
countervailing strategy" of the Carter administration or its minor refine-
ments under President Reagan offer a sufficiently persuasive theory of
deterrence or of damage limitation should prewar deterrence fail.[33] Defense professionals may debate the rival merits of this and that strategy for
the quality of deterrence and the limitation of damage, but what matters is
that the U.S. government should commit itself to the goal of major

reduction in the damage that the United States might suffer at home in the event of war. The quality of U.S. support for distant allies, and certainly the quality of deterrent effect in Soviet minds with respect to the credibility of that support, is tied umbilically to the issue of putative U.S. self-deterrence.[34]

The practice of containment over the past twenty years has reflected a disregard for likely American operational needs in time of acute crisis and war. Dynamic containment would require the United States to evaluate its strategy and posture not according to peacetime standards but in the light of predictably stressful circumstances. It suggests that theater defenses should be better capable than they are at present of actually defending friendly territory, because no plausibly achievable improvement in the U.S. strategic posture can restore the relationship between local and central forces that obtained in the 1950s. Further, it urges the modernization of strategic offensive forces and the construction of strategic defenses in order to deter any Soviet leader who may need deterring, to minimize the possibility that U.S. nuclear forces will frighten an American president more than a Soviet leader, and to provide some measure of insurance against adverse events that may not lend themselves to deterrence at all.

The recommendation of dynamic containment—or a dynamic perspective on containment—requires recognition of change in international history. The adjective "dynamic" is not intended to suggest across-the-board frenetic activism in U.S. policy; rather, it recognizes that relations of power are ever-changing, that the strategic meaning of geography does change or may change with technology and politics, and that the security concerns of the day need to be seen in a historical context.

Following that recognition, a dynamic containment suggests a willingness on the U.S. part to play an active role in restricting the growth of the Soviet imperium. In need of containment are both Soviet ability to brandish its military power for the purpose of strengthening its geostrategic position vis-à-vis the United States, and Soviet ability actually to employ its military power for the purpose of forcibly restructuring its external and probably internal security. In addition, the United States should have no problem in policy principle with aiding and abetting local elements among Soviet clients who wish to reverse the course of their incorporation into the socialist commonwealth. Just as the Soviet Union opportunistically invests aid and assistance in potential imperial expansion, so should the United States and its major allies be prepared—as opportunity arises, and it certainly will—both to seek to thwart such Soviet expansion and to provide aid and assistance for the destabilization of Moscow's clients.[35]

Dynamic containment, including selective destabilization of the Soviet overseas imperium, would not be an anti-Communist or even an anti-

Soviet crusade. In moral or religious terms individual Americans who find the Soviet Union an embodiment of evil may believe that the recognition of evil carries an obligation to attempt its extirpation. However, anyone calling today for a more dynamic containment of Soviet power and influence should not be permitted to think of himself or herself as a latter-day Pope Urban II. For one policy reason only should the United States seek to contain the Soviet Union in a power-balanced condition in Eurasia with as few extra-Eurasian security dependents of geostrategic note as possible: specifically, the Soviet Union is a threat to U.S. security interests. Geopolitically, popular local concepts of political right conduct in Africa, Latin America, and Asia are important to the United States because political authorities who function in violation of those concepts are certain to be unstable. As a great power with a strong political ideology, the United States understandably wishes to extend the benefits of American, indeed Western, values abroad. But the policy challenge of containment for the United States is geostrategic, not ideological.

It is through selfish determination to protect its own national interests first and foremost that the United States is in fact protecting the longevity of the values of Western civilization. Halford Mackinder made his geopolitical assessments with tough-minded realism, but he was never confused over the salience of the outcome of persisting continental/ East–maritime/West conflict for the quality of civilization.[36] In this secular and nuclear-armed age, however, the American public will not tolerate the expenditure of economic resources and lives in pursuit of ideological goals alone. U.S. armed forces deployed abroad are defending U.S. security interests; they are not committed to a *mission civilisatrice* on a grand and global scale. Dynamic containment sees the U.S. political and military commitment to NATO-Europe as a determination through maintenance of a balance of power in Europe and Asia to keep the Soviet Union continentally distracted and thereby vastly constrained in its conduct of extra-Eurasian *Weltpolitik*. It sees the countries of Central America and the Caribbean as being of strategic importance because they border on the United States, but also because they provide highly strategic real estate that flanks the sea routes to Europe and to Asia.

Above all else, it is essential that the strategic nuclear forces of the United States function effectively under any and all circumstances as a counterdeterrent to nuclear assault upon the American homeland. But the political and economic realities of the American scene almost certainly mean that the days of heavy reliance upon extended nuclear deterrence have passed. Soviet outposts of empire in Vietnam, South Yemen, Angola, and Cuba, for example, could be of importance for the most probable East-West conflicts of the next fifty years. For strategic freedom of action in peace and in war it will matter to the United States whether its access to Rimland Eurasia is challenged by Soviet, or Soviet-client, air-sea power deployed in regions remote from the center of gravity of the Soviet empire. But the prospective inability of the continental power to break out of a blockaded position in Euasia would translate into the rapid demise of the extended imperium as a strategic factor.

Dynamic containment is not cheap, but neither is running the Soviet empire. (The Reagan doctrine of assistance to freedom fighters, which amounts to a policy of highly selective imperial destabilization, must increase the costs of empire to the Soviet Union considerably.[37]) The respect for history that is central to dynamic containment precludes the assumption of a happy ending to East-West conflict. But dynamic containment should strengthen the capacity for sustained and suitable collective action in U.S. national security policy, by explaining with unprecedented frankness to Western publics the nature of that conflict, and the architecture of geopolitical argument should help policymakers and the public understand precisely why particular foreign military commitments are of importance to U.S. security.

12

Disengagement

Given the current structure of responsibilities and allocation of military contributions, it is probably fair to say that the NATO Alliance is living dangerously on borrowed time. The danger is two-edged. First, the absence of reform of a strategy (or its material basis) that reflects a very different era of assumptions about the military balance means that the mismatch between plans and expectations on one side and prospective crisis or wartime reality on the other grows ever wider.[1] The theories of deterrence that undergird flexible response and controlled escalation resolved the dilemma of U.S. assumption of survival-level risks on behalf of only vital interests by presuming a permanent margin of U.S. strategic nuclear superiority. But an alliance strategy that is good enough in peacetime could well come unraveled precipitately in time of acute crisis or war. Second, if the alliance does not seek to lead and manage a process of purposeful change, it is likely to find itself the victim of rapid change that it neither collectively endorsed nor could easily survive in roughly familiar shape and effectiveness of operation.

In the previous chapter, while endorsing the policy concept of a dynamic containment, I was careful not to specify with precision what the U.S. defense policy, implementing strategy, and quantity and quality of armed forces should be to express this concept. One hopes that a very rapid process of major change in the terms and conditions of the alliance connection will not be necessary, but the case for a cumulatively major change—particularly in the relative scale and geographical foci of the military contributions of alliance members—is not a trivial one.[2]

This book has argued as follows thus far: that containment of Soviet power is a geopolitical necessity for the United States—meaning that a Soviet Union no longer contained in a landlocked condition by severe balance-of- power distractions within Eurasia would pose a severe danger to U.S. survival interests; that the balance of power in Eurasia can be maintained only with the backing of U.S. economic and military strength and can be organized, at least for the time being, only by the United States; that there are no panaceas to the U.S.-Soviet problem (or condition)—the Soviet Union willl not evolve rapidly into an ordinary status quo great power (indeed the Soviet Union is a distressingly and all too ordinary, if anachronistic, *imperial* power, by contemporary Western standards); and that neither emerging conventional weapon technologies nor new strategic defensive devices will exorcise the Soviet military threat as by magic.

Geopolitically, containment is the correct guiding concept for U.S. national security policy. The concept of containment and the geopolitical ideas behind it have not been overtaken by changes in weapon technologies or by the limited Soviet geostrategic success in establishing a handful of outposts of empire in Africa, the Middle East, southeast Asia, the Caribbean, and Central America. But containment as a policy in attempted action, rather than as a concept, is in serious danger of being overtaken by political, economic, and military change. What is at issue is the political viability under stress, and the plain military feasibility, of U.S. military strategy in the expression and implementation of containment.

I have chosen to risk being accused of erecting "straw men" in this and the succeeding chapter. After all, readers already know that dynamic containment is favored in this analysis; the policy concepts of devolution, fortress America, and rollback are in part presented in order to demonstrate error. It is also important to deal with the two disengagement concepts discussed in this chapter because they enjoy cogently argued support on the Left and the Right of the American political spectrum, and one or the other could quite plausibly become policy over the next several decades, either by purposeful political design or under the pressure of events.

"Devolution" is intended as a strictly descriptive term for the major restructuring of the particulars of U.S. alliance ties. It is consistent with the basic concept of the containment of Soviet power and influence, but if pursued rigorously it could very easily become a de facto change in concept as well as a major shift among policy means. The central idea of devolution is that the United States would devolve upon its principal security partners many of the forward military power-balancing duties that are currently U.S. responsibility. It is important to identify the leading motives and purposes for such a shift in policy.

First, devolution would be intended to restore a long-absent quality of flexibility, or freedom of action, to U.S. foreign policy. The United States would continue to be an ally of countries in Europe and Asia, but— as in the case of Great Britain with respect to France in 1914 and again in the late 1930s—those allies would not be able to assume automatic U.S. military involvement in their local defense.[3]

Second, the United States would change the terms of alliance to a condition wherein its more or less full, and certainly immediate, military support could not be taken for granted. NATO-Europeans always have assumed that the United States has no practical security alternative to maintaining its military frontier in central Europe. Devolution would say, and mean, that U.S. support of a kind carrying high risks to the American homeland via the powder trail of escalation would have to be deserved by local countries and would be considered as an option in Washington in the light of global security factors.

Third, devolution would be expected to transform into true allies the security dependents who are currently mistermed security partners. Security dependency is a fundamentally unhealthy relationship that places undue burdens on all parties involved.[4]

Fourth, devolution would mark a U.S. determination to effect a more accurate match between risks and the calculated worth of foreign interests. The terms of the NATO Alliance, as interpreted over the years, require the United States to regard an attack upon the sovereign territory of any of its members as being the equivalent to an attack upon the United States. Whatever its merit for Soviet deterrence, such a formula rests upon very shaky geopolitical ground. An important consequence of the promulgation of this precept of "one (that is, the United States) for all" is NATO's inability to design and effect a defense strategy that makes much operational sense. NATO's strategy is a compromise among the differently defined survival and vital interests of its geopolitically distinctive members.[5]

Fifth, devolution would express an American determination no longer to subsidize unduly the heavily self-regarding preferences of others. U.S. defense expenditure, strategy, and force structure is affected very significantly by the military missions whose accepted purpose is to contain Soviet military power in and around Europe. The prospective central European combat environment is uniquely stressful and influences or dominates most of the U.S. military effort.[6] NATO-European countries are able to afford a quantity of social welfare because the United States has agreed to function as their security blanket. Also, NATO-European countries have strengthened their domestic economies by engaging in a quantity and quality of trading connections with Warsaw Pact states which have a dual cost to the United States: first, the Pact states are able partially to finance their anti-NATO military preparations as a result of their trading relations with western Europe, a result that the United States must shoulder the lion's share of countering; second, NATO-European countries increasingly become politically hostage to the domestic economic benefits of these trading relations,[7] thereby greatly complicating the U.S. task as alliance leader in proposing, coordinating, and effecting Western security policy.

Melvyn Krauss, forceful proponent of a full-blooded variant of the devolution concept, has argued: "The fact that our allies spend—in some cases substantial amounts—on their own defense in no way indicates they aren't free-riding, as European apologists and accommodationists argue. The difference between the ratio of the West European defense expenditure to GNP that would exist if the U.S. were to follow a "Fortress America" policy, and that existing today, measures the present level of West European defense free-riding. One might guesstimate that defense free-riding adds perhaps two to three percentage points to West European GNP."[8] Krauss's economic judgment is as arguable as his implicit military judgment, but he does point to a potentially serious political problem in alliance relations. The U.S. political system has chosen to live for more than three decades with the perception, accurate or not, that its European allies are persistent underachievers.[9] European politicians and officials probably believe that in company with death and taxes, American complaints about allies' defense contributions are a permanent feature of the human condition. To date, the security consequences of American exhortations have been very modest. Declarations of good faith, promises to do better in the future, and—above all else—deft maneuvering by Atlanticist elements in Washington have sufficed to keep U.S. irritation within manageable bounds.

American critics of NATO-European defense efforts wax indignant over the allocation of NATO-allied public monies among welfare and security functions but rarely notice that free riding, if such it be, is the logical expression of a quite rational perspective upon security. European governments do not simply choose to "pass (some of) the buck" of security production to the United States in order to liberate national resources for more attractive purposes. They believe that their natioinal security is maximized by purposeful underinvestment in regional defense: in this situation Soviet leaders confront a NATO that has no plausible regional defense capability, beyond the important—indeed essential—abilities to deny options for *coups de mains* and to compel an invader to wage war on a very large scale. The U.S. extended nuclear deterrent is thus coupled with the defense of Europe through the enduring fact of military weakness in that local defense.

Finally, devolution would or could require that the NATO-European allies take what many commentators view as a more mature and responsible view of their own security needs, a view not strictly required so long as they remain in a very dependent condition. In the context of devolution, those allies would know that if they failed to make adequate provision for their national security, they could not count on somebody else being willing to step in and take up the slack. Behind this line of reasoning is the thought that free goods are rarely appreciated appropriately;[10] *ergo,* NATO-European countries would be likely to place a correct value upon their security if they had to provide it and pay for it almost entirely themselves. Moreover, the help they would hope the United States would provide in time of dire need should also be assayed accurately in the new security context.

The points specified above contain a measure of truth; what is more, they reflect a general though dormant American attitude that few NATO-Europeans have elected to take very seriously. Because contemporary variants of isolationist sentiment may one day achieve political dominance in Washington, the devolutionist argument continues, it is preferable that that event be anticipated—if it cannot totally be precluded—by a careful and deliberate restructuring of the terms of the Atlantic alliance. Such a restructuring, they argue, should be in the direction of greater local self-reliance, thus defusing American isolationist impulses and preventing a wholesale and very abrupt American withdrawal that would leave no security arrangement worthy of the name to help manage a transition. Such a view is not without logical merit, but it is still fatally flawed. I believe, first, that the present structure and defensive arrangements of the Western Alliance work well enough in peacetime but, second, that the NATO structure can and should be improved as to the quality of its likely performance in time of crisis and war. Third, there is no credible alternative structure for the security of the Eurasian Rimlands to an alliance led by the United States. Fourth, the United States cannot be a full-fledged member, let alone the leader, of the Western Alliance unless it is militarily present in the zones of Soviet pressure. Finally, it is a geopolitical fallacy to contend that the United States can enhance its security either by washing its hands of its current Eurasian security responsibilities or by dramatically altering their military terms.

Although devolution is not intended to be synonymous with the concept of an isolationist fortress America, in practice it would likely precipitate political circumstances at home and abroad that would lead to an isolated stance. In principle, however, devolution (or alliance restructuring, if one prefers) is intellectually compatible with the proposition that the United States would be altering its strategy and military posture rather than its basic national security concept. If the idea of devolution were to guide U.S. policy, it would not mean that the United States had decided it was no longer concerned to contain Soviet power and influence. Instead, it would mean that the United States had decided that containment should be effected differently in the future. A wide variety of policy options could be accommodated by the concept of devolution, among them the following are leading examples.

First, the United States could announce that it would withdraw all of its armed forces from current forward deployment in and around Eurasia on a set schedule, protracted over perhaps five to ten years. It would offer to remain politically allied, as at present, but would insist that it seeks to regain freedom of action with respect to the possible fact and kind of its future mililary involvement in foreign conflict.[11] In conception, this would be American Gaullism. Like France today, the United States would proclaim both its steadiness as a firm ally and its resolve to control its own destiny and protect its own interests.[12]

This most rigorous variant of devolution would express a determination not to have a large fraction of the U.S. armed forces locked into an overseas garrison status or tied to the need to sustain, reinforce, or rescue garrisons in predetermined locations. In conception, at least, it would be not a retreat—analogous to Constantine's legions leaving Britain to its fate in 407 A.D.—but a recognition that the potential for regional self-help in general-purpose forces can never be tapped appropriately so long as the United States contributes to regional defense as it has in the postwar period to date. The U.S. armed forces would be organized, equipped, and trained so as to pose a more formidable global threat to Soviet power and influence. Those forces would emphasize maritime/air strength for amphibious flexibility,[13] against the backcloth of a first-class strategic forces' posture. An all-too-obvious prerequisite for this form of devolution would have to be the U.S. determination to carry through its military redeployment design regardless of regional consequences.[14] Devolution would be a gamble that the allies would choose to accept the regional security responsibilities relinquished by the United States. Of course, the allies might decline to pick up the baton.

A second possibility would be a substantial thinning out, rather than total withdrawal, of U.S. forces deployed in and about western Europe, Korea, and Japan—a sufficient reduction (perhaps one-half to two-thirds) to make a noteworthy adverse difference, absent local compensation, in the strength of the allied order of battle.[15] Reasonable though this second possibility may appear, given the mobilizable assets and ability to pay of western Europe and Japan, in practice it might produce the worst of all security worlds for the United States. Rather than responding by filling the preparedness gap left by the large U.S. force withdrawals, the forward-placed allies of the United States might prefer to consider the residual American military deployment sufficient for the extant military strategy and tactics of the alliance still to obtain. Thinner NATO defenses might not much trouble Europeans who have never fully defined their security in relation to the putative ability of the alliance actually to defend their territory.

With some reason, West Germany would argue that its manpower pool for military service is shrinking and that it cannot provide additional standing forces (even though it could greatly increase the effectiveness of its reserves).[16] France, apart from being predictably unenthusiastic about any large-scale increase in the size and effectiveness of the *Bundeswehr*, would respond to partial U.S. devolution by reaffirming its current defense policy, particularly the nuclear theme. Britain could fill a part of the gap, but only by reintroducing the draft and shifting resources from social welfare to security functions. Indeed, it is very likely that Britain, far from assuming new continental burdens, would follow the American example and itself begin a process of continental disengagement. Rather than send additional forces to Germany, Britain would probably prefer to invest in modernization of its national nuclear deterrent, in revitalization of its grossly inadequate home air defenses, and in the strengthening of its navy.

Despite these probable developments, which would likely not meet with American favor, a U.S. thinning-out process would have some advantages. The fact that half or more of the U.S. garrison had been withdrawn would demonstrate a determination to restructure alliance military arrangements that could not be matched by any number of speeches. Yet by way of major contrast to the plan of total military withdrawal, the retention of up to half its military assets in western Europe would give the United States a large bargaining chip with the allies. As Owen Harries has argued, NATO- Europe has come to take its American partner for granted as a net security producer.[17] If the United States should decide to take the path of measured devolution, it will be able to persuade the allies that it means what it says only by actually withdrawing forces on a more than token scale. To withdraw all of its forces from Europe would be to take itself out of the game of European force-posture politics, but with a substantial fraction of its forces remaining, the United States could convincingly link the continued forward deployment of those forces to the actions taken, or not taken, by its European allies.

A third possibility is to retain strictly token U.S. forces in western Europe and northeast Asia. By symbolizing American commitment, these should have a deterrent value out of all proportion to their military significance. Yet they would be sufficiently small (perhaps some tactical air squadrons, an armored brigade or two, and a small permanent naval presence) to free the hands of U.S. defense planners with respect to the design of a truly global strategy that would emphasize exploitation of the American long suits of maritime and air power.

The potential benefits to the United States of devolution options cannot be doubted. Clearly, it would be very desirable for Americans were the local defense of western Europe to repose almost entirely in western European hands. It would be in the interest of the United States were its military commitments to NATO-Europe to be so modest that a military defeat in that theater would not fatally limit the country's ability to wage war effectively elsewhere. However, the United States cannot select prudently a particular national security concept without believing that it could live with the consequences of that concept's failure—this is the fatal flaw in punitive theories of nuclear deterrence. The dissolution of the Western Alliance would be a highly plausible consequence of total or substantial U.S. force withdrawals from western Europe and northeast Asia—together with the loss of that local confidence in the strength of U.S. security commitments which is a large, though far from guaranteed, barrier to nuclear proliferation.[18] A NATO-Europe deprived of a convincing U.S. security commitment could evolve in any of three basic directions: "superpower Europe"; *"Europe des patries"*; or "accommodationist Europe" (contracting what Walter Laqueur has termed the malady of "Hollanditis").[19]

I do not believe that a "superpower Europe" is lurking in the wings waiting to come on stage once the United States has taken its final bow. Such a superpower is certainly feasible in terms of resources, but history suggests that Europe lacks the creative political assets and the basic sense of essential common interests to reorganize in its own defense. *"Europe des patries,"* the idea that a non-communist Europe comprising proud, well-armed (read *nuclear*-armed) states would be willing and able to resist Soviet intimidation on an individual basis, is almost certainly sheer fantasy. One American devolutionist has casually observed that "the French model of defense policy could serve as a basis for a reconstituted Europe and Western alliance. Each European country, but especially France, West Germany and the United Kingdom, would have [its] own national nuclear force whose prime responsibility would be to defend the motherland."[20] One does not know whether to laugh or cry! Very few events might plausibly provoke a deliberate Soviet military lunge into West Germany, but a whole range of scenarios can be composed for such an eventuality should Bonn acquire truly national nuclear forces in the absence of American military power from West German soil.

"Accommodationist Europe" is the most likely outcome of total or very substantial U.S. military withdrawal. The real action in the Soviet-American rivalry in Europe is taking place in the minds of Europeans.[21] It is not difficult to conclude that the policy preference of an average European—faced with the realities of American military withdrawal, French material limitations and rigorous self-regard, German anxiety concerning its military vulnerability and German dreams of reunification, and British weakness and insular yearnings—would be *sauve qui peut*. There would be no principal guardian to organize and direct the Western end of the European security order. Some, perhaps many, Americans will not be unduly disturbed by this analysis. They may believe that should a U.S. troop withdrawal reveal a pusillanimous NATO-European willingness to accommodate the Soviet Union, it is better to know it now than to have it revealed in the midst of some terrible military crisis. But they cannot evade the implications of the apparent fact that western Europe will not have the political assets in the foreseeable future to organize itself as a regional security pact with sufficient military muscle of all kinds to withstand Soviet intimidation.

American proponents of the variants of devolution, as well as those western Europeans who are seriously interested in restructuring the Atlantic alliance in the direction of greater regional self-help, have to consider the meaning for security of the trends in European political culture. Overall, it is by no means obvious that the societies of western Europe have the moral vitality, or even the sense of civic virtue, necessary to preserve a condition of political independence vis-à-vis Soviet hegemonism. The experience of a sustained prosperity in the wake of two devastating and protracted wars, set against the backcloth of nuclear fears, may have so completely debellicized the welfare democracies of western Europe that they no longer possess the cultural attributes necessary for self-defense.[22] The adherence of European countries to NATO may not be evidence of will to resist the barbarians to the East, because to western Europeans the function of NATO is not preparation for war in the service of deterrence, order, and peace; instead, the mere existence of NATO—particularly the comforting security connection to an offshore superpower—is itself viewed as a guarantee of peace.

The popular anxiety in western Europe about the structure of its contemporary security condition is a mirror image of the principal neo-isolationist concern in the United States. On both sides of the Atlantic there are people who fear that the entangling alliance will function as a handcuff to the severe risk of a war initiated by the attitudes and actions of others. A transatlantic difference is that whereas in the United States alienation from the NATO enterprise is largely confined to handfuls of intellectuals and policy commentators on the Left and the Right, in some European countries it has attained the character of a mass movement. The European peace movements express both the belief that Europe has a right to peace and the perception that the contemporary U.S. direction of alliance security policies constitutes a threat to the exercise of that right.

It is certainly true that nuclear defense questions have been the catalysts for popular protest in western European countries. But one should not neglect the implications of the fact that some NATO allies have in effect come to reject war as an instrument of policy—possibly even in the strictest conditions of self-defense. In their view, war has become unacceptable and unthinkable for the complex, densely populated, and enormously vulnerable societies of western Europe. Prosperity and an understandable nuclear dread have completed the process of debellicization that was begun and advanced by the nightmares of 1914-18 and 1939-45.[23]

Just as neither the willingness of the United States to mobilize its power to save the world for democracy (or, in effect, to restore a favorable balance of power in Eurasia) twice in this century nor the ability of the Soviet system to withstand teutonic assault were confidently predictable long ahead of time, so the capacity for sufficient collective action in self-defense on the part of western Europe cannot be confidently predicted today. The visible trends are not comforting, however. If it is true or possible that NATO-Europe at the popular level is more disturbed by its perceptions of U.S. belligerence than it is by the course of the Soviet imperium, then there is serious doubt of the European political ability to effect functional substitutes for the American legions. For the near-term future at least, I believe that the societies and certainly the governments of NATO-Europe much prefer to live with what they discern as their American problem rather than launch the bold venture of trying to live without that problem.

Americans secure in their political and strategic culture—and, one hopes, clear-eyed about the geopolitical realities of the global contest for power, influence, and the exercise of preferred values—understandably have the universal problem of failing to see themselves as others see them. Whatever the future course of U.S. national security policy, American policymakers should recognize the potential for damage of a politically significant, strongly negative strain in European attitudes toward the United States. Michael Vlahos somewhat, but only somewhat, overstates the case:

The degradation of European perceptions of America since Vietnam has influenced trans-Atlantic relations in two ways: First, American savagery [the longstanding European image of America as "the savage land"] means America represents a dangerous variable in the equation of world peace and stability. Reagan as a wild cowboy, with his brace of Colts, is the metaphor underlying European views of unleashed American patriotic emotion. The image of the frontiersman as the pathfinder expanding civilization has been replaced by the evocative symbol of the manic, amoral gunfighter: The United States of America. Second, America the barbarian is unfit for democratic leadership in a complex international system that requires cultural sensitivity and emotional restraint. All this, America lacks. A powerful but brutal people, Americans have no right to determine European policy.[24]

The attitudes of many young Europeans, to which Vlahos refers, are not really so much a rejection of distasteful and allegedly dangerous American policy (even cultural) traits as an attempted rejection of the distasteful and certainly dangerous enduring facts of international politics. However unsure its grasp of the rules of the game of international conflict and, as a consequence, however inept it may be on occasion, by virtue of its power position in the international system the United States has been somewhat inoculated by responsibility against rejection of power politics in favor of fantasies of perpetual peace (or of detente *as* defense). Devolution, as a conceptual guide for national security policy, requires either that European (and perhaps Japanese) societies respond to a far more conditional and less locally visible *Pax Americana* by meeting regional security challenges with suitable regional effort, or that there be a persuasive explanation of how vital American interests can be protected in the context of a security-defaulting Rimland.

Habits of security dependence evolved over a long period of peace can hardly help breeding confusion about what is tolerable in the search for international order. American theorists of all tendencies can find evidence of the NATO-Europe that fits their prejudices and supports their case for this or that recommended course in U.S. policy. No amount of careful historical research can reveal with certainty how western Europe and Japan would behave with respect to regional organization and provision for military security in the face of a devolutionary shift in U.S. strategy.

Analysis of the concept of devolution suggests that it has some merit as a way for the United States to secure a better fit between means and ends within the ambit of containment, but its highly problematical benefits would seem to be quite out of balance with its certain risks. In some key respects, military withdrawal is puzzling *even in the context of an intended continuation of containment.* A United States liberated from heavy garrison duties in the direct defense of western Europe should indeed nominally have regained much of its freedom of strategic action. But what would a United States so liberated wish to accomplish? While it should be better prepared in some respects to conduct an essentially maritime strategy, where and to what purpose would U.S. military power be applied in the event of a military conflict in Europe? Would it be the U.S. intention to rush forces to Europe should an acute crisis occur there? No great imagination is required to foresee the political and logistic difficulties of such a proposal. Is it the idea that a United States substantially free of European defense burdens would enjoy freedom of action to threaten the Soviet Union elsewhere? If so, where, and for what purpose?[25]

There is a case to be made for a U.S. effort to obtain substantial relief from those forward defense duties in Europe that could far more economically be assumed by continental European allies, and to adopt a national military strategy more suitable for the prosecution of a genuinely global conflict. However, the benefits of a greater freedom to act strongly in regions aside from central-western Europe would be purchased too dear if as a consequence the geostrategic advantages of the current security structure in non-Soviet-controlled Eurasia were placed at severe risk. To the degree to which devolution is sensible, it points to the desirability of strategy adjustments and postural evolution rather than of wholesale change.

In debating the future course of U.S. national security policy, one should not permit confusion to emerge as between means and ends or lose sight of the need to guard the primacy of the latter. To debate the desirability and feasibility of devolving some U.S. forward defense duties upon regional allies is to debate policy instrumentalities. The ultimate purpose of security policy is not to seek relief from unwanted burdens but to contain Soviet power and influence.

Proponents of strategic withdrawal from containment concerns to a "fortress America" have to address the question of how the vital interests of the United States should be defined in geographical terms. Would the defense perimeter be rigorously Jeffersonian in definition, strictly the coasts and borders of U.S. territory?[26] Would it embrace the "quarter-sphere" of the United States, Canada, Central America, and the Caribbean? or the bicontinental hemisphere from the Drake Passage to the Arctic Ocean? An expansive definition might even include Greenland, Iceland, and the Azores, as well as the Marshall and Mariana islands in the western Pacific. The core of the idea of fortress America is plain enough, but any plan for its implementation raises a host of practical difficulties.

Typically, fortress America means a fortress *Americas*, with sentimental if somewhat astrategic reference to the Monroe Doctrine. The pertinent model probably would be Franklin Roosevelt's security policy conception of 1938-41: "We must have a large airforce in being to protect any part of the North or the South American continents...to deter anyone from landing there."[27] It is one thing to have a hemispheric view of U.S. security when domestic opinion permits no other, but it is quite another deliberately to choose such a policy concept. In terms of U.S. military security, the current barrier allies of Eurasia—preminently Norway, Britain, Turkey, and Japan—are vastly more important and worth supporting against Soviet hegemonic pressure than are the countries of South America below the equator. U.S. attachment to the idea of an American hemisphere substantially unsullied by Old World imperialism is far more emotional than geostrategic in origin.

This is not to say that no modern variant of fortress America could make strategic sense in an age of nuclear weapons capable of delivery on an intercontinental scale. Indeed, some people argue that the very technologies that have shrunk strategic distance and created a global security system have rendered a national security policy of wholesale withdrawal to the Americas strategically feasible and prudent as never before. Because the strategic context has been dominated by the size and diversity of superpower nuclear arsenals, it is not at all clear what the deterrent (as opposed to inward-looking political) benefits of national nuclear forces have been for France and Britain. However, it is not necessarily the case that national nuclear forces, tasked with homeland protection duties, can invariably function satisfactorily as an existential deterrent in the face of Soviet political and military pressure. Looking to the end of this century, it is predictable that small national nuclear forces will increasingly lose a strictly technical credibility in prospective response, just as they have always lacked political credibility from the perspective of isolated national action.[28]

The concept of fortress America should not be dismissed too lightly as an archaic idea that has been obviated by a new American maturity as well as by the alleged facts of global security interdependence. The concept's proponents may argue that the new American maturity is really nothing of the kind, that attempted performance of a global guardianship role on behalf of a compatible international order is evidence not of sophistication or international political adulthood but of protracted hubristic adolescence.[29] In this view, U.S. forward military diplomacy around the Rimland of Eurasia has generated threat perception in the Soviet Union that belies the true defensive character of U.S. foreign policy; it has vastly reduced local European and Asian incentives to construct and pay for security structures and policies well adapted to local needs; and, most important of all, it has generated potentially fatal dangers to U.S. survival interests.[30]

The fortress America concept comprises certain central features. First, there is the determination to protect the survival interests of the American people, if need be at the expense of vital (and lesser) interests.[31] Second, the United States would explicitly eschew a global, indeed any extrahemispheric, military guardianship role on behalf of international order. Third, the United States would have no alliance ties beyond the Western Hemisphere of a kind that carry, or might encourage, expectations of military assistance. Fourth, the United States would strive to achieve the maximum feasible measure of freedom of international action (or inaction). Fifth, a critical corollary to the others, the United States would refuse to play any security role (unilaterally, or in bilateral or multilateral contexts) outside the Western Hemisphere that would be likely to generate or fuel political antagonism toward itself.[32]

A United States seeking to practice the fortress America concept as policy would not need to forswear all political or military interests in Eurasia. Indeed, given the values of the American people, the cultural and sentimental ties that many of them feel for the homelands of their forebears, and the facts of economic interdependence,[33] to do so would be unrealistic. Nor would it need to resemble an isolated, let alone an isolationist, America. The United States could remain militarily a very strong power and could state its willingness, indeed its determination, to defend its most important interests whenever and wherever those interests might be threatened. However, those interests would not be defined in anti-Soviet terms so as to include the territorial integrity of countries around the Rimland of Eurasia from Norway to South Korea; neither would they be defined as embracing the security of oil supply from the

Persian Gulf region to the non-Communist economies of western Europe and the Far East.[34]

In the context of this discussion, the term "fortress" is probably as misleading as the term "isolationism." It could be argued that this policy course need not compel the United States to evolve a siege economy or to mobilize and regiment the American people like a beleaguered garrison. Even in the event of Soviet domination of virtually the whole "World-Island" of Eurasia-Africa, the United States would be protected by vast oceanic distances from the newly expanded base of Soviet power. A very heavily nuclear-armed United States would need have no fear of Soviet invasion.

Michael Vlahos has argued with considerable eloquence that the interventionist geopolitical logic of Nicholas Spykman,[35] with its Mackinderesque foundations, spoke more to the constraints imposed by U.S. political culture—national ethos, perhaps—than to strategic realities. Vlahos has objected that the domestic debate in the United States in 1940-41 was constrained culturally to the all-or-nothing choice between global interventionism to "save" the Old World and a very muscular defense of the New World (and its transpacific holdings) according to popular interpretation of the Monroe Doctrine. Geostrategically, though not culturally, a United States with a navy second to none—looking to the products of the construction envisaged in the Two Ocean Naval Expansion Act of 1940—and long-range airpower on a scale unmatched and probably unmatchable by any hostile coalition, could have considered very seriously the policy option of permitting the wars in Eurasia to run their course.[36]

Such speculation is idle, however, because American political culture, notwithstanding its preference for strategic disengagement from Old World quarrels, was incapable of acquiescing in the implications for China of Imperial Japan's design for a Greater East Asia Co-Prosperity Sphere. The attack on Pearl Harbor and Hitler's gratuitous declaration of war served to write finis to the political authority of hemispheric conceptions of the U.S. defense perimeter. Nonetheless, prior to Pearl Harbor, or prior to the trade embargo imposed on Japan in July 1941 in response to its occupation of French Indochina, it is probably true that in theory the United States had policy options intermediate between a hemispheric fortress America and a crusade to defeat the Axis powers in Eurasia. In practice, the intermediate options would have required the United States to behave imperially in a very un-American manner, moved by considerations of prudential strategic advantage or of disadvantage to be precluded.[37] Nonetheless, the debate over isolation and intervention in 1940-41 showed American democracy capable of contemplating seriously only two concepts for national security policy. There was a missing middle to the debate, and I suspect strongly that American political culture today is little different in its essentials. If true, this would mean that even strategically more rewarding options than the stark alternatives of global containment and fortress America may not exist in the reality of domestic political supportability. Americans can understand and empathize with either a mission of global resistance to Soviet hegemony or the concept of standing aside from the sullying disputes of unworthy foreigners. But to promote very selective U.S. intervention applied as needed for the protection of strictly vital U.S. interests may be to ask too much, or too little, of the American people.

The fortress America concept can be approached from two quite different directions. On the one hand, it could be argued that although the United States would be withdrawing from entangling alliances in Eurasia, it would have carefully considered in advance the quantity and quality of likely substitute elements in European and east Asian security communities. On the other hand, it might be more politically realistic to argue that a United States determined to be master of its own fate would be interested, but no more than interested, in the character and details of European and east Asian defense.

At root, a United States opting for fortress America would be saying that henceforth it would accept the most dire of risks only on behalf of the most important of its national interests.[38] An American president who decided to implement this concept should have little difficulty explaining the choice in suitably ideological terms to the American public, dramatic though the change would be from the practice of U.S. statecraft since the 1940s. The point would be made that while the United States has *vital* interests at stake in the Rimlands of Eurasia, the countries in question have *survival* interests at issue.[39]

The United States would prefer that the major western European and eastern Asian powers should be organized so as to face the Soviet Union with a solid local barricade of political and military opposition—but it would have to be prepared for a failure of regional nerve. To give the concept of fortress America full integrity, proponents would have to insist that its adoption as policy should not be contingent upon the creation of alternative security structures for Rimland Eurasia. Absent that insistence, NATO-Europe and Japan would be provided with strong incentives not to invest in security alternatives. The potential regional organizers of security almost all prefer the continuation of their long-standing alliance ties to the United States to any of the more likely alternatives.[40]

In practice, though not in principle, rigorous forward security-duty devolution and fortress America could be close to indistinguishable policies. A pure application of fortress America would leave no formal U.S. security connections whatsoever in Eurasia because, it could be argued, it would be unhelpful to soften the security shock of U.S. military withdrawal by leaving political connections in place; such a diplomatic lifeline could negatively affect the local determination to design and pay for a new security framework. According to this line of thought, the only security shock strong enough to trigger the creation of local defense communities plausibly capable of resisting Soviet intimidation would be local recognition that Europeans and Asians were unambiguously on their own.

Several major uncertainties pertain to fortress America. First, would the former allies of the United States, cast adrift at last without the U.S. security blanket that they have enjoyed and chafed under for the better part of forty years, attempt to organize themselves in such a way that Soviet hegemony could be prevented? Second, if they attempted to organize regionally for defense, would they be likely to succeed? Third, could the American people live with the distinct possibility that the unintended consequence of such a radical shift in their national security policy would be to donate the whole of Eurasia to Soviet imperialism? In short, how strong a case can be presented for the concept of fortress America?

First, it may be argued that adoption of such a concept could not fairly be characterized as an American retreat, or as evidence of an American failure of will or nerve. On the contrary, it would constitute a return to the traditional and most genuinely American national security policy—the policy pursued from the time of George Washington until Franklin Delano Roosevelt's third term of office, though with varying geographical referents.[41] Furthermore, the most probable consequences would be consistent with the underlying U.S. foreign policy intention in the early years of the NATO Alliance. People today, so the argument proceeds, tend to forget that the U.S. military commitment to (and in) Europe was not intended to be permanent. In the early 1950s it was recognized that a U.S. military shield had to be provided, temporarily, behind which the war-shattered non-Communist countries of Europe could recover, rebuild, and regain the strength to defend themselves. The NATO treaty per se does not commit the United States to any particular forms or quantity of military commitment. Adoption of a fortress America policy would be less a rejection of the global-guardian role of the past forty years than long overdue action in recognition of the substantial success of that role. Unfortunately, although NATO-Europe and Japan have regained the economic and political assets needed for evolution from security adolescent to security adult, the habit of military dependence upon the United States has taken deep root.

Second, although the forward security commitments of the United States have the comforting quality of long familiarity, is it really very radical to suggest that the United States should not deploy well in excess of 400,000 military personnel abroad *prospectively forever?* Do opponents of the several variants of fortress America propose that the American taxpayer should subsidize the national security of western European countries and of Japan indefinitely? What is the ethical, political, economic, or military basis for the proposition that wealthy Europeans and Japanese should not foot the full bill for their own defense? At a generic level of policy discussion, one need not decide whether implementation of fortress America would be effected over a period of months or of years. Similarly, although the United States must be adamant on the principle that it would not commit itself to assist automatically in the defense of any country in Eurasia, there could be variants of fortress America wherein the United States would continue to function as a more or less active player in the politics, and perhaps the defense economics, of regional security in Eurasia.[42]

Third, it may be argued that the United States, like other Western countries, needs freedom of action in order to define and protect its own interests in the world. NATO-Europe is perennially distressed by the consequences of the fact that the United States has truly global security-supportive roles to play; for example, European officials have been very critical of what they discern as a "Pacific tilt" to U.S. grand strategy in the 1980s.[43] They do not want the political stability achieved in Europe to be threatened by tensions manufactured or expressed elsewhere in the world—yet the very fact of alliance with the United States provides an unwanted connection with distant security problems. Moreover, in European perspective, the virtue of being allied to a country as strong as the United States is further offset by the perceived vices of American political culture. In successive general elections (1976 and 1980) that culture produced two very different but uniquely American presidents who were novices in the field of international statecraft. The burden of this argument is that NATO-European countries should be unleashed to design and conduct the security policies for Europe that they believe best meet their local needs. Their criticism of trends in American strategic weapons policy—indeed, denunciation of nuclear weapons per se—would have to be conducted against a new backcloth of realization that the only nuclear weapons directly pertinent to their security would be the ones aimed at them by the Soviet Union and any that they choose to build for themselves.[44]

Proponents of fortress America need not profess indifference to the security of Europeans and Asians (though many undoubtedly would); they need say only that their concern stops short of a willingness to commit the United States, in advance, to go to war on behalf of other countries. They could also argue that western Europe is more likely to design and sustain a lasting and effective regional security structure than is a NATO Alliance permanently riven with political tensions among its current, geopolitically diverse membership. As to the prospect of an "accommodationist Europe," the opinon could be offered that on the evidence of their histories, Germans, Frenchmen, Britons, Spaniards,

Norwegians, and others are not natural candidates for appeasement roles. Once the first shock of being cast adrift had worn off, these old socially and ethnically homogeneous countries would realize that they have ample resources with which to thwart Soviet hegemonial ambitions.

Fourth, the Soviet motive for its ever-renewed political offensive against the coherence of NATO may have had less to do with a desire to dominate western Europe than with the ambition to separate the United States from its European allies. While it is not in the nature of Soviet/ Russian political culture to be a good neighbor, the Soviet Union might adopt a more relaxed defense posture toward a western Europe that was no longer a Trojan horse for the real enemy across the Atlantic; it might ask of a western Europe bereft of plausible American military support only that it stand on the sidelines with respect to Soviet-American competition. The United States would like western Europe and eastern Asia to continue to provide continental military distraction on a major scale for Soviet imperialism, but should a superpower quality of defense capability prove to be beyond the ambition and political strength of western Europe, some widespread functional analogue of Swiss, Yugoslav, and Swedish deterrence might be entirely feasible. Provided its neutrality were not unduly benign toward the Soviet Union, a relatively militarily weak though nuclear-armed western Europe that would not add its economic strength or its strategic geography to the Soviet imperium would be distinctly tolerable for a thoroughly disengaged America.[45]

Finally, proponents of fortress America may contend that even should the pessimists be proved correct and the Rimland countries of Eurasia fail to provide alternative security structures to a defunct NATO, the consequences need not be so terrible. It could be argued that the Soviet Union lacks the material strength to achieve hegemony over all of Eurasia. Expanding empires acquire more and more of the seeds of their own destruction. While the Soviet Union could intimidate and even physically coerce any country or countries in Eurasia that it found to be unacceptably uncooperative, it could not possible occupy western Europe, and/or China, and so on, *and profit by the deed.* Even if the Soviet Union enjoyed substantially unchallenged strategic primacy throughout Eurasia, the value of that primacy would be far less than might be supposed in the correlation of forces with a United States strategically self-excluded from the World- Island.

There is some abstract merit in the fortress America argument, some validity to the criticisms offered by partisans of devolution and fortress America of the seemingly enduring fragility in NATO's defense posture and its resulting risks to the American homeland—but not enough to warrant very serious public interest. For six major reasons I recommend rejection of fortress America and its close affiliates.

First, a U.S. withdrawal on the scale and of the quality under discussion here would constitute a geopolitical revolution in the structure of international security in the Soviet favor. Although the Soviet Union defines the United States as its principal enemy, as it must on grounds of capability, Soviet strategy appears to have the proximate goal of expelling U.S. power and influence from the Rimland of Eurasia and, *ipso facto*, of isolating the United States from potential sources of support. A disengaged America, while it would pose the Soviet Union some difficult problems, would plainly provide Soviet leaders with strategic opportunities of historic dimensions. The United States, in withdrawing voluntarily from many of the fields of greatest economic and strategic significance, would effectively be inviting the Soviet Union to exploit the newly created imbalance of power in Eurasia and thus to strengthen itself for the long-term struggle against a United States which would have chosen to stand alone.

Second, it is not at all obvious that the United States would want to remain militarily isolated under all circumstances. Repeatedly in this century it has permitted events to teach that it does have interests in Europe and Asia worth fighting to protect. Far from purchasing peace—and nuclear peace in particular—through disengagement, the United States would be encouraging an upheaval in Eurasian security structures that would greatly reduce deterrent effect in Soviet minds and thus place vital U.S. interests at severe risk. One can predict that the United States would still want to intervene militarily should traditional friends and former allies become subject to aggression, but—intervening late and lacking a regional logistics infrastructure—it might confront a military task more offensive (in the interests of liberation) than defensive in character.[46] Moreover, it should be recalled that there has not been a resolution of the dilemma posed by Germany: that united, it would be too powerful for the peace of mind of most of its neighbors; divided, it constitutes the major item of unresolved security business in Europe. The prospect of West Germany essentially let loose from the NATO framework to see to its own security has potentially catastrophic implications for the peace of Europe.

Third, NATO without the United States would have no leader, and there are no likely European candidates for that role.[47] The degree of Franco-German reconciliation has been remarkable, but neither country could accept the leadership of the other. Similarly, Britain would veto either French or German leadership yet would lack the strength, not to mention the confidence and trust of others, to assert leadership itself.

Fourth, I believe that disengagement would not be viable as a policy theme in American political culture today. One must admit that an American politician can usually secure a hearing for claims that Uncle Sam is being exploited by free-riding, overly self-regarding, and ungrateful foreigners. An American politician could probably attract a following also for the proposition that the United States should declare peace with the outside world and retire to its well-defended island continent (or bi-continent, à la James Monroe) to engage in virtuous American pursuits. Day by day in normal times these sentiments could well dominate policy consideration. But how well would they play if and when South Korea were overrun by North Korea? or if Israel faced a military catastrophe? or if Soviet forces intervened in West Germany? Interventionism in truly worthy causes and security guardianship overseas have taken sufficiently deep root in the U.S. worldview and in Americans' views of themselves that truly rigorous disengagement is simply not viable in U.S. domestic politics—at least once the consequences of that policy are brought home. This argument is astrategic; in this particular context I do not challenge the strategic rationality of fortress America. I do suggest that the United States has been changed as a country by the events and trends of the twentieth century. Although an isolationist and certainly unilateralist impulse remains and should not be dismissed lightly by foreigners, in practice Americans would demand that their government *do something* were Soviet or North Korean tanks to celebrate the American departure from Rimland Eurasia in a traditional Soviet or North Korean manner.

Fifth, trite though it may sound, history does teach that predatory countries abhor a power vacuum. It is as certain as anything in politics can be that the Soviet Union would hasten to exploit an American withdrawal. (There would be good reason for its haste: the withdrawal would be so foolish in geopolitical terms that Soviet leaders would probably anticipate a U.S. policy reversal following the next general election.)[48] Proponents of any variant of fortress America whose position rests on the belief that the Soviet Union would behave in a more benign fashion toward its regional neighbors in the absence of local U.S. security complications should be reminded of the enduring cultural and stylistic features of the Soviet imperial system.[49] Recall the security arguments advanced in defense of appeasement of Hitler over Czechoslovakia in 1938.[50] The United States today, like Britain in 1938-39, cannot achieve "real peace," because a general and lasting settlement of political differences is not possible with the character of adversary that we face in the Soviet Union. In 1938 Britain chose to buy peace, meaning a postponement of war, by abandoning a well-armed friend. Fortress America would not achieve peace, because the United States affronts the Soviet Union by its very existence.[51] Rather, it would achieve the removal of the only power capable of organizing effective collective resistance to Soviet ambitions around the periphery of Eurasia, and the deletion from the American column of a number of wealthy and—in many cases—heavily armed allies. The pertinent question is whether or not those allies contribute more to American insecurity than security.

Fortress America, devolution, disengagement, America First—whatever rhetorical preference is exercised—would in fact be a policy rooted in fear and would constitute in geostrategic terms an American defeat of historically unprecedented proportions. If a fortress America policy were implemented on the terms advocated by its more logically rigorous proponents, it would amount to granting the Soviet Union a free hand in Eurasia. The central geostrategic point is that the United States is locked into a long-term, potentially deadly struggle with the Soviet Union, and it is not in the U.S. interest vastly to simplify Soviet security problems. Furthermore, it cannot be in the U.S. interest knowingly to risk creating an insecurity condition in Eurasia that would virtually invite the Soviet Union to press for unilateral advantage over the economically well-endowed former security clients of the United States.

Some readers may wonder why the family of disengagement concepts discussed here under the headings of devolution and fortress America have been analyzed in such detail, given the strength of judgment expressed to their disfavor. The reasons are that these concepts can be presented with a superficially acceptable face; that they are enjoying something of a resurgence of public attention (if not widespread popularity) at the present time;[52] that they do have an enduring appeal to some deeply American cultural traits; and that they are so dangerous. A book such as this must discuss fortress America seriously for much the same reasons that a study of U.S. security problems must focus more than passing attention upon the prospects for general nuclear war. The low probability of occurrence is more than counterbalanced by the prospective horrors of the hypothetical event.

13

Rollback

As a concept for the guidance of national security policy, "rollback" lends itself to a wide range of definitions. In principle it could refer to a policy of political warfare scarcely distinguishable from that announced by President Reagan in his Westminster speech of June 8, 1982,[1] or it could denote a determination to effect a shrinkage in the scale of the Soviet empire by whatever means are found to be necessary.

Three elements of the Soviet empire that might be targeted for rollback or destabilization comprise the ethnically non–Great Russian areas of the Soviet Union;[2] the eastern European countries first liberated and then secured by the Soviet Army from 1944 to 1948;[3] and the former European colonial dependents (Syria, Libya, Angola, South Yemen, Ethiopia, Vietnam, Kampuchea), quasi-colonial dependents (Cuba, Nicaragua), and neutral states (Afghanistan) that have joined the Soviet security sphere.[4] Contemporary American discussion of rollback options *in peacetime* is generally confined to consideration of the opportunities that present themselves in the Third World imperium of the Soviet Union. The Reagan Doctrine of October 24, 1985,[5] which pledged U.S. support to "democratic resistance forces," plainly was applicable only to Central America, Africa, Afghanistan, and south east Asia.

The essence of this concept is a commitment to proceed beyond the mere containment of Soviet power and influence, to seek its forced retreat. Given that Soviet leaders cannot be bribed or persuaded voluntarily to retreat, more or less coercion would need to be applied. Although rollback sounds dangerously adventurous and lends itself easily to (mis)representation as such, mild variants of it have been attempted. And it is well to remember that the commitment to compel a retreat of U.S. power and influence to, and indeed within, the Western Hemisphere, is a major element of Soviet grand strategy.

Strategically rational motives for a U.S. rollback policy are not difficult to identify. Such a policy could usefully focus Soviet attention and energy on internal imperial difficulties, thereby weakening Soviet ability to prosecute the long-term struggle against the United States in areas beyond the current boundaries of the Soviet imperium. Also, a Soviet Union heavily engaged in restoring and maintaining comradely discipline in Poland or Afghanistan would yield the initiative to the West in the public relations war of ideas. Undeniable disturbance within the Soviet empire should enable the United States to focus attention on the visible sins of misrule. The true nature of Soviet imperialism would be revealed even to the most skeptical by Soviet misdeeds within an empire that is unmistakably troubled.[6] Given that the principal problem of Western defense is political will and not a scarcity of material assets, evidence of Soviet brutality should help to rally the troops of democracy.

A policy of selective imperial destabilization could force Moscow to invest very heavily in imperial subsidization and policing duties. Empires run on prestige as well as on coercive power, and the Soviet state would appear to derive considerable domestic prestige, as well as strategic value, from the success story of socialist allies in the Third World. The nonterritorially contiguous imperium that has been acquired in the wake of European decolonization is a distinctively Soviet achievement adding to the inherited continental empire of czarist Russia. But the economic costs of empire are not light. For example, RAND Corporation analysts have estimated that the total costs to the Soviet Union in 1980 lay in the range of $35.88 to $46.48 billion (in 1981 dollars).[7] By assisting "democratic resistance forces" on a modest scale, the United States has the ability to raise those costs noticeably. Scarce economic resources allocated to the subsidization of Cuba, Angola, and Vietnam or to the protracted endeavor to pacify Afghanistan are resources unavailable for more productive tasks.

The economic impact of a rollback policy needs to be considered in the context of a stagnant Soviet economy. The former chairman of the U.S. National Intelligence Council, Henry Rowen, has claimed that the Central Intelligence Agency's estimate of 2.5 percent average Soviet GNP growth from 1975 to 1985 "is probably the upper bound of performance. Actual growth overall might have been less, perhaps close to zero." The CIA, he says, "forecasts a growth rate of 1.5 to 2.4 percent annually for the rest of the 1980s. This range may be too high and one should not rule out the possibility of declining per capita output over the next decade."[8] The point is not that Soviet leaders will find the costs of empire an intolerable burden but rather that those costs are very likely to have a growing negative impact upon Soviet domestic living standards, or upon the availability of resources for military modernization.[9] Notwithstanding the reform program of the Gorbachev leadership, substantial improvement in Soviet economic performance would require a scale of economic redirection toward market practices that is not likely to be sanctioned.[10]

There is a complacent assumption popular in the U.S. defense community that such strategically exposed and highly vulnerable allies of the

Soviet Union as Cuba and Vietnam would be likely, if not to defect, at least to declare their neutrality in any direct Soviet-American clash of arms. Further, it is assumed that such expedient neutrality would take the practical form of denying Soviet forces the use of local facilities. Both assumptions are plausible, but the second presumes a greater local military competence on the part of erstwhile clients than may be the case. Regardless of the political wishes of the local governments, the Soviet Union may be able to make timely and effective use of its facilities in regions far distant from the epicenter of a war on the Central Front in Europe. Cuba is of particular concern because Soviet submarines operating in the Gulf of Mexico and particularly in the Florida Straits would be in a position to inflict great damage upon U.S. reinforcement efforts for Europe.

Given the uncertainty that must surround consideration of the course of a war in Europe, it is impossible to predict with confidence the importance or otherwise of small Soviet and Soviet-allied forces operating in and from southern Africa, South Yemen, Afghanistan, and Vietnam. Should a war be lost by NATO, or should a Soviet invasion of western Europe be contained and limited to a war of attrition, the flexibility inherent in the maritime power of the West would assume preponderant significance as the United States maneuvered worldwide in search of military advantage.[11] In a protracted conflict it would matter enormously what forces of their own or of others the Soviet Union could apply against chokepoints on the sea lines of communication that knit together the maritime coalition led by the United States.[12]

If it is important to deterrence for the United States to persuade Soviet leaders that they may be compelled to wage a protracted global war no matter how well they fare in central-western Europe, it is also incumbent upon American leaders to remember that some outposts of the Soviet empire might be difficult and expensive to neutralize. One should recall that in German East Africa (Tanzania today) Lt. Col. Paul von Lettow-Vorbeck, admittedly an unusually gifted guerrilla strategist, defied the might of the British Empire throughout the entire course of the First World War: "With an original force of only 5,000, five percent being Europeans, he...caused the employment of 130,000 enemy troops and the expenditure of £72,000,000."[13] Should World War III comprise five days of intense theater combat in Europe and perhaps a day of central nuclear combat, then it will not matter at all whether the Soviet Union has any latter-day Lettow-Vorbecks functioning in southern Africa, Central America, or elsewhere. But should the war be protracted, it could matter very much indeed.

A commitment to the vigorous conduct of ideological struggle, as in the first Reagan administration,[14] need betoken no serious expectation that Soviet power will be rolled back—though it may betoken determination to roll back Soviet influence over the minds of individuals in western Europe and elsewhere outside the Soviet empire. Certainly, the *threat* to roll back Soviet power from its extended empire, from eastern Europe, and even from the non–Great Russian Soviet Union is an essential element in the deterrence of war and for intrawar deterrence. There should be scant reason to doubt the efficacy for the deterrence of war of Soviet leaders' uncertainty that they could wage a war of only limited liability against the West; indeed, it would be difficult to exaggerate the importance of a Soviet conviction that the United States and its allies have the means and the contingent (last-resort) intention to shake the edifice of the entire power structure of the Soviet state. To some degree that power structure can be targeted by U.S. strategic forces,[15] but it can also be imperiled by military defeat in the field and, above all else, by the insertion of Western combat forces into the Soviet empire—in eastern Europe and even in the territorial periphery of the Soviet Union proper.[16]

U.S. policymakers should not need to be reminded of the perils that can accompany an invasion of Mother Russia, but they may benefit from being reminded of the opportunities for liberation, rather than conquest/exploitation, that Nazi Germany denied itself by its misconduct in 1941-42. In an analysis of the importance of a policy of rollback in wartime, Stephen Rosen has argued persuasively that eastern European armies could function as a critical weakness for the Soviet Union, but he warns, wisely, that "the reliability of the non-Russian Warsaw Pact soldiers is a *latent* problem, one that can only be brought out by Western military success" (original emphasis).[17] It is one thing to identify a potential vulnerability that would faciliate rollback; it may be quite another to be able to exploit that vulnerability. Eastern European military units are not likely to mutiny if they are participating in a brief and successful sweep to the English Channel.

Attempts to effect the demise of the Soviet state by direct military means have been launched twice: in the civil war that followed the Bolshevik coup, and by Nazi Germany in 1941.[18] The most serious instance of a military attempt at (very limited) rollback since 1945 was the U.S.-U.N. decision in the fall of 1950 forcibly to reunite the whole of Korea and to hold subsequent free elections. That venture was brought to naught by the Chinese eruption across the Yalu river in October. The Bay of Pigs fiasco of spring 1961 should serve for all time as an object lesson in how a superpower should not conduct its foreign military business. More recently the U.S. military operations on October 24, 1983, that placed Grenada under new management was a classic exercise in rollback, not to mention a belated muscular application of the Monroe Doctrine.

From time to time throughout the postwar period the United States has sought more or less actively to destabilize and bring down regimes which, while far removed geographically from Soviet Eurasia, have been judged to pose dangers to important U.S. interests (if only by the potential power of their example, in some instances). Prominent cases in this category include Guatemala in 1954, Chile in 1970 (when the United States failed to prevent the inauguration of Salvador Allende as president), and Nicaragua, Afghanistan, Angola, and Kampuchea today. It is worth noting that the United States formally denied any ambition to bring down the government of North Vietnam in the 1960s. Concerned to wage a limited war for limited political objectives, the United States believed it had learned from Korea that the danger of active intervention by the Communist great powers could be much reduced by the absence of challenge to an established Communist government.

With respect to the Soviet state itself, the U.S. government since 1945 has never even come close to considering seriously the merits and demerits of the case for waging a preventive war—notwithstanding some historians' suspicions to the contrary.[19] As one would expect of a political system and a national security bureaucracy as diverse, even unruly, as those of the United States, some papers were written and speeches delivered by individuals who did urge consideration of preventive war. However, quite aside from prudential concerns (that is, would it work?), American political culture simply would not permit truly serious contemplation of a surprise nuclear attack on the Soviet Union. This is not to deny that for a period in the late 1950s and early 1960s, when the U.S. strategic nuclear deterrent comprised essentially the manned bomber force, the United States was prepared to attack preemptively, but there is a major difference between being prepared to attack if one learns that an assault is being mounted (preemption: launch on tactical or strategic warning) and being prepared to attack because one believes that war is very likely to occur (prevention: launch in anticipation).[20]

U.S. policymakers have long been attracted to the idea of rollback on the grounds (*inter alia*) that it would help establish a more healthy symmetry of concerns between the rival alliance leaders. It is frustrating to be engaged, *faute de mieux*, in a long-term struggle wherein it is only areas of predominant U.S. interest that are in live political contention. U.S. officials from the days of President Truman to the present have quite rightly rejected the proposition that what is theirs is theirs, whereas what is ours is negotiable; however, the structure of the contest has not permitted much action in support of that rejection.

For many years after the initial Soviet occupation and/or domination of east-central Europe (1944-48), there was U.S. and some allied support of romantic ventures for the liberation of the Baltic states, Albania, and even the Ukraine—not to mention U.S. backing for the regime of the Kuomintang that Chiang Kai-shek established on Taiwan following his defeat on the mainland. Yet for all the plots that were hatched and the words of sympathy that were issued by American politicians and officials, the plain fact remains that the United States has taken no action worthy of note to challenge the Soviet ability to hold its imperium in Europe. The United States (and NATO) did nothing to assist the East Germans in their rising in 1953, the Hungarians (and Poles) in 1956, or the Czechs in 1967-68. The more recent case of Poland again saw the United States fairly strong on gestures but notably weak in direct support. An arguably important contextual distinction between Poland in 1981-82 and Hungary and Czechoslovakia in the 1950s and 1960s is that the Soviet Union had acquired military parity-plus over the West by the later date; the United States has no plausible theory of compellence in the 1980s. Also, Poland is far more important geostrategically to the Soviet Union than is Hungary or even Czechoslovakia.

The worldwide public that is attentive to Soviet-American rivalry should have concluded from the events of 1956 that if the United States was not prepared to fight for "free Hungary" then, it will hardly choose to assume even moderate risks on behalf of any other satellite in revolt. Hungary in 1956 constituted the best political cause, in the context of the most advantageous state of Soviet-American strategic (im)balance, that is likely ever to obtain. The United States did not back the new government of Imre Nagy in Hungary for the excellent reason that the American interest in Hungary was well short of vital, whereas the Soviet imperial interest was probably of a survival character. The Soviet Union had to fight to retain control of Hungary if it was to restore respect for its power throughout eastern Europe and not risk losing authority at home. Nikita Khrushchev himself would have been at political risk had the Hungarian revolution not been suppressed in a suitably exemplary manner.

The American and NATO role with respect to Hungary in 1956 and Czechoslovakia in 1968 was profoundly inglorious, but it was prudent. The United States is not going to challenge the Soviet Union over an issue that a Soviet government, any Soviet government, is obliged as an imperial power to contest *à outrance*. It is stirring rhetoric to talk, as did John F. Kennedy in his inaugural speech, of being prepared to "pay any price, bear any burden, meet any hardship, support any friend, oppose any foe to assure the survival and the success of liberty." But such rhetoric is not and cannot be true. Khrushchev might have blinked in the face of an American military guarantee to the Nagy regime in Hungary, but he would have had good reasons not to do so. The balance of military power is always important, but it can be dominated in significance by the balance in the quality of political interests.

The fact of the matter is that the United States has not been prepared to risk military confrontation with the Soviet Union over the issue of Soviet control of any of the countries liberated by the Soviet Army in 1944-45. Many Hungarians failed to appreciate this fact in 1956, but the Czechs certainly recognized it in 1967-68. It is worth nothing that in its turn the Soviet Union has been scarcely less cautious than has the United States in directing policy against countries in Europe that are recognized to be within the security orbit of the other superpower. The recurring Soviet offensives against the cohesiveness of the Western Alliance are political, not overtly military. It is the strong Soviet preference to destroy NATO by a judicious mix of intimidation and bribery. Catalysts for the break-up or massive erosion of Western Alliance ties would include the self-regarding actions of western Europeans fearful of Soviet military power; the apparent provocation of Soviet power that might occur as a result of vigorous defense preparation in the West; and high anxiety over the functioning of the nuclear-dependent security system itself, which, like the interlocking alliance systems of 1914, seems to some people to carry a high risk of war.

If a U.S. government decided to carry the political offensive against the Soviet imperium to the point where it would stand behind a revolutionary anti-Soviet regime in eastern Europe, then essentially it would have taken a decision for war. It is just barely possible to argue that the Soviet government paced its reaction to events in Hungary in the fall of 1956, waiting to see how resolute the United States would be. But it is inconceivable that any Soviet government would retreat from empire under American threat in the late 1980s and the 1990s. If there are U.S. enthusiasts for the peacetime rollback of Soviet power from eastern Europe today, they should understand that the same strength of the political defensive that provides some compensation for NATO's military deficiencies also applies on the other side of the dividing line. In order to offset the quality of Soviet imperial interests in East Germany or Poland for example, the United States would require strategic superiority of the most splendid kind—and even that would probably not suffice, because it is exceedingly unlikely that any U.S. president would be able to explain satisfactorily why he *chose* to wage a nuclear war over an issue that was less than vital to U.S. interests, however central it might have been to U.S. principles.

Soviet authority does not retreat voluntarily from positions gained, and Soviet success in the military competition over the past twenty years insures that there is no predictable reason why Soviet authority should be compelled to retreat in the near future. Nevertheless, the United States does have a rollback option that warrants endorsement as policy. Beyond the east-central European core regions of the Soviet empire, particularly in the Middle East, Africa, and Central America, there is a Soviet military-backed, political action offensive that can indeed be rolled back with little or no risk of direct Soviet-American military confrontation. Unlike an eastern European country, Third World countries can be offered, at little U.S. risk, whatever kind and quantity of American assistance may be needed in order to turn back KGB and Soviet-surrogate influence.

Such a policy of imperial destabilization does pose several dilemmas. First, a low-intensity war (as in Afghanistan) is not necessarily a low-technology war. The U.S. military establishment, while enthusiastic about the imperial embarrassment of the Soviet Union, is typically reluctant to funnel high-technology weapons to combat zones where eventually they are certain to fall into Soviet hands for examination and possible replication and improvement. Second, if the United States supplies "freedom fighters" through a territorially contiguous friendly country, that country may risk Soviet military retaliation (Pakistan is a case in point). Third, the United States is uncomfortable in simultaneously managing a phase of positive political engagement with the Soviet Union and a campaign of selective negative political-military engagement, as at present in Afghanistan, Angola, and Central America. Publicly noticeable efforts to roll back the extended Soviet imperium are held by many U.S. officials and policy commentators to risk poisoning the well of good feeling necessary to the allegedly greater issues of the day which may be at stake in arms-control talks. Finally, the manifestation of U.S. political culture in the oversight prerequisites of a Congress that insists upon the micro-management of foreign policy does not lend itself to the effective conduct of a secret war-in-peace against the extended imperium of the Soviet Union.

It is interesting to note that even a modest rollback policy of imperial destabilization, is continually challenged on a criterion that American colonists in the mid-1770s and the British people in 1940 would have failed to satisfy. Specifically, the U.S. government is tasked to demonstrate that the various insurgencies it supports or wishes to support in the Soviet empire really can succeed. Should the United States encourage apparently hopeless causes? If one wills and encourages the end—the demise of Soviet authority—then one could be held to have some responsibility to provide the means. It seems entirely appropriate for the United States to provide material support to the Afghan freedom fighters (for example) on the excellent grounds that it is not for the United States to decide whether or not a cause is hopeless. Western and Chinese arms admittedly help sustain the revolt, and some moral responsibility pertains thereto. But if a brave people want to fight, even knowing that the U.S. cavalry will not come to rescue them, then I believe they should be provided with the tools to fight effectively.

The United States has no prudent alternative other than to wage political warfare against the Soviet Union. The rollback that is feasible, if difficult, is with respect to the intimidating potential of Soviet military power and the direct and indirect political action of the KGB and its local instruments (the willing and knowing—that is, treasonable—as well as the ignorant). This is not to deny that U.S. endeavors at rollback can be frustrated at source by American ethnocentrism. Communist regimes are very tenacious in their power-holding, and U.S. political culture ever-impatient for swift results is not at all well adapted to provide the kind of steady long-term support that insurgencies typically require.

Nonetheless, the United States has enormous assets vis-à-vis its Soviet rival. For example, it can preach what it attempts to practice and can admit to imperfections. In other words, it has the greatest assets of a propagandist on its side: the truth and the confidence to let the truth be told. If the United States is honest about itself and about its purposes abroad, if it endeavors to confine its expressed ambitions to the scope of its means, and if it respects the interests of others as those others choose to define them, American spokesmen have nothing to fear in the realm of political warfare.

This book has already commented on the U.S. proclivity, to indulge, irregularly and inconsistently, in missionary activity for the great abstractions of freedom and democracy. In practice the United States has neither the physical means nor the political-cultural skills to inoculate every candidate victim of Soviet and Soviet-proxy imperialism with the vaccine of Western enlightenment. In many of the countries that are at risk to the predatory activities of Soviet foreign policy, effective resistance would be better fueled by a hatred of foreigners, by religious zeal, by the plain excitement of insurgency, and by the resentment of a particular kind of oppression than by any love for freedom or democracy recognizable as such in the terms of American political culture. Americans may feel more comfortable and certainly more legitimate in dealing with recognizable democratic political structures as instruments of containment or selective rollback policy. But the U.S. purpose in promoting destabilization in the Soviet extended imperium is to contain and effect some retraction in Soviet power and influence so that Americans may be more secure. Therefore, for the United States as for other countries, "the enemy of my enemy is my friend" (at least in most circumstances; some strategically objective friends can be so malodorous in their domestic political values and practices that they would be a net liability as allies).

While the United States cannot sensibly aspire to roll back the Soviet imperium in Europe either by direct military action from without or sponsored revolution from within, there is a great deal to recommend a reasonably high U.S. profile of political activism in denial of the legitimacy of Soviet authority elsewhere. This analysis has sought to show that a peacetime rollback policy worthy of the name would carry military risks out of all proportion to any reasonable anticipation of gains except with reference to the Soviet extended imperium in the Third World. A satisfied status quo country like the United States (and its allies) can take the political offensive only for profoundly defensive reasons, and the United States has no strong defensive motivation to take high risks in order to challenge the Soviet political writ in east-central Europe. Indeed, it would not be healthy for international peace and security for a Soviet government to believe that it faced an imminent collapse of its *glaçis* in east-central Europe; such a belief stands perpetually as the leading candidate motive for the Soviet Union to decide to go to war. But Soviet anxiety over the reliability of its allies and nervousness over the robustness of the domestic respect and awe in which it is held can be beneficial to international security. Up to a point, but only to a point, the insecurity of empire restrains the imperialist. Beyond that uncertain point—with Austria-Hungary as the classic example[21]—insecurity can prompt external adventure.

To be translated into effective practice, the concept of dynamic containment requires a political offensive. The challenge for U.S. spokesmen is not to defeat Soviet ideas; rather it is to show that Soviet ideas and Soviet practices are far apart, to demonstrate that the United States stands for the right of all countries to develop the institutions they choose, and to thwart by appropriate means those Soviet political actions that could damage U.S. security interests. In many cases those means will not include the prominent American promotion of *American* beliefs. While there is much that is generic to human aspiration in American political ideology, there are also many elements too native to the American experience to flourish in foreign soil.

14

Strategy and Military Power

One is obliged to agree with Secretary of Defense Caspar Weinberger when he writes: "By a truly gargantuan effort—now consuming more than 15 percent of its gross national product—the Soviet Union has become a one-dimensional [i.e., military] superpower. The issue today is whether the United States and its allies are prepared to permit the Soviet Union to establish military superiority it can use for territorial or political advantage."[1] There are grounds for debate over how much deterring Soviet leaders may need, but there is no basis for disputing the proposition that to the degree to which the Soviet Union is a national security problem for the United States, that problem is military for most practical purposes. There are political roots and manifestations, as U.S. allies, friends, and neutrals devise foreign policies in the shadow of Soviet military power, but the proximate source of the problem—Soviet military power—is not in doubt.

The U.S. defense debate rarely if ever proceeds holistically.[2] The essential indivisibility of strategy in operational reality is not well reflected in the heat of public contention. Just as the German general staff enjoyed an excellence in military performance at what is termed the operational level (that is, the planning and conduct of war at the level of army and army group)[3] but was persistently deficient in its approach to strategy (the planning and conduct of war above the level of an army group), so the U.S. defense establishment today gives the appearance of being incapable of grasping the scope and structure of war as a whole.

Much of the strategic thinking in the U.S. Department of Defense and in the separate armed services reflects parochial concerns to provide rationales for desired programs, to protect roles and missions (whence come programs) and hence budgets. Typically, that thinking does not accommodate a reasonably coherent vision of a genuinely national, let alone inter-allied, military strategy for deterrence and defense. The total architecture of national security policy, its driving commitments, and national military strategy need to constitute a tolerably harmonious whole if individual service initiatives are not to present more difficulties than solutions.

Writing early in 1986, Weinberger advised: "Today, we face the challenge of *the third phase of containment: containment of the Soviets' massive military power*. Having failed to achieve its ideological or geopolitical ambitions, the Soviet Union in the early 1960s, launched the largest military buildup in world history" (emphasis added). In the first or ideological phase, in the middle to late 1940s, the United States prevented "a combination of ideological appeal and internal subversion from seizing power in nations vital to U.S. interests." The second or geopolitical phase of containment, which Weinberger rightly associates with the 1950 policy document NSC-68, "reflected our fundamental interest in preventing the Eurasian landmass from being dominated by a hostile power."[4] To date, the maritime alliance between continental-insular and Rimland states has effected this Mackinderesque policy successfully. Notwithstanding Weinberger's somewhat fanciful and oversimple labeling of phases, his historical schema does have the merit both of pointing to the military character of the contemporary Soviet problem and of highlighting the geopolitical meaning of containment policy.

The Soviet quest for total security will be thwarted and contained neither by superior Western GNP performance nor by superior appeal in Western political ideas. The Roman threat to Carthage and the Nazi-German threat to Europe were both military in kind. The success of the former and the failure of the latter say nothing about the quality of the civilizations and cultures of the societies in conflict. There are many historical analogies to Weinberger's "third phase of containment," though American political culture certainly is not steeped in historical consciousness—a long-standing condition in large measure produced by the distinctive American experience in creating a new nation but accelerated by a deplorable antihistorical (or ahistorical, at best) trend in public school curricula. As a result, deficiencies in the historical scope of official explantions of policy are not likely to be made up from the educational resources of many individual Americans. They lack the training.[5]

The national security policies of tribes, nations, states, and empires are not eternal. The Soviet Union is most unlikely to modernize in a liberal direction, selectively embracing elements of a free market economy and developing institutions for the manifestation of political pluralism. But political, economic, and technological forces within and without the Soviet imperium are certain to alter the terms of security relations between the Soviet state and the outside world. To believe that there will not be any Historic Compromise, Grand Bargain, or general political settlement that would benignly redefine the terms and instruments of the security relations of East and West is not to believe that there can be no relief from the perils of the arms race or, more accurately, from the perils of the political antagonism that fuels competition in armaments.

Dreams of universal imperium, missionary zeal derived from a historic duty to spread a faith, very powerful internal pressures to enhance security through imperial expansion, and the like neither began nor likely will conclude with the Soviet Union—barring a general nuclear catastrophe. Soviet power as a military problem for the West is not dissimilar from the thousand-year threat (in the third to thirteenth centuries) that nomadic tribes from central Asia posed first to the Roman Empire and then to Christian Europe.[6] As further examples, militant Islam posed a military threat to the warrior kings of Christian Europe from the seventh century to the tenth, just as a resurgent Christian Europe posed a military threat to the Mediterranean littoral of the Islamic world from the close of the eleventh century to late in the thirteenth.[7]

In all of the cases cited the threat was military, not economic or ideological (religious), and in none of the cases was a potentially definitive military solution available as a policy option. Geography and the "loss-of-power gradient" precluded a quest for clear-cut solutions to the Romans' "Barbarian problem," the Franks' "Islamic problem," and the Moslems' "Frankish problem"; today the existence of nuclear weapons precludes even the contemplation of any attempt to dismantle the Soviet imperium definitively.

When Caspar Weinberger and others make somewhat disparaging reference to the military unidimensionality of Soviet superpower, one should not be misled into believing that the Soviet empire has about run its course because it has *only* military-coercive strength in its favor. The glory of medieval Kievan Russia was razed by Subedei's Mongols in 1240; the culturally spectacular final phase of the Byzantine experience was terminated by the superior military power of Mohammed II, "the Conqueror," in 1453. Mohammed completed the work of destruction so ably begun by the Fourth Crusade with its sack of Constantinople in 1204. History does not demonstrate that the pen and the brush are consistently mightier than the sword.

The evidence indicates both that Soviet state ideology is tired and can inspire only those who are heroically ignorant or conveniently stupid, and that the Soviet economic system is endemically ill conditioned to compete effectively in the long run with free-market systems. Unfortunately for the Western democracies, the undeniable weaknesses in the Soviet empire are not likely to effect a benign transformation in the Soviet state, or in Soviet national security policy, in the near future. Though history records that totalitarian states can be tranformed forcibly as a consequence of thoroughgoing defeat in war—Nazi Germany, Imperial Japan—transformation from within is not at all a reliable prospect (contemporary China may, just possibly, prove to be the exception). Political philosophers and economic historians may note the internal inconsistencies and demonstrable fallacies of Marxist theory, and Western observers may notice the cynicism of Soviet citizens toward their state religion, but the declining political potency of the state ideology may be a matter of little practical consequence. An obligatory state religion, to which one accords occasional and nominal conformity, may have the stabilizing and comforting quality of familiarity. In addition to legitimizing Soviet authority, Soviet ideology undoubtedly benefits by its identification with (some of) the deeds and symbols of a Soviet state that Great Russians equate with historic Russia. The Soviet state and Soviet state power are deemed inevitable; no practical alternatives are even conceivable to Soviet citizens who have no personal memory of any other political system and who lack even a myth of some lost golden age.

With respect to the world beyond the territorially contiguous Soviet imperium in Eurasia, one should not forget that Soviet methods and material strengths are far more important sources of influence for Moscow than are Soviet political and economic ideas. Americans like to believe that American-style democracy is on the march and that a more or less free-market economy is an essential precondition for the functioning of a pluralistic political system. These beliefs are neither unworthy nor wholly untrue, but in much of the world they are simply irrelevant.[8] The client-state structure of an extended imperium that the Soviet Union has acquired over the past quarter-century derives scarcely, if at all, either from the clients' conviction that Marxist-Leninist ideology is somehow more true than its doctrinal rivals or from the belief that Soviet economic ideas and practice are in any abstract sense superior to the alternatives. Soviet clients in Central America, Africa, the Middle East, and Asia have signed up for relationships of reciprocal net advantage. The Soviet Union, directly or indirectly, provides the physical means and administrative methods whereby their local clients can consolidate internal authority and possibly, with a variable measure of Soviet support, expand that authority over neighboring lands.

It is a matter of only limited interest to Americans, then, to be told that "in 1986, as we watch the embers of communist ideology burning low, this threat [of ideological appeal and internal subversion] has been met. Never since 1917 has communist ideology appealed less and to fewer, and for better reasons, that it does today."[9] Empire has a way of providing its own justification. The Roman Empire managed adequately for three centuries with a state religion/ideology focused upon the deification of the emperor, to which few thinking people paid more than occasional and nominal obeisance. There is no good reason to doubt that Marxism-Leninism is more than capable of handling the modest amount of political traffic required of it.[10] Those in the West who point with satisfaction to the structural weaknesses in the Soviet economy that persist for reasons of the political control needs of the CPSU, as well as to the economic disadvantages imposed by an unfriendly Russian physical geography, are on far more solid ground than are those who choose to be heartened by the declining vibrancy of Soviet ideological appeal. Even so, caution is very much in order.

First, prosperous societies with dynamic economies are not, *ipso facto*, well defended. If the Soviet state is able and willing to channel scarce economic resources into national security functions, at the expense of popular living standards, it may succeed in sustaining a tolerable or even favorable military balance with its external foes. The Western world does enjoy a commanding economic advantage over the Soviet Union. The most relevant national economies in 1984 (1983 for Japan) have been priced as follows: United States, $3.6 trillion; NATO (non–U.S.), $2.7 trillion; Japan, $1.1 trillion; Soviet Union, $1.6-$1.9 trillion; and Warsaw Pact (non–Soviet Union), $394-$739 billion.[11] But wealth and national security are very different properties. The Soviet Union copes with a U.S. economy that is approximately twice the size of its own by devoting to defense some two and a half to three times the U.S. proportion of economic resources. The percentage of GNP allocated to defense in the United States is hovering just above 6 percent; the comparable figure for the Soviet Union (granted the great difficulty in accounting) appears to lie in the range of 15 to 18 percent.[12]

Second, although on narrow economic grounds the long-run competitive prospects for the Soviet Union do not look bright, Western policymakers should never forget the sources of compensating advantage upon which the Soviet Union can draw. These include the long-demonstrated ability to hold down living standards in the interest of defense preparation; the ability to seek military-technological excellence on a very selective basis through concentration of effort; the ability to provide quantity in lieu of quality, again selectively; the political feasibility of employing tactical, and perhaps even strategic, surprise as a force multiplier;[13] a relatively favorable geostrategic context for threat and *invasion on the ground* in west-central Europe; and, finally, the force-multiplying benefit of unity in political-military command.[14]

Third, the economic underpinnings of military competition, let alone of the actual conduct of war, have a way of changing under the pressure of events. As British and French defense planners discerned correctly in 1938-39, the German economy was in key respects—particularly in ready access to critical raw materials—fundamentally ill conditioned to support a long war.[15] Hitler managed (one cannot say solved) his economic problems through expansion of his economic base (the acquisition of Czechoslovakia);[16] through securing economic tribute from the Soviet

Union between August 1939 and June 1941 in return for territorial concessions (naturally, at the expense of others);[17] and by massive innovation
in the development of substitute materials.

The German example of 1939-45 in the waging of a war that the
country was so economically ill equipped to conduct[18] should recommend some caution on the part of those western analysts who are inclined
to be optimistic about the future course of the Soviet-American competition. The steady U.S. conduct of a national security policy of dynamic
containment could eventually see the effective demotion of the Soviet
Union to the status of a second-class superpower. But like Nazi Germany
in 1938 and 1939, the Soviet Union does have several options—of varying
feasibility and risk—for achieving more effective competition.

- First, it might undertake thoroughgoing domestic economic reform to raise dramatically the productivity of the Soviet economy.
  This is very unlikely, because it would threaten central political
  control by the CPSU. The newest leadership in Moscow has given
  no persuasive indication of a willingness to dismantle thoroughly
  the essentially Stalinist structure and ethos of centralized economic management.[19]
- Second, it might improve efficiency through tighter worker discipline and marginally improved economic incentives, as well as
  redouble efforts to improve productivity through selective, highly concentrated infusions of new Western technology (purchased
  or stolen) and, where politically tolerable, management methods.
- Third, over the long run, Moscow could seek favorable terms of
  trade with advanced Western economies through the manipulation of perceptions of military threat. While there is always a
  danger that Soviet statecraft might overplay its hand, intimations
  of security or insecurity on the part of western Europeans are
  very substantially in the gift of the Soviet Union.
- Finally, it might physically seize control of an economic base more
  suitable than its present one for the conduct of global military
  competition with the United States. Given the risks to its homeland and the damage that might be wrought to the economic
  "prizes" at issue, however, one would expect Soviet leaders to be
  far more interested in securing gain through intimidation than
  through an old-fashioned attempt at territorial conquest. War as a
  policy carries the dangers of nuclear escalation, peril to the victor's inheritance, and subsequent difficulties for reliable imperial
  policing.

Commentators may speculate on the ability of the Soviet system that
favors reliability of political control over economic productivity and effi-

ciency to compete satisfactorily with the Western Alliance. But the indications are that given their respective strengths and weaknesses, there is likely to be a balance (or worse, for the West) between the two parties. Recognizing as a "third revolution in military affairs" the military significance of electronic microcircuitry, directed-energy technologies, and genetic engineering,[20] the Soviet defense establishment has concentrated its efforts so as to achieve clear leadership in the field of genetic engineering for chemical/biological warfare (CBW) application;[21] it may well be ahead of the United States in directed energy; and it is buying and stealing what it can in the area of rapid information processing.

The Soviet Union today has armament in depth.[22] Moreover, notwithstanding the general Western lead in high technology, the Soviet Union has succeeded in applying high enough technology where it matters most: "The West has largely lost the technological edge in conventional equipment which allowed NATO to believe that quality could substitute for numbers."[23] The technological superiority of a society can be militarily decisive only if it is reflected on a large scale in the military establishment or the enemy is technologically very backward or the enemy lacks powerfully compensating advantages of its own. New technology for military application can be assessed responsibly only in some particular, postulated military environments. Too much of the promise of new emerging technology for NATO defense remains promise rather than weapons in the arsenal, and it is debated as a panacea more than as a vital element in a well-rounded combined-arms theory of war.

The "third phase of containment" should see the maritime alliance of the West seek and adopt those "competitive strategies" that play to Western strengths and to Soviet vulnerabilities, as the U.S. Department of Defense has been emphasizing.[24] But the competitive strategies must yield exploitable advantages vis-à-vis a Soviet military threat that is global, prospectively permanent, and directed by political leaders who, should they ever come to consider seriously the use of military power directly against the West, would likely be exceedingly difficult to deter.

There is some truth in the proposition that since strategy is an output of organization, to improve the organization should be to improve the strategy it produces. Belief in this proposition is fundamental to the advice tendered by the various bodies exploring the realm of U.S. military reform and defense reorganization. The most heavyweight of these, the President's Blue Ribbon Commission on Defense Management, in its report of February 28, 1986, set forth this damning indictment: "Today, there is no rational system whereby the Executive Branch and the Congress reach coherent and enduring agreement on national military strategy, the forces to carry it out, and the funding that should be provided—

in light of the overall economy and competing claims on national resources. The absence of such a system contributes substantially to the instability and uncertainty that plague our defense program."[25]

There is a great deal to be said in favor of rationality and coherence, but there is even more to be said in favor of selecting the right strategy. The German general staff under Alfred von Schlieffen in 1891-1906 and then under Helmuth von Moltke ("the Younger") in 1906-14 devised a rational and coherent strategy—which was fundamentally flawed for the rapid, sequential destruction of French and then Russian military power.[26] I am concerned at the growing popularity of the fallacious assumption that the route to sensible strategy must lie through this or that preferred form of defense reorganization. Organizational improvement is no panacea; it will not necessarily facilitate greater competence in strategic thought.

It is not difficult to see why coherence in national military strategy— or even the existence of anything worth calling national military strategy—tends to be elusive for the United States.[27] U.S. policymakers must endeavor to cope with some major complications. First, their base is a U.S. political and strategic culture that is ahistorical in its worldview, that expects near-term happy endings, and that is not reliably reconciled to a policy involving prospectively permanent U.S. containment of Soviet power and influence.

Second, the principal external problem is an adversary that is about as remote from the American experience and condition—geopolitically, geostrategically, and culturally—as any fiction writer could have imagined. From 1941 to 1945, Japan was a vastly overextended insular empire that could be strangled economically by superior maritime-air power, as well as outmaneuvered by the country that enjoyed the initiative and the resources to exploit that initiative. Nazi Germany was a continental landpower that the United States alone could not have overcome.[28] But Hitler's statecraft was so inept that his armed forces were grossly overextended on land and mightily distracted on the Eastern Front, making the allied invasion of France possible. By way of contrast, the enemy of the United States today is *the* first-class continental landpower, is economically self-sufficient to a degree not remotely approached by the Central and Axis Powers that Western navies blockaded in the two world wars, and would be unlikely to be distracted for long in continental Eurasian campaigns by extra-U.S. efforts (always presuming that the Soviet Union sensibly declines to campaign deep in China).

Third, warfare today is unprecedentedly complex. The United States must plan to play a leading role in combat on land, at sea, in the air, and in space for the purpose of deterring, and if need be defending against, a landpower with a central geostrategic position, an intercontinental nuclear reach, and at least the beginnings of a global maritime capability.[29]

Furthermore, whether or not they are actually used, nuclear weapons will cast a shadow over any and every clash of Soviet-American arms. Should a Soviet *attaque brusquée*[30] in Europe fail after the fashion of the Schlieffen Plan, the Soviet High Command (unlike Erich von Falkenhayn, who had to answer the question of what to try next when the great offensive in the West was beaten back early in September 1914) would have the option of vertical escalation as an alternative to an armistice, to horizontal escalation,[31] or to acceptance of a long war of attrition.

Fourth, in geopolitical perspective, U.S. national security policy is very much a coalition enterprise. Given the insularity and the irregular crusading preference of its political culture, the United States has performed better as principal Western guardian of an international order keyed to the persistent containment of Soviet power than anyone could reasonably have expected in the mid-1940s. However, the alliance performance of U.S. security partners in Europe and the Pacific reflects the terms and conditions of the late 1940s and early 1950s rather than those of the 1980s. Basic military relations between the United States and its Eurasian allies remain essentially those of a guardian and its wards. The European allies dare not cut free from the U.S. security guarantee, but the societies of western Europe neither steadily share the most widely held U.S. view of the Soviet threat nor place much trust in the wisdom of the U.S. government's global practice of containment. The difficulties of coalition management embrace the U.S. need to accommodate or resist both local assertions of security priorities in Europe and Asia and the wishes and complaints of the U.S. political system concerning the proper conduct of collective security. The U.S. government must deal simultaneously with allies whose definition of interests is not identical to Washington's and with a domestic public and its elected political representatives frequently insensitive to the force of necessity in international security affairs.[32]

In the face of these complexities, it is hardly surprising that officials, legislators, and expert commentators talk more about priorities and the virtues of strategy than about the content of priorities and the actual detail of preferred strategy. U.S. military priorities must be rank-ordered at the most general and important of levels. This ordering should be seen as only the conceptual foundation for national military strategy; it is not such a strategy itself. Nevertheless, sensitive though I am to potential charges of geopolitical determinism, I believe that rank-ordering is geostrategically inescapable if the United States is prepared to pay more than lip service to rigorous strategic thinking. *In descending order of importance, the United States must attend to its strategic forces, maritime forces, and ground and tactical air forces.* The fact that the Soviet adversary remains above all else a continental landpower does not mean that U.S. landpower is necessarily the measure of effective military containment.[33]

Without prejudice toward particular theories of nuclear deterrence, it has to be the case that should U.S. strategic forces be unable through deterrence to fence a conflict against deliberate vertical escalation by the Soviet Union, or alternatively provide for the physical defense of the American homeland, U.S. national survival would be highly improbable.[34] It is no overdramatization to assert, simply and really irrefutably, that it is the strategic forces—in whatever mix of offensive and defensive elements—and only the strategic forces that directly protect the United States from the sole immediate military threat to its national survival. Additional threats to U.S. political survival do lurk in the possibly adverse evolution of the balance of power in Eurasia; indeed, it is these threats that provided the structure of Mackinder's and Spykman's geopolitical theories, and that explain the sense in a U.S.-Rimland coalition strategy for Eurasia.[35] Nonetheless, the one temporally immediate military threat to U.S. national survival is posed by the strategic offensive forces of the Soviet Union.

It would be highly desirable for U.S. strategic forces to have coercive, compellent value. Under the rubric of extended deterrence and controlled and flexible response, the United States and NATO both hope and pretend that such value does obtain. However, in the absence of a very convincing ability to limit damage to the American homeland,[36] U.S. policymakers would be wise to confine their strategic-force ambitions to the deterrence of Soviet intercontinental attack.[37] Strategic forces should be considered carefully in both negative and positive roles. In their negative role strategic forces function as a *counter*deterrent. They would deny the Soviet Union the rational use of its own strategic forces for prompt military effect in a search for quick victory. The threats to be deterred include both coercive strikes for political intimidation and counterforce assault intended physically to arrest U.S. ability to prosecute the war. In their positive role strategic forces would have credible—or not incredible—utility in first use.[38] First use has not been emphasized in U.S. public pronouncements, but it remains the key to NATO's theory of deterrence.[39] The emphases on countermilitary and counterpolitical control in U.S. nuclear strategy make sense virtually no matter how extensive the scope of the missions for the strategic forces, but they are close to an absolute requirement if compellent first-use duties for extended deterrence obtain.

It is essential that the United States should have a nuclear strategy and matching forces that are suitably fearsome in terms of Soviet values. It is no less important for Soviet leaders to believe that U.S. offensive forces just might be employed in a desperate endeavor to restore deterrence should the West suffer an unfolding military disaster in some regional conflict. However, in the absence of a clear measure of U.S. strategic superiority, the positive, compellent duties of strategic forces ought to be regarded as an atavistic example of wishful thinking, even if they are a regrettable strategic necessity. Strategic superiority can be defined both relatively—as a very healthy imbalance in the U.S. favor in the ability to wreak harm upon a superpower homeland; and absolutely—as a U.S. ability physically to protect itself against virtually all nuclear threats. The contemporary pretense that extended nuclear deterrence is a realistic and vital component of NATO strategy is harmful because it serves as an excuse for Western countries not to confront actual defense problems and explore possible strategic opportunities.

Nuclear reliance, or rather the pretence of nuclear reliance, gives the appearance of being cheap. But in practice a Western Alliance that dwarfs its Soviet antagonist economically has persuaded itself that it can tolerate both nonnuclear defense capabilities that most likely could hold for only a matter of days and, as a consequence, the threat of having to resort rapidly to what it hopes would be controlled nuclear escalation—even though such escalation would make little military or political sense for NATO. As long as the Soviet motive to attack is healthily very low, the dangerous and fundamentally irresponsible military doctrine of NATO has major merits: it is relatively cheap; it is familiar; and no one in the West in peacetime can demonstrate the probable scale of its folly.

The U.S. strategic-force posture strictly required to play an extended deterrent role in NATO's doctrine of flexible response is one that would deny the Soviet Union militarily attractive first-use options (let alone a first-strike opportunity); could do much damage to the Soviet ability to wage war (regional and central); as the basis of hope for early war termination and the restoration of deterrence, would leave the Soviet state with a great deal left to lose—preeminently its own continued existence. The U.S. problem would be so to employ its strategic offensive forces that the Soviet Union would withdraw its invading armies from western Europe and choose not to strike back at the United States on a scale or in a manner excessive to the level of U.S. interests in the conflict in Europe. Even in the possible context of evolving strategic defenses, the responsible path for U.S. national security policy would seem to be one that restricts the duties of strategic forces to the realm of counterdeterrence. Any value they may have for extended deterrence should be regarded only as a welcome bonus.

As should be plain by this juncture, the granting of first military priority to the strategic forces is not at all keyed to an extravagant notion of the deterrent effect that those forces might be expected to secure.[40] This discussion simply affirms that policy errors with respect to strategic forces, unlike policy errors in other military areas, could place the physical survival of American society immediately at terminal risk. Furthermore, deficiencies in strategic-force posture could negate the value of U.S. and U.S.-allied strengths in seapower and landpower.

It may appear idiosyncratic, or at least highly contentious, to identify maritime and ground (plus tactical air) forces respectively as second and third defense priorities for the United States. Of course seapower and landpower must function synergistically, and advantage at sea has strategic value only for its consequences on land.[41] Nonetheless, notwithstanding the development of nuclear weapons, the rise of "rail-power,"[42] the growth in motor transportation, and the evolution of air travel, the geostrategic fact remains that an insular United States is as dependent in the 1980s upon a working command of the (relevant) sea for the successful prosecution of most military enterprises as was Britain during the Napoleonic Wars.[43] Maritime preponderance is an absolute prerequisite if the United States is to assert its landpower overseas. This is not to deny that weakness in U.S. and U.S.-allied landpower could more than negate the value of U.S. preponderance at sea; certainly, it would diminish the geographical scope of maritime preponderance by rendering "closed seas"—such as the Sea of Japan or the Aegean—and other continental coastal waters intolerably dangerous for naval forces because of land-based air threats.

The case for according maritime forces priority over ground and land-based tactical air forces is thus generically identical to the case for according strategic forces first priority overall. The United States cannot move, reinforce, supply, or rescue expeditionary ground forces or overseas garrisons unless it controls the relevant sea lines of communication. Similarly, no matter how potent the synergism between U.S. seapower and landpower, a war will be lost if the Soviet Union believes it can win a regional or multiregional conflict through a direct nuclear assault upon the U.S. homeland.[44]

The maritime strategy of the U.S. Navy that has evolved in the 1980s transcends, and in my judgment usefully transcends, the strict bare logic of the seapower-landpower connection as specified above. Seapower as a prerequisite for the exercise of landpower by an insular country like the United States need imply only a more or less expansive set of duties in sea-lane protection and perhaps convoy escort. In principle, SLOC protection can be secured by a range of alternative strategies, including close or distant escort, close or distant blockade of the maritime threat to the SLOC, or direct assault upon that maritime threat wherever it may be lurking. Whatever the strategy and tactics preferred, it must be understood that the United States and its allies can use sea lines of communication freely only if they first enjoy a working military command of the seas of most relevance. Relatively unimpeded use of the sea is the principal benefit that accrues from command.[45] For the first time since the Second World War, the U.S. Navy in the 1980s has designed a maritime strategy intended to direct naval power as an offensive instrument critical for the conduct of global war.[46]

The United States and the global alliance that it leads require a grand strategy for the support of dynamic containment in peace and in war.[47] The great debate currently booming on the subject of strategic defense pertains strictly, if importantly, to one element of one dimension of such a grand strategy.[48] Strategic defenses for NATO would protect allied military assets in the European theater against preemptive assault,[49] would help police a regional conflict to discourage escalation, and would enable the Western world to mobilize for war without suffering a fatal nuclear interdiction of that process. The Western Alliance would both mobilize general-purpose military power and, in the high-technology realm, place strategic offensive and defensive developments on a managerial basis somewhat akin to that of the Manhattan Project. To assert these benign consequences, however, is only to set the stage for a global strategy of deterrence through effective defense of all kinds.

The dominant landpower of the age could not easily be deterred from local aggression should it come to believe that such military action could be fenced off from more geographically extensive military consequences. To date, as reflected in NATO's authoritative strategic concept of flexible response, the Western Alliance has sought to deter such aggression as might need deterring by coupling a putative local conflict in western Europe with the central nuclear arsenal of the United States. Since this policy device manifestly has yet to fail and is relatively cheap to sustain, the alliance has been unwilling to assume the risks of major innovation in strategy.

Unfortunately, flexible response enjoys a sharply declining credibility, at least in U.S. minds (one can only speculate concerning Soviet opinions), and there is no dispute worthy of note concerning its prospective undesirability in action. The SDI, if it proceeds to weapons procurement, may well be confined in practice largely to strengthening the prelaunch survivability of the nuclear deterrent, but it is unlikely to restore political and military utility to first nuclear use.[50] For the long term, the West needs a military strategy that is effective and prudent as well as morally tolerable.[51] The solution, albeit an imperfect one, is an attempt increasingly to substitute the threat of long duration and global geographical scope of conflict for that of nuclear escalation at the end of the sputtering fuse from war in Europe.

The extended deterrent of the Western Alliance for an age of strategic nuclear parity or marginal inferiority should no longer be thought and planned to repose primarily in strategic nuclear offensive forces. Rather, the extended deterrent should be the total mobilizable defense potential of the United States and its allies. That defense potential would be knit together, transported, and capable of flexible application in maneuver on a global scale by preponderant Western maritime power. Soviet leaders should understand that if they elect to begin a war in Europe, they will be igniting a global conflict that they are unlikely to be able to win.

This long-term defense design for the West is as easily identified in theory as it would be politically difficult to effect in practice. Its essential elements would be these:

- Maintenance of what should be a definitively discouraging strategic-forces' counterdeterrent (with an evolving mix of offensive and defensive elements).[52]
- Significant improvement in NATO's ability to hold (initially unreinforced) on the Central Front, given the danger of a Soviet surprise attack.[53]
- Enhanced security for U.S. and British reinforcements and resupply on the European continent, from port and airfield to equipment holding points to operational deployment areas.[54]
- Much greater sustainability in war for all NATO ground and tactical air combat formations.[55]
- Serious defense mobilization—of manpower and near- and farther-term equipment—plus plans, organization, and exercises (where suitable) to provide credibility for the protracted conflict with which the West (plus some Asian allies) would wish to threaten the Soviet Union.
- Revival of the mercantile marine assets of the United States.
- Campaign and force planning for the "trailing edge" as well as the "leading edge" of a global war.[56] Because of the risks of nuclear escalation and in recognition of the prospective brevity of NATO's continental resistance, even U.S. maritime strategists tend to eschew campaign planning for a conflict of more than a few weeks' duration. But for deterrent purposes, the Western Alliance requires a theory of victory for a protracted war with the Soviet Union. With some caveats to be noted, the Soviet Union should be placed in a geostrategic position where its military assets would be seriously overextended. The Soviet Union would not enjoy the military superiority that can flow from interior lines of land communication within the Heartland, given the scope of the geography of the conflict in and around Eurasia (from Norway's North Cape to Kamchatka).[57]

The first important caveat is that NATO's Central Front should hold so as to function as an anvil for the blunting of Soviet offensive strength. NATO need not aspire to achieve the military overthrow of Soviet landpower in a war in Europe, but it should aspire so to grind down Soviet military power in that region that the prospect of Soviet defeat elsewhere would be greatly enhanced.[58] U.S. maritime strategists are wont to describe military action on the flanks of the Soviet Union's Western Front as valuable distractors of scarce Soviet resources, energy, and command attention, but such thinking is the linear descendant of much abortive planning and relatively ill-considered and ill-executed action in the two world wars.[59] It is probably more sensible for U.S. defense planners to consider NATO's Central Front as the great distractor, the magnet that should attract the major part of the Soviet general-purpose forces' effort. A Western Alliance at liberty to move forces and project power from the sea where it will should plan and threaten to insert its own forces in strength, to assist local allies, to liberate Soviet subject peoples, and the like, wherever there are objectives of strategic importance that can be secured at reasonable cost.[60]

The second caveat, complementary to the first, is that as little U.S. general-purpose military power be precommitted to the battle for continental Europe as is both politically feasible in the peacetime politics of the alliance and militarily essential for deterrence and defense. Prominent among the long suits of the Western Alliance is its prospective command of the world's oceans. The less the military power of the United States is locked into the territorial defense necessities of continental Europe, the greater the Western power for intervention on the flanks of the Soviet landlocked imperium.[61]

A third caveat is that the United States should balance realistically the military needs of the "anvil" of continental European defense (including reinforcement and resupply) and the "hammer" of force projection from the sea. Readers should not imagine that I am willing to write off NATO-Europe and U.S. assets there in pursuit of what some critics might disparage as idle yet dangerous fantasies of glittering opportunities elsewhere. To do so might, in practice, repeat the errors of Gallipoli and Salonika (in planning and execution) or Mesopotamia (in conception, planning, and execution) in the First World War.[62]

Necessarily, this chapter is very speculative; however, for comparison, there is the fixed element of the current deterrence-defense design. I have sketched in bare outline a global strategy that speaks to Western strengths and Soviet vulnerabilities, that could preclude the need for Western statesmen to face intolerable early wartime decisions on nuclear-weapon employment, and (most important of all) that should be both eminently credible and suitably fearsome in Soviet perspective. Consider the principal alternative in the light of the probable as opposed to the aspiration. I recognize the authority of Clausewitz's concept of "friction" in war and acknowledge readily that war is always a very uncertain enterprise.[63] This book aspires only to help point the way to a national military strategy for the United States that is in keeping with its political and strategic culture yet fits actual and prospective geostrategic needs. In short, the strategy should have a better than even chance of working successfully: preferably, to deter; if need be, to defend and actually to carry a realistic promise of creating conditions in which the Soviet state could be brought down.

Already the United States has adopted a maritime strategy that is global in conception and looks to the aggressive forward application of sea-based power against Soviet landpower;[64] it has adopted operational concepts for integrated conventional ground and air warfare radically more offensive in orientation than those of the 1970s (although, as noted in a previous chapter, the new AirLand Battle doctrine may not be practicable, given the discernible changes in Soviet theater-operational concepts)[65]; it has endeavored (albeit with very limited success) to revitalize mobilization planning for protracted conflict;[66] it recognizes the problems of relying upon strategic nuclear forces as the extended deterrent; it has enhanced the capabilities of and increased operational dependence upon reserve forces;[67] and, finally, it has set in train with SDI what may well become a technically and militarily irresistible tide of diminishing utility for nuclear offensive forces, providing thereby strong fences for the containment of conventional conflict against (vertical) nuclear escalation.

The United States is still a long way from achieving the protracted war capability for deterrence and effective military containment that has been sketched lightly in this chapter. Today, Soviet leaders could aspire to attack in central Europe with a measure of surprise adequate to deny SACEUR (Supreme Allied Commander, Europe) the minimum counter-mobilization time (perhaps ten days) he would need to stand a good chance of thwarting an invasion. Furthermore, Moscow might well anticipate that in such a context any use of nuclear weapons in Europe by NATO would be too little and too late to affect significantly the military outcome of the campaign. As a bonus, Soviet leaders would have some grounds for hoping that Western naval power would take such heavy losses in a short war for Europe that the United States subsequently would lack the means to maneuver globally in the conduct of a protracted war.

It is ironic that a potentially very unstable Soviet empire—surrounded by hostile *Communist (inter alia)* states, commanding by force and habit of obedience a myriad of dissatisfied nationalities, having a state religion of no vitality and an economy that cannot be reformed systemically for reasons of security of central political control, and locked in a condition of antagonism with the major sources of the gross world product—is yet able to confront the Western Alliance with the most terrible of security dilemmas. As an unreformed legacy of the long period of major U.S. nuclear advantage, the Western Alliance leans unnecessarily heavily upon a nuclear crutch that would likely play to the net advantage of Soviet, rather than Western, political culture in time of crisis or war. After all, which states are more likely to be intimidated (deterred or self-deterred) by nuclear threats, those wherein the prospect of "collateral damage" to society can generate popular opposition to state policy or those wherein it cannot?

When one considers the geography of East-West conflict, how can it be that a coalition and its functional allies with economic assets three or four times the scale of those of the Warsaw Pact can yet permit itself to be dependent upon incredible and, if exercised, almost certainly self-defeating threats of nuclear use? The answer lies in the politics of NATO, the unwillingness of the European members of the alliance to change the terms of their security, and the acquiescence of the United States in a strategic grand design that meets the interests of the allies as those allies choose to define them.

Recognizing the political realities behind flexible response, and appreciating the possible negative effects of the security shock of any precipitate change in U.S. declaratory strategy,[65] I nonetheless recommend that the United States should seriously consider eschewing (as operational strategy) the *initiation* of central nuclear operations. Furthermore, as a vital complement to nuclear deemphasis, the United States should so modernize its strategic forces that Soviet leaders could calculate no advantage in *their* initiating such operations. As always, the problem would be the territorial defense of western Europe. The United States should make it plain to its European allies that it would not execute its plan for central nuclear war in the event of defeat in Europe.[69] The extended deterrent of the United States and any of its allies willing and able to fight on would be the capability to mobilize for and to conduct a protracted global war. The core of deterrence would be Soviet understanding that however well they might fare in a campaign in Europe, they could not guarantee that the campaign would be synonymous with the war as a whole.

Such a shift in emphasis in military strategy would reflect far more accurately the true balance between intensity of risks and quality of interests for the United States. It need not promote a decline in deterrent effect, since gain in prospective credibility should compensate for loss of Soviet anticipation of a dangerous gallop to nuclear holocaust, and it should be politically and ethically far more tolerable for Western political culture than is the shaky reed of an incredible and irresponsible nuclear dependency.

The NATO-European countries would be very restrained in their enthusiasm for the new strategy. Should their hostility pose a fundamental threat to the integrity of the strategy—as is entirely possible—the United States would need to decide whether to acquiesce in the fact of a deficiency of cooperation or to effect a radical restructuring of its military commitments. Given the importance of the barrier role of some of the European allies in keeping Soviet power landlocked, given the absolute economic importance of western Europe, and given the strength of the western European interest in maintaining a tangible transatlantic security nexus, the United States should be able, and would be able, and would be wise, to implement much of its new strategy design in an evolutionary fashion, avoiding a formal challenge to flexible response. In some important respects, after all, the United States is already well on the strategy road recommended here.

15

Conclusions

This book has explained that U.S. national security policy first, must be responsive to geopolitical realities; second, must be tolerable for American political and strategic culture; and third, sets requirements for strategy which, in its turn, has implications for the force posture and deployment that must implement strategy. In addition, this book has explained that basic national security concepts reflect fundamental judgments concerning the identity and worth of those national interests that merit military support in the last resort. Ideally, national security policy, strategy, and military force would interrelate harmoniously, but in practice there is often disharmony. It might be argued that the choice of a basic national security concept is of less importance for the safety and well-being of Americans than is the achievement of an appropriate match between ends and means. I have rejected the various U.S. disengagement options discussed in Chapter 12 under the headings of devolution and fortress America, but those concepts would likely serve Americans better as policy guides than would forward, global containment ideas that were not backed by appropriate strategy and forces.

If the United States, in close collaboration with its Eurasian allies, is unable to sustain the defense equilibrium (which is not to be confused with an arithmetic notion of an even military balance) that is needed to offset Soviet military power and deny success to Soviet policies of intimidation, then discussion of national interests, national security concepts, and even of strategy is largely irrelevant. It does not much matter what goals American statesmen believe the United States should pursue for international order; what matters is what the United States and its allies are prepared to pay for.[1] A global policy requires global capabilities for its effective implementation.

For the foreseeable future the Soviet Union will remain committed irrevocably to the conduct of political warfare against the West. It has sought and acquired the military means substantially to balance the political value of American military power, insofar as that power is intended to help sustain the political independence of countries around the periphery of Eurasia. Soviet military power certainly has a primary defensive mission: to secure the extant holdings of the insecure Soviet empire. But for both defensive and offensive reasons that power is also intended, *faute de mieux*, to be the primary instrument for Soviet advantage in the long-term struggle with the United States. Soviet leaders will not gamble gratuitously with the assets of their patrimony, but neither will they cease to work to restrict the effectiveness of the United States as the linchpin of the only international security order alternative to their own.

Contrary to the enduring aspirations of some American scholars and commentators, a general settlement—though not a tactical *modus viven-di*—in Soviet-American relations is structurally impossible pending fundamental change in the nature of the Soviet state (and perhaps not even then). The United States cannot accord the Soviet Union the Soviet definition of its proper place in the sun. That definition of its rightful place shifts with Soviet assessment that the correlation of forces has altered, and this *Realpolitik* theme is complicated by Soviet ideological necessities that bear upon the fundamental legitimacy of the CPSU's right to rule in Greater Russia.

Since there has never really been a general settlement, or peace, of more than transient authority in the recorded history of international politics,[2] I am not being unduly pessimistic in asserting the prospective permanence of a condition of war-in-peace, or occasionally violent peace, between the superpowers. The extraordinary feature of the present geopolitical scene is the likely duration of an essentially bipolar system of military competition and very limited cooperation. In past systems of international order in Europe-oriented security politics, the great powers were always in more or less rapidly shifting constellations of rival alliance entanglements. The rigidity of the present system—and the reason for the long dark tunnel of Soviet-American struggle that drives some commentators in search of panaceas—derives from the military preeminence of the superpowers. Because of the weight of its national security assets, the source of the U.S. guardianship role for international order, the United States cannot help but function as the principal object of Soviet hostility: it is capable of thwarting or—in Soviet perspective—delaying the march of progress in history.

Although unrelenting political struggle is the essence of the Soviet-American relationship, partial accommodation and tactically convenient settlement of particular issues is ever possible because of nuclear anxieties or economic strain.[3] Detente as a theme in U.S. foreign policy is fully compatible with the concept of containment. However, an easing of tensions symbolized by limited agreements for limited purposes must not be permitted to mislead Western polities into believing that a *basic* settlement of differences is possible between East and West. The Soviet Union employs policies of tactical accommodation as an instrument of political warfare, intended over the long term to contribute usefully to the demise of security structures that stand in its way. The Soviet Union defines its relations with the United States in the very existence of the United States as the principal organizer of and security producer for a security system alternative to its own.

The portrait is grim, but it is the only portrait of the Soviet Union that the evidence will support. The monstrous tyranny of the CPSU, sustained cynically and ironically in the name of the people, is by no means the first and is unlikely to be the last state-organized threat to the humane values of Western civilization, or to the physical existence or political independence of its peoples.[4] Far from being pessimistic, the discussion in this book suggests that the security problems posed by Soviet power are eminently solvable—at least in the sense that those problems can be treated as a condition that no prudent Soviet leaders should be able to transform greatly to the Soviet advantage by intimidation or by overt violence.

The central themes of this book—geopolitics, strategic culture, and national security—have been developed so as to articulate the view that there is a reasonably well-settled structure to the U.S. national security context. This structure is of long standing, can be presented at varying levels of sophistication, and has identifiable implications for U.S. policy. The Soviet Union is the Heartland superpower. It is the still-landlocked continental superstate that has been bequeathed by its distinctive history a political culture and strategic style which—when married to a permissive balance of power[5]—is profoundly threatening to the security of the "Marginal Crescent"[6] of peripheral Eurasia and, ultimately, even to the insular continental-scale democracy that is the United States. The Soviet Union of this book is not a quasi-theocratic empire masquerading as a normal great power; neither is it a superpower-sized organized conspiracy run by gangster-statesmen. Instead, the Soviet Union delineated here is the Great Russian imperium organized by and for the greater satisfaction of patriotic Great Russians, legitimized by a transnational ideology that is entirely a tool of control for the ruling political elite. The question of the degree to which the rulers of the Soviet Union believe in Marxism-Leninism is as unanswerable as it is ultimately uninteresting. Indeed, so rich were the voluminous writings of the founding theorists and theorist-practitioners, and so continuous is the process of ideological revelation, that faith and expediency can always achieve a convenient accommodation.

The Soviet-American rivalry is but the latest manifestation of the landpower-seapower antagonism of which Halford Mackinder wrote so eloquently more than eighty years ago.[7] In dereliction of geopolitical duty, the Western leaders of the Grand Alliance permitted Nazi Germany to be defeated in such a way that the Red Army would liberate most of the

Balkans, occupy Prague, take Vienna and Berlin, and advance to the Elbe. The manner in which Churchill and Roosevelt won the war guaranteed that their countries, and indeed the Western world in general, would be in severe danger of losing the peace.[8]

The Soviet Union is both a territorial and an expanding hegemonic empire. The problems of security, even survival, that it poses for the United States are both immediate and long term. There is an immediate danger that some planned or unplanned crisis might explode through a process of very rapid escalation to the level of a central nuclear war; however implausible the political scenarios for the triggering of such a war, it is an ever-present possibility. Over the long term there is a danger to U.S. national security, even to U.S. physical or political survival, in the dynamic working of the contemporary balance-of-power system. Through a variety of nonexclusive means the Soviet Union could become the more and more undisputed organizer of security in Eurasia.[9] The instruments of expanding imperium include subtle and unsubtle intimidation, exemplary punishment or disciplining of recalcitrant allies and neutrals, and old- fashioned military intervention. In fear of Soviet power, out of distress at U.S. policy, or in attempted reassertion of national or regional independence, U.S. clients could cut adrift from the maritime alliance. Alternatively, the United States could decide that the risks and economic costs of forward security commitments in Eurasia were no longer in step with the evolving identity and quality of U.S. interests.

This book is not much concerned with the detail of prediction; the forward and global containment policy of the United States could come unraveled for a variety of reasons. After all, that policy has remained unaltered in its essentials while the economic position of the United States vis-à-vis its major allies and military position vis-à-vis its principal antagonist have both shifted cumulatively to the U.S. disadvantage. Nonetheless, the containment concept as broadly conceived since the late 1940s recognizes a long-enduring geopolitical truth that U.S. policymakers would deny only at great peril to the national security. Peripheral Eurasian security structures alternative to the U.S.-organized alliance and compatible with U.S. vital interests are, and prospectively will long remain, almost pure fantasy. The most plausible alternative is not a genuinely multipolar world, wherein Soviet ambitions would be checked by a Sino-Japanese alliance, a European defense community, and the like. Instead, the most probable alternative to U.S.-led forward containment of Soviet Power around the Eurasian Rimland would be a process of gain for Soviet hegemonic influence throughout Eurasia— perhaps not by crude territorial conquest but by more or less gradual local accommodation to expressed or anticipated Soviet strategic wishes.

Understandably and prudently, the power of the Soviet Union that has the greatest psychological impact upon Americans is the destructive potential of its strategic nuclear forces. If the use of that potential is not suitably deterred, then U.S. defense arrangements overall cannot be adequate. However, if Americans will accept the notion of the impracticality of strategic nuclear forces as an instrument of policy except in the context of deterring attack upon their homeland, the national security threats that lurk in geopolitics should become much clearer.[10]

If the Western coalition were to fracture definitively, if perhaps only in Europe, the geostrategic terms of the Soviet-American security relationship could shift dramatically to the medium- or long-term disadvantage of the United States. For all the military dangers and deterrent implausibilities that attend U.S. global strategy today, the Soviet Union is both massively distracted on land in the East and West and landlocked by the barrier functions of those forward-placed U.S. allies whose territory constitutes gateways to the open oceans, through which Soviet seapower must seek transit if it is to escape coastal confinement. The issue is not Soviet seapower per se but the strategic uses to which a no longer reliably landlocked Soviet Union could apply its seapower to influence events ashore.

It has been observed that Americans are a warlike nation but not a military people.[11] Consideration of the geopolitical dimension of Soviet-American relations cannot neglect the domestic political feasibility of alternative national security policies. A question mark must hang over the willingness of the American people, with their insular proclivities, to sustain on an indefinite basis a global policy of forward containment. Steady maintenance of a global balance-of-power policy that eschews even the idea of a happy ending is at variance with important features of American political culture. For example, the American people tend to define conditions to be managed or endured as problems to be solved; to seek in technology the answers to political problems; to simplify into either/or terms issues that really involve a multitude of choices; and to be optimistic about the future.

As explained earlier, American political culture is characterized by the understandable, if erroneous, attitude that peace is the normal condition of humankind; an inclination to personalize international politics (witness the interpretations of the Gorbachev succession offered by the U.S. mass media); a happy conviction that agreement is always possible between people of good will (even if the other side is not obviously led by such folk); and a projection of the American preference for order and stability upon foreign statesmen who may, in practice and by cultural inclination, have a very different world view and agenda. None of these tendencies is particularly helpful to U.S. policymakers, who cannot, responsibly, either effect a U.S. resignation from global security politics and its dangers and costs or take on the Soviet "focus of evil in the modern world" and compel or teach it to mend its ways.

Nonetheless, there are means and a style by which U.S. policymakers can work with American culture without mortgaging the national security unduly. Admittedly, the ideological style in U.S. declaratory policy can be abrasive in its consequences for inter-allied as well as East-West politics. But that style is so deep-rooted in American political culture, speaking as it does to the way Americans conceive of the purposes of their polity, that one is wise to regard it as necessary fuel for the engine of U.S. domestic mobilization for defense. Furthermore, as Caspar Weinberger has recognized, there is an American way in the *effective* use of force that U.S. policymakers ignore at their peril.[12] The U.S. armed forces are the extension and instrument of a popular democracy which requires very considerable convincing that the cause is good and the resort to force necessary before it will sanction the evil of war; American soldiers should be deployed in action only in response to a clear and present danger to vital U.S. interests, and in pursuit of a definable and unmistakable success or victory.[13] American strategic theorists and policymakers must recognize the cultural flaws in the ideas on limited war with which the civilian hierarchy in the defense establishment attempted to validate a very un-American style of war in Vietnam in the 1960s.[14] Those who ignore the constraints of their political culture will not succeed.

The U.S. and alliance strategy recommended in Chapter 14 is not by any means a call for revolution in U.S. military doctrine or security commitments. The key would be the *gradual* replacement of U.S. strategic nuclear forces as the extended deterrent of the West by defense- economic mobilization potential, *in the context of ready military cover against short-war defeat (conventional or nuclear).* However, the strategy does imply a cumulatively noteworthy measure of Europeanization of NATO's forward defense arrangements;[15] much more careful planning of the middle and end games of a global conflict; and provision of a very dissuasive nuclear counterdeterrent to discourage possible Soviet incentives to escalate. Last-ditch dynamic containment would be sustained by Moscow's belief that it could not enforce a sufficiently favorable change in the correlation of forces at the beginning of a war whose duration it would be unable to restrict. This concept addresses the most dire of geopolitical dangers and would enable the United States and the alliance it leads to exploit the geostrategic advantages granted (in principle) by preponderance in a globe-uniting seapower.

In the future, as in the past, it will be the American way to oscillate between surge and coast in military preparedness; to design a strategy for the United States which rested upon any other assumption would be futile. Nonetheless, in the light of the generally adequate U.S. performance in national security policy over the past four decades, a net assessment of Soviet versus Western strengths and weaknesses provides considerable grounds for optimism. Even without a great statesman at the policy helm—though with policymakers who are, one hopes, familiar with the ideas of Halford Mackinder and Nicholas Spykman—Americans should be able to remember that the Soviet Union is going to be an enemy for a long time to come; that Soviet power needs to be distracted by major military tasks on the ground in Eurasia; and that Soviet seapower should be denied access at will to the world's oceans.

Notes

1. Introduction

1. See Edward N. Luttwak: *The Grand Strategy of the Roman Empire: From the First Century A.D. to the Third* (Baltimore; Md.: Johns Hopkins Univ. Press, 1976); and *The Grand Strategy of the Soviet Union* (London: Weidenfeld & Nicolson, 1983).

2. A collection of outstanding essays that address questions of U.S. grand strategy is Robert E. Osgood *et al.*, *Containment, Soviet Behavior, and Grand Strategy*, Policy Papers in International Affairs No. 16 (Berkeley, Calif.: Institute of International Studies, 1981). A useful definition of grand strategy has been suggested by Barry R. Posen: "A grand strategy is a political-military, means-ends chain, a state's theory about how best it can 'cause' security for itself": *The Sources of Military Doctrine: France, Britain, and Germany between the World Wars* (Ithaca, N.Y.: Cornell Univ. Press, 1984), p. 13.

3. Official sensitivity to the charge that national security policy lacks coherence may be gauged by Ronald Reagan, *National Security Strategy of the United States* (Washington, D.C.: White House, 1987).

4. The doctrine of American exceptionalism is still very much alive: the idea that God has ordained "the American experiment" for some distinctive purpose related to the betterment of all humankind.

5. An abiding precept of strategic history is that a great conflict need not be triggered by a great proximate event.

6. See Paul M. Kennedy, *The Rise and Fall of British Naval Mastery* (New York: Scribner, 1976); and Richard Pares, "American versus Continental Warfare, 1739–63," in *The Historian's Business and Other Essays* (Oxford: Clarendon Press, 1961), pp. 130-72.

7. See Sir Julian S. Corbett: *Some Principles of Maritime Strategy* (1911; Annapolis, Md.: Naval Institute Press, 1972), chap. 4; and *The Campaign of Trafalgar* (London: Longmans, Green, 1910), esp. pp. 11-16.

8. Corbett, *Some Principles of Maritime Strategy*, p. 259.

9. See Alfred T. Mahan, *The Influence of Sea Power upon the French Revolution and Empire, 1793-1812*, (1892; Boston: Little, Brown, 1898), 1: 338-46, 2: 118-21. Also see the maps illustrating the "Ushant Position" in Corbett, *Campaign of Trafalgar*, pp. 184, 302.

10. Robert V. Daniels, *Russia: The Roots of Confrontation* (Cambridge, Mass.: Harvard Univ. Press, 1985), p. 358.

2. Sir Halford Mackinder and Geopolitics

1. Saul B. Cohen, *Geography and Politics in a Divided World* (London: Methuen, 1964), p. 24. For a recent overview, see the essays in Ciro E. Zoppo and Charles Zorgbibe, eds., *On Geopolitics: Classical and Nuclear* (Dordrecht: Martinus Nijhoff, 1985).

2. See George F. Kennan, "Moscow Embassy Telegram No. 511: 'The Long Telegram,'" Feb. 22, 1946, in Thomas H. Etzold and John Lewis Gaddis, eds., *Containment: Documents on American Policy and Strategy, 1945-1950* (New York: Columbia Univ. Press, 1978), pp. 50-62; and "X" [George F. Kennan], "The Sources of Soviet Conduct," *Foreign Affairs* 25 (July 1947): 566-82. Gaddis has observed: "There soon developed a line of reasoning reminiscent of Sir Halford Mackinder's geopolitics, with its assumption that none of the world's 'rimlands' could be secure if the Eurasian 'heartland' was under the domination of a single hostile power": *Strategies of Containment: A Critical Appraisal of Postwar American National Security Policy* (New York: Oxford Univ. Press, 1982), p. 57.

3. The critics are weighed and found wanting in W.H. Parker, *Mackinder: Geography as an Aid to Statecraft* (Oxford: Clarendon Press, 1982), chap. 8.

4. Ibid., p. 175.

5. Mackinder's major geopolitical writings are presented in his *Democratic Ideals and Reality* (New York: Norton, 1962). This book contains the 1919 title work and three additional papers, including "The Geographical Pivot of History" (1904) and "The Round World and the Winning of the Peace" (1943). All references to these titles cite this collection of his writings.

6. For this and some other details concerning Mackinder's life and influence, I am greatly indebted to Parker, *Mackinder*, esp. chap. 7. Mackinder's ideas are outlined briefly in Colin S. Gray, *The Geopolitics of the Nuclear Era: Heartland, Rimlands, and the Technological Revolution* (New York: Crane, Russak for the National Strategy Information Center, 1977), and at considerable length in James Trapier Lowe, *Geopolitics and War: Mackinder's Philosophy of Power* (Washington, D.C.: University Press of America, 1981).

7. Mackinder's Heartland thesis of 1904 was borrowed and employed as policy advice by Gen. Karl Haushofer, professor of geography at the University of Munich in the 1920s and 1930s and (as Adolf Hitler's appointee) president of the German Academy (1934-37); he influenced Rudolf Hess (who was to be Hitler's deputy) and visited Hitler while he was writing *Mein Kampf* in Landsberg prison. Haushofer accepted the Heartland thesis with great enthusiasm and vigorously promoted the idea of a German (-dominated) alliance with Russia as the preferred method of Heartland unification. The allied authorities seriously considered indicting Haushofer as a war criminal, but although he was the leading philosopher of German expansionism and *Lebensraum*, he was not in any direct sense responsible for the crimes of the Third Reich. (His son Albrecht was killed at Dachau in 1945 for involvement in attempts to negotiate peace.) A fascinating discussion of Haushofer's role is Edmund A. Walsh, S.J. (his principal interrogator at Nuremberg), *Total Power: A Footnote to History* (Garden City, N.Y.: Doubleday, 1949). Walsh writes: "[Haushofer's] specific denial of complicity with Hitler in writing *Mein Kampf* is correct in a technical sense. What he contributed at a given point in

Hitler's psychological evolution was a line of argument, a thesis, and a series of geographical facts heavily weighted with political significance" (p.41). Also see Parker, *Mackinder,* pp. 176-83; Robert Strausz-Hupé, *Geopolitics: The Struggle for Space and Power* (1942; New York: Arno Press, 1972); Andreas Dorpalen, *The World of General Haushofer: Geopolitics in Action* (1942; Port Washington, N.Y.: Kennikat Press, 1966); Derwent Whittlesey, *German Strategy of World Conquest* (London: Robinson, 1942); and Jean Klein, "Reflections of Geopolitics: From Pangermanism to the Doctrines of Living Space and Moving Frontiers," in Zoppo and Zorgbibe, *On Geopolitics,* pp. 45-75.

8. "The British way in warfare," the allegedly traditional peripheral strategy of a maritime power, had been resurrected after what was viewed widely as the ghastly error of continental commitment to land combat on a major scale in 1914-18. In Feb. 1938 the Minister for the Co-ordination of Defence presented a memorandum reflecting the doctrine of "limited liability": the Army's first-priority mission was home (largely air) defense; the second was "the discharge of overseas commitments" (imperial defense, largely in India and Burma); "continental commitments" came third. See N.H. Gibbs, *History of the Second World War: Grand Strategy, Vol. 1, Rearmament Policy* (London: Her Majesty's Stationery Office, 1976), pp. 474-76. See also Michael Howard, *The Continental Commitment; The Dilemma of British Defence Policy in the Era of the Two World Wars* (London: Temple Smith, 1972).

9. Mackinder, "The Geographical Pivot of History," in *Democratic Ideals and Reality,* pp. 241-64.

10. See Antony Preston and John Major, *Send a Gunboat! A Study of the Gunboat and Its Role in British Policy, 1854-1904* (London: Longmans, Green, 1967), pp. 9-31; and John Shelton Curtiss, *Russia's Crimean War* (Durham, N.C.: Duke Univ. Press, 1979), esp. p. 287.

11. Mackinder, *Democratic Ideals and Reality,* pp. 73-74, 260.

12. Ibid., p. 62.

13. "But trans-continental railways are now [1904] transmuting the conditions of land-power, and nowhere can they have such effect as in the closed heart-land of Euro-Asia" (Mackinder, *Democratic Ideals and Reality,* p. 259).

14. It should be recalled that Germany was prostrate in defeat and Russia convulsed in civil war.

15. See Nicholas J. Spykman, *The Geography of the Peace* (New York: Harcourt, Brace, 1944), pp. 37-38, 40-41. A valuable critical analysis is David Wilkinson, "Spykman and Geopolitics," in Zoppo and Zorgbibe, *On Geopolitics,* pp. 77-129.

16. Mackinder, *Democratic Ideals and Reality,* p. 150. Spykman redrafted these *obiter dicta* as follows: "Who controls the rimland rules Eurasia; who rules Eurasia controls the destinies of the world" (*Geography of the Peace,* p. 43). Spykman intended to convey the point that the Rimland, rather than Mackinder's Heartland, was the key to Eurasian and ultimately to global dominance. However, a loyal follower of Mackinder could argue that there is no essential opposition between these apparently rival theses: the holder of the Heartland is likely to be the hegemonic ruler of the Rimland.

17. See Halford J. Mackinder, *Britain and the British Seas* (1902; Oxford: Clarendon Press, 1915), chap. 20; and Parker, *Mackinder,* chap. 3.

18. Mackinder, *Democratic Ideals and Reality,* p. 70. On the same page he had asked: "What if the Great Continent, the whole World-Island or a large part of it, were at some future time to become a single and united base of sea-power. Would not the other insular bases be outbuilt as regards ships and outmanned as regards seamen?"

19. By 1919 Mackinder had introduced a strategic as well as a physical-geographical criterion: "The Heartland is the region to which, under modern conditions, sea-power can be refused access" (*Democratic Ideals and Reality,* p. 110.)

20. "The Round World and the Winning of the Peace," ibid., pp. 272-73.

21. Mackinder's classification of the Americas as insular and echeloned satellites of the World Island of Eurasia-Africa has limited his appeal to American geostrategists. In 1919 he wrote: "Thus, the three so-called new continents are in point of area merely satellites of the old continent. There is one ocean covering nine-twelfths of the globe; and there are many smaller islands, whereof North America and South America are, for effective purposes, two, which together cover the remaining one-twelfth": *Democratic Ideals and Reality,* pp. 64-65. Hemispheric defense advocates have long held that there is a north-central American Heartland at least as meaningful strategically as Mackinder's Eurasian Heartland—particularly in the nuclear age. This thesis is relevant to the U.S. withdrawal options discussed in Chapter 12.

22. And that none too competently. See Williamson Murray, *The Change in the European Balance of Power, 1938-39: The Path to Ruin* (Princeton, N.J.: Princeton Univ. Press, 1984); and Wesley J. Wark, *The Ultimate Enemy: British Intelligence and Nazi Germany, 1933-1939* (Ithaca, N.Y.: Cornell Univ. Press, 1985). The agility and persistence in the British pursuit of antihegemonism from the sixteenth to the mid-twentieth century is worthy of great respect, actual British performance somewhat less so. British statecraft has displayed a repeated affinity for the (over-) balancing of yesterday's principal hegemonic menace: in the seventeenth century its anti-Spanish policy contributed to the growth of France as a superstate; in the nineteenth century it facilitated the growth of German power, owing to its habitual hostility to France (plus fond memories of Marshal Blücher at Waterloo and of Prussian grit and reliability under the Great Frederick, as well as the Teutonic royal connection); in the first four decades of the twentieth century it provided repeated examples of how not to function in a balance-of-power system.

23. See Parker, *Mackinder,* pp. 167-72.

24. Field Marshal Friedrich von Paulus surrendered the remnants of the encircled Sixth Army at Stalingrad on Feb. 2, 1943.

25. Mackinder, "The Round World," pp. 276-77.

26. Quoted in Parker, *Mackinder,* p. 175.

27. See esp. Alfred Thayer Mahan, *The Problem of Asia and Its Effects upon International Policies* (Boston: Little, Brown, 1905). An excellent commentary is William E. Livezey, *Mahan on Sea Power* (1947; rev. ed., Norman: Univ. of Oklahoma Press, 1981).

28. Mackinder, *Democratic Ideals and Reality,* p. 111.

29. This subject is probed in Colin S. Gray, *The Wartime Influence of Sea Power Upon Land Power* (Fairfax, Va.: National Institute for Public Policy, 1987).

3. The Problem of Security

1. On the 1904-5 reorientation of British military strategy away from imperial defense and toward a continental commitment, see John Gooch, *The Plans of War: The General Staff and British Military Strategy, c. 1900-1916* (London: Routledge & Kegan Paul, 1974), chaps. 6, 9; and J. McDermott, "The Revolution in British Military Thinking from the Boer War to the Moroccan Crisis," in Paul M. Kennedy, ed., *The War Plans of the Great Powers, 1880-1914* (London: Allen & Unwin, 1979), pp. 99-117.

2. As Douglas Porch has argued: "'The spirit of the offensive' was born not so much out of confidence in French superiority, as out of anxiety over French weaknesses": *The March to the Marne: The French Army, 1871-1914* (Cambridge: Cambridge Univ. Press, 1981), chap. 11.

3. See Jan Karl Tanenbaum, "French Estimates of Germany's Operational War Plans," in Ernest R. May, ed., *Knowing One's Enemies: Intelligence Assessments before the Two World Wars* (Princeton, N.J.: Princeton Univ. Press, 1984), pp. 150-71.

4. "The French Plan of Campaign: Plan 17," Appendix 9 in Sir James E. Edmonds, *The British Official History of the Great War: Military Operations, France and Belgium, 1914,* (rev. 3d ed. 1935; Woking, Surrey: Shearer, 1984), 1:501.

5. In the words of Martin van Creveld, "The size of armies and the rise of the General Staff, the need for mobilization and the dependence on railways, and the effects of a prolonged peace all led to a belief in the feasibility of planning and control as a means for attaining certainty in war": *Command in War* (Cambridge, Mass.: Harvard Univ. Press, 1985), p. 152.

6. Robert Jervis, *The Illogic of American Nuclear Strategy* (Ithaca, N.Y.: Cornell Univ. Press, 1984); McGeorge Bundy, "Maintaining Stable Deterrence," *International Security* 3 (Winter 1978-79): 5-16; and McGeorge Bundy, "Existential Deterrence and Its Consequences," in Douglas MacLean, ed., *The Security Gamble: Deterrence Dilemmas in the Nuclear Age* (Totowa, N.J.; Rowman & Allenheld, 1984), pp. 3-13.

7. Classic examples include Thomas C. Schelling, *Arms and Influence* (New Haven, Conn.: Yale Univ. Press, 1966); and Herman Kahn, *On Escalation: Metaphors and Scenarios* (New York: Praeger, 1965).

8. Carl H. Builder, *The Prospects and Implications of Non-nuclear Means for Strategic Conflict,* Adelphi Papers No. 200 (London: IISS, 1985).

9. McGeorge Bundy, "To Cap the Volcano," *Foreign Affairs* 48 (Oct. 1969): 13.

10. This thesis is developed in detail in Colin S. Gray, *Nuclear Strategy and National Style* (Lanham, Md.: Hamilton Press, 1986).

11. Of the British performance during the third battle of Ypres (1917), British historian John Terraine has observed, "The familiar but bitter lesson was that strategy ignores tactics at its peril": *The Western Front, 1914-1918* (London: Hutchinson, 1964), p. 158.

12. The relationship between strategy and tactics is easily misassessed if undue focus is placed on one or the other. "Reformist" scholars in the 1980s have tended to show greater sensitivity to tactical and operational than to strategic matters. E.g., van Creveld states that *"While the overall strategic direction of the German campaign* [the Ludendorff offensive, launched on March 21, 1918] *thus left something to be desired* in failing to provide the required flexibility, on the tactical level it

was an immense...triumph" (*Command in War,* p. 183; emphasis added); in fact, the offensive was a strategic disaster for Germany.

13. A superior and generally very balanced analysis of the character and origins of the Soviet approach to security is presented in Daniels, *Russia.*

14. Thomas Powers, "What Is It About?" *Atlantic,* 253 (Jan. 1984): 35-55. Powers's article plainly was the inspiration for Norman A. Graebner, "The Soviet-American Conflict: A Strange Phenomenon," *Virginia Quarterly Review* 60 (Fall 1984): 656-86.

15. See Frank L. Klingberg: "The Historical Alternation of Moods in American Foreign Policy," *World Politics* 4 (Jan. 1952): 239-73; and *Cyclical Trends in American Foreign Policy Moods: The Unfolding of America's World Role* (Lanham, Md.: University Press of America, 1983). Jack E. Holmes has expanded upon Klingberg's work and analyzed in detail the thesis that *"There is a fundamental conflict between the moods manifested in the liberal American ideology and the dictates of United States politico-military interests"* (original emphasis): *The Mood/Interest Theory of American Foreign Policy* (Lexington: Univ. Press of Kentucky, 1985), p. 6.

16. See Michael Howard; *The British Way in Warfare: A Reappraisal,* 1974 Neale Lecture in English History, (London: Jonathan Cape, 1975); and *The Continental Commitment.* On the subsidization of continental allies, see John M. Sherwig, *Guineas and Gunpowder: British Foreign Aid in the Wars with France, 1793-1815* (Cambridge, Mass.: Harvard Univ. Press, 1969).

17. On the *ultimately* decisive role of seapower (the blockade) in the defeat of Germany, see Basil H. Liddell Hart, *History of the First World War* (1934; London: Pan, 1972) pp. 460,464; Richard Hough, *The Great War at Sea, 1914-1918* (Oxford: Oxford Univ. Press, 1983), p. 321; and Gray, *Wartime Influence of Sea Power.*

18. The relevance of the case of the Imperial German Navy for U.S. and NATO strategy today is argued in Colin S. Gray, "Maritime Strategy," *U.S. Naval Institute Proceedings* 112 (Feb. 1986): esp. 37-38.

19. In the fall of 1905, in the context of the Tangier (or First Morocco) Crisis, the British general staff recommended that in the event of German violation of Belgian neutrality, two army corps be dispatched to Antwerp within twenty-three days. See McDermott, "The Revolution in British Military Thinking," p. 110. Also of interest is Winston S. Churchill, *The World Crisis* (New York: Scribner, 1931), chap. 13, "Antwerp and the Channel Ports."

20. Edward N. Luttwak, "On the Meaning of Strategy...for the United States in the 1980s," in W. Scott Thompson, ed., *National Security in the 1980s: From Weakness to Strength* (San Francisco: Institute for Contemporary Studies, 1980), pp. 260-61.

21. The sharply contrasting consequences of territorial expansion for the U.S. and Russian political systems are explained superbly in Daniels, *Russia,* pp. 37-38.

22. The meaning of the SDI for NATO-Europe is discussed most usefully in Keith B. Payne, *Strategic Defense: "Star Wars" in Perspective* (Lanham, Md.: Hamilton Press, 1986), chap. 10. Also see Trevor Taylor, "Europe and the SDI," *Rusi Journal,* 130 (March 1985): 41-44; Phil Williams, "West European Security and the Strategic Defense Initiative," paper prepared for Workshop on the American Strategic Defense Initiative, Netherlands Institute of International Relations, The Hague, April 1985; and, from a different perspective, David S. Yost, "Soviet Ballistic Missile Defense and NATO," *Orbis* 29 (Summer 1985): 281-92.

23. See Brian Caven, *The Punic Wars* (London: Weidenfeld & Nicolson, 1980), chap. 1. On Roman strategic culture, see William V. Harris, *War and Imperialism in Republican Rome, 327-70 B.C.* (1979; Oxford: Clarendon Press, 1985).

24. It is correct to maintain that the balance-of-power system had order, not peace, as its highest value but quite wrong to argue that the necessary sanction of war was regarded with equanimity in nineteenth-century Europe. This point is explained well in F.R. Bridge and Roger Bullen, *The Great Powers and the European States System, 1815-1914* (London: Longman, 1980), esp. pp. 10-11. The construction of rival coalitions, beginning with the Triple Alliance of 1882 (Germany, Austria, and Italy) and followed by the Franco-Russian Alliance of 1891, very significantly increased the prospect that any war in Europe involving a great power would be transformed rapidly into a general conflict. See George F. Kennan, *The Fateful Alliance: France, Russia, and the Coming of the First World War* (New York: Pantheon Books, 1984); but also the powerful critique in Paul Seabury and Patrick Glynn, "Kennan: The Historian as Fatalist," *National Interest*, no. 2 (Winter 1985-86): 97-111.

25. See Gaddis, *Strategies of Containment*, chap. 3; and Terry L. Deibel and John Lewis Gaddis, *Containment: Concept and Policy*, 2 vols. (Washington, D.C.: National Defense Univ. Press, 1986).

26. Henry R. Luce, "The American Century," *Life*, Feb. 17, 1941, pp. 61-65.

27. One such commentator is Earl C. Ravenal; see his article, "The Case for a Withdrawal of Our Forces," *New York Times Magazine*, March 6, 1983, pp. 58-61, 75. A sophisticated survey of contemporary American thought on the U.S. role in the world is Robert W. Tucker, "Isolation and Intervention," *National Interest*, no. 1 (Fall 1985): 16-25.

28. E.g., in Leon Wieseltier, *Nuclear War, Nuclear Peace* (New York: Holt, Rinehart & Winston, 1983).

29. Luttwak, "On the Meaning of Strategy," p. 261.

30. This charge has permeated the writings of Edward Luttwak and John Collins in particular. See, e.g., Edward N. Luttwak, "SALT and the Meaning of Strategy," *Washington Review*, 1 (April 1978): 18-28; Edward N. Luttwak, *The Pentagon and the Art of War: The Question of Military Reform* (New York: Simon & Shuster, 1984); and John M. Collins, *U.S. Defense Planning: A Critique* (Boulder, Colo.: Westview Press, 1982). Also relevant is Harry A. Summers, Jr., *On Strategy: A Critical Analysis of the Vietnam War* (Novato, Calif.: Presidio Press, 1982).

31. For enlightening explanations of the concept, see Arnold Wolfers, *Discord and Collaboration: Essays on International Politics* (Baltimore, Md.: Johns Hopkins Univ. Press, 1962), chap. 10; and Charles F. Herrmann, "Defining National Security," in John F. Reichart and Steven R. Sturm, eds., *American Defense Policy*, 5th. ed. (Baltimore, Md.: Johns Hopkins Univ. Press, 1982), pp. 18-21.

32. Wolfers, *Discord and Collaboration*, esp. p. 150. A broad view is elaborated in Lester R. Brown, "An Untraditional View of National Security," in Reichart and Sturm, *American Defense Policy*, pp. 21-25.

33. See Arnold Wolfers, *Britain and France between Two Wars: Conflicting Strategies of Peace from Versailles to World War II* (1940; New York: Norton, 1960) chap. 1.

34. See Robert Gilpin, *War and Change in World Politics* (Cambridge: Cambridge Univ. Press, 1981), chap. 5.

35. George F. Kennan, "Morality and Foreign Policy," *Foreign Affairs* 64 (Winter 1985-86): 206.

36. This was a condition wherein deterrence could be rooted in the prospect of successful defense, not a condition of deterrence *contrasted* with defense. The historical fragility of defense-based deterrence is well illustrated in John J. Mearsheimer, *Conventional Deterrence* (Ithaca, N.Y.: Cornell Univ. Press, 1983): "My central proposition in this book is that, in a crisis, deterrence is likely to fail" (p. 203), but "deterrence is likely to hold when a potential attacker is faced with the prospect of employing an attrition strategy, largely because of the associated exorbitant costs and because of the difficulty of accurately predicting ultimate success in a protracted war" (p. 207).

37. The early years of the American republic demonstrated both the need for a U.S. Navy and the degree to which American security depended upon divisions within the Old World. See Terry Sharrer, "The Search for a Naval Policy, 1783-1812," in Kenneth J. Hagan, ed., *In Peace and War: Interpretations of American Naval History, 1775-1984*, 2d ed. (Westport, Conn.: Greenwood Press, 1984), pp. 27-45; and Allan R. Millett and Peter Maslowski, *For the Common Defense: A Military History of the United States of America* (New York: Free Press, 1984), chap. 4. The problems posed by trans-oceanic distance for a continental European power are drawn vividly in Holger H. Herwig, *Politics of Frustration: The United States in German Naval Planning, 1889-1941* (Boston: Little, Brown, 1976).

38. Alexander Hamilton, James Madison, and John Jay, *The Federalist Papers* (1787-88); (New York: Bantam Books, 1982), p. 21: "Nay it is far more probable that in America, as in Europe, neighbouring nations, acting under the impulse of opposite interest, and unfriendly passions, would frequently be found taking different sides. Considering our distance from Europe, it would be more natural for these confederacies to apprehend danger from one another, than from distant nations, and therefore that each of them should be more desirous to guard against the others, by the aid of foreign alliances, than to guard against foreign dangers by alliances between themselves. And here let us not forget how much more easy it is to receive foreign fleets into our ports, and foreign armies into our country, than it is to persuade or compel them to depart."

39. See Rebecca V. Strode and Colin S. Gray, "The Imperial Dimension of Soviet Military Power," *Problems of Communism* 30 (Nov.-Dec. 1981): 1-15.

40. Luttwak, *The Grand Strategy of the Soviet Union*, p. 92.

41. Edward N. Luttwak, "Q and A: The Soviet Union Seen as a Classic Land Empire," *Washington Times*, Sept. 16, 1983, p. 4C.

42. For a powerful attack on "strategic romanticism," see Richard K. Betts, "Dubious Reform: Strategism versus Managerialism," in Asa A. Clark IV et al., eds., *The Defense Reform Debate: Issues and Analysis* (Baltimore, Md.: Johns Hopkins Univ. Press, 1984), pp. 67-74. With Luttwak particularly in mind, Betts charges that reformist critiques of much mainstream defense analysis promote "an almost mystical apotheosis of strategy as a vocation" (p. 68).

43. Stephen M. Walt, "Alliance Formation and the Balance of World Power," *International Security* 9 (Spring 1985): esp. 8-9. The term "political velocity" is mine, not Walt's.

44. For the thesis that military doctrines can be classified as offensive, defen-

sive, or deterrent, see Posen, *The Sources of Military Doctrine,* This tripartite classification is thoroughly unsound. Posen degrades the meaning of a deterrent doctrine by equating it with a doctrine of punishment.

45. See the discussion in Michael Howard, *War and the Liberal Conscience* (New Brunswick, N.J.: Rutgers Univ. Press, 1978), chaps. 2-3.

46. The impact of Watergate on executive authority is assessed thoughtfully, though of course far from disinterestedly, in Henry Kisinger, *Years of Upheaval* (Boston: Little, Brown, 1982), chaps. 4, 22.

47. A thin but prescient literature questions the necessity for a formal arms-control negotiating process or for formal agreements. Examples, written nearly two decades apart, are Jeremy J. Stone, *Strategic Persuasion: Arms Limitations through Dialogue* (New York: Columbia Univ. Press, 1967); and Kenneth L. Adelman, "Arms Control with and without Agreements," *Foreign Affairs* 63 (Winter 1984-85): 240-63.

48. "In the West, Finlandization of Western Europe may still be Washington's nightmare, but the more compelling reality is that the U.S.S.R.'s security buffer in Eastern Europe is disintegrating....The U.S.S.R. can, of course, prop up its East European empire with bayonets. But the stark reality remains: Eastern Europe is no longer a springboard for pressuring the West or even a security buffer, but an area of primary infection for the Soviet system": William G. Hyland, "Clash with the Soviet Union," *Foreign Policy,* no. 49 (Winter 1982-83): 8.

49. This is not to ignore the legitimacy that flows from simple longevity of rule; from the leading role of the Party in organizing and effecting the defense of Mother Russia against the German invasion, from the industrial and scientific modernization of the country and from the international standing of the Soviet state as a superpower.

50. Paul H. Nitze, "Living with the Soviets," *Foreign Affairs* 63 (Winter 1984-85): 365.

51. Ideological goals can be dressed in national security clothing, but in reality they tend to function either as legitimizing rationales obscuring more or less predatory motives or as a source of conveniently expansive missions for the nations that have capabilities surplus to the needs of a strictly defined national security.

52. See A.P. Thornton, *Doctrines of Imperialism* (New York: Wiley, 1965); Wolfgang J. Mommsen, *Theories of Imperialism* (1977; New York: Random House, 1980); Tony Smith, *The Pattern of Imperialism: The United States, Great Britain, and the Late-Industrializing World since 1815* (Cambridge: Cambridge Univ. Press, 1981); and Charles Reynolds, *Modes of Imperialism* (Oxford: Martin Robertson, 1981). Readers who find my claim of the imperial need for a "legitimizing rationale" unduly mundane may prefer the complementary judgment of the late French historian Fernand Braudel: "For no empire could exist without some mystique and in Western Europe, this mystique was provided by the crusade, part spiritual, part temporal, as the example of Charles V was soon to prove." See *The Mediterranean and the Mediterranean World in the Age of Philip II* (1949; New York: Harper & Row, 1976), 2:659.

53. As often as not the allies of the United States serve not only to caution restraint but actually to subvert U.S. ability to defend its interests. These observa-

tions apply broadly to the fields of counterterrorism, trade in "strategic" goods with the Soviet Union, economic sanctions more broadly, and some critical elements of arms control (e.g. coping effectively with Soviet noncompliance).

54. See Benjamin S. Lambeth, "The Political Potential of Soviet Equivalence," *International Security* 4 (Fall 1979): 22-39.

4. Statecraft: Retrospect and Prospect

1. Michael Howard, "Nuclear Bookshelf," *Harper's* 266 (Feb. 1983), pp. 65-70.

2. See Howard, *War and the Liberal Conscience;* and Norman Cohn, *The Pursuit of the Millennium: Revolutionary Millenarians and Mystical Anarchists of the Middle Ages* (London: Paladin, 1970).

3. Dexter Masters and Katherine Way, eds., *One World or None* (New York: McGraw-Hill, 1946).

4. Jonathan Schell, *The Fate of the Earth* (New York: Knopf, 1982). The sequel is no less unsatisfactory; see *The Abolition* (New York: Knopf, 1984).

5. Schell, *The Fate of the Earth,* p. 227.

6. Probably the most rigorous endeavor to describe and explain great-power phenomena is Jack S. Levy, *War in the Modern Great Power System, 1495-1975* (Lexington: Univ. Press of Kentucky, 1983), chap. 2. Also see Bridge and Bullen, *The Great Powers,* chap. 1; and Gordon A. Craig and Alexander L. George, *Force and Statecraft: Diplomatic Problems of Our Time* (New York: Oxford Univ. Press, 1983), chap. 1.

7. The strategic problem is to find the material and tactical basis for "extended deterrence" in a nuclear arsenal that one is willing to shape according to negotiated guidelines intended (by U.S. officials) to produce the net effect of a rough parity. In theory the solution is simple enough. First, NATO provides sufficient regional defense capability to reduce dramatically the burden of erstwhile extended-deterrence duties on strategic nuclear forces. Second, through a process of "constructive engagement" the Soviet Union should be in need of less deterring. The real world has proved reluctant to be manipulated by the power of these ideas. NATO-Europe has consistently declined to construct a truly robust regional defense, and the Soviet Union is not, strategically, in the "constructive engagement" business. This was demonstrated to any in the West who were confused on the matter *immediately* after the superpowers had erected allegedly important pillars of a new architecture of detente in 1972. See Walter Slocombe, "Extended Deterrence," *Washington Quarterly* 7 (Fall 1984): 93-103; and Gray, *Nuclear Strategy and National Style,* chap. 8. A new approach to extended deterrence is developed in Chapter 14, below.

8. On October 4, 1985, former Secretary of Defense Robert S. McNamara delivered an impassioned attack upon the alleged sins of strategic defense vis-à-vis stability. His speech had one critical flaw: it took no realistic account of the actual Soviet polity with which the United States has to contend. See McNamara, "Reducing the Risk of Nuclear War: Is Star Wars the Answer?" in Craig Snyder, ed., *The Strategic Defense Debate: Can "Star Wars" Make Us Safe?* (Philadelphia: Univ. of Pennsylvania Press, 1986), pp. 121-30.

9. For reasons ably outlined in Charles Burton Marshall, "Arms Control: History and Theory," in Richard F. Staar, ed., *Arms Control: Myth versus Reality* (Stanford, Calif: Hoover Institution Press, 1984), pp. 180-88.

10. For contrasting analyses, see Michael Mandelbaum, *The Nuclear Revolution: International Politics before and after Hiroshima* (Cambridge: Cambridge Univ. Press, 1981); and Colin S. Gray, "Across the Nuclear Divide—Strategic Studies, Past and Present," *International Security* 2 (Summer 1977): 24-46.

11. Gilpin, *War and Change*, p. 7.

12. A classic case against American isolation in the Western Hemisphere is Nicholas J. Spykman, *America's Strategy in World Politics: The United States and the Balance of Power* (1942; Hamden, Conn.: Archon Books, 1970).

13. See Gray, *The Geopolitics of the Nuclear Era;* and Paul Kennedy, *Strategy and Diplomacy, 1870-1945: Eight Studies* (London: Allen & Unwin, 1983), pp. 43-85.

14. See Edward V. Gulick, *Europe's Classical Balance of Power System: A Case History of the Theory and Practice of One of the Great Concepts of European Statecraft* (Ithaca, N.Y.: Cornell Univ. Press, 1955).

15. In the course of the eighteenth century two states, Spain and Sweden, left the column of great powers, never to return; and two states, Prussia and Russia, joined.

16. Imperial Roman frontier policy is treated comprehensively in Luttwak, *The Grand Strategy of the Roman Empire*. Frontier policy under the Republic is detailed in Stephen L. Dyson, *The Creation of the Roman Frontier* (Princeton, N.J.: Princeton Univ. Press, 1985).

17. For a highly critical study of the "defensive imperialism" thesis, see Harris, *War and Imperialism in Republican Rome*. Harris concludes: "For a war against some enemy or other, with some 'justification' or other, the Romans intended and expected every year" (p. 254).

18. See Richard Pipes, *Survival Is Not Enough: Soviet Realities and America's Future* (New York: Simon & Schuster, 1984); and Marshall I. Goldman, *USSR in Crisis: The Failure of an Economic System* (New York: Norton, 1983).

19. Thucydides, *The Peloponnesian Wars*, trans. Rex Warner (London: Cassell, 1962), pp. 360,363.

20. See Walter Laqueur, *A World of Secrets: The Uses and Limits of Intelligence* (New York: Basic Books, 1985), chap. 5. A work of lasting merit is Arnold Horelick and Myron Rush, *Strategic Power and Soviet Foreign Policy* (Chicago: Univ. of Chicago Press, 1965).

21. See Gaddis, *Strategies of Containment*, chaps. 4-6; and David Alan Rosenberg, "The Origins of Overkill: Nuclear Weapons and American Strategy, 1945-1960," *International Security* 7 (Spring 1983): 3-71.

22. Readers attracted to analogies may find some points to ponder in the following words by Brian Caven: "At the end, Carthage made the fatal mistake of failing to gauge the inveteracy of Rome's malevolence towards her. For her own part national animosities were laid aside when she surrendered her empire; she asked for nothing better than amicable, and profitable, relations with Massinissa and with Rome. When at last, goaded beyond further endurance, she defied Rome...she was unaware that she was giving to a mortal enemy the excuse that he had been looking for not simply to punish but to destroy her" (*The Punic Wars*, p. 272).

23. It remains an open question whether or not German leaders planned to wage a preventive war in 1912-14. See L.L. Farrar, Jr., *Arrogance and Anxiety: The Ambivalence of German Power, 1848-1914* (Iowa City: Univ. of Iowa Press, 1981), pp. 142-48. A collection of outstanding essays is H.W. Koch, ed., *The Origins of the First World War: Great Power Rivalry and German War Aims*, 2d ed. (London: Macmillan, 1984).

24. See Murray, *Change in the European Balance of Power.*

25. For a stimulating commentary on Germany's lack of preparedness for a protracted war, see Ronald Lewin, *Hitler's Mistakes* (London: Leo Cooper, 1984), chap. 7.

26. Stalingrad in the Winter of 1942-43 *appeared* to be the highwater mark of German military achievement in its great Russian adventure. It is evident in retrospect, as it was to many people (particularly German soldiers) at the time, that the German Army had ruined itself in Russia as early as the 1941 campaign. The lunges in 1942, across the Don bend to the Volga and toward the Caucasus, served to compound German military problems rather than help resolve them. Excellent studies include Albert Seaton, *The Russo-German War, 1941-45* (New York: Praeger, 1971); John Erickson, *The Road to Stalingrad* (1975; Boulder, Colo.: Westview Press, 1983); and John Erickson, *The Road to Berlin* (Boulder, Colo.: Westview Press, 1983).

27. See Paul Fussell, *The Great War and Modern Memory* (New York: Oxford Univ. Press, 1975).

28. See Martin Wight, *Systems of States*, ed. Hedley Bull (Leicester, U.K.: Leicester Univ. Press, 1977).

29. See United States Strategic Bombing Survey, *Over-all Report: European War* (Washington, D.C.: U.S. Government Printing Office, 1945).

30. See the outstanding collection of essays in Michael Howard, ed., *Restraints on War: Studies in the Limitation of Armed Conflict* (Oxford: Oxford Univ. Press, 1979).

31. See Colin S. Gray, *Maritime Strategy, Geopolitics, and the Defense of the West* (New York: Ramapo Press for the National Strategy Information Center, 1986).

32. This is not to assume that states always seek a clear, favorable military decision. Plainly, Egypt did not attack Israel in October 1973 intent upon a definitive victory. Moreover, as the British demonstrated in the Falklands in 1982, there are occasions when force, the *ultima ratio regum*, is the only instrument that can produce a satisfactory outcome to a political conflict.

33. Important modern interpretations of Karl von Clausewitz include Raymond Aron, *Clausewitz: Philosopher of War* (1976; London: Routledge & Kegan Paul, 1983); Michael Howard, *Clausewitz* (New York: Oxford Univ. Press, 1983); and *Journal of Strategic Studies* 9 (June-September 1986), a special double issue edited by Michael I. Handel.

34. See Howard, *War and the Liberal Conscience;* Henry F. Graff, ed., *American Imperialism and the Philippines Insurrection* (Boston: Little, Brown, 1969); and Sam C. Sarkesian, *America's Forgotten Wars: The Counterrevolutionary Past and Lessons for the Future* (Westport, Conn.: Greenwood Press, 1984), pp. 165-83.

35. Louis J. Halle, *The Elements of International Strategy* (Lanham, Md.: University Press of America, 1984), p. 15.

36. See Daniel J. Boorstin, *The Americans: The Colonial Experience* (New York: Vintage Books, 1958), 1, 1. A very useful discussion of American self-images is Michael Vlahos, *America: Images of Empire*, Occasional Papers in International

Affairs (Washington, D.C.: Johns Hopkins Foreign Policy Institute, School of Advanced International Studies, 1982).

5. Geopolitics and Strategic Culture

1. See John Shy, "The American Military Experience: History and Learning," *Journal of Interdisciplinary History* 1 (Winter 1971): 205-28.

2. Those "oppositions" were outlined at the close of Chapter 1: landpower vs. seapower; Heartland vs. Rimland; center vs. periphery; individualist vs. authoritarian/totalitarian values; and East vs. West.

3. See Alastair Horne, *To Lose a Battle: France 1940* (London: Macmillan, 1969); and *The French Army and Politics, 1870- 1970* (New York: Peter Bedrick, 1984), esp. chap. 3. Also useful, for a military analysis, is Bradford A. Lee, "Strategy, Arms and the Collapse of France, 1930-40," in Richard Langhorne, ed., *Diplomacy and Intelligence during the Second World War: Essays in Honour of F.H. Hinsley* (Cambridge: Cambridge Univ. Press, 1985), pp. 43-67.

4. See Gray, *Geopolitics of the Nuclear Era,* chap. 4.

5. An intriguing if somewhat forced historical perspective is provided by Robert Dallek, *The American Style of Foreign Policy: Cultural Politics and Foreign Affairs* (New York: Knopf, 1983).

6. Donald E. Nuechterlein, *America Overcommitted: United States National Interests in the 1980s* (Lexington: Univ. Press of Kentucky, 1985).

7. Robert W. Tucker, "Containment and the Search for Alternatives: A Critique," in Aaron Wildavsky, ed., *Beyond Containment: Alternative American Policies toward the Soviet Union* (San Francisco: Institute for Contemporary Studies Press, 1983), pp. 81-82.

8. In the words of Williamson Murray: "While British strategic policy rested on a 'worst case analysis,' Chamberlain based his foreign policy on the most optimistic interpretation of German motives and aims. On the one hand the prime minister received advice that Britain should avoid war at all costs because of a desperate military situation. On the other hand he believed that relatively minor concessions would guarantee peace and world order" (*Change in the European Balance of Power,* p. 58). See also Donald C. Watt, "British Intelligence and the Coming of the Second World War," in *Knowing One's Enemies,* pp. 237-70; and Wark, *Ultimate Enemy.*

9. See the discussion in Chapter 2.

10. See Pipes, *Survival Is Not Enough,* pp. 51-60.

11. See Michael McGiffert, ed., *The Character of Americans: A Book of Readings* (Homewood, Ill.: Dorsey Press, 1964); and Dean Peabody, *National Characteristics* (Cambridge: Cambridge Univ. Press, 1985).

12. This thesis is pursued in Gray, *Nuclear Strategy and National Style,* esp. chap. 2. Robert Daniels has observed that "Americans, grasping little of the peculiar sources of Soviet behavior, oscillate between fear of a moribund ideology and naive faith in expressions of peaceful intentions" (*Russia,* p. 358).

13. E.g., Zbigniew Brzezinski, Henry Kissinger, George Liska, Edward Luttwak, Hans Morgenthau, Nicholas Spykman, and Arnold Wolfers.

14. It has been argued strongly that the leaders of the American Revolution, true to their time and their European heritage, thought of war as a limited endeavor in the service of state policy. The all-or-nothing crusading spirit most commonly held to be "the American way" of war was allegedly the product of the change in political and strategic circumstances wrought by the Revolution. See Reginald C. Stuart, *War and American Thought: From the Revolution to the Monroe Doctrine* (Kent, Ohio: Kent State Univ. Press, 1982). For a view from cultural anthropology, see Marvin Harris, *Cultural Materialism: The Struggle for a Science of Culture* (New York: Random House, 1979), pp. 260-62, "The Mutability of National Character."

15. In a somewht specialized context, I have attempted to identify the cultural roots of U.S. strategic thinking in "American Strategic Culture and Military Performance," in Asa A. Clark IV *et al.*, eds., *Defense Technology* (forthcoming). For a study as rich with insight as it is provocative, see Ken Booth, *Strategy and Ethnocentrism* (London: Croom, Helm 1979).

16. Cohen, *Geography and Politics*, p. 24.

17. Booth, *Strategy and Ethnocentrism*, p. 14.

18. It should not be forgotten that Halford Mackinder was a geographer first and a geopolitical grand theorist only distantly second. See Parker, *Mackinder*, chap. 5.

19. See Harold Sprout and Margaret Sprout, *The Ecological Perspective on Human Affairs, with Special Reference to International Politics* (Princeton, N.J.: Princeton Univ. Press, 1965), chap. 7.

20. Booth, *Strategy and Ethocentrism*, p. 144.

21. An outstanding study is Norman Rich, *Hitler's War Aims: Ideology, the Nazi State, and the Course of Expansion* (New York: Norton, 1973). Also helpful is Lewin, *Hitler's Mistakes*. For a more sympathetic view of Hitler's statecraft, see the trilogy by David Irving: *The War Path: Hitler's Germany, 1933-1939* (1978; London: Macmillan, 1983); *Hitler's War, 1939-1942* (1977; London: Macmillan, 1983); and *Hitler's War, 1942-1945* (1977; London: Macmillan, 1983).

22. This is the central message in Alan Tonelson, "The Real National Interest," *Foreign Policy*, no. 61 (Winter 1985-86): 49-72.

23. F.S. Northedge, quoted in Paul Kennedy, *The Rise of the Anglo-German Antagonism* (London: Allen & Unwin, 1980), p. 425.

24. "Within the limits set by its size, an army's worth as a military instrument equals the quality and quantity of its equipment multiplied by...its 'Fighting Power'...'Fighting Power,' in brief, is defined as the sum total of mental qualities that make armies fight": Martin van Creveld, *Fighting Power: German and U.S. Army Performance, 1939-1945* (Westport, Conn.: Greenwood Press, 1982), p.3. Also see Trevor N. Dupuy, *A Genius for War: The German Army and General Staff, 1807-1945* (London: Macdonald's & Jane's, 1977).

25. Distance, climate, and logistic problems constrain—or should constrain—choice in strategy. The Union victory in the American Civil War was far more a victory in logistic management than a product of any superiority in strategy. See Herman Hattaway and Archer Jones, *How the North Won: A Military History of the Civil War* (Urbana: Univ. of Illinois Press, 1983), pp. 684-86. Of Hitler's adventure in Russia, Albert Seaton has said that "the part played by the Red Army in 1941 in

halting the enemy advance has been exaggerated by Soviet historians. Success was due mainly to geography and climate and thereafter to Stalin's determination" (*The Russo-German War*, p. 221).

26. See Paul S. Dull, *A Battle History of the Imperial Japanese Navy, 1941-1945* (Annapolis, Md.: Naval Institute Press, 1978); and H.P. Willmott, *The Barrier and the Javelin: Japanese and Allied Pacific Strategies, February to June 1942* (Annapolis, Md.: Naval Institute Press 1983), esp. pp. 44, 516-17. Willmott observes: "Because the Japanese lacked an adequate pool on which to draw for their island air garrisons in the first place, they were condemned to attempt too much with too little over too great an area; individual bases were no more than hostages to fortune, since there was never a chance of making the all-important first contact with the enemy on a basis remotely approaching equality" (p. 57).

27. On "working command," see Geoffrey Till, *Maritime Strategy and the Nuclear Age* (London: Macmillan, 1982), pp. 128-37, 189. The classic discussion is Corbett, *Some Principles of Maritime Strategy*, pp. 87-104.

28. Writing in 1942, Spykman noted that "the Continent of Europe can engage in distant naval operations only with the consent of Britain, not against her" (*America's Strategy in World Politics*, p. 98). This thought was expressed with typical vigor by Admiral Sir John Fisher, who insisted that "5 keys lock up the world! Singapore, the Cape, Alexandria, Gibraltar, Dover. These five keys belong to England, and the five great Fleets of England...will hold these keys": quoted in Arthur Marder, *The Anatomy of British Sea Power: A History of British Naval Policy in the Pre-Dreadnought Era, 1880-1905* (1940; Hamden, Conn.: Archon Books, 1964), p. 473. The United States today, with its Eurasian Rimland allies, "locks up" Soviet seapower in the sense intended by Spykman and Fisher.

29. The "knockout blow" from the air of 1938 vintage was a hypothetical strategic catastrophe, but it was a light-year removed from the concept of assured destruction of thirty years later. See Brian Bond, *British Military Policy between the Two World Wars* (Oxford: Clarendon Press, 1980), pp. 282-83; Malcolm Smith, *British Air Strategy between the Wars* (Oxford: Clarendon Press, 1984), chap. 7; and John Terraine, *A Time for Courage: The Royal Air Force in the European War, 1939-1945* (New York: Macmillan, 1985), chaps. 6-7.

30. See Herbert W. Richmond, *The Invasion of Britain: An Account of Plans, Attempts and Countermeasures from 1586 to 1918* (London: Methuen, 1941).

31. Mahan, *The Influence of Sea Power*, 2:118-19.

32. Corbett, *Some Principles of Maritime Strategy*, p. 258.

33. For a superior example, see Kenneth Macksey, *Invasion: The German Invasion of England, July 1940* (London: Corgi Books, 1981).

34. See Gray, *the Wartime Influence of Sea Power*.

35. See Norman Friedman, "U.S. Maritime Strategy," *International Defense Review* 18, no. 7 (1985): 1071-75; F.J. West, Jr., "Maritime Strategy and NATO Deterrence," *Naval War College Review* 38 (Sept.-Oct. 1985): 5-19; the testimony in House Armed Services Committee, Seapower and Strategic Critical Materials Subcommittee, *The 600 Ship Navy and the Maritime Strategy*, Hearings, 99th Cong., 1st sess. (Washington, D.C.: U.S. Government Printing Office, 1986); Admiral James D. Watkins *et al.*, *The Maritime Strategy*, *U.S. Naval Institute Proceedings Supplement* (Jan. 1986); and F.J. West, Jr., "The Maritime Strategy: The Next Step," *U.S. Naval Institute Proceedings* 113 (Jan. 1987): 60-69.

36. Napoleon's empire was far more vulnerable to maritime pressure than the Third Reich was or the Soviet Union would be, yet Julian Corbett could write: "By universal assent Trafalgar is ranked as one of the decisive battles of the world, and yet of all the great victories there is not one which to all appearance was so barren of immediate result. It had brought to a triumphant conclusion one of the most masterly and complex sea campaigns in history, but in so far as it was an integral part of the combined campaign its results are scarcely to be discerned. It gave to England finally the dominion of the seas, but it left Napoleon dictator of the Continent. So incomprehensible was its apparent sterility that to fill the void a legend grew up that it saved England from invasion" (*The Campaign of Trafalgar*, p. 408). When American advocates of the forward maritime strategy indicate that "glittering opportunities" would beckon following victory in the Norwegian Sea, they need to be interrogated closely. See, e.g., Hugh K. O'Donnell, Jr., "Northern Flank Maritime Offensive," *U.S. Naval Institute Proceedings* 111 (Sept. 1985): 41-57.

37. See Colin S. Gray "Global Protracted War: Conduct and Termination," in Stephen J. Cimbala, ed., *Strategic War Termination* (New York: Praeger, 1986), pp. 75-96.

38. This point can be taken too far. In practice, Britain was obliged to send an army to fight on the continent in all of its major conflicts: e.g., in the wars against France from 1689 to 1815 except in 1778-83, and against Germany twice in the twentieth century. The British Army, traditionally, has been starved in time of peace and has had to be revived, with minimal lead time, in war. See Correlli Barnett, *Britain and Her Army, 1509-1970: A Military, Political, and Social Survey* (1970; London: Penguin, 1974), pp. xvii-xix.

39. Robert W. Komer, "Maritime Strategy vs. Coalition Defense," *Foreign Affairs* 60, (Summer 1982): 1124-44.

40. Michael Vlahos, "Maritime Strategy versus Continental Commitment?" *Orbis*, 26 (Fall 1982): 583-89.

41. George Ott, "Geopolitics for an Uncertain Era," *Air University Review* 33 (Sept.-Oct. 1982): 29-35.

42. Spykman, *America's Strategy in World Politics*, pp. 179-80.

43. Barnett has observed that "the British army has always enjoyed in its continental wars an advantage denied to Europeans: it can legitimately run away" (*Britain and Her Army*, p. xix).

44. This has been the long-standing Gaullist position, enduring long past Charles de Gaulle's period of authority. Both the British and the French national nuclear deterrent forces have been understood to function as insurance against the possibility of an American wish to enforce a "firebreak" between war in central Europe and war involving the superpower homelands. Also, it has long been believed that these national deterrents could have a "trigger" effect upon U.S. strategic nuclear forces; see Lawrence Freedman, *Britain and Nuclear Weapons* (London: Macmillan, 1980), pp. 131-32.

45. See Hans Speier, "Magic Geography," *Social Research*, Sept. 1941, pp. 310-30; Spykman, *Geography of the Peace*, chap. 2; Alan K. Henrikson, "The Map as an 'Idea': The Role of Cartographic Imagery during the Second World War," *American Cartographer* 2, no. 1 (1975): 19-53; and Alan K. Henrikson, "The Geographical 'Mental Maps' of American Foreign Policy Makers," *International Political Science Reivew* 1, no. 4 (1980): 495-530.

46. Moreover, naval power can prove to be a dangerous luxury. The British decision to end its "splendid isolation" and align against Imperial Germany was triggered in good part by recognition of the threat posed by "the luxury fleet" (Churchill's term) that Germany declared its intention to build. See Holger H.Herwig, *"Luxury Fleet": The Imperial German Navy, 1888-1918* (London: Allen & Unwin, 1980); and Churchill, *World Crisis,* pp. 11, 25-27. A recent study judges that "the construction of the German fleet had failed to provide Germany with the opportunity of becoming a major world power and had substantially contributed to her so-called encirclement": Ivo Nikolai Lambi, *The Navy and German Power Politics, 1862-1914* (Boston: Allen & Unwin, 1984), p. 427.

47. Under the new forward-pressure maritime strategy of the U.S. Navy, Soviet bastions in the far north and in the Sea of Japan would be at early risk in war. See David B. Rivkin, Jr., "No Bastions for the Bear," *U.S. Naval Institute Proceedings* 110, (April 1984): 36-43; R.T. Ackley, "No Bastions for the Bear: Round 2," *U.S. Naval Institute Proceedings* 111 (April 1985): 42-47; and Watkins *et al., Maritime Strategy.*

48. Corbett, *Some Principles of Maritime Strategy,* p. 116. See Corbett also on "general" and "local" command.

49. See Jeffrey Record, "Sanctuary Warfare," *Baltimore Sun,* March 26, 1985, p. 7. For the full set of criticisms of the maritime strategy, see John. J. Mearsheimer, "A Strategic Misstep: The Maritime Strategy and Deterrence in Europe," *International Security* 11 (Fall 1986): 3-57.

50. See Gray, "Maritime Strategy," pp. 34-42.

51. Albert Wohlstetter, "Illusions of Distance," *Foreign Affairs* 46, (Jan. 1968): 242-55. Essential historical background is provided in Martin van Creveld, *Supplying War: Logistics from Wallenstein to Patton* (New York: Cambridge Univ. Press, 1977).

52. An excellent discussion is Gooch, *Plans of War,* chaps. 6-7.

53. The Soviet Union has developed the sea route from its Baltic republics to East Germany in order to help reduce the scale of its potential Polish problem.

54. E.g., Clark et al., *Defense Reform Debate;* Luttwak, *Pentagon and the Art of War;* James Coates and Michael Kilian, *Heavy Losses: The Dangerous Decline of American Defense* (New York: Viking, 1985); Robert J. Art, Vincent Davis, and Samuel P. Huntington, eds., *Reorganizing America's Defense: Leadership in War and Peace* (Washington, D.C.: Pergamon-Brassey, 1985); Senate Committee on Armed Services, *Defense Organization: The Need for Change, Staff Report,* 99th Cong., 1st sess. (Washington, D.C.: U.S. Government Printing Office, 1985); and William J. Lynn and Barry R. Posen, "The Case for JCS Reform," *International Security* 10 (Winter 1985-86): 69-97.

55. E.g., "in June 1944, 54.35 percent of the German army consisted of fighting soldiers, against 38 percent of the American army. Forty-four point nine percent of the German army was employed in combat divisions, against 20.8 percent of the American. While the U.S. army became a huge industrial organization, whose purpose sometimes seemed to be forgotten by those who administrated it, the German army was designed solely as a machine for waging war": Max Hastings, *Overlord: D-Day and the Battle for Normandy* (New York: Simon & Schuster, 1984), p. 184.

56. Ibid., pp. 186-95. Compare Hastings's sweeping judgments with the au-

thoritative firsthand "sharp-end" opinions in the report of Maj. Gen. Isaac D. White (2nd Armored Division), *"United States vs German Equipment"* (March 20, 1945), prepared for Gen. Dwight D. Eisenhower.

57. The standard work is Russell F. Weigley, *The American Way of War* (New York: Macmillan, 1973). A perceptive review essay is Reginald C. Stuart, "War and the American Experience: Some New Perspectives," in Brian Bond and Ian Roy, eds., *War and Society: A Yearbook of Military History* (London: Croom, Helm, 1975), pp. 243-51.

58. See Luttwak, *Pentagon and the Art of War,* chap. 5, for a brilliant assault on the inappropriate application of the criteria of business efficiency to military issues. A no less brilliant critique of reformers' theses is Richard K. Betts, "Conventional Strategy: New Critics, Old Choices," *International Security* 7 (Spring 1983): 140-62.

59. Outstanding statements of this argument are MacKubin Thomas Owens, "The Utility of Force," *Backgrounder,* no. 370 (Aug. 1, 1984); and "The Hollow Promise of JCS Reform," *International Security* 10 (Winter 1985-86): 98-111.

60. Neglect of this basic point is one of the systematic weaknesses in Luttwak, *Pentagon and the Art of War.* See Samuel P. Huntington, "Playing to Win," *National Interest,* no. 3 (Spring 1986): 8-16.

61. The outstanding text of the maritime school is Corbett, *Some Principles of Maritime Strategy.*

62. The Reagan administration has not, let it be emphasized, endeavored to downplay its major continental commitment to NATO-Europe or promulgated a maritime unilateralist alternative to a continental coalition strategy. The Eurasian commitments, with their very long sea and air lines of communication, mandate U.S. supremacy at sea. For a strongly worded statement that the plans of the U.S. Navy are nevertheless a threat to the military integrity of NATO strategy, see Robert W. Komer, *Maritime Strategy or Coalition Defense?* (Cambridge, Mass.: Abt Books, 1984).

63. See Gregory D. Foster, "Missing and Wanted: A U.S. Grand Strategy," *Strategic Review* 13 (Fall 1985): 16.

6. The American Way

1. Booth, *Strategy and Ethnocentrism,* p. 147.

2. See Daniels, *Russia,* pp. 84-89, 281-89.

3. Michael Howard, "The Bewildered American Raj: Reflections on a Democracy's Foreign Policy," *Harper's,* March 1985, pp. 56-57.

4. An interesting set of essays relevant to this claim is Richard Rosecrance, ed., *America as an Ordinary Country: U.S. Foreign Policy and the Future* (Ithaca, N.Y.: Cornell Univ. Press, 1976).

5. See Vlahos, *America.*

6. An outstanding analysis is Edward L. Keenan, "Russian Political Culture," unpublished paper, July 1976 (Russian Research Center, Harvard University). On the perils of approaching Russian history with a modern agenda, see Keenan's review article, "Russian History and Soviet Politics," *Problems of Communism* 33 (Jan.-Feb. 1984): 68-72.

7. Booth, *Strategy and Ethnocentrism,* p. 17.

8. The government's foreign policy performance was impressive in the late 1940s, with the achievement of the Truman Doctrine (aid to Greece and Turkey, in the first instance), the Marshall Plan, Point Four, and the NATO Alliance. But President Truman did not develop a military policy adequately supportive of the foreign policy commitments the United States acquired in those years. See Gaddis, *Strategies of Containment*, chaps. 3-4. For some historical perspective upon the quality of U.S. performance in defense preparedness, see James L. Abrahamson, *America Arms for a New Century: The Making of a Great Military Power* (New York: Free Press, 1981); Russell F. Weigley, *History of the United States Army*, enlarged ed. (1967; Bloomington: Indiana Univ. Press, 1984); and Millett and Maslowski, *For the Common Defense*.

9. It has been "the American Way" to employ hastily improvised mass armies in time of dire need. Until Vietnam the U.S. Army always managed to do well enough to win, but its record is noticeably short of first-rate performances. In World War I, at St. Mihiel and in the Meuse-Argonne, American soldiers compensated with enthusiasm and in casualties for what they lacked in combat skills—against a German Army in sharp decline. In World War II, fortunately, the U.S. Army rarely met the German Army on anything close to equal terms; when they did, as in Italy, the results were not flattering to American self-esteem. I believe that political constraints were fatal to U.S. prospects of success in Vietnam but do not subscribe to the opinion that the Army waged that war as effectively as it could, given the constraints of sanctuaries in Cambodia, Laos, and North Vietnam. The student of Vietnam should recall that the U.S. Army's hundred-year performance in policing the frontier against the Indians was rarely of five-star quality. Unlike the British on their North West Frontier, the Americans persistently failed to acknowledge that the Indian problem was essentially a matter of imperial police work. "Though frequently criticized, the standard [U.S.] offensive method [against the Indians] was never seriously threatened. Heavy columns of infantry and cavalry, locked to slow-moving supply trains, continued to crawl about the vast western distances in search of an enemy who could scatter and vanish almost instantly": Robert M. Utley, *Frontier Regulars: The United States Army and the Indian, 1866-1891* (New York: Macmillan, 1973), p. 53. Elsewhere, Utley has claimed that "even though the regular army found its principal sanction in the frontier, its leaders, from the dropsical general in chief Winfield Scott—'Old Fuss and Feathers'—on down, steadfastly refused to face up to the realities of the frontier mission. They seemed to have learned nothing from earlier experiences with eastern Indians": Robert M. Utley and Wilcomb E. Washburn, *Indian Wars* (New York: American Heritage, 1985), p. 172. Similarly, the U.S. Army in the 1960s declined to recognize that it might have something to learn from the failure of the French Army in Indochina.

10. On strategic nuclear doctrine, see Lawrence Freedman, *The Evolution of Nuclear Strategy* (London: Macmillan, 1981); Thomas Powers, "Choosing a Strategy for World War III," *Atlantic* 250 (Nov. 1982), pp. 82-110; and Leon Sloss and Marc Dean Millot, "U.S. Nuclear Strategy in Evolution," *Strategic Review* 12 (Winter 1984): 19-28. A positive description of change in the strategic thinking of the U.S. Navy is provided in Friedman, "U.S. Maritime Strategy," pp. 1071-75; a negative assessment pervades Komer, *Maritime Strategy or Coalition Defense?* For an interesting cultural perspective on recent changes in the doctrine of the U.S.

Army, see Herbert I. London, *Military Doctrine and the American Character: Reflections on AirLand Battle*, Agenda Paper No. 14 (New York: National Strategy Information Center, 1984).

11. There is no generally acknowledged standard text on the history of U.S. postwar national security policy, but three books, published roughly ten years apart, are of particular value: Samuel P. Huntington, *The Common Defense: Strategic Programs in National Politics* (New York: Columbia Univ. Press, 1961); George H. Quester, *Nuclear Diplomacy: The First Twenty-Five Years*, 2d ed. (1970; New York: Dunellen, 1983); and Gaddis, *Strategies of Containment*.

12. See Holmes, *Mood/Interest Theory*.

13. Ironically, perhaps, the optimism in American culture is congruent with the optimism mandated, indeed exhorted, in the state ideology of the Soviet Union. A more genuine area of cultural congruence has been noted by Robert Daniels: "The Russian Revolution, like the American, put an end to a society of deference in which ordinary people acknowledged the natural superiority of the elite. Psychologically, Americans often find that they have much in common with Russians—personal openness, informality, simplicity of manner, and lack of ceremony, in contrast to the greater polish and protocol that embellish life in Europe" (*Russia*, p. 318).

14. Foster, "Missing and Wanted," p. 15.

15. Gen. Daniel O. Graham, in a question-and-answer session at a conference on SDI at the Georgia Institute of Technology, Atlanta, Nov. 17, 1985.

16. For a different view, see Ken Booth, "American Strategy: The Myths Revisited," in Booth and Moorhead Wright, eds., *American Thinking about Peace and War* (New York: Barnes & Noble, 1978), pp. 7-13.

17. From 1776 to the present day, the United States has been at war for 37.3 years (including such undeclared wars as Korea and Vietnam). The comparable figure for Prussia/Germany is only 26.1 years (van Creveld, *Fighting Power*, p. 12).

18. See Richard Pipes, "Militarism and the Soviet State," *Daedalus* 109 (Fall 1980): 1-12.

19. Tibor Szamuely, *The Russian Tradition* (New York: McGraw-Hill, 1974), p. 23.

20. This belief intrudes in the most unlikely places. For example, in an otherwise perceptive, even pathbreaking essay, Gregory Foster could write: "Ethnocentrism lies at the root of misperception, and misperception lies at the root of conflict (even among presumed allies)" ("Missing and Wanted," p. 21). Ethnocentrism and the misperception it feeds do unquestionably stoke the fire of international conflict and in some instances may lie at its root, as Foster claims. But the greatest conflicts in Western history—between Athens and Sparta, Rome and Carthage, Christian and Moslem, Catholic and Protestant, Revolutionary/Imperial France and Great Britain, France and Germany, Britain and Germany, and now the United States and the Soviet Union—can all be explained with scant reference to the malign effects of ethnocentrism and consequent reciprocal misperception.

21. The Soviet concept of a true peace is remarkably similar to the Roman concept of *pax*. "The Roman peace meant world empire with security from outside interference, law and order within": Chester G. Starr, *The Roman Empire, 27 B.C.–A.D. 476: A Study in Survival* (New York: Oxford Univ. Press, 1982), p. 16.

22. Luttwak, *Grand Strategy of the Roman Empire*, p. 137.

23. Speech printed in *Pravda*, Nov. 30, 1920, quoted in William E. Odom,

"Soviet Force Posture: Dilemmas and Directions," *Problems of Communism* 34 (July-Aug. 1985): 2.

24. Ibid.

25. "President's Speech on Military Spending and a New Defense," *New York Times*, March 24, 1983, p. 20. See Colin S. Gray, "The Transition from Offense to Defense," *Washington Quarterly* (Summer 1983): 59-72.

26. For an unintended parody of the American faith in the negotiating process, see William L. Ury, *Getting to Yes* (Boston: Houghton, Mifflin, 1981). A classic treatment is Fred Charles Ikle, *How Nations Negotiate* (1964; New York: Praeger, 1967). Recent analyses of Soviet negotiating behavior include Joseph G. Whelan, *Soviet Diplomacy and Negotiating Behavior: The Emerging New Context for U.S. Diplomacy* (Boulder, Colo.: Westview Press, 1983); Richard Pipes, "Diplomacy and Culture: Negotiation Styles," in Richard F. Staar, ed., *Arms Control: Myth versus Reality* (Stanford, Calif.: Hoover Institution Press, 1984), pp. 154-62; and Leon Sloss and M. Scott Davis, eds., *A Game for High Stakes: Lessons Learned in Negotiating with the Soviet Union* (Cambridge, Mass.: Ballinger, 1986). For a generally persuasive argument that the U.S. Department of State is wrongly organized—indeed, inappropriate in its basic diplomatic ethos—for the conduct of foreign policy toward any totalitarian great power, see Pipes, *Survival Is Not Enough*, pp. 273-77.

27. Richard Pipes has observed: "The Department of State is the branch of government specifically responsible for diplomacy in all its aspects, and this involves, first and foremost, the peaceful resolution of disagreements and conflicts with other sovereign states. The task has a great deal in common with law. And indeed, on closer acquaintance, the Department gives the impression of a giant law firm.... Essentially, diplomacy is a device for settling disputes out of court, the court, in the case of international conflicts, being the battlefield" (*Survival Is Not Enough*, pp. 273-74).

28. For a highly unauthorized and unflattering discussion, see Strobe Talbott, *Deadly Gambits: The Reagan Administration and the Stalemate in Nuclear Arms Control* (New York: Knopf, 1984).

29. E.g., by the spring of 1983, Soviet leaders had a ringside seat for the spectacle of the NATO Alliance negotiating publicly within itself on the question of how soon and in what way the United States should abandon its "zero-zero" negotiating position in the INF (Intermediate-Range Nuclear Force) negotiations.

30. Hamilton, Madison, and Jay, *Federalist Papers*, p. 36.

31. I have developed this thesis in "Reflections on Empire: The Soviet Connection," *Military Review* 62 (Jan. 1982): 2-13. For a superb, terse discussion of Soviet imperialism, see Luttwak, "Q and A."

32. For a noteworthy late Vietnam-era tract sympathetic to noninterventionism, see Bruce M. Russett, *No Clear and Present Danger: A Skeptical View of the United States Entry into World War II* (New York: Harper and Row, 1972). On the policy connections between Left and Right on the subject of interventionism, see Tucker, "Isolation and Intervention."

7. Of National Interests

1. E.g., Jeffrey Record, *Revising U.S. Military Strategy: Tailoring Means to Ends* (Washington, D.C.: Pergamon-Brassey 1984).

2. See Nuechterlein, *America Overcommitted*.

3. For an interesting alternative view, see Walt, "Alliance Formation," pp. 3-41. Walt writes: "This analysis stands many familiar notions of geopolitics on their heads. For example, Halford Mackinder suggested that Russia gained great advantages from its geographic position at the center of the world 'Heartland.' The implications of alliance theory are that while this *may* provide some military advantages, it also greatly increases the number of potential enemies the centrally placed power will face" (p. 36 n.100; original emphasis). Walt argues that states prefer to balance threatening power rather than "bandwagon" with it—if the prospects for "balancing" success are at all reasonable. For all his praiseworthy recognition of the importance of geography, his argument as phrased is ridiculous: "More than any other factor, geography explains why so many of the world's significant powers have chosen to ally with the U.S." (p. 36). The attractiveness of the United States is its strength, not its distant location, else why not ally with New Zealand or Australia? In fact, Walt does not stand Mackinder on his head. Had he read geopolitical theory carefully, he could not have failed to notice that Mackinder did not predict that peripheral Eurasia would be unable to resist outward pressure from the Heartland. Far from challenging the Mackinderesque framework, Walt actually, though apparently unknowingly, advances arguments compatible with Spykman's variant of it.

4. Hamilton, Madison, Jay, *Federalist Papers*, p. 10.

5. An important recent study is Rosemary Foot, *The Wrong War: American Policy and the Dimensions of the Korean Conflict, 1950-1953* (Ithaca, N.Y.: Cornell Univ. Press, 1985).

6. It should not be supposed that the Chamberlain government was determined actually to fight over the issue of Poland in 1939. The British decision of March 31, 1939, to guarantee Poland's independence was a response as much to domestic criticism of the appeasement policy as to any conviction that a line had to be drawn. Furthermore, throughout the summer Chamberlain proceeded on the premise that Hitler was a statesman with finite goals and with whom business could be conducted. The casually issued Polish guarantee initiated a policy intended to effect the political rather than the military containment of Germany. See Murray, *Change in the European Balance of Power*, pp. 283, 289-90, 366.

7. By definition, there cannot be a Marxist government in the Third World. "Marxism," to the limited degree to which the *corpus* of Karl Marx's voluminous writings constitute a coherent system, posits a necessary relationship between a historically progressive capitalism and the creation by that maturing capitalism of an increasingly class-conscious proletariat. Countries with little industry cannot have a politically significant class-conscious proletariat in a Marxist sense. So-called Marxist governments have either been imposed by Soviet bayonets or involved dictatorship by a self-ascribed Marxist party on behalf of a yet-to-be-created proletariat.

8. "A Note on *The National Interest*," *National Interest*, no. 1 (Fall 1985): 3.

9. See Elvin Hatch, *Culture and Morality: The Relativity of Values in Anthropology* (New York: Columbia Univ. Press, 1983).

10. See the title essay in Michael Howard, *The Causes of Wars and Other Essays* (1983; London: Counterpoint, 1984), pp. 7-22.

11. Spykman, *Geography of the Peace*, p. 45.

12. Spykman, *America's Strategy in World Politics*, p. 461.

13. Ibid.

14. A view endorsed strongly in A.E. Campbell, "Franklin Roosevelt and Unconditional Surrender," in Langhorne, *Diplomacy and Intelligence*, pp. 219-41.

15. Kenneth Boulding usefully formalized the concept that power should diminish with the distance to its application as the "loss-of-strength gradient": *Conflict and Defense: A General Theory* (New York: Harper and Brothers, 1962), pp. 78-79, 245-47. Albert Wohlstetter challenged this traditional idea vigorously in his important article "Illusions of Distance," *Foreign Affairs* 46 (Jan. 1968): 242-55.

16. Even at the level of general nuclear war, geographical and geopolitical relationships are far from irrelevant; see the essays by Ciro Zoppo, Desmond Ball, Albert Legault, and Hubert Moineville in Zoppo and Zorgbibe, *On Geopolitics*, chaps. 5-8. Professional soldiers understandably wax indignant when academic strategists prescribe ground warfare while ignoring such mundane factors as climate, terrain, distance, and their attendant logistic difficulties. Maps can deceive. An example of grand strategic conception and geographical absurdity was the Balkan project of 1944, dear to some British hearts. The idea was to effect a breakout from the Po valley to Austria via the so-called "Ljubljana Gap." If any Balkan option for Britain and the United States made sense in 1943-44, it was not an advance from northern Italy. See Michael Howard, *The Mediterranean Strategy in the Second World War* (London: Weidenfeld & Nicolson, 1968), pp. 65-68; and Henrikson, "The Map as an 'Idea.' "

17. The most recent major foray of reinterpretation is Deborah Welch Larson, *Origins of Containment: A Psychological Explanation* (Princeton, N.J.: Princeton Univ. Press, 1985).

18. Daniels, *Russia*, p. 355.

19. See P.H. Vigor, "Doubts and Difficulties Confronting a Would-be Soviet Attacker," *RUSI Journal* 125 (June 1980): 32-38; and Benjamin S. Lambeth, "Uncertainties for the Soviet War Planner," *International Security* 7 (Winter 1982-83): 139-66.

20. Parker, *Mackinder*, p. 203.

21. Luttwak, *Grand Strategy of the Soviet Union*, p. 87.

22. An important study that emphasizes the harmful effect upon cohesiveness and continuity in policymaking of the rise of an ideologically committed professional elite, in place of traditional "establishment" people, is I.M. Destler, Leslie H. Gelb, and Anthony Lake, *Our Own Worst Enemy: The Unmaking of American Foreign Policy* (New York: Touchstone, 1985), esp. chap. 2. The authors argue that the new policy "professionals" of both Left and Right are far more committed to the promotion of particular ideas in policy than to the conduct of the business of government per se.

23. "The Young Emperor William II and his advisers made their debut in foreign policy by refusing to renew the famous Reinsurance Treaty with Russia, an

agreement which was, in every sense of the term, the cornerstone of the Bismarckian alliance system": William L. Langer, *The Diplomacy of Imperialism, 1890-1902*, 2d ed. (1935; New York: Knopf, 1968), p. 3. Though it would seem that the new Kaiser did not intend any shift in the substance of Berlin's policy toward Russia, the refusal to renew the Reinsurance Treaty, closely followed by a marked warming in Anglo-German relations (Germany traded major claims in East Africa for the small but supremely strategic island of Heligoland), produced understandable feelings of isolation and vulnerability in St. Petersburg; these found expression in the Franco-Russian Military Convention of August 1892 and alliance of 1894. See ibid., chap. 2; and Kennan, *The Fateful Alliance*. By 1894 anti-Russian rhetoric in Berlin and rumors (particularly out of Italy) that Britain might welcome some form of association with the Triple Alliance (of Germany, Austria-Hungary, and Italy—1882, renewed in 1887) had served to alarm both Russia and France.

24. With the benefit of hindsight, it is easy to condemn a policy of appeasement that seemed to many intelligent people at the time no more than a realistic recognition of the restoration of Germany's quite proper power position. In itself, German rearmament after 1933 was neither alarming nor surprising. It was the Versailles arms control restraints on the defeated Germany that were extraordinary and, many British officials believed, in need of amendment as Germany returned to the normal run of great-power diplomacy. This is not to exonerate the imprudence of British policy in 1938 but to suggest that the true monstrousness of the Nazi regime and the scope of its ambitions are infinitely plainer in the 1980s than they were through most of the 1930s. See Watt, "British Intelligence"; and Wark, *Ultimate Enemy*.

25. Winston S. Churchill, *The Second World War*, vol. 1, *The Gathering Storm* (1948; London: Reprint Society, 1950), pp. 178-79.

8. Organizing the Rimland

1. Gregory F. Treverton, *Making the Alliance Work: The United States and Western Europe* (Ithaca, N.Y.: Cornell Univ. Press, 1985).

2. See the overview in Tucker, "Isolation and Intervention."

3. Historical perspective is provided in the brilliant essay by Michael Howard, "War in the Making and Unmaking of Europe," in Howard, *Causes of Wars*, pp. 171-88.

4. Notwithstanding the rapidity of U.S. demobilization in 1945 and the trivial scale of its atomic armament at the time, it seems probable that Stalin accepted a near-global U.S. hegemony—beyond eastern Europe—as a regrettable fact of life resting upon both U.S. warmaking potential and U.S. military technology. NATO was essential for the rational organization of military containment in Europe, but it is doubtful that it clarified Stalin's appreciation of his geopolitical problems and opportunities. "What the Second World War established was not a new British hegemony, but a Soviet hegemony over the Euro-Asian land mass from the Elbe to Vladivostok; and what was seen, at least from Moscow, as an American hegemony over the rest of the world; one freely accepted in Western Europe as a preferable alternative to being absorbed by the rival hegemony" (Howard, "Causes of Wars,"

p. 20). "Until well into the postwar period America did not have to concern itself with the balance of power, for it was by itself the balance of power" (Henry Kissinger, "The Long Journey," *Washington Post*, Dec. 17, 1985, p. A19).

5. See Odom, "Soviet Force Posture," pp. 1-14; and John Hines, Phillip A. Petersen, and Notra Trulock III, "Soviet Military Theory from 1945-2000: Implications for NATO," *Washington Quarterly* 9 (Fall 1986): 117-37.

6. See Gray, *Wartime Influence of Sea Power*.

7. Not infrequently, the opinion is expressed in the U.S. defense community that NATO is essentially a U.S.–West German alliance. The critical nature of West German contributions is beyond question, but proponents of the Washington-Bonn linchpin theory should consider the strategic geography of a NATO without Britain. If a neutralist Britain were to tilt toward Moscow, the northern—and hence western—flanks of NATO-Europe would be uncovered; Norway would be isolated behind the Soviet strategic frontier; Soviet maritime and air power would have very much easier access to the North Atlantic sea lines of communication; and the United States could not fight in continental Europe unless it first neutralized an actually or potentially hostile Britain. A similar judgment pertains to the strategic necessity for the United States to neutralize Cuba as a base for Soviet military power at the outset of any armed conflict in Europe.

8. Steven F. Kime, "Warsaw Pact: Juggernaut or Paper Tiger?" *Air Force Magazine* 65 (June 1982): 67-69.

9. See the collection of essays in David Holloway and Jane M. O. Sharp, eds., *The Warsaw Pact: Alliance in Transition?* (Ithaca, N.Y.: Cornell Univ. Press, 1984).

10. The merits of NATO are very well summarized in Morton H. Halperin, "Keeping Our Troops in Europe," *New York Times Magazine*, Oct. 17, 1982, pp. 82-84, 86-88, 93-97. On the troubles of the alliance set in historical perspective, see Michael Howard, "Reassurance and Deterrence: Western Defense in the 1980s," *Foreign Affairs* 61 (Winter 1982-83): 309-24; and Eliot A. Cohen, "The Long-Term Crisis of the Alliance," *Foreign Affairs* 61 (Winter 1982-83): 325-43.

11. See Laurence Martin, *NATO and the Defense of the West: An Analysis of America's First Line of Defense* (New York: Holt, Rinehart & Winston, 1985), pp. 121, 126.

12. The maritime element of U.S. national security policy under President Reagan is intended explicitly to strengthen deterrence in Europe by the threat of a horizontal escalation to and in regions of comparative Western military advantage (see West, "Maritime Strategy and NATO Deterrence"). There is no strategic novelty in this idea. Defending the "Carter Doctrine" of U.S. interests in the security of the Persian Gulf region (enunciated on January 23, 1980), Zbigniew Brzezinski has written: "In our private contingency preparations, I made the point of instructing the Defense Department to develop options involving both 'horizontal and vertical escalation' in the event of a Soviet military move toward the Persian Gulf, by which I meant that we would be free to choose either the terrain or the tactic or the level of our response": *Power and Principle: Memoirs of the National Security Adviser, 1977-1981* (New York: Farrar, Straus & Giroux, 1983), p. 445. See also Brzezinski, *Game Plan: A Geostrategic Framework for the Conduct of the U.S.-Soviet Contest* (Boston: Atlantic Monthly Press, 1986).

13. The most substantial broadside of recent years is delivered in Melvyn Krauss, *How NATO Weakens the West* (New York: Simon & Schuster, 1986).

14. Per capita defense expenditures for 1983 (in current U.S. dollars) were $1,023 for the United States, $272 for Belgium, $439 for Britain, $394 for France, $363 for West Germany, $172 for Italy, and $300 for the Netherlands: International Institute for Strategic Studies, *Military Balance, 1985-1986*, p. 170.

15. Martin, *NATO and the Defense of the West*, p. 121.

16. Brzezinski has defended the means-ends mismatch that characterized the strategic context for the Carter Doctrine: "As a practical matter there is no way for the United States to reach the conclusion secretly that the Persian Gulf is in our vital interest, then to build up our military forces in order to have the capability of responding locally, and only then to announce that the United States is committed to such a defense. In a democracy such as ours, only a public commitment is capable of generating the necessary budgetary support and the other decisions that are needed to implement a commitment. In the meantime, the very awareness in Moscow and elsewhere of America's engagement serves as the immediate deterrent" (*Power and Principle*, p. 446). Fortunately for the United States and for world peace, the Carter Doctrine was designed to cope with the Soviet Union rather than the Third Reich. Carter in 1980 and Chamberlain in 1939 were both in the business of political rather than military containment. In the words of Williamson Murray: "In the last half of March 1939 the Chamberlain Cabinet feared that war was at hand. It panicked and decided that it could deter the Germans by guaranteeing the independence of Poland" (*The Change in the European Balance of Power*, p. 366). While the "art of commitment" (Schelling, *Arms and Influence*, chap. 2) has to be practiced differently in the face of an Adolf Hitler rather than a Leonid Brezhnev, *and in the context of nuclear arms*, the fact remains that the voluntary accumulation of security commitments far ahead of military capability for their protection is a dangerous enterprise. The outstanding brief treatment of the security problem posed by Hitler's purpose and style is Alan Bullock, "Hitler and the Origins of the Second World War," in Hans W. Gatzke, ed., *European Diplomacy between Two Wars, 1919-1939* (Chicago: Quadrangle, 1972), pp. 221-46.

17. For AirLand Battle doctrine, see *Operations, FM 100-1* (Washington, D.C.: Department of the Army, 1981); *Operations, FM 100-5* (Washington, D.C.: Department of the Army, 1982); and *Airland Battle 2000* (Ft. Monroe, Va.: U.S. Army Training and Doctrine Command, 1982). The spirit of AirLand Battle is conveyed well in William S. Lind, "The Case for Maneuver Doctrine," and Huba Wass de Czege, "Army Doctrinal Reform," both in Clark et al., *Defense Reform Debate*, pp. 88-100, 101-20.

18. For the American rediscovery of the operational level of war, which is a key to AirLand Battle doctrine, see Edward N. Luttwak, "The Operational Level of War," *International Security* 5 (Winter 1980-81): 61-79. An excellent discussion of NATO-European reactions to AirLand Battle is Jacqueline K. Davis, "Europe's Edgy Approach to Strategy," *Air Force Magazine* 68 (Dec. 1985): 82-88.

19. Brzezinski, *Power and Principle*, p. 446.

20. D.W. Brogan, *The American Character* (New York: Knopf, 1944), p. 150.

21. See Record, *Revising U.S. Military Strategy*.

22. A useful discussion is William T. Tow, "NATO's Out-of-Region Challenges and Extended Containment," *Orbis* 28 (Winter 1985): 829-55.

23. The defensive cast to French military doctrine in the 1930s was in part predetermined by French concern lest an offensive strategy discourage the British

from making a firm continental commitment. The strategic logic of the Maginot Line was "to incite the Germans to invade through Belgium" (Gen. Maurice Chauvineau, quoted in Posen, *Sources of Military Doctrine*, p. 114) and hence to structure a conflict geostrategically in such a way that British intervention would be well-nigh inevitable.

24. GNP for 1984 (in U.S. dollars): U.S.A., $3,619.2 billion; U.S.S.R., $1,672-$1,920 billion; NATO-Europe, $2,429.5 billion. Population: U.S.A., 239,600,000; U.S.S.R., 276,500,000; NATO-Europe, 373,177,000. NATO-Europe is NATO less the U.S.A., Canada, and Iceland. Source: IISS, *Military Balance, 1985-1986*.

25. With periodic variations in detail, the U.S. government has long envisaged approximately 60 percent of its ground divisions (17 percent of 28⅓, on mobilization) and tactical fighter wings (25 of 41) as having primarily a NATO role. Most of the U.S. Navy has been assigned, more or less directly, to North Atlantic SLOC protection, while the extended deterrence mission of the strategic nuclear forces has always been a major source of budgetary justification. See William W. Kaufmann, *Planning Conventional Forces* (Washington, D.C.: Brookings, 1982), p. 7. Comparative military effort among NATO countries is treated competently in Martin, *NATO and the Defense of the West*; and in Caspar W. Weinberger, *Report on Allied Contributions to the Common Defense* (Washington, D.C.: Department of Defense, 1986).

26. British historian Michael Howard has observed: "I do not believe that Western Europe ever could create for itself an independent centre of military power, and I emphatically do not believe that it should" ("War in the Making and Unmaking of Europe," p. 187).

27. See Krauss, *How NATO Weakens the West*.

28. Many Americans understand their having to pay a "leadership premium," but they wonder if they are underwriting a substantial fraction of the welfare state structures so generously entrenched in the budgets of their European allies.

29. See Harlan Cleveland, *NATO: The Transatlantic Bargain* (New York: Harper & Row, 1970).

30. Switzerland has been able to maintain a condition of heavily armed neutrality since the Napoleonic wars in good part because its terrain lends itself to territorial defense. Denmark and the Netherlands are less fortunate, geographically. Alfred von Schlieffen, in the design of his famous plan, seriously considered a "left hook" through Switzerland around the frontier defense that faced (then) German Alsace-Lorraine, but he judged the difficulty of the terrain to be too great.

31. The shocked NATO-European reactions to the Reykjavic, Iceland, summit of 1986 highlighted the tension between the enthusiasm of NATO-European (Atlanticist) elite opinion for nuclear deterrence and the absence of enthusiasm in elite and more popular opinion for actual nuclear use should prewar deterrence fail. European elites do not favor a conventional build-up that might diminish deterrence writ large. But in the event of war the absence of robust conventional defensive capability would inexorably propel NATO toward early nuclear use.

32. It is somewhat curious, though true in my experience, that of all the NATO allies France is the one that most often elicits admiration (privately) on the part of American officials and defense commentators. Despite its formal military with-

drawal from NATO and persisting residual doubts of French reliability in the event of war in Europe, France has bought, by its determinedly independent course, a quality of American respect that is unequaled for other European allies. A partial exception is the American view of the British armed forces and especially the British Army (in staggering contrast with World War II): notwithstanding the near-fatal technical inadequacies of the task force that Britain sent to the Falklands, American observers recognized behind the superior performance of the British light infantry in that campaign a unit cohesiveness and degree of tactical skill that are objectives for serious military reform in the United States.

33. Outstanding sympathetic American treatment of French strategic policy is David Yost, *France's Deterrent Posture and Security in Europe:* pt. 1, *Capabilities and Doctrine*, and pt. 2, *Strategic and Arms Control Implications*, Adelphi Papers Nos. 194 and 195 (London: IISS, 1984-85). A stimulating French perspective is Pierre Lellouche, *L'Avenir de la guerre* (Paris: Mazarine, 1985).

34. See Colin S. Gray, "Theater Nuclear Weapons: Doctrines and Postures," *World Politics* 28 (Jan. 1976): 300-314.

35. In fairness, it should be noted that although NATO-Europe is disquieted by the U.S. enthusiasm for operational maneuver—both backward (*trading NATO territory* for time and better counterattack possibilities) and forward (waging part of the war on Pact soil)—and for deep strike against uncommitted Soviet armies, that disquiet rests on fears of an unduly rapid escalation *and* of military inutility. With respect to the latter point, some European officials have noticed that AirLand Battle and FOFA are designed to defeat a form of Soviet theater offensive and operational method that may be in the process of being discarded. The deep echeloning of armies was an important part of the Soviets' 1960s and 1970s answer to the threat posed by NATO theater nuclear forces to the massing of troops for World War II–style breakthrough operations. But M.A. Gareyev, *Frunze: Military Theoretician* (Moscow: Voyenizdat, 1985) proclaims the obsolescence of the operational ideas that AirLand Battle and FOFA are designed to defeat. To summarize: while scarce NATO deep-strike assets (the purchase of which may shortchange NATO's direct battlefield support assets) were looking for Soviet second- and third-echelon armies, to destroy the timetable for their introduction into battle, a very much strengthened Soviet (and Pact-allied) first echelon would be attempting decisively and irreversibly to unravel the whole NATO defense. A nightmare vision for NATO planners is the possibility of a Pact offensive analogous to the Manstein plan unleashed by Germany on May 10, 1940: the Anglo-French (plus Belgian and Dutch) forces, though numerically superior and enjoying at least rough parity in quality of equipment, were defeated precipitately because they were often caught out of prepared positions in encounter battles (a form of combat in which the Germans excelled); they lacked strategic reserves (these were squandered in inactivity behind the Maginot Line and on an adventurous and strategically irrelevant foray into the south of the Netherlands); and they wasted their large air assets both in inactivity and in pitifully ineffective attacks against scattered German line-of-communication targets. AirLand Battle and FOFA could have disturbing potential similarities in action. On the actual and possible changes in Soviet theater doctrine, see Odom, "Soviet Force Posture." Also see Martin, *NATO and the Defense of the West*, esp. pp. 90-91, 117-19.

36. In practice, only the United States, Britain, Canada, and France have met

the 1978 goal of 3 percent sustained real growth. See IISS, *The Military Balance, 1985-1986*, pp. 38-39, 168, 195-98; and *The Military Balance, 1986-1987* (London: IISS, 1986), pp. 55-56, 234-35.

37. See Howard, "Reassurance and Deterrence," pp. 321-22.

38. The link between the targeting strategy appropriate for U.S. strategic nuclear forces and extended-deterrence ties is not as well appreciated as it should be. Useful analyses include Edward N. Luttwak, "The Problems of Extending Deterrence," in *The Future of Strategic Deterrence*, pt. 1, Adelphi Papers No. 160 (London: IISS, 1980), pp. 31-37; Earl C. Ravenal, "Counterforce and Alliance: The Ultimate Connection," *International Security* 6 (Spring 1982): 26-43; Anthony H. Cordesman, *Deterrence in the 1980s*, pt. 1, *American Strategic Forces and Extended Deterrence*, Adelphi Papers No. 175 (London: IISS, 1982); and Earl C. Ravenal, *NATO: The Tides of Discontent*, Policy Papers in International Affairs No. 23 (Berkeley, Calif.: Institute of International Studies, 1985), pp. 19-34.

39. Richard K. Betts has emerged as the apostle of the strategic virtues of the uncertainty principle: see his "Conventional Deterrence: Predictive Uncertainty and Policy Confidence," *World Politics* 37 (Jan. 1985): 153-79; "Security and Solidarity: NATO's Balancing Act after the Deployment of Intermediate-Range Nuclear Forces," *Brookings Review*, Summer 1985, pp. 26-34; and "Compound Deterrence vs. No-First-Use: What's Wrong Is What's Right," *Orbis* 28 (Winter 1985): 697-718. Betts on theater defense, much like Robert Jervis on strategic nuclear issues, has the rare distinction of being wrong for most of the right reasons. Unlike many American defense commentators, Betts understands how strategic improvements in alliance defense can undermine the political confidence in Europe that is essential for the very functioning of the alliance as an instrument of deterrence. But—a large and fatal "but"—his sophisticated analyses lead him to endorse a strategy and posture for NATO that would almost certainly fail militarily were it ever to be tested in combat. Betts's argument is clear, politically astute, but fundamentally irresponsible. The same judgment applies to Lawrence Freedman, "NATO Myths," *Foreign Policy*, no. 45 (Winter 1981-82): 48-68. Betts and Freedman should recall the price paid by all of Europe for the success of French grand strategy in the late 1930s (see Posen, *Sources of Military Doctrine*, chap. 4): France succeeded in constructing a deterrent so inoffensive that Britain was again ensnared in a continental commitment—while the deterrent both failed to deter and proved incapable of defense.

40. See Henry S. Rowen, "The Evolution of Strategic Nuclear Doctrine," in Laurence Martin, ed., *Strategic Thought in the Nuclear Age* (Baltimore, Md.: Johns Hopkins Univ. Press, 1979), pp. 131-56; Aaron L. Friedberg, "A History of the U.S. Strategic 'Doctrine'—1945 to 1980," *Journal of Strategic Studies* 3 (Dec. 1980): 37-71; Lawrence Freedman, *The Evolution of Nuclear Strategy* (London: Macmillan, 1981), esp. chap. 25; Desmond Ball, "U.S. Strategic Forces: How Would They Be Used?" *International Security* 7 (Winter 1982-83): 31-60; Desmond Ball, *Targeting for Strategic Deterrence*, Adelphi Papers No. 185 (London: IISS, 1983); and the essays collected in Desmond Ball and Jeffrey Richelson, eds., *Strategic Nuclear Targeting* (Ithaca, N.Y.: Cornell Univ. Press, 1986).

41. The point is stressed rigorously in Ravenal, "Counterforce and Alliance."

42. On this and related issues, see Colin S. Gray: "Nuclear Strategy: The Case

for a Theory of Victory," *International Security* 4 (Summer 1979): 54-87; and *Nuclear Strategy and National Style*, chap. 9.

43. Thoughtful critics of the war-fighting school of deterrence theory have considerable difficulty praising discrimination and flexibility, while worrying that the search for more discriminating strategic capabilities may fuel aspirations for a chimerical military advantage. This tension pervades Jervis, *The Illogic of American Nuclear Strategy*. In the heat of political debate, proponents of Reagan's SDI have endorsed the proposition that "offensive doctrines increase the probability and intensity of arms races and of wars" (Posen, *The Sources of Military Doctrine*, p. 16). But some NATO-Europeans, contemplating an indefinite period of transition in U.S. strategic posture from offense dominance to defense dominance, worry that an American president would come to see strategic defenses as permitting bold offensive actions. On the offense-defense relationship, see the rigorous discussion in Karl von Clausewitz, *On War*, ed. Michael Howard and Peter Paret (1832; Princeton, N.J.: Princeton Univ. Press, 1976), bk. 6, chaps. 1-7; bk. 7, chaps. 1-3. The sins of the more thoroughgoing contemporary American critics of offensive doctrines have been well exposed in Scott Sagan, "1914 Revisited: Allies, Offense, and Instability," *International Security* 11 (Fall 1986): 151-75.

44. Although reunification is nowhere in sight, the government of West Germany declines to take even modest defensive measures that might appear to symbolize a permanence to the inner-German boundary. Bonn has consistently refused to construct or permit construction of field fortifications in aid of the forward defense commitment of the alliance, upon the integrity of which it insists rigidly.

45. Soviet commentators can point to articles in the American press advocating one or another variant of U.S. military disengagement from western Europe. For a superior recent example, see Eliot A. Cohen, "Do We Still Need Europe?" *Commentary* 81 (Jan. 1986): 28-35.

46. See Jeffrey D. Boutwell, Paul Doty, and Gregory F. Treverton, *The Nuclear Confrontation in Europe* (Dover, Mass.: Auburn House, 1985).

47. See David Yost, "European Anxieties about Ballistic Missile Defense," *Washington Quarterly* 7 (Fall 1984): 112-29; and Payne, *Strategic Defense*, chap. 10.

48. "Final Manuscript of the Farewell Address," reprinted in Felix Gilbert, *To the Farewell Address: Ideas of Early American Foreign Policy* (Princeton, N.J.: Princeton Univ. Press, 1961), p. 145.

49. Selig Adler, *The Isolationist Impulse: Its Twentieth Century Reaction* (1957; New York: Collier, 1961), p. 17.

50. Cohen, "Do We Still Need Europe?" p. 34.

51. The theme is advanced in much more muted form in Betts, "Security and Solidarity," p. 32: "Incremental change is the alternative to fundamental change."

52. Cohen, "Do We Still Need Europe?" pp. 32-34.

53. Ibid., p. 35.

54. Spanish landpower never recovered from its smashing defeat at Rocroi on May 19, 1643. In that battle the young Duc d'Enghien (the Great Condé to be) inflicted irreparable loss upon the Spanish infantry.

55. See Derek McKay and H.M. Scott, *The Rise of the Great Powers, 1648-1815* (London: Longman, 1983), chap. 1.

56. For speculation on this possibility, see Colin S. Gray, "Maritime Strategy and the Pacific: The Implications for NATO," *Naval War College Review* 30 (Winter 1987): 8-19.

57. In 1904 Mackinder wrote: "Were the Chinese, for instance, organized by the Japanese, to overthrow the Russian Empire and conquer its territory, they might constitute the yellow peril to the world's freedom just because they would add an oceanic frontage to the resources of the great continent, an advantage as yet denied to the Russian tenant of the pivot region" ("Geographical Pivot of History," p. 264).

58. Spykman, *Geography of the Peace*, p. 43. However, as he made brutally plain, Spykman insisted that the United States required a condition of balanced power in Eurasia, allowing neither a superior Rimland nor a superior Heartland. In 1942 Spykman wrote: "If the peace objective of the United States is the creation of a united Europe, she is fighting on the wrong side. All-out aid to Mr. Hitler would be the quickest way to achieve an integrated transatlantic zone" (*America's Strategy in World Politics*, p. 466).

59. Cohen recognizes this point perhaps too generously: "Command of the sea is the sine qua non of successful American containment of the Soviet Union and its allies, but (as England discovered in each of its wars against Spain, France, and Germany) command of the sea can accomplish nothing without continental power" ("Do We Still Need Europe?" p. 29). The valid point lurking here is almost buried beneath the weight of excess in the claim. For example, British command of the sea in 1940—resting upon a contested dominion in the air—did preclude the feasibility of a German invasion. That is "something" in anybody's book.

9. The Course of Soviet Empire

1. See Paul A. Seabury, ed., *Balance of Power* (San Francisco: Chandler, 1954); Kenneth N. Waltz, *Theory of International Politics* (Reading, Mass.: Addison-Wesley, 1979); and Gilpin, *War and Change*.

2. See Ernest B. Haas, "The Balance of Power: Prescription, Concept, or Propaganda?" *World Politics* 5 (July 1953): 446-88.

3. In multipolar power systems there is a tendency to "buck-passing" and to the hope that other states will incur the major costs of balancing behavior. Recent scholarship includes Kenneth A. Oye, "Explaining Cooperation under Anarchy: Hypotheses and Strategies," *World Politics* 38 (Oct. 1985): 1-24; and Robert Jervis, "From Balance to Concert: A Study of International Security Cooperation," *World Politics* 38 (Oct. 1985): 58-79.

4. Mackinder, "The Geographical Pivot of History," pp. 260-62.

5. "Letters to the Editor," *London Times*, Dec. 30, 1985, p. 9.

6. Of course, the czars, and later the hierarchy of the Communist Party of the Soviet Union, achieved a fusion of religion/ideology and state that was not approximated in Byzantium, but "the Czarist concept of imperial power was that of Byzantium": Charles Diehl, *Byzantium: Greatness and Decline* (New Brunswick, N.J.: Rutgers Univ. Press, 1957), p. 296. See also Adda B. Bozeman, *Politics and Culture in International History* (Princeton, N.J.: Princeton Univ. Press, 1960), pp. 340-56, on the Byzantine impact on Russia.

7. "From the present time forth, in the post-Columbian age, we shall again have to deal with a closed political system, and none the less that it will be one of world-wide scope. Every explosion of social forces, instead of being dissipated in a surrounding circuit of unknown space and barbaric chaos, will be sharply re-echoed from the far side of the globe, and weak elements in the political and economic organism of the world will be shattered in consequence" (Mackinder, "The Geographical Pivot of History," p. 242).

8. Aaron Wildavsky, "America First," *National Interest*, no. 1 (Fall 1985): 117.

9. Such judgment is susceptible to influence by U.S. policy. The con-sequences of Soviet treaty noncompliance are at the discretion of the U.S. govern-ment, which to date has had policy regarding verification but not sanctions. For contrasting analyses, see Colin S. Gray, "Verification of Non-compliance: The Problem of Response," *Defense Science 2003 + 4* (Oct.-Nov. 1985): 29-39; and Jeanette Voas, "The Arms Control Compliance Debate," *Survival* 28 (Jan.-Feb. 1986): 8-31.

10. See Jack L. Snyder, *The Soviet Strategic Culture: Implications for Limited Nuclear Operations*, R-2154-AF (Santa Monica, Calif.: RAND, 1977); and Archie Brown, ed., *Political Culture and Communist Societies* (1984; Armonk, N.Y.: M.E. Sharpe, 1985).

11. See "X" [Kennan], "The Sources of Soviet Conduct."

12. E.g., Seweryn Bialer: *Stalin's Successors: Leadership, Stability, and Change in the Soviet Union* (Cambridge: Cambridge Univ. Press, 1980), chap. 9; and *The Soviet Paradox: External Expansion, Internal Decline* (New York: Knopf, 1986), pp. 36-38.

13. In the vast literature on the Russian revolution(s) I have leaned heavily on Adam B. Ulam, *The Bolsheviks: The Intellectual and Political History of the Triumph of Communism in Russia* (New York: Macmillan, 1965); Robert V. Daniels, *Red October: The Bolshevik Revolution of 1917* (1967; Boston: Beacon, 1984); Edward Crankshaw, *The Shadow of the Winter Palace: The Drift to Revolution, 1825-1917* (London: Mac-millan, 1976); Harrison E. Salisbury, *Black Night, White Snow: Russia's Revolutions, 1905-1917* (Garden City, N.Y.: Doubleday, 1978); Adam B. Ulam, *Russia's Failed Revolutions: From the Decembrists to the Dissidents* (New York: Basic Books, 1981); and Leonard Shapiro, *The Russian Revolutions of 1917: The Origins of Modern Com-munism* (New York: Basic Books, 1984).

14. Lenin's blueprint for an elitist party of dedicated and, above all else, disciplined revolutionaries appears in his 1902 polemic *What Is to Be Done?* See the excellent discussion in Ulam, *The Bolsheviks;* It is interesting that, according to Ulam, "Lenin thought of himself and wrote as a humble disciple of Karl Marx. His orderly and prosaic mind would have rebelled at the idea that his vision of the Party was closer to that of a collective superhuman Nietzschean hero or some medieval order of chivalry than to that of a humdrum political association, which the Social Democratic Party was supposed to be" (p. 179). But as Ulam has observed elsewhere: "The dazzling success which Lenin's organizational and tactical blueprint was to bring him in 1917 and 1918 ought not hide the fact that its formulation in 1902 was a serious blow to Russian Marxism. The Bolsheviks' attempts to put this blueprint in effect between 1903 and 1914 were to bring them to the verge of extinction as a serious political force and did considerable harm to the unity of the Russian working class, as well as the cause of political freedom in Russia" (*Russia's Failed Revolutions*, p. 144).

15. With Leninism in major key and Marxism in only a minor key.

16. The Anglo-Russian Convention demarcated spheres of influence in Persia, Afghanistan, and Tibet.

17. See Bridge and Bullen, *Great Powers*, pp. 159-62; and D.C.B. Lieven, *Russia and the Origins of the First World War* (London: Macmillan, 1983), chap. 2.

18. Notwithstanding the worthy endeavors of the American Catholic bishops in 1982-83 to provide moral guidance on the subject of nuclear deterrence. See National Conference of Catholic Bishops, "The Challenge of Peace: God's Promise and Our Response," *Origins* (National Conference Documentary Service) 13 (May 1, 1983).

19. See Samuel L. Sharp, "National Interest: Key to Soviet Politics," in Erik P. Hoffmann and Frederic J. Fleran, Jr., eds., *The Conduct of Soviet Foreign Policy*, 2d ed. (New York: Aldine, 1980), pp. 108-17.

20. Useful discussions of Soviet concepts and terminology are Benjamin S. Lambeth, "The Sources of Soviet Military Doctrine," in Frank B. Horton III et al., eds., *Comparative Defense Policy* (Baltimore, Md.: Johns Hopkins Univ. Press, 1984), pp. 200-216; Harriet Fast Scott and William F. Scott, *The Armed Forces of the U.S.S.R.* (Boulder, Colo.: Westview Press, 1979), chap. 3; Harriet Fast Scott and William F. Scott, eds., *The Soviet Art of War: Doctrine, Strategy, and Tactics* (Boulder, Colo.: Westview Press, 1982), pp. 1-15; John J. Dziak, *Soviet Perceptions of Military Power: The Interaction of Theory and Practice* (New York: Crane, Russak for National Strategy Information Center, 1981), chap. 3. On the general staff, see John Erickson, *The Russian Imperial/Soviet General Staff*, College Station Papers No. 3 (College Station: Texas A&M University, 1981).

21. The references to Mikhail Frunze tend to be more substantive, and his contribution to the Soviet military tradition is a serious one. See Mikhail V. Frunze, "A Unified Military Doctrine for the Red Army," in Scott and Scott, eds., *Soviet Art of War*, pp. 27-31; William E. Odom, "Soviet Force Posture: Dilemmas and Directions," *Problems of Communism* 34 (July-Aug. 1985): 1-14; and Condoleezza Rice, "The Making of Soviet Strategy," in Peter Paret, ed., *Makers of Modern Strategy: From Machiavelli to the Nuclear Age* (Princeton, N.J.: Princeton Univ. Press, 1986), pp. 648-76.

22. See Henry Steele Commager, *The Empire of Reason: How Europe Imagined and America Realized the Enlightenment* (New York: Oxford Univ. Press, 1977). For a stunning contrast in ethos and style, compare Lenin's influential pamphlets (*What Is To Be Done?*, *State and Revolution*, *Imperialism: The Highest Stage of Capitalism*) with *The Federalist Papers*. Both were polemical in purpose, but there the similarity ends.

23. "I have conceived of grand strategy as a chain of political ends and military means. Its effectiveness is highly dependent on the extent to which the ends and means are related to one another. The 'knitting-together' of political ends and military means I call political-military integration" (Posen, *Sources of Military Doctrine*, p. 25).

24. An excellent brief treatment of Soviet grand strategy is Pipes, *Survival Is Not Enough*, pp. 51-60.

25. A superb treatment is provided in Robert Conquest, ed., *The Last Empire: Nationality and the Soviet Future* (Stanford, Calif.: Hoover Institution Press, 1986). Also see Brzezinski, *Game Plan*.

26. The strategic significance of Cuba and Vietnam is illustrated graphically in

James D. Watkins, "The Maritime Strategy," in Watkins et al., *Maritime Strategy*, p. 7. See also Caspar W. Weinberger, *Soviet Military Power, 1986*, 5th ed. (Washington, D.C.: U.S. Government Printing Office, 1986), pp. 126-27.

27. I have been taken to task for seeing merit (in Soviet terms) in Soviet strategic policy, and taken even more severely to task for suggesting that the United States might be able to learn some useful things from Soviet practice. See Donald W. Hanson, "Is Soviet Doctrine Superior?" *International Security* 7 (Winter 1982-83): 61-83; and Wieseltier, *Nuclear War, Nuclear Peace*, pp. 47-53. Readers may judge for themselves from Gray, *Nuclear Strategy and National Style*, esp. chap. 3. As to whether the Soviet Union believes it could win a nuclear war, the rival schools of thought are well represented in Richard Pipes, "Why the Soviet Union Thinks It Could Fight and Win a Nuclear War," *Commentary* 64 (July 1977): 21-34; and Robert Arnett, "Soviet Attitudes towards Nuclear War: Do They Really Think They Can Win?" *Journal of Strategic Studies* 2 (Sept. 1979): 172-91. Understanding is better served by Fritz Ermath, "Contrasts in American and Soviet Strategic Thought," *International Security* 3 (Fall 1978): 138-55; and Dan L. Strode and Rebecca V. Strode, "Diplomacy and Defense in Soviet National Security Policy," *International Security* 8 (Fall 1983): 81-116.

28. Through the summer and fall of 1941 the Soviet Union had good reason to fear that Japan might emulate Mussolini's example and rush to the aid of the anticipated victor. But at the high tide of German optimism in late summer, Berlin positively discouraged Japanese assistance. The German invasion of Russia on June 22, 1941, was as much a surprise to Japan as was the Japanese attack on Pearl Harbor to the Germans; see Seaton, *The Russo-German War*, pp. 168-70. Stalin was not sure of Japanese intentions until after the direction of Japanese expansion was revealed in Dec. 1941 by the attacks on Pearl Harbor, the Philippines, and the British and Dutch East Indies. In fact, the trade embargo on strategic materials, particularly oil, imposed on Japan by the United States, Britain, and the Netherlands on July 22, 1941, had rendered the Siberian option logistically impractical. It is known now that "just three days after the start of the German invasion of the USSR at an army-navy liaison meeting the two [Japanese] services settled matters by adopting the southwards expansion option before turning to face whatever situation arose as a result of the Nazi-Soviet conflict. This decision was formalized at an imperial conference on 2 July": H.P. Willmott, *Empires in the Balance: Japanese and Allied Pacific Strategies to April 1942* (Annapolis, Md.: Naval Institute Press, 1982), p. 64.

29. An outstanding study is Norman Rich, *Hitler's War Aims: The Establishment of the New Order* (New York: Norton, 1974).

30. Pipes, *Survival Is Not Enough*, pp. 21-22.

31. Exceptions are the peoples of the Baltic states, of formerly Rumanian Bessarabia, and of Czechoslovakian Ruthenia. The massive population migrations of 1944-45 substantially emptied eastern Poland and East Prussia of their Polish and German inhabitants.

32. Concerning Nicholas I, the brother and successor of Alexander I, Crankshaw has written: "Nicholas followed Frederick of Prussia and Napoleon, preceded the young Franz Joseph of Austria and William II of Germany, in reversing the proper order of things by regarding their armies not as necessary and regrettably expensive shields for the civilian state, but as the supreme expressions of the

state for the support of which the civilian economy was designed" (*Shadow of the Winter Palace*, p. 52). For valuable background, see Christopher Duffy, *Russia's Military Way to the West: Origins and Nature of Russian Military Power, 1700-1800* (London: Routledge & Kegan Paul, 1981). From Waterloo to the Crimean War (1854-56), Russia was generally regarded as the preponderant landpower in Europe.

33. John Lewis Gaddis, *Russia, the Soviet Union, and the United States: An Interpretive History* (New York: Wiley, 1978), p. 18.

34. See "NSC 7: The Position of the United States with Respect to Soviet-Directed World Communism," March 30, 1948, reprinted in Etzold and Gaddis, *Containment*, pp. 164-69. The original containment concept is outlined in Kennan, "Moscow Embassy Telegram No. 511."

35. In his magisterial study of the Russian revolutionary tradition, Ulam observes that "the Russian countryside was, to the Marxist, a veritable kingdom of darkness, for unlike the Populists, he had never believed in the people being a repository of socialist virtue and thus viewed the villager's mentality with a mixture of puzzlement and apprehension" (*Russia's Failed Revolutions*, p. 321).

36. Daniels, *Russia*, p. 157.

37. Presumably the transition from socialism to communism cannot be effected until the class enemy has been defeated worldwide.

38. See Gilpin, *War and Change*.

39. E.g., Charles Krauthammer, "The Illusion of Star Wars," *New Republic*, May 14, 1984, p. 16. For a detailed discussion of why the Soviet Union would, or should, lack the opportunity to act effectively on an incentive to fight, see Payne, *Strategic Defense*, chap. 6.

40. See Alfred Vagts, *Defense and Diplomacy: The Soldier and the Conduct of Foreign Relations* (New York: King's Crown, 1957), chap. 9, "The Promise of Victory"; and Jack Snyder, *The Ideology of the Offensive: Military Decision Making and the Disasters of 1914* (Ithaca, N.Y.: Cornell Univ. Press, 1984).

41. The unflattering terms "useful idiots" and "deaf-mutes" were coined by Lenin; see Vladimir Bukovsky, "The Peace Movement and the Soviet Union," *Commentary* 73 (May 1982): esp. 38. Writing in 1921, Lenin said: "As a result of my observation during my emigration, I must say that the so-called cultivated elements in Western Europe and America are incapable of understanding the present state of things and the balance of forces today; these elements should be thought of as deaf and dumb and treated accordingly": quoted in Jean-François Revel, *How Democracies Perish* (1983; New York: Harper & Row, 1985), pp. 215-16.

42. Luttwak, *Grand Strategy of the Soviet Union*, p. 26.

43. See Vernon V. Aspaturian, "The Anatomy of the Soviet Empire: Vulnerabilities and Strengths," in Keith A. Dunn and William O. Staudenmaier, eds., *Military Strategy in Transition: Defense and Deterrence in the 1980s* (Carlisle Barracks, Pa.: U.S. Army War College, 1984), pp. 97-146; and Pipes, *Survival Is Not Enough*. Soviet problems range from the restlessness of client states in eastern Europe, through economic inefficiency and political corruption at home, to widespread alcoholism and the alienation of Soviet youth from the official values of the state.

44. Daniels, *Russia*, p. 159.

45. For sharply contrasting views of Soviet military power in the 1980s, see

Andrew Cockburn, *The Threat: Inside the Soviet Military Machine* (New York: Random House, 1983); and Luttwak, *Pentagon and the Art of War*, chap. 4.

46. People in the West today tend to be more impressed by the facts of the revolutions of 1917 than by the resiliency of a system that withstood two and a half years of terrible punishment in war. Moreover, one should recall that the relatively brief and geographically distant conflict with Japan in Manchuria had already triggered an abortive revolution in 1905. Of the March Revolution, Winston Churchill said: "It was primarily a patriotic revolt against the misfortunes and mismanagement of the war. Defeats and disasters, want of food and prohibition of alcohol, the slaughter of men, joined with inefficiency and corruption to produce a state of exasperation among all classes which had no outlet but revolt, could find no scapegoat but the Sovereign....No people had suffered and sacrificed like the Russians. No state, no nation, had ever gone through trials on such a scale and retained its coherent structure" *The Unknown War: The Eastern Front* (New York: Scribner, 1931), pp. 375, 376). An authoritative modern study is Norman Stone, *The Eastern Front, 1914-1917* (London: Hodder & Stoughton, 1975). Also useful is W. Bruce Lincoln, *Passage through Armageddon: The Russians in War and Revolution, 1914-1918* (New York: Simon & Schuster, 1986).

47. On the geopolitical and cultural roots of Soviet attitudes and practices, see Szamuely, *Russian Tradition*; Richard Pipes, *Russia under the Old Regime* (New York: Scribner, 1974); and Ronald Hingley, *The Russian Mind* (New York: Scribner, 1977). In the essentials of the relationship between state and individual, the Soviet Union is not only the linear descendant of Imperial Russia but indistinguishable from it. Western commentators both Left and Right notice the absence from the Soviet scene of some of those human rights that help define Western civilization. It is less common for them to notice that, aside from a minute number of dissident intellectuals, there is no evidence that downtrodden masses of exploited Soviet citizens are yearning seriously to be set free. The dissident movement is noticeable more for its political lack of consequence than for the fact of its existence. There have always been dissident intellectuals in Russia (as everywhere else); more impressive and politically significant is the continuing evidence of popular fear of disorder and respect for strong leadership.

48. See Crane Brinton, *The Anatomy of Revolution* (1952; New York: Random House, 1965).

49. See Robert Conquest, *The Great Terror: Stalin's Purge of the Thirties*, rev. ed. (New York: Collier, 1973); and Helene Carrere D'Encausse, *Stalin: Order through Terror* (1979; London: Longman, 1981).

50. Typical of the judgements by historians are those of S.J. Lewis that "January 1942 would find the German Army bleeding to death, leaderless, and in the vast expanses of Western Russia"; and: "The spring of 1942, by which time the Russian winter counteroffensive had ended, found the German Army a spent force, incapable of undertaking major military operations": *Forgotten Legions: German Army Infantry Policy, 1918-1941* (New York: Praeger, 1985), pp. 145, 163. Also see van Creveld, *Supplying War*, chap. 5; Matthew Cooper, *The German Army, 1933-1945: Its Political and Military Failure* (New York: Stein & Day, 1978), chaps. 18-21; Lewin, *Hitler's Mistakes*, chaps. 6-7; and Albert Seaton, *The German Army, 1933-45* (1982; London: Sphere, 1983), chaps. 7-9.

51. See Edward B. Atkeson, "Hemispheric Denial: Geopolitical Imperatives and Soviet Strategy," *Strategic Review* 4 (Spring 1976): 26-36. Weinberger has expressed the same thought: see Richard Halloran, "Weinberger Says Soviet Seeks Retreat to 'Fortress America,' " *New York Times*, March 14, 1983, p. A4. But see Peter Vigor, "The Soviet View of Geopolitics," in Zoppo and Zorgbibe, *On Geopolitics*, pp. 131-39.

52. V.I. Lenin, quoted in Caspar W. Weinberger, *Annual Report to the Congress, Fiscal Year 1987* (Washington, D.C.: U.S. Government Printing Office, 1986), p. 55.

53. The term was applied in the context of European responses to the irrefutable evidence of Libyan support of terrorism; see Charles Krauthammer, "Getting to Qaddafi," *Washington Post*, Jan. 10, 1986, p. A23. The Soviet Union, of all countries, takes a supremely political view of conflict and is most unlikely to confuse battlefield success with enduring victory. A perceptive treatment is Robert Bathurst, "Two Languages of War," in Derek Leebaert, ed., *Soviet Military Thinking* (London: Allen & Unwin, 1981), pp. 28-49.

54. Walt, "Alliance Formation," pp. 3-41.

10. Containment

1. See the historical survey by Cecil V. Crabb, *The Doctrines of American Foreign Policy* (Baton Rouge: Louisiana State Univ. Press, 1982).

2. See John Foster Dulles, "A Policy of Boldness," *Life*, May 19, 1952, 146-60. The 1952 Republican Platform declared that a Republican victory "will mark the end of the negative, futile and immoral policy of 'containment' which abandons countless human beings to a despotism and Godless terrorism which in turn enables the rulers to forge the captives into a weapon for our destruction": *Annals* 283 (Sept. 1952): 163.

3. See George F. Kennan, *Russia, the Atom and the West* (London: Oxford Univ. Press, 1958); *Memoirs, 1925-1950* (London: Hutchinson, 1968), esp. chap. 15; and *The Nuclear Delusion: Soviet-American Relations in the Atomic Age* (New York: Pantheon, 1982)—to cite but a fraction of Kennan's output. For a comprehensive list through 1982, see Barton Gellman, *Contending with Kennan: Toward a Philosophy of American Power* (New York: Praeger, 1984), pp. 159-64.

4. This topic runs like a thread though the excellent study by Shelford Bidwell and Dominick Graham, *Fire-Power: British Army Weapons and Theories of War, 1904-1945* (London: Allen & Unwin, 1982). Military reform theorists should ponder the wealth of meaning in Bidwell and Graham's historical judgment that "the generals of 1942-5 did not take long to discover that it was of little use to weave tactical arabesques round such soldiers as the Germans and Japanese" (p. 288). Enthusiasts for maneuver doctrine also might benefit from the observation that "thirty years after these now remote battles [of World War II] the idea persists, and among men learned enough not to deceive themselves, that there is some elegant formula for the overthrow of a powerful opponent" (p. 291).

5. Posen, *Sources of Military Doctrine*, p. 13.

6. See the discussion in Gray, *Maritime Strategy, Geopolitics, and the Defense of the West*, pp. 43-53.

7. See Freedman, *Evolution of Nuclear Strategy*, chap. 25; and "The First Two

Generations of Nuclear Strategists," in Paret, *Makers of Modern Strategy*, pp. 735-78.

8. See Colin S. Gray and Jeffrey G. Barlow, "Inexcusable Restraint: The Decline of American Military Power in the 1970s," *International Security* 10 (Fall 1985): 27-69.

9. Note the cautionary words in Simon Hornblower, *The Greek World, 479-323 BC* (London: Methuen, 1983), pp. 256-57.

10. Demosthenes, *Olynthiacs, Philippics, Minor Public Speeches, Speech against Leptines*, trans. J.H. Vince (Cambridge, Mass.: Harvard Univ. Press, 1970), pp. 233, 235.

11. See the discussion in Chapter 2, and the essays in Deibel and Gaddis, *Containment*.

12. Outstanding studies are Sherwig, *Guineas and Gunpowder*; and Piers Mackesy, *War without Victory: The Downfall of Pitt, 1799-1802* (Oxford: Clarendon Press, 1984).

13. "NSC 7: The Position of the United States with Respect to Soviet-Directed World Communism," p. 166.

14. "NSC 20/4: U.S. Objectives with Respect to the USSR to Counter Soviet Threats to U.S. Security," Nov. 23, 1948, in Etzold and Gaddis, *Containment*, p. 209.

15. "Keep That Gap from Getting Any Bigger" (interview with General Bernard Rogers), *U.S. News and World Report*, Jan. 20, 1986, p. 29.

16. See Howard, "Reassurance and Deterrence"; and Henry A. Kissinger, "Nuclear Weapons and the Peace Movement," *Washington Quarterly* 5 (Summer 1982): 31-39.

17. See the strong words in Richard Perle, "Color It Pallid for NATO," *Washington Times*, Feb. 5, 1987, pp. 1D-2D.

18. See J. Michael Legge, *Theater Nuclear Weapons and the NATO Strategy of Flexible Response*, R-2964-FF (Santa Monica, Calif.: RAND, 1983); Paul Buteux, *Strategy, Doctrine, and the Politics of Alliance: Theater Nuclear Force Modernization in NATO* (Boulder, Colo.: Westview Press, 1983); Treverton, *Making the Alliance Work*, chap. 2; and Betts, "Conventional Deterrence."

19. Brogan, *American Character*, p. 156.

20. Edward N. Luttwak, "On the Meaning of Victory," *Washington Quarterly* 5 (Autumn 1982): 18.

21. See Booth, *Strategy and Ethnocentrism*. Also relevant are Brogan, *The American Character*; Gray, *Nuclear Strategy and National Style*; and Carnes Lord, "American Strategic Culture," *Comparative Strategy* 5 (1985): 269-93.

22. Debating protagonists tend to organize theoretical and policy arguments into such opposed and allegedly incompatible pairs as mutual assured destruction *or* war fighting (as approaches to deterrence), continental (Europe-focused) *or* maritime (global) strategies, arms control *or* arms race, conventional *or* nuclear emphasis in NATO/Soviet regional defense posture for Europe—even war *or* peace.

23. There is a large literature on the implications of technological change for policy and strategy. For a diverse sampling, see Bernard Brodie, "Technological Change, Strategic Doctrine, and Political Outcomes," in Klaus Knorr, ed., *Historical Dimensions of National Security Problems* (Lawrence: Univ. Press of Kansas, 1976), pp. 263-99; Bryan Ranft, ed., *Technical Change and British Naval Policy, 1860-1939* (London: Hodder & Stoughton, 1977); T.H.E. Travers, "Technology,

Tactics, and Morale: Jean de Bloch, the Boer War, and British Military Theory, 1900-1914," *Journal of Modern History* 51 (June 1979): 164-88; Karl Lautenschläger, "Technology and the Evolution of Naval Warfare," *International Security* 8 (Fall 1983): 3-51; Maurice Pearton, *Diplomacy, War, and Technology since 1830* (1982; Lawrence: Univ. Press of Kansas, 1984); Franklin D. Margiotta and Ralph Sanders, eds., *Technology, Strategy, and National Security* (Washington, D.C.: National Defense Univ. Press, 1985), esp. chaps. by Irving B. Holley and Ralph Sanders; and Steven E. Miller, "Technology and War," *Bulletin of the Atomic Scientists* 41 (Dec. 1985): 46-48.

24. See Christopher Thorne, *Allies of a Kind: The United States, Britain, and the War against Japan, 1941-1945* (Oxford: Oxford Univ. Press, 1978).

25. See Maurice Matloff and Edwin M. Snell, *The War Department: Strategic Planning for Coalition Warfare, 1941-1942*, and Maurice Matloff, *The War Department: Strategic Planning for Coalition Warfare, 1942-1944*, both in United States Army in World War II series (Washington, D.C.: Office of the Chief of Military History, Department of the Army, 1953, 1959); and Millett and Maslowski, *For the Common Defense*, chaps. 13-14.

26. Lack of historical perspective on the process of competitive armament and deficient comprehension of its functions and standing vis-à-vis a more normal pattern in defense preparation are prominent among the sources of intellectual and policy weakness of the United States as a superpower. "The perils of the arms race" is a popular theme in criticism of military doctrines, weapons, and arms-control proposals, but U.S. political elites show a less than secure grip of understanding on the phenomenon. See Charles H. Fairbanks, Jr., "Arms Races: The Metaphor and the Facts," *National Interest* 1 (Fall 1985): 75-90.

27. There is a sense in which nothing fails like success: "It takes only one generation of successful peacekeeping to engender the belief among those not concerned with its mechanisms, that peace is a natural condition threatened only by those professionally involved in preparations for war" (Howard, "Reassurance and Deterrence," p. 316).

28. Secretary of Defense Caspar Weinberger has said that "should deterrence fail, U.S. strategy seeks the earliest termination of conflict on terms favorable to the United States, its allies, and its national security objectives. *Favorable means that if war is forced upon us, we must win—we cannot allow aggression to benefit the aggressor*" (emphasis added): *Annual Report to the Congress, Fiscal Year 1986* (Washington, D.C.: U.S. Government Printing Office, 1985), p. 27. Pertinent to this issue are Gray, "Nuclear Strategy"; and Luttwak, "On the Meaning of Victory."

29. Adda B. Bozeman, "U.S. Foreign Policy and the Prospects for Democracy, National Security, and World Peace," *Comparative Strategy* 5, no. 3 (1985): 241. See also Bozeman, *Politics and Culture*, pp. 340-56.

30. Bozeman, "U.S. Foreign Policy," p. 240.

31. See Caspar W. Weinberger, *Annual Report to the Congress, Fiscal Year 1988* (Washington, D.C.: U.S. Government Printing Office, 1987), pp. 85-98.

32. See the articles (by Melvin R. Laird, Colin S. Gray, and Jeffrey G. Barlow, and Robert W. Komer) that debate this "decade of neglect" thesis in *International Security* 10 (Fall 1985).

33. For a devastating in-house critique of 1980s-style congressional oversight of

the executive in defense matters, see Jim Courter, "Micromanaging Defense," *Washington Times*, Jan. 21, 1986, p. 2D.

34. For a very different opinion, see Robert S. Cooper, "The Coming Revolution in Conventional Weapons," *Astronautics and Aeronautics*, Oct. 1982, pp. 73-75, 84: "They [new conventional weapons] will render obsolete manned tactical forces and should make regional warfare untenable" (p. 73). Strongly contrasting views, con and pro respectively, are presented by Steven L. Canby, and Donald R. Cotter as a two-part article, "New Conventional Force Technology and the NATO-Warsaw Pact Balance," in *New Technology and Western Security Policy*, pt. 2, Adelphi Papers No. 198 (London: IISS, 1985), pp. 7-24 and 25-38.

35. Admirable recognition of this point drives the analysis in Robert P. Meehan, *Plans, Programs, and the Defense Budget* (Washington, D.C.: National Defense Univ. Press, 1985).

36. Schelling, *Arms and Influence*, chap. 1. An uncompromising critique of the tendency to replace military strategy with coercive diplomacy is Eliot A. Cohen, "Why We Should Stop Studying the Cuban Missile Crisis," *National Interest*, no. 2 (Winter 1986): 3-13.

37. I have discussed this issue at length in Colin S. Gray, *Strategic Studies and Public Policy: The American Experience* (Lexington: Univ. Press of Kentucky, 1982), chap. 4. Also see David Alan Rosenberg: "A Smoking Radiating Ruin at the End of Two Hours: Documents on American Plans for Nuclear War with the Soviet Union, 1954-55," *International Security* 6 (Winter 1981-82): 3-38; and "The Origins of Overkill," pp. 3-71. For a well-reasoned analysis skeptical of the diplomatic utility of the 1950s United States nuclear advantage, see Richard K. Betts, "A Nuclear Golden Age? The Balance before Parity," *International Security* 11 (Winter 1986-87): 3-32.

38. On the value of strategic forces for extended deterrence, see Carl H. Builder, *The Case for First-Strike Counterforce Capabilities*, P-6179 (Santa Monica, Calif.: RAND, 1978).

39. Quoted in van Creveld, *Fighting Power*, p. 29.

40. See Seaton, *German Army*; and Dennis E. Showalter, "A Dubious Heritage: The Military Legacy of the Russo-German War," *Air University Review* 36 (March-April 1985): 4-23.

41. In 1952 in Lisbon the North Atlantic Council approved a plan for the alliance to raise ninety-six divisions, active and reserve, within two years. In less than a year this ambitious program was defunct, overtaken by economic anxieties, by a sharp diminution in perception of the Soviet threat, and by eager acceptance of nuclear weapons as a cure-all substitute for the conventional forces that none of the major allies wished to be obliged to afford.

42. See Fen Osler Hampson, "Groping for Technical Panaceas: The European Conventional Balance and Nuclear Stability," *International Security* 8 (Winter 1983-84): 57-82; Martin, *NATO and the Defense of the West*, pp. 51-56.

43. Intellectual support for this proposition is provided in Robert Jervis: "Why Nuclear Superiority Doesn't Matter," *Political Science Quarterly* 94 (Winter 1979-80): 617-33; and *Illogic of American Nuclear Strategy*. For an attempt to bridge the gap between the logic of punitive and war-fighting deterrents, see Robert J. Art, "Between Assured Destruction and Nuclear Victory: The Case for the 'Mad-Plus'

Posture," in Russell Hardin et al., eds., *Nuclear Deterrence: Ethics and Strategy* (Chicago: Univ. of Chicago Press, 1985), pp. 121-40.

44. See Richard Ned Lebow, "The Soviet Offensive in Europe: The Schlieffen Plan Revisited?" *International Security* 9 (Spring 1985): 44-78.

45. I have explored this subject in Gray, "Global Protracted War." To date, there has been very little careful study of the possible conduct of protracted war in the shadow of central nuclear capabilities.

46. A valuable and rare exception is Record, *Revising U.S. Military Strategy*, esp. chap. 8.

47. See Gray, *Wartime Influence of Sea Power.*

48. *Operations, FM 100-5* (1982).

49. See Watkins et al., *Maritime Strategy*; and Reagan, *National Security Strategy*, pp. 29-30.

50. A Polish businessman, publishing and lecturing between 1899 and 1901, who predicted the general shape and much of the detail of the Great War. See I.S. Bloch, *Modern Weapons and Modern War* (London: Grant Richards, 1900); Travers, "Technology, Tactics, and Morale"; and Michael Howard, "Men against Fire: The Doctrine of the Offensive in 1914," in Paret, *Makers of Modern Strategy*, pp. 510-26.

51. See Nikolay Ogarkov, *Always in Readiness to Defend the Homeland*, trans. JPRS L/10412, March 25, 1982 (Moscow: Voyenizdat, 1982); Gareyev, *Frunze*; and M.A. Gareyev, "The Creative Character of Soviet Military Science in the Great Patriotic War," *Voenno-istoricheskii zhurnal*, no. 7 (1985).

52. From the time he became prime minister on Dec. 7, 1916, until (at least) the summer of 1918, David Lloyd George was in search of strategic schemes that might enable the British Army to scale down its efforts—and hence its casualties—on the Western Front in France and Belgium. The notes of a War Cabinet meeting held on June 10, 1917, record that in Lloyd George's view "the great defect of the War had been that we hit the enemy at his strongest instead of his weakest side": quoted in John Terraine, *The Road To Passchendaele: The Flanders Offensive of 1917, A Study in Inevitability* (London: Leo Cooper, 1977), p. 130. In a letter of Aug. 22, 1917, to the chief of the Imperial General Staff (Sir William Robertson), the commander of the British Expeditionary Force (Sir Douglas Haig) expressed his general opinion of "Eastern" schemes: "The one black spot in the whole picture of the war is our P.M.'s [Prime Minister's] desire to gain ground in secondary theatres as if he did not believe in our ability to beat the Germans themselves and wished to gain something with which to bargain at a Peace Conference" (p. 242). British preferences for a Mediterranean emphasis in allied strategy in 1942-44, while certainly reflecting some parochial interests, also stemmed from a genuine military conviction that a frontal amphibious assault upon an enemy fortress (the coast of northern France) was an unsound operation of war. The thesis that "Easterners" in reality proposed a "strategy of evasion"—a pejorative perspective on the strategy of "indirect approach"—see B.H. Liddell Hart, *Strategy: The Indirect Approach*, rev. ed. (London: Faber & Faber, 1967)—runs from the strategy debates of the two world wars to current arguments over whether the United States should accord first priority to the defense of NATO's Central Front.

53. Whereas the English word control means detailed direction, the French *contrôle* means general supervision.

54. In the times of Caesar Augustus the imperium meant the power to com-

mand armies. There was also a proconsular imperium (authority over approximately half of the provinces) and a "greater" imperium (*imperium maius*) that permitted the emperor (or *princeps*, first citizen) to interfere in, or control, the administration of those provinces formally under the jurisdiction of the Senate. See Starr, *The Roman Empire*, p. 13.

55. See Bozeman, "U.S. Foreign Policy," p. 241.

56. See George F. Kennan, *American Diplomacy: 1900-1950* (New York: New American Library, 1951); Stanley Hoffman, *Gulliver's Troubles; or, The Setting of American Foreign Policy* (New York: McGraw-Hill, 1968); and Dallek, *American Style of Foreign Policy*.

57. Holmes, *Mood/Interest Theory*, p. 6.

58. There is much to recommend the following judgments by Raymond Price: "Successful foreign policy is the domain of the head, not of the heart. Its focus is on the future, not the past. And in the long run, the morality of our choices will be judged by their consequences" ("America's Foreign Policy Dilemma," *Washington Times*, Jan. 15, 1987, p. 1D).

59. This point pervades the excellent article by Makubin Thomas Owens, "The Hollow Promise of JCS Reform."

11. Dynamic Containment

1. Long after I had settled upon the verbal formulation "dynamic containment," I discovered that a friend and former colleague had also made it his preference. See Max Singer, "Dynamic Containment," in Wildavsky, *Beyond Containment*, pp. 169-99. A good idea will bear multiple analysis and advocacy.

2. See S. Tyushkevich, "The Methodology for the Correlation of Forces," *Voyennaya Mysl*, FPD 0009/70 (June 1969): 26-39; and Michael Deane, "The Soviet Assessment of the Correlation of Forces: Implications for American Foreign Policy," *Orbis* 20 (Fall 1976): 625-36. For authoritative Soviet claims that the correlation of forces has shifted in their favor, see the references in Dziak, *Soviet Perceptions of Military Power*, p. 21. For some Soviet analytical disagreements over the correlation of forces, see entries 36 and 37 in Scott and Scott, *The Soviet Art of War*, pp. 186-90, 191-94. One should not forget the claim issued by Leonid Brezhnev in 1973: "A decisive shift in the correlation of forces will be such that by 1985 we will be able to exert our will whenever we need to" (quoted in Weinberger, *Annual Report, 1987*, p. 55).

3. Whether or not Soviet leaders think explicitly in terms of hegemony over Eurasia and eventually the world is less important than is the long-term logic of their policies, which is consistent with this characterization. For pertinent commentary, see Vigor, "The Soviet View of Geopolitics."

4. This is not to suggest that a dynamic containment policy strictly requires a shift of emphasis from the strategic offense to the strategic defense; moreover, the American public should be inoculated by the historical perspective of *dynamic* containment against unreasonable expectations of very near-term defensive solutions to the problems of nuclear risk. Strategic defense and political commitment to a containment task that is understood to be long term should function synergistically for the enhancement of national security. Strategic defense could help

render perception of nuclear risk more manageable in American domestic politics, and the respect for history implied by dynamic containment should provide the U.S. defense community, politically, with the time necessary to make strategic defense as much a physical reality as technology and considerations of cost-effectiveness will permit.

5. Valuable discussion of the questions of continuity in Russian/Soviet history may be found in the prepared statements of Cyril E. Black and Richard Pipes in Senate Committee on Armed Services, Subcommittee on Strategic Arms Limitation Talks, *The Limitation of Strategic Arms, Hearings*, 91st Cong., 2d sess. (Washington, D.C.: U.S. Government Printing Office, 1970), pp. 3-18, 18-25. Black advised: "The leaders of a nation can modify historically evolved institutions and values only to limited degree, and at any given moment the genuinely new elements in a nation's life are relatively few and those that have deep roots in the past are inevitably more influential" (p. 3). Pipes offered some background from Russia's colonial experience: "As a result of these acquisitions [the territorial conquests of the sixteenth through the nineteenth century], the Moscow government acquired early a great deal of expertise in handling foreigners; but this expertise it gained from administering subject peoples, Western and Oriental, not from dealing on equal terms with other sovereign states. The Office of Ambassadors in Moscow knew less, comparatively speaking, about foreigners than did the various administrative offices charged with responsibility for administering immense territories inhabited by peoples of differing races and religions. In some measure this also held true of the Imperial government and of the Soviet government; for techniques of administration tend to survive changes of elite" (p. 22).

6. See Richard B. Foster and Francis P. Hoeber, "Limited Mobilization: A Strategy for Preparedness and Deterrence," *Orbis* 24 (Fall 1980): 439-57. Also useful is Paul Bracken, "Mobilization in the Nuclear Age," *International Security* 3 (Winter 1978-79): 74-93.

7. For an attempted step in the right direction, see Reagan, *National Security Strategy*.

8. See Robert W. Komer, "Strategymaking in the Pentagon," and Robert J. Art, "Congress and the Defense Budget: Enhancing Policy Oversight," both in Art, Davis, and Huntington, *Reorganizing America's Defense*, pp. 207-29, 405-27; and Meehan, *Plans, Programs, and the Defense Budget*.

9. Senate Committee on Armed Services, *Defense Organization*, p. 15, also pp. 622-24, 637. See also President's Blue Ribbon Commission on Defense Management (the Packard Commission), *A Quest for Excellence*, Final Report to the President (Washington, D.C.: White House, 1986).

10. The benefits of parity are abundantly advertised in Jerome H. Kahan, *Security in the Nuclear Age: Developing U.S. Strategic Arms Policy* (Washington, D.C.: Brookings, 1975). A classic statement of the rationale for—indeed, the alleged technological inevitability of—parity is Wolfgang K.H. Panofsky, "The Mutual Hostage Relationship between America and Russia," *Foreign Affairs* 52 (Oct. 1973): 109-18.

11. See Betts, "Conventional Deterrence."

12. See Gray, "Verification of Non-Compliance." The principal safeguard against covert Soviet deployments of offensive arms in the context of a radical disarmament regime would have to be strategic defense.

13. Useful analyses include *Defense Planning and Arms Control*, Proceedings of a Special NSAI Conference, June 12-14, 1980 (Washington, D.C.: National Security Affairs Institute, National Defense University, 1980); and Richard Burt, "The Relevance of Arms Control in the 1980s," *Daedalus* 110 (Winter 1981): 159-77.

14. Mikhail Gorbachev has demonstrated that he can trump, politically, any attractive-sounding scheme for disarmament that the United States can advance. On Jan. 15, 1986, he proposed the complete elimination of all the nuclear weapons on earth, to be accomplished in three stages by the end of 1999 (see "Excerpts from the Soviet Leader's Statements on Arms Control Proposals," *New York Times*, Jan. 17, 1986, p. A8), a ploy designed not to advance negotiations in Geneva but to cause maximum embarrassment in Washington. A powerful voice of realism is Eugene V. Rostow, "Why the Soviets Want An Arms-Control Agreement, and Why they Want It Now," *Commentary* 83 (Feb. 1987): 19-26.

15. Bernard Brodie, *War and Politics* (New York: Macmillan, 1973), p. 452.

16. George T. Dennis, trans., *Maurice's Strategikon: Handbook of Byzantine Military Strategy* (Philadelphia: Univ. of Pennsylvania Press, 1984), p. 113. The subtitle promises more than the text delivers.

17. See Cleveland, *NATO.*

18. Pipes, *Survival Is Not Enough*, pp. 250, 256-57.

19. Ibid., p. 220.

20. See Fritz Fischer, *Germany's Aims in the First World War* (1961; New York: Norton, 1967), chaps. 1, 23 (esp. pp. 586-91); Kennedy, *British Naval Mastery*, chaps. 8-9; Ruddock F. Mackay, "Historical Reinterpretations of the Anglo-German Naval Rivalry, 1897-1914," in Gerald Jordan, ed., *Naval Warfare in the Twentieth Century, 1900-1945: Essays in Honour of Arthur Marder* (New York: Crane, Russak, 1977), pp. 32-44; Lambi, *Navy and German Power Politics;* and Clark G. Reynolds, *Command of the Sea: The History and Strategy of Maritime Empires, vol. 2, Since 1815* (1974; Malabar, Fla.: Robert E. Krieger, 1983), chap. 14.

21. See Watkins et al.

22. Quoted in C.J. Bartlett, "Statecraft, Power, and Influence," in Bartlett, ed., *Britain Pre-eminent: Studies in British World Influence in the Nineteenth Century* (London: Macmillan, 1969), p. 182.

23. Fred Charles Ikle, "NATO's 'First Nuclear Use': A Deepening Trap?" *Strategic Review* 9 (Winter 1980): 8-23; and John D. Steinbruner and Leon V. Sigal, eds., *Alliance Security: NATO and the No-First-Use Question* (Washington, D.C.: Brookings, 1983).

24. See Gray, *Nuclear Strategy and National Style*, chaps. 6, 8.

25. The length of the fuse can be only a matter of speculation. It is certainly the official view of SHAPE that NATO ground forces would be in need of tactical nuclear assistance after only a few days of combat. Partly in recognition of this probability, Soviet ground and tactical air forces are being trained and equipped to attempt a classic, nonnuclear *Blitzkrieg* for the purpose of effecting NATO's regional military ruin in a matter of days: that is to say, with such celerity that nuclear employment by NATO could not preclude success for Warsaw Pact forces. See C.J. Dick, "Catching NATO Unawares: Soviet Army Surprise and Deception Techniques," *International Defense Review* 19, no. 1 (1986): 21-26.

26. See Barry Blechman, "Is There a Conventional Defense Option?" *Washington Quarterly* 5 (Summer 1982): 59-66; European Security Study, *Strengthening*

Conventional Deterrence (New York: St. Martin's Press, 1983); Hampson, "Groping for Technical Panaceas"; and Barry Posen, "Measuring the Central European Conventional Balance," *International Security* 9 (Winter 1984-85): 47-88. The debate within NATO over conventional deterrence should recognize possible Soviet incentives as well as Western wishes. Richard Pipes has advised: "Improving NATO's conventional forces is certainly desirable, but it is unlikely of itself to prevent a war from turning nuclear. The assumption that underlies Western strategy—that the decision whether to resort to nuclear weapons will be for the West to make—may have made sense when first devised, but it seems unrealistic today in the light of what is known of Soviet plans and capabilities in this regard. A military command that has built its armed forces around a nuclear core is unlikely to defer use of it until the enemy has given it an excuse to do so"; once the Soviet Union sees war as unavoidable then in order to avoid a war of attrition "it will almost certainly have prompt recourse to nuclear weapons, since they alone offer it a chance of gaining a rapid and decisive victory" (*Survival Is Not Enough,* pp. 349-40). Pipes is out of step here with the views of some leading U.S. and British scholars concerning the latest developments in Soviet operational art and tactics; still, he might be correct. See John Erickson, Lynn Hansen, and William Schneider, *Soviet Ground Forces: An Operational Assessment* (Boulder, Colo.: Westview Press, 1986), pp. 87,215.

27. I am not sufficiently persuaded by the more optimistic elements of the analysis in Mearsheimer, *Conventional Deterrence.*

28. This tension is clearly emerging in European anxieties concerning SDI.

29. See Daniel O. Graham, *High Frontier: A New National Strategy* (Washington, D.C.: High Frontier, 1982).

30. Present trends in the willingness of the U.S. Congress to license tactical nuclear modernization are not particularly encouraging. Antinuclear sentiment among the publics of the European members of NATO sits uncomfortably with the nuclear reliance favored by NATO-European governments.

31. See Nathan Leites, *Soviet Style in War* (New York: Crane, Russak, 1982); and P.H. Vigor, *Soviet Blitzkrieg Theory* (New York: St. Martin's Press, 1983).

32. This concept is among the strongest developed in Clausewitz, *On War,* p. 119: "Everything in war is very simple, but the simplest thing is difficult. The difficulties accumulate and end by producing a kind of friction that is inconceivable unless one has experienced war....Friction is the only concept that more or less corresponds to the factors that distinguish real war from war on paper."

33. See Colin S. Gray, "War-Fighting for Deterrence," *Journal of Strategic Studies* 7 (March 1984): 5-28.

34. By far the best detailed exposition of a contrasting view is Jervis, *Illogic of American Nuclear Strategy.*

35. The problem with policy *practice* can be severe indeed. See Raymond W. Copson and Richard P. Cronin, "The 'Reagan Doctrine' and Its Prospects," *Survival* 29 (Jan.-Feb. 1987): 40-55. One should beware of crusading rhetoric and practice, but the core of the policy idea is plain enough. See Jack Wheeler, "Destabilizing the Soviet Empire," *National Security Record* (Heritage Foundation), no. 87 (Jan. 1986): 1-3.

36. See Parker, *Mackinder,* pp. 152-54, 245.

37. See Charles Wolf, Jr., *et al., The Costs of the Soviet Empire,* R-3073/1-NA

(Santa Monica, Calif.: RAND, 1983). A useful summary is Charles Wolf, Jr., "The Costs of the Soviet Empire," *Science* 230 (Nov. 29, 1985): 997-1002.

12. Disengagement

1. Problems are treated in Slocombe, "Extended Deterrence." The central difficulty is that NATO has a military strategy in the 1980s that was appropriate for the 1960s—when the doctrine of flexible response was debated at length and formally adopted in 1967. A 1968 Senate report said: "Since Hiroshima, our nuclear posture vis-à-vis the Soviet Union has moved progressivley from monopoly to massive superiority to exploitable superiority to our present posture of what is at best marginal superiority. The current tend is toward parity and a condition which some have characterized as 'unconditional mutual deterrence' under which no provocation short of a nuclear attack on the homeland would trigger a deliberate exchange of strategic nuclear weapons. . . . In general, our national policy has reflected our military posture. When we had massive nuclear superiority, our policy was massive retaliation. When we had an unambiguous or 'exploitable' superiority, our policy was flexible response": Senate Committee on Armed Services, Preparedness Investigation Subcommittee, *Status of U.S. Strategic Power, Report*, 90th Cong., 2d sess. (Washington, D.C.: U.S. Government Printing Office 1968), p. 3.

2. Some American military reformers believe that critically significant improvements in NATO's ability to hold or restore the Central Front in Europe could be achieved within projected defense budgets if military methods were improved. Landmark statements of this belief are Luttwak, "The Operational Level of War"; and Steven L. Canby, "Military Reform and the Art of War," *Survival* 25 (May-June 1983): 120-27. Canby argues: "United States and Western military inferiority is purely self-inflicted. It is a case of dated doctrine causing too few combat units, misuse of technology and manpower, and poor strategy and integration with allies" (p. 127).

3. But one must presume that the details of military staff talks would not be withheld from responsible officials and political leaders, as they were in Britain. As late as July 1914 the British Parliament and most cabinet ministers were as ignorant concerning the military talks with France as was the British Army's general staff concerning the details of the French war plan (with which the British Expeditionary Forces were to conform). For the full story, see Samuel R. Williamson, Jr., *The Politics of Grand Strategy: Britain and France Prepare for War, 1904-1914* (Cambridge, Mass.: Harvard Univ. Press, 1969).

4. The ill effects of a protracted relationship of security dependence are well recognized. See Jeffrey Record, "The Europeanization of NATO: A Restructured Commitment for the 1980s," *Air University Review* 23 (Sept.-Oct. 1982): 23-28; Howard, "Reassurance and Deterrence," pp. 309-24; Cohen, "Long-Term Crisis of the Alliance"; and Krauss, *How NATO Weakens the West*.

5. A sophisticated West German treatment of the structural problems of NATO is Uwe Nerlich, "Change in Europe: A Secular Trend?" *Daedalus* 110 (Winter 1981): 71-103.

6. For an attempt at calculating the influence of European contingencies, see

Ravenal, "Case for a Withdrawal of Our Forces." A leading historian of U.S. nuclear planning, David Alan Rosenberg, is entirely correct when he advises that *"U.S. nuclear strategy has been strongly shaped by the commitment to defend Western Europe"* (original emphasis): "U.S. Nuclear Strategy: Theory vs. Practice," *Bulletin of the Atomic Scientists* 43 (March 1987): 26.

7. Benefits are primarily in the realm of the most political of all economic issues, jobs, but are also related to the ability of eastern European countries to pay the service charges on their debts to Western banks.

8. Melvyn B. Krauss, "It's Time to Change the Atlantic Alliance," *Wall Street Journal*, March 3, 1983, p. 24. For the official reply, see Richard R. Burt, "Europe Pullout Isn't Deserved or Desirable," *Wall Street Journal*, March 28, 1983, p. 22. Krauss develops his thesis at length in *How NATO Weakens the West*.

9. For a carefully reasoned and computed analysis challenging this perception, see Klaus Knorr, "Burden-Sharing in NATO: Aspects of U.S. Policy," *Orbis* 29 (Fall 1985): 517-36. Knorr asserts that "with one exception [extended nuclear deterrence], any careful analysis will find it hard to conclude that the United States has been carrying, relative to national economic capacity, an inequitable share of the burdens that the major members of NATO (Class I and II) have assumed for purposes of military deterrence and defense vis-à-vis the U.S.S.R. Even a comparison limited to budgetary data cannot show inequity once allowance is made for the high cost of military manpower in the United States, and for the proportion of American forces earmarked for missions outside Europe and the Atlantic" (p. 534).

10. See G. Mancur Olson and Richard Zeckhauser, "An Economic Theory of Alliances," *Review of Economics and Statistics* 48 (1966): 266-79.

11. For one vision of a more flexible U.S. military posture, see Vlahos, "Maritime Strategy versus Continental Commitment?" Another vision is presented in Record, *Revising U.S. Military Strategy*. An analysis that strives for the exact center of the controversy is Keith A. Dunn and William O. Staudenmaier, *Strategic Implications of the Continental-Maritime Debate*, Washington Papers, vol. 12, no. 107 (New York: Praeger, 1984). See the discussion in Gray, *Maritime Strategy, Geopolitics, and the Defense of the West*, pp. 43-56.

12. A variant of this idea, stressing the necessity for the United States to be willing and able to act alone, is advanced in Simon Serfaty, "Atlantic Fantasies," *Washington Quarterly* 5 (Summer 1982): 74-81. Also relevant is Charles Krauthammer, "The Multilateralist Fallacy," *New Republic*, Dec. 9, 1985, pp. 17-20.

13. See the classic argument in B.H. Liddell Hart, "Marines and Strategy," *Marine Corps Gazette*, Jan. 1980, pp. 23-31 (first published in 1960).

14. This is not strictly true, but if the United States resolved to experiment with military disengagement on a "try it and see" basis, the allies would be motivated strongly to insure that the experiment failed.

15. The most common figure specified by NATO "restructurers" is a reduction of U.S. Army personnel in Europe from some 220,000 to roughly 100,000.

16. Given its pool of recently trained manpower, with suitable augumentation of equipment the *Bundeswehr* should be able to achieve a mobilized strength of twenty-four divisions (half of which would be armored), as contrasted with the current and long-standing count of twelve (plus six Territorial Army brigades). Always assuming adequate mobilization time, a force of twenty-four heavily

armed West German divisions fighting for their national territory would virtually guarantee that Pact forces could not achieve a walkover.

17. See Owen Harries, "The Uncertainty Principle," *National Interest*, no. 2 (Winter 1985-86): 125-28.

18. This argument is advanced persuasively in Lewis A. Dunn, *Controlling the Bomb: Nuclear Proliferation in the 1980s* (New Haven, Conn.: Yale Univ. Press, 1982).

19. Walter Laqueur, "Hollanditis: A New Stage in European Neutralism" *Commentary* 72 (Aug. 1981): 19-26. A contrasting perspective is Richard Eichenberg, "The Myth of Hollanditis," *International Security* 8 (Fall 1983): 143-59.

20. Krauss, "It's Time to Change the Atlantic Alliance." Also see Krauss, *How NATO Weakens the West*.

21. There is some merit in Michael Vlahos's claim that "military force in Europe since 1945 has focused on testing the cohesion of alliance systems (ours) and unacknowledged empires (theirs)" (*America*, p. 73).

22. There is some irony in the fact that the United States was second to none in 1945 in requiring barriers against any resurgence of militarism in postwar Germany and Japan. Given the importance of West Germany and Japan for the balance of power in Eurasia—indeed, their criticality should the United States disengage from most of its forward defense duties—Americans may come to believe that their pro-consuls in the late 1940s did their job too well.

23. For a fascinating comparative study, see Robert Wohl, *The Generation of 1914* (London: Weidenfeld & Nicolson, 1980).

24. Vlahos, *America*, p. 71. Vlahos, or perhaps his European youth in "gothic jeans" (it is not clear which, from the text), would seem to have confused Ronald Reagan with Gen. George S. Patton, Jr. Cf. the relatively optimistic analysis in Gebhard L. Schweigler, "Anti-Americanism in Germany," *Washington Quarterly* 9 (Winter 1986): 67-84.

25. The bare outline of an answer to this question may be found in Watkins et al., *Maritime Strategy*. Watkins writes: "As prudent military planners, the Soviets would, of course, prefer to be able to concentrate on a single theater; a central premise of U.S. strategy is to deny them such an option....The Soviets will probably focus their offensive on Central Europe, while attempting to maintain a defensive posture elsewhere. Instead, we must dilute their effort, divert their attention, and force them to divide their forces. We must control the type and tempo of conflict, making sure the Soviets understand that they can take no area for granted" (pp. 7, 11). For historical perspective, see the thoughtful studies by C.E. Callwell: *The Effect of Maritime Command on Land Campaigns since Waterloo* (Edinburgh: William Blackwood, 1897); and *Military Operations and Maritime Preponderance: Their Relations and Interdependence* (Edinburgh: William Blackwood, 1905).

26. It is reasonable to ponder the contemporary equivalents of coastal artillery and "coast-line battleships." Writing about the naval debate of the early 1880s, Harold and Margaret Sprout observed that "the prevailing defensive strategy still rested on the ancient doctrine of stopping an enemy at the coast. This strategy envisaged little more than defending our principal seaports from actual bombardment and hostile occupation, and practically ignored the problem of dealing with commercial blockades such as those which played so decisive a role in the War of

1812 and the Civil War": *The Rise of American Naval Power, 1776-1918* (1939; Princeton, N.J.: Princeton Univ. Press, 1967), p. 196. A useful essay is Lance C. Buhl, "Maintaining 'An American Navy,' 1865-1889," in Hogan, *In Peace and War,* pp. 145-73. The United States might choose to reduce very dramatically the offensive arsenal of its strategic forces and move to a defense-dominant posture, regardless of developments in Soviet strategic forces—always provided that the defense could achieve the requisite technical and tactical competence. Similarly, the United States could so fashion its general-purpose forces that expeditionary adventures much beyond the Caribbean would be beyond its ability. The U.S. Navy certainly could not justify fifteen carrier battle groups or four battleship surface-action groups if national security policy were only quarterspheric or hemispheric. See John Lehman, "The 600-Ship Navy," in Watkins et al., *Maritime Strategy,* pp. 32-36.

27. Statement of Nov. 18, 1938, quoted in Vlahos, *America,* p. 50.

28. The French theory of proportional deterrence would call for national courage of a suicidal quality, resting as it does upon the proposition that France need only threaten retaliatory damage disproportionate to the strategic value to the Soviet Union of a French defeat (by whatever means). One should recognize that a different quality of risk attends the conduct of hostilities against a nuclear-armed state as contrasted with a state not so armed; still, superpower strategic defenses that might be of marginal value for protection of the national territory against thousands of nuclear weapons ought to perform very successfully against relatively small third-party attacks.

29. For budgetary and force-planning purposes the U.S. Department of Defense in the 1960s adopted the "two and a half war" concept, which envisaged the waging of major land wars in Europe and the Far East and a minor conflict elsewhere, *simultaneously.* This expressed a political culture of optimism shorn of strategic judgment. On the political Left the practice of global containment since the late 1940s has predictably triggered the charge that the United States has become an imperial power; see, e.g., Ronald Steel, *Imperialists and Other Heroes: The Imperial Generation and the End of the American Dream* (New York: Random House, 1971). An instructive analysis is George Liska, *Career of Empire* (Baltimore, Md.: Johns Hopkins Univ. Press, 1978). The imperial theme is prominent in Brzezinski, *Game Plan.*

30. A forceful discussion of the actual and potential costs of a global containment policy is Robert W. Tucker, *The Purposes of American Power: An Essay on National Security* (New York: Praeger, 1981). Tucker has a discomforting knack of framing questions that threaten the jugular of orthodox thinking: e.g., "Why should we persist in commitments whose sacrifice would not risk our physical survival but whose retention does?" (p. 121).

31. See Nuechterlein, *America Overcommitted.*

32. It is a central tenet of revisionist theories of postwar Soviet-American relations that U.S. strategic encirclement of the Soviet Union, resting upon a misperception of Stalin's intentions (allegedly to expand his domain), generated countervailing Soviet hostility. By the logic of this model of reciprocal threat perception, it should follow that if the United States were to dismantle the political and military architecture of Eurasian containment, some approximation of peace could break out in Soviet-American relations. It may well be that Stalin was not

overeager to expand his empire beyond the reach of prompt discipline by his tanks and that the Soviet threat was exaggerated in the late 1940s and very early 1950s; however, it does not necessarily follow that an American policy course very different from containment could have precluded Soviet definition of the United States as an enemy. For a new study on this seemingly inexhaustible subject, see Larson, *Origins of Containment*.

33. Great trading states, as contrasted with old-fashioned military empires, may be the wave of the future, but international trading and financial systems are exceedingly vulnerable to interruption by conflict. See Richard Rosecrance, *The Rise of the Trading State: Commerce and Conquest in the Modern World* (New York: Basic Books, 1986).

34. See David A. Deese, "Oil, War, and Grand Strategy," *Orbis* 25 (Fall 1981): 525-55.

35. See Spykman, *America's Strategy in World Politics*, pp. 447-48: "The Old World is 2½ times as large as the New World and contains 7 times the population....industrial productivity is almost equally divided, but in terms of relative self-sufficiency, the Eurasian Continent with the related continents of Africa and Australia is in a much stronger position. If the three land masses of the Old World can be brought under the control of a few states and so organized that large unbalanced forces are available for pressure across the ocean fronts, the Americas will be politically and strategically encircled. There is no war potential of any size in any of the southern continents and South America can, therefore, offer the United States no compensaton for the loss of the balance of power in Europe and Asia." Spykman went on to warn: "There is still a danger that the erroneous ideas regarding the nature of the Western Hemisphere inherent in the isolationist position may tempt people to urge a defensive strategy in the belief that the New World could survive a German-Japanese victory abroad" (p. 450).

36. Vlahos, *America*, pp. 51-56.

37. Strategic culture is a scarcely less important theme of this book than geopolitics. Strategically interesting ideas for policy that affront the culture of the nation are not policy options; they are simply ideas. As Millett and Maslowski said of Emory Upton's 1870s scheme to "Germanize" the U.S. military establishment, policy "reflects a nation's characteristics, habits of thought, geographic location, and historical development. Built upon the genius, traditions, and location of Germany, the system he [Upton] admired could not be grafted onto America" (*For the Common Defense*, p. 258). Teutonophilia has recurred in some of the writings of the contemporary military reform caucus.

38. See Tucker, *The Purposes of American Power*, p. 118: "Our alliances do not contribute to our physical security. Instead, they constitute perhaps the principal threat to that security, since the prospect of using nuclear weapons is most likely to arise as a result of threats to their security."

39. "The preservation of a free Europe is vital to American security, but American power is vital to European survival" (Cohen, "Long-Term Crisis of the Alliance," p. 328).

40. This is unlikely to be true in eastern Asia. See Colin S. Gray, "Western Security and the Pacific: A Geopolitical Perspective," in *NATO's Sixteen Nations* 32 (April 1987): 42-47.

41. For an interesting historical review of the issue of foreign entangle-

ments, see Harvey Starr, "Alliances: Tradition and Change in American Views of Foreign Military Entanglements," in Booth and Wright, *American Thinking about Peace and War*, pp. 37-57.

42. In a very important sense the United States would still stand behind the political independence of Rimland Eurasia, whatever the degree of contraction of its formal alliance ties. Soviet leaders know that democracies tend to be politically volatile. A United States capable of disengaging, perhaps precipitately, from forward containment duties would be quite capable, no less precipitately, of reengaging. Even if it were unable to do so in sufficiently short order to preclude Soviet imperial gain, it could redraw its defense perimeter in such a way as to contain recent Soviet advances. Michael Vlahos has sketched (interestingly, if—as he himself implies—none too convincingly) "an emerging American realm," alternative to the NATO-focused structure of today, comprising "four spheres— the Anglo-Oceanic, the Latin American, the Bantu African, and the East Asian" (*America*, pp. 80-85). Optimistic prognoses for European security in the event of U.S. disengagement from NATO should be exposed to the following cautionary thoughts of Barry Posen: "While it is true that, from a theoretical perspective, the world would remain bipolar even in the absence of NATO, and many of the beneficial effects of bipolarity would probably remain, it also seems likely that the dissolution of NATO would spell a major decline in U.S. attention to European affairs. The United States' engagement in Europe could—at least for a time—be as ambivalent and erratic as Britain's during the 1920s and 1930s.... In the absence of NATO, and after a U.S. withdrawal from continental affairs, it seems likely that these peacetime and wartime problems [lack of coordination among prospective co-belligerents] could reemerge. As they did for Hitler, such problems might provide temptations for a future Soviet leader more daring than those we have seen recently" (*Sources of Military Doctrine*, pp. 241-42).

43. See Ernest Conine, "Germans Could Tilt Us toward Asia: Anti-Americanism Threatens Continued Support for Europe," *Los Angeles Times*, Dec. 15, 1986, p. II-5.

44. See E.P. Thompson, *Beyond the Cold War: A New Approach to the Arms Race and Nuclear Annihilation* (New York: Pantheon, 1982). Useful commentary on nuclear protest in Europe is Kissinger, "Nuclear Weapons and the Peace Movement."

45. I am not persuaded that even a well-armed and neutralist multinational western Europe would be able over the long run to avoid functional cooperation as an agent of Soviet *Weltpolitik*. The Soviet Union could not venture forth on the high seas in quest of greater and greater imperial security, leaving a powerful and potentially hostile western European garrison in its rear. While a western Europe independent of direct Soviet control must always have continental-distraction value, one should assume that the Soviet Union would strive to achieve the necessary degree of *contrôle*. Both for Moscow and for the European rump of erstwhile NATO members, *contrôle* would be far preferable to the costs of securing, and resisting, control.

46. In 1914 Germany was encouraged by the absence of formal alliance ties between Britain and France to hope, if not quite believe, that the former would stand aside. In 1940 the absence of alliance ties between the United States and

Britain, France, and the Netherlands fed a (temporary) belief in Tokyo that Japan might have an option for expansion in colonial southeast Asia that would not require the conduct of war with the United States. The point is that although the existence of formal commitments can never guarantee a sufficiency of deterrence—witness Hitler's invasion of Poland—their absence must function to breed hope in the minds of potential aggressors that the uncommitted nations will not intervene.

47. In the words of Barry Posen: "The continued existence of NATO presents the would-be aggressor with a difficult situation. The presence of the United States, a leader willing and able to take on a disproportionate share of the risks and costs of maintaining the status quo, ensures speedy reaction to expansionist gambits. The presence of a single great power in the alliance also helps secure and manage the defensive contributions of smaller states, who fear being left in the lurch should their futures be entrusted to the less dynamic middle powers" (*Sources of Military Doctrine*, pp. 242-43).

48. Fritz Ermath has argued that "policies of strategic retreat especially entail a risk of war as the favored party drives for irreversible gains while the loser reconsiders the cost of his retreat" ("Sources of Dispute Over Containment Strategy," pp. 37-38).

49. On the character of the Soviet system, see the monumental and chilling work by Mikhail Heller and Aleksandr M. Nekrich, *Utopia in Power: The History of the Soviet Union from 1917 to the Present* (1982; New York: Summit Books, 1986).

50. See Murray, *Change in the European Balance of Power*, esp. pp. 245, 365-66.

51. In the uncompromising words of Heller and Nekrich: "The Soviets are congenitally hostile to the West and reject its right to exist in its present form" (*Utopia in Power*, p. 730).

52. As Charles Krauthammer has observed, neoconservative opinion in the United States is advocating "an isolationism of ends: it will provide means, but only for a constricted set of interests, principally those required for American security narrowly defined"; by way of contrast, "Left isolationism is an isolationism of means: it still has internationalist aspirations but will not supply the means to carry them out": "Isolationism: A Riposte," *National Interest*, no. 2 (Winter 1985-86): 115.

13. Rollback

1. In this speech the president declared ideological warfare against nondemocratic regimes of the Right *and the Left*. He said, amidst some very strong anti-Soviet rhetoric, that "we must take actions to assist the campaign for democracy." President Reagan, "Promoting Democracy and Peace," speech before the British Parliament, June 8, 1982, *Current Policy*, no. 399 (Washington, D.C.: Department of State, Bureau of Public Affairs, Office of Public Communication, June 1982): 3.

2. It is assumed here that the Soviet Union is essentially an empire run by and for the benefit of Great Russians. See Luttwak, *Grand Strategy of the Soviet Union*, esp. chap. 1.

3. On Soviet–east European relations, see Charles Gati, "The Soviet Empire: Alive but Not Well," *Problems of Communism* 34 (March-April 1985): 73-86; and Milovan Djilas, "Eastern Europe within the Soviet Empire," in Conquest, *The Last Empire,* pp. 369-77.

4. I do not intend to suggest that the security clients of the Soviet Union in the Third World are mere passive pawns in the extended Soviet empire. A careful historical case study that demonstrates the importance of a client's own definition of its interests is W. Raymond Duncan, *The Soviet Union and Cuba: Interests and Influence* (New York: Praeger, 1985).

5. In a speech commemorating the fortieth anniversary of the United Nations, the president enunciated what was promptly called, inevitably, the Reagan Doctrine; in effect, he declared U.S. open season on the extra-European imperium of the Soviet Union. With reference to Afghanistan, Cambodia, Ethiopia, Angola, and Nicaragua, he called for negotiated settlements but then proceeded to assert: "Of course, until such times as these negotiations result in definitive progress, America's support for struggling democratic resistance forces must not and shall not cease" ("The President's Message of Hope at the General Assembly of the United Nations," *Congressional Record,* Oct. 24, 1985, p. E4790). This was a statement of dynamic containment, even of rollback, with a vengeance.

6. Another view is possible: namely, that evidence of Soviet willingness to suppress revolt is a source of the respect, awe, and fear that are essential for the authority of the Soviet state. Luttwak has made this same point about the Romans: "The lesson of Masada was that the Romans would pursue rebellion even to mountain tops in remote deserts to destroy its last vestiges, regardless of the cost" (*Grand Strategy of the Roman Empire,* p. 6).

7. "The Costs of the Soviet Empire," p. 999.

8. Henry S. Rowen, "Living with a Sick Bear," *National Interest,* no. 2 (Winter 1985-86): 14-15.

9. See Henry S. Rowen and Charles Wolf, Jr., "Soviet Economy and U.S. Opportunity," *Wall Street Journal,* Dec. 11, 1986, p. 32.

10. But see Vladimir Kontorovich, "Discipline and Growth in the Soviet Economy," *Problems of Communism* 34 (Nov.-Dec. 1985): 18-31. Kontorovich argues: "If a discipline drive does indeed succeed in accelerating economic growth, Lenin's dictum on the primacy of politics over economics under socialism will receive ringing confirmation. If Gorbachev succeeds, this will be an instance of a reinvigorated political system coming to the rescue of a sick economy. It will also demonstrate why the Soviet economy cannot collapse under the weight of its own problems. As long as the political system works, it simply will not allow the economy to collapse but will help it back to its feet in its idiosyncratic, yet workable, ways" (p. 31).

11. An outstanding analysis is Henry Young, *General War and Its Naval Implications,* HY80-0060F, Final Report for the Office of the Chief of Naval Operations, OP-65, Department of the Navy (Andover, Mass.: Henry Young, 1981).

12. In a press conference on Feb. 11, 1986, Reagan referred to sixteen choke points. See Michael R. Gordon, "Reagan's 'Choke Points' Stretch from Sea to Sea," *New York Times,* Feb. 13, 1984, p. 12; the map, with indicated choke points supplied by the Navy, is curious for its commissions and omissions. For a far more comprehensive, even somewhat indiscriminate, specification of maritime choke

points, see John Keegan and Andrew Wheatcroft, *Zones of Conflict: An Atlas of Future Wars* (New York: Simon & Schuster, 1986), pp. 152-53.

13. Liddell Hart, *History of the First World War*, p. 308.

14. See Reagan's "Darth Vader" speech in Orlando on March 7, 1983, in which he made explicit reference to "the aggressive impulses of an evil empire" *(New York Times*, March 9, 1983, p. 18).

15. See Gray, "Nuclear Strategy." But note the caveats that are stressed in Colin S. Gray, "Targeting Problems for Central War," *Naval War College Review* 33 (Jan.-Feb. 1980): 3-21.

16. See Samuel P. Huntington, "Conventional Deterrence and Conventional Retaliation in Europe," *International Security* 8 (Winter 1983-84): 32-56.

17. Stephen Peter Rosen, "Mutiny and the Warsaw Pact," *National Interest*, no. 2 (Winter 1985-86): p. 79.

18. The interventions by Russia's former allies, more or less explicitly in support of anti-Soviet forces, are all-but-forgotten episodes of twentieth-century history in Western policy debates, but the memory of them has been kept very much alive in the Soviet Union by careful official nurturing.

19. See Gaddis, *Strategies of Containment*, pp. 149, 174. In my opinion Gaddis makes too much of Eisenhower's passing references to preventive war as a possible option. Also relevant are Rosenberg, "The Origins of Overkill," pp. 25, 33-35; and Betts, "Nuclear Golden Age."

20. With reference to the 1961 revision of the Single Integrated Operational Plan (SIOP-63, approved finally in June 1962), one study has noted that there was "provision that Options I and II be exercised in pre-emptive fashion in response to unequivocal strategic warning of impending major Sino-Soviet Bloc attack upon the U.S. or her allies" (Ball, *Targeting for Strategic Deterrence*, p. 11).

21. Very much to the point is Paul W. Schroeder, "World War I as 'Galloping Gertie': A Reply to Joachim Remak," *Journal of Modern History* 44 (Sept. 1972): 319-45.

14. Strategy and Military Power

1. Weinberger, *Annual Report, 1987*, p. 29.

2. There are no true counterparts in other countries to the extra-official U.S. defense experts who testify before congressional committees, write openly, and speak publicly. The United States is unique in the requirement its political culture places upon government to be open. Only in the United States is open policy debate on defense issues conducted by people on all sides with tolerably equivalent access to specialized, and even highly classified, information. See Gray, *Strategic Studies and Public Policy*, chap. 11; Fred Kaplan, *The Wizards of Armageddon* (New York: Simon & Schuster, 1983); and Greg Herken, *Counsels of War* (New York: Knopf, 1985).

3. See Seaton, *The Russo-German War*, p. 212. Seaton notes, accurately for the time of his writing in the late 1960s, that "in British or United States terminology there is no equivalent for this use of the word operations (or the operative art)." However, this has changed with the latest version of *Operations, FM 100-5* (Washington, D.C.: Headquarters, Department of the Army, 1986). See Jay Luvaas,

"Thinking at the Operational Level," *Parameters* 16 (Spring 1986): 2-6; and David Jablonsky, "Strategy and the Operational Level of War," pt. 1, *Parameters* 17 (Spring 1987): 65-76.

4. Weinberger, *Annual Report, 1987*, pp. 28-29. Weinberger rightly associates the second phase with the policy document "NSC 68: United States Objectives and Programs for National Security," April 14, 1950, reprinted in Etzold and Gaddis, *Containment*, pp. 385-442.

5. See U.S. Department of Education, *What Works: Research about Teaching and Learning* (Washington, D.C.: U.S. Government Printing Office, 1986). For an intriguing description of one endeavor, the "Uses of History" course taught at Harvard, to help remedy the problem, see Richard E. Neustadt and Ernest R. May, *Thinking in Time: The Uses of History for Decision-Makers* (New York: Free Press, 1986). The Harvard course, worthy though it is, can assist only *la crème de la crème*. Peter McGrath, reviewing *Thinking in Time* for *Newsweek* (April 14, 1986, p. 71), made the following culturally penetrating observations: "Respectful of history as they are, Neustadt and May still treat it in the American way—pragmatically. And pragmatic history is founded on an unhistorical point of view, in that it implicitly denies the past any reality independent of present needs and wants. It puts the past in service to the present and thus abandons any attempt to give a disengaged account of events. In short, pragmatic history belongs more to rhetoric than to social science." Also see John Gooch, "Clio and Mars: The Use and Abuse of History," *Journal of Strategic Studies* 3 (Dec. 1980): 21-36. The real problem, and the area in need of urgent attention, lies in the public schools.

6. The Goths invaded the Balkans in 251, and although the integrity of the Roman Empire was restored, under Aurelian (270-75) it abandoned its forward positions beyond the Danube and the Rhine in Dacia and Germany. The Huns, who first appeared in Europe from central Asia in 370, put such pressure on the Goths and the Vandals that those tribes sought and were granted sanctuary in the Roman Empire (for whose armies they provided large numbers of thoroughly unreliable soldiers). A barbarian confederacy crossed the Rhine in 406; the Goths sacked Rome in 410; the Vandals repeated the exercise in 455; and the Roman Empire in the West ceased to exist even in form—the substance having long since vanished—with the death of Romulus Augustus in 476. See J.B. Bury, *Invasion of Europe by the Barbarians* (New York: Norton, 1967); and Arthur Ferrill, *The Fall of the Roman Empire: The Military Explanation* (London: Thames & Hudson, 1986).

7. See Stephen Runciman, *A History of the Crusades*, 3 vols. (Cambridge: Cambridge Univ. Press, 1951-54); Jonathan Riley-Smith, *What Were the Crusades?* (London: Macmillan, 1977); and Ronald C. Finucane, *Soldiers of the Faith: Crusaders and Moslems at War* (New York: St. Martin's Press, 1983). For the crusades in northern Europe, see Eric Christiansen, *The Northern Crusades: The Baltic and the Catholic Frontier, 1100-1525* (Minneapolis: Univ. of Minnesota Press, 1980). The *Reconquista*, the Christian reconquest of the Iberian peninsula, began in the first half of the eighth century (with Alfonso I of the Asturias) and was not complete until 1492, when the Moslems lost their toehold in Granada.

8. Furthermore, these ideas may be dangerous to U.S. national security. In the interests of promoting democracy, the United States is quite capable of helping to destabilize authoritarian regimes, even when the emergence of a friendly successor government is most unlikely. In addition, the legal genesis of many of

the new polities in Asia and Africa predated that process of genuine nation-building which is essential for the growth of a sense of community and almost prerequisite for Western-style democracy. See Henry Kissinger, "Too Much Euphoria?" *Washington Post*, March 14, 1986, p. A19. Of the tension and need for balance between "American values and American security," Kissinger notes: "Security without values is like a ship without a rudder; but values without security are like a rudder without a ship."

9. Weinberger, *Annual Report, 1987*, p. 28.

10. Jan Sejna and Joseph D. Douglass, Jr., accord Marxist ideology rather more importance than I do—*in political circumstances where the Communists are not fully in control*. They argue that "Marxism, communism and socialism are exploited by the Soviet Union in the quest for power. The Marxist-Leninist ideology is the sales pitch, the 'sugar that makes the medicine go down.' The target audience is the people, the working class, the uncommitted and unsuspecting, the poor and uneducated, as well as the intellectual middle class. By the time they understand what is happening, that they have been deceived, it is too late because the controls, i.e., the dictatorship of the proletariat, have been established and they are trapped. But the ideology that governs Soviet actions and policies is alive and well, and ready to be used against the next unsuspecting or vulnerable target country": *Decision-Making in Communist Countries: An Inside View* (Washington, D.C.: Pergamon-Brassey for Institute for Foreign Policy Analysis, 1986), p. 7.

11. IISS, *The Military Balance, 1985-1986*.

12. Ibid., pp. 17-20; Weinberger, *Annual Report, 1987*, pp. 14-19; and Weinberger, *Annual Report, 1988*, p. 17.

13. See John Gooch and Amos Perlmutter, eds., *Military Deception and Strategic Surprise* (London: Frank Cass, 1982); and Dick, "Catching NATO Unawares."

14. History-conscious planners on the Soviet general staff will not need reminding that the declining unity of command on the Axis side was of considerable value in 1944 in the clearing of the western Ukraine and the invasion of the Balkans. Axis unity of command eroded and then vanished as Hitler's fair-weather allies in Rumania, Hungary, and Slovakia came to recognize that the war was lost and that *sauve qui peut* should be the order of the day. There may be hope in Moscow that the 1944 example would be followed by some NATO members, but Soviet planners must recognize also that defection can be a two-way street: in the event of a NATO counterinvasion of Warsaw Pact territory, Soviet generals could be greatly embarrassed by a revolt of pact allies. Undersecretary of Defense Fred Charles Ikle raised the counterinvasion possibility at the 1986 *Wehrkunde* conference—to be met, predictably, with no little European consternation. See "U.S. Aide Faults NATO Strategy," *New York Times*, March 3, 1985, p. A2.

15. This point is emphasized in Murray, *Change in the European Balance of Power.* Also see Gibbs, *History of the Second World War, Grand Strategy*, 1:658-60. For "official history" at its best, see W.N. Medlicott, *History of the Second World War (Civil Series): The Economic Blockade*, 2 vols. (London: Her Majesty's Stationery Office, 1952, 1959). Medlicott observes, judiciously: "No one expected the blockade to win the war single-handed: for no one imagined that so strong an industrial state as Germany, which had entered a war in all the glory of its armed might and economic power, could be brought to surrender merely by the cutting off of its foreign supplies" (2:630).

16. "The führer's strategic problem was how to break out from Germany's narrow economic base to gain the resources required to fight a great war" (Murray, *Change in the European Balance of Power*, p. 362).

17. With reference to the Ribbentrop-Molotov Non-Aggression Pact of Aug. 23, 1939, Seaton goes so far as to claim that "in the event of war, Germany became an economic dependency of the Soviet Union, since a British blockade would cut off most of its sea-based imports" (*Russo-German War*, p. 9). This relationship of economic dependency was to contribute significantly to Stalin's conviction that Germany could not afford to wage war upon the Soviet Union.

18. The Third Reich committed itself by decree to mobilization for total war only on Jan. 13, 1942, when it was unmistakably plain that Stalingrad could neither be held nor relieved.

19. A very different opinion has been expressed by Jerry F. Hough in a letter to the editor ("Something Will Change in the Soviet Union," *Washington Post*, March 15, 1986, p. A21) with reference to Gorbachev's speech to the 27th Party Congress: "Why should Gorbachev lay out all the details? He wants to rule for 15 years. Let others work with the details and get blamed if they don't work out quite right. His job is to say there will be radical reform and to accumulate the power to ensure that it is done. He has, in fact, committed himself to reform in a way that none of us thought possible a year ago."

20. See Odom, "Soviet Force Posture," p. 7.

21. See Neil C. Livingstone and Joseph D. Douglass, Jr., *America the Vulnerable: The Threat of Chemical/Biological Warfare* (Lexington, Mass.: Lexington Books, 1986).

22. For example, Soviet tanks are calculated to total 53,000, including 33,600 that are obsolescent though still useful (IISS, *Military Balance, 1986-1987*, p. 37).

23. Ibid., p. 185.

24. Weinberger, *Annual Report, 1987*, pp. 85-88; *Annual Report, 1988*, pp. 65-69.

25. President's Blue Ribbon Commission on Defense Management, *An Interim Report to the President* (Washington, D.C.: White House, 1986), p. 5.

26. The flaws of the Schlieffen plan lay in its underestimation of the superior mobility and logistic circumstances of the defending party (which would be falling back upon its lines of communication); its neglect of the practical problems of operational command; and (as actually exercised in Aug.-Sept. 1914) a deficiency in strength where it was most required, on the right wing. Rather than enveloping the Anglo-French deployment, the German right wing—because of a paucity of field intelligence and of numbers—itself was threatened with envelopment.

27. To be fair, one could amend this sentence without fracturing the truth by deleting the phrase "for the United States." In the words of J.C. Wylie, "There is as yet no accepted and recognized general theory of strategy": *Military Strategy: A General Theory of Power Control* (1967; Westport, Conn.: Greenwood Press, 1980), p. 66.

28. The Soviet Union alone probably could not have overcome Nazi Germany either. Aside from the large distraction of scarce German military assets (perhaps 42 percent of the German Army's field divisions) promoted by the campaign in the Mediterranean and by preparations to meet the long-anticipated second front, the German ability in 1943-44 to conduct an orderly fighting withdrawal from its territorial conquests of 1941-42 was handicapped fatally by the combination of Hitler's insistence upon standing fast to the last man and the last bullet, and by the

superior tactical mobility of an increasingly motorized Red Army—a critical advantage largely made possible by the abundant supply of U.S. trucks. "At the end of the war the equipment holdings of the Soviet Armed Forces amounted to 665,000 motor vehicles. Of these, 427,000 had been provided mainly from United States sources during the war years" (Seaton, *The Russo-German War*, p. 589).

29. On the Soviet Navy, see Bryan Ranft and Geoffrey Till, *The Sea in Soviet Strategy* (Annapolis, Md.: Naval Institute Press, 1983); Office of the Chief of Naval Operations, Department of the Navy, *Understanding Soviet Naval Developments*, 5th ed. (Washington, D.C.: U.S. Government Printing Office, 1985); Bruce W. Watson and Susan M. Watson, eds., *The Soviet Navy: Strengths and Liabilities* (Boulder, Colo.: Westview Press, 1986); and Norman Polmar, *Guide to the Soviet Navy* (Annapolis, Md.: Naval Institute Press, 1986).

30. The idea of the *attaque brusquée* is to preempt the enemy's mobilization plans. The term is associated historically with General Hans von Seeckt, the unofficial chief of the German general staff, 1920-26. Seeckt needed a strategy that would buy Germany time to expand its 100,000-man "treaty" *Reichswehr* so that it could cope on more even terms with the mass conscript armies of France and Poland. See Posen, *The Sources of Military Doctrine*, pp. 185-88.

31. World War I did see some vertical escalation in types of weaponry, most notably with the German introduction of poison gas at Ypres on April 2, 1915. Following its defeat on the Marne and its retreat in good order to the Aisne, the German Army and its Franco-British enemy sought to envelop the (briefly) open flank to the West: this was the so-called "race to the sea" that concluded with the first battle of Ypres. The allied amphibious descent upon the Gallipoli peninsula in 1915 was a classic example of horizontal escalation, as was the subsequent development of a front in Macedonia (with Salonika as the base for operations).

32. The contemporary politics of NATO are well handled in Treverton, *Making the Alliance Work*. For valuable historical perspectives, see Sir Nicholas Henderson, *The Birth of NATO* (Boulder, Colo.: Westview Press, 1983); and Andre de Staercke et al., *NATO's Anxious Birth: The Prophetic Vision of the 1940s* (New York: St. Martin's Press, 1985).

33. An alternative view pervades Luttwak, *Pentagon and the Art of War*, esp. pp. 64, 111, 120.

34. See Desmond Ball, *Can Nuclear War Be Controlled?* Adelphi Papers No. 169 (London: IISS, 1981); Paul Bracken, *The Command and Control of Nuclear Forces* (New Haven, Conn.: Yale Univ. Press, 1983); Bruce G. Blair, *Strategic Command and Control: Redefining the Nuclear Threat* (Washington, D.C.: Brookings, 1985); and Gray, *Nuclear Strategy and National Style*.

35. See Chapter 2; Mackinder, *Democratic Ideals and Reality;* Spykman, *America's Strategy in World Politics*; and Spykman, *Geography of the Peace*. However, note the critique of Spykman in Vlahos, *America*, pp. 51-56.

36. See Colin S. Gray and Keith B. Payne, "Victory Is Possible," *Foreign Policy*, no. 39 (Summer 1980): 14-27. Critics of our thesis that the United States could win a nuclear war have tended to be so appalled by the very notion of winnable nuclear war that they have neglected to notice our specified prerequisite of a capability to limit homeland damage.

37. A deterrent rather than a compellent focus need not mean, however, that some variant of a societal-punitive nuclear strategy can suffice for the United

States. See Scott D. Sagan's contribution to "Correspondence: The Origins of Offense and the Consequences of Counterforce," *International Security* 11 (Winter 1986-87): 197-98.

38. See Schelling, *Arms and Influence*, pp. 69-91; Gray, *Nuclear Strategy and National Style*, chap. 8; and Paul Stockton, *Strategic Stability between the Super-powers*, Adelphi Papers No. 213 (London: IISS, 1986), pp. 55-71.

39. See Steinbruner and Sigal, *Alliance Security*. Quite inexcusably, many Western commentators provide quotable fuel for Soviet propagandists by being careless in their terminology as between first *use* and first *strike*. First use, meaning the initiation of nuclear conflict, is employed in contrast to the concept of first strike, which means the initiation of nuclear conflict *with the intention of attempting to disarm the enemy*. This distinction is sufficiently clear, so critically important, and of such long standing that one should be suspicious when a commentator confuses the two terms.

40. Paradoxically, perhaps, Jervis, *The Illogic of American Nuclear Strategy*, is willing to place far more reliance on the ripple or trickle-down effects of strategic nuclear deterrence than I am.

41. See Gray, *Wartime Influence of Sea Power*.

42. Mackinder, "Geographical Pivot of History," pp. 259-60. The classic study is Edwin A. Pratt, *The Rise of Rail-Power in War and Conquest, 1833-1914* (Philadelphia: Lippincott, 1916).

43. In the apposite words of G.J. Marcus, "Strategically, the significance of the blockading squadrons is that they formed the essential covering screen for the multitudinous activities of our warships and merchantmen all over the world. It was the blockades which secured the small divisions and single ships guarding the far-flung territories of the British Empire. Without these covering squadrons the operation of the convoy system would have been impossible. So, too, would have been the numerous conjunct expeditions against the French colonies, and the continual flow of supply-ships which nourished the British Army in the Peninsula. In short, the blockades did the work that was expected of them. Gradually but surely, Napoleon was urged on to his destruction. The abiding and determining factor in the chapter of events between Nelson's last and greatest victory and the crucial Russian campaign of 1812 was the maritime supremacy of Great Britain and the unremitting blockade of the enemy's ports": *The Age of Nelson: The Royal Navy, 1793-1815* (New York: Viking Press, 1971), pp. 439-40. Also see the classic essay by J. Holland Rose, "Sea Power *versus* Land Power, 1803-14," in *Man and the Sea: Stages in Maritime and Human Progress* (Cambridge: W. Heffer, 1935), pp. 219-39.

44. Such a nuclear (or chemical) assault might not have the strategic counter-force character that is so familiar in the arsenal exchange models. Instead, the Soviet Union might confine itself to attacking very selectively those assets in the continental United States that would be critical for the training, arming, assembly, and transportation of general-purpose military power abroad; e.g., the arrival of several handfuls of Soviet ICBM warheads on U.S. Gulf and Atlantic ports would utterly wreck NATO's prompt-reinforcement schedule. The value of strategic defenses for the preclusion or at least complication of this Soviet option is developed in Keith Payne: "The Deterrence Requirements for Defense," *Washington Quarterly* 9 (Winter 1986): 139-54; and *Policy Implications of Enduring Warfighting*

Capability: Prolonged War and Strategic Defense, report prepared for the Defense Nuclear Agency (Fairfax, Va.: National Institute for Public Policy, 1986).

45. The classic treatment is Corbett, *Some Principles of Maritime Strategy*, pt. 2.

46. See Friedman, "U.S. Maritime Strategy"; Watkins et al., *The Maritime Strategy*; and Linton F. Brooks, "Naval Power and National Security: The Case for the Maritime Strategy," *International Security* 11 (Fall 1986): 58-88.

47. For an ambitious endeavor to outline such a design, see Helmut Schmidt, *A Grand Strategy for the West: The Anachronism of National Strategies in an Interdependent World* (New Haven, Conn.: Yale Univ. Press, 1985).

48. See Payne, *Strategic Defense*.

49. The significance of this mission is well treated in Dennis M. Gormley, "A New Dimension to Soviet Theater Strategy," *Orbis* 29 (Fall 1985): 537-69; and Manfred Wörner, "A Missile Defense for NATO Europe," *Strategic Review* 14 (Winter 1986): 13-19.

50. But *if* relatively near-term Western strategic defensive deployments could deny the Soviet Union the ability to enforce a short-war condition, the United States might achieve the technological basis to reassert strategic superiority. I must hasten to add that I recognize both the problematic character of the all-important *if* and the strength of the Soviet incentive to preclude (whether by preventive military action or negotiated war termination) U.S. wartime restoration of strategic superiority. It is for these reasons, *inter alia*, that the national and allied military strategy recommended in this chapter requires of the strategic forces only that they function very robustly as a counterdeterrent to possible Soviet strategic nuclear initiatives.

51. See Fred Charles Ikle: "Can Nuclear Deterrence Last Out the Century?" *Foreign Affairs* 51 (Jan. 1973): 267-85; "NATO's 'First Nuclear Use,' " pp. 18-23; and "Nuclear Strategy: Can There Be a Happy Ending?" *Foreign Affairs* 63 (Spring 1985): 810-26.

52. Enthusiasts for a redefined extended deterrent should not be permitted to pass casually over the essential precondition of maintaining a strategic forces' counterdeterrent. Since the "revolution in military affairs" of the 1950s, Soviet general staff theorists have asserted a war-fighting theory of strategic-force military utility that might not easily be denied under the press of dire events. Soviet authors have argued: "The Strategic Rocket Forces have become the basis of the Soviet armed forces' combat power by virtue of their ability to accomplish in the shortest time possible their mission of destroying the enemy's nuclear attack forces, to demolish the main groupings of his troops, and to devastate his entire military-economic potential.... At the foundation of the new means of conducting armed struggle is the concerted effort to annihilate the strategic nuclear forces of the aggressor, but also to strike the most important military-economic targets, groupings of troops, and organs of political and military control. Toward the fulfillment of this mission are directed the efforts of all the services, with the leading role belonging to the SRF, atomic submarines, and long-range aviation": M.M. Kirian et al., *Voennotekhnicheskii progress i Vooruzhennye sily SSSR* (Moscow: Voenizdat, 1982), pp. 295, 314. Should Soviet leaders anticipate defeat in a protracted conflict, they would probably require a great deal of dissuasion from a selective attack on U.S. military power at source. U.S. strategic defensive deployments could be critical to sustaining a sufficient level of Soviet dissuasion: see

Payne, *Policy Implications of Enduring Warfighting Capability*. Furthermore, U.S. official understanding of the Soviet theory of war might prove gravely deficient: see Benjamin S. Lambeth, "On Thresholds in Soviet Military Thought," *Washington Quarterly* 7 (Spring 1984): 69-76; and John Van Oudenaren, *Deterrence, Warfighting, and Soviet Military Doctrine*, Adelphi Papers No. 210 (London: IISS, 1986).

53. See Vigor, *Soviet Blitzkrieg Theory*.

54. See the growing threat detailed in Gormley, "A New Dimension to Soviet Theater Strategy."

55. There is, and will likely long remain, a basic problem for NATO in quantities—of soldiers, ammunition, fighting vehicles, and territory. For an optimistic appraisal, see Mearsheimer, *Conventional Deterrence*, p. 188: "Certainly NATO does not have the capability to win a conventional war on the Continent against the Soviets. NATO does have, however, the wherewithal to deny the Soviets a quick victory and then to turn the conflict into a lengthy war of attrition, where NATO's advantage in population and GNP would not bode well for the Soviets. In short, NATO is in relatively good shape at the conventional level." Another relatively optimistic survey is "NATO's Central Front," *Economist*, Aug. 30, 1986, supplement, pp. 46ff. A clear-eyed view of NATO's problems in implementing its Conventional Defense Initiative is Stephen J. Flanagan, "Emerging Tensions over NATO's Conventional Forces," *International Defense Review* 20, no. 1 (1987): 31-39.

56. I am indebted for these terms to my colleague Roger Barnett of the National Institute for Public Policy.

57. The classic treatment of interior and exterior lines of operation is Baron Antoine-Henri de Jomini, *The Art of War* (1838; Westport, Conn.: Greenwood Press, 1971), pp. 100-132. Whether or not lines of operation are interior is a function of time as well as of geographic distance; e.g., given the probable ease with which Soviet overland lines of communication to its Far Eastern provinces could be interdicted, the U.S. Navy would likely be acting on interior lines vis-à-vis Soviet military power in eastern Asia. Working control of the sea can provide the advantage of operations on interior lines even against a country whose central land position is well served by railroads. Anglo-American maritime (and air—denying the enemy timely reconnaissance) command in 1942-44 forced a severely resource-constrained Nazi Germany to garrison *Festung Europa* from the North Cape to the Dodecanese with scarce military assets that could not prudently be moved. While fighting for its life on the Eastern Front with 2,800,000 men as of Dec. 31, 1943, Germany had no fewer than 2,440,000 men deployed beyond its frontiers in the West (Seaton, *The Russo-German War*, p. 396). B.H. Liddell Hart asserts that *"amphibious flexibility is the greatest strategic asset that a sea-based power possesses. It creates a distraction to a continental enemy's concentration that is most advantageously disproportionate to the resources employed"* (original emphasis): "Marines and Strategy," p. 31. Liddell Hart should be amended to read that "amphibious flexibility is the *second* greatest asset"; the greatest is a major continental ally.

58. Historical analogies include, first, the relationship between the Russo-German war and the Anglo-American campaign against Germany in the Mediterranean and then in France; and, second, the relationship between Grant's campaign in the Wilderness, and then before Petersburg and Richmond, and

Sherman's progress in Georgia and the Carolinas. See Gray, *Wartime Influence of Sea Power*, chap. 13.

59. I have in mind the Gallipoli and Salonika enterprises of World War I, and the campaigns in Sicily and Italy in World War II. Orthodox opinion notwithstanding, the Germans were probably fortunate that the Western allies elected to crawl from the toe of Italy to the Po rather than invade the Balkans—where they would have threatened to turn the flank of the German military position in the East and endangered Germany's supply of oil and other strategic raw materials from Rumania and Hungary. Facing an increasingly powerful Anglo-American alliance that enjoyed a historically unusual measure of command of the sea and relevant air space (and whose heavy bomber force almost fully occupied the fighter assets of the *Luftwaffe* in defense of the German homeland), Hitler could not have dared to strip bare his garrisons in France and Norway in order to concentrate against an allied invasion of the Balkans.

60. Wylie has observed: "Prior to the middle of the twentieth century no one had set forth in writing the second half of the maritime theory of warfare, the exploitation of control at sea toward the establishment of control on the land" (*Military Strategy*, p. 39). In the context of a nuclear-armed Soviet enemy much work remains to develop the theory of how maritime command can be translated into favorable military decisions ashore.

61. For a parallel analysis, see Vlahos, "Maritime Strategy versus Continental Commitment?"

62. "Glittering opportunities" are promised in Hugh K. O'Donnell, Jr., "Northern Flank Maritime Offensive," *U.S. Naval Institute Proceedings* 111 (Sept. 1985): 42-57.

63. "But planning for certitude is the greatest of all military mistakes, as military history demonstrates all too vividly" (Wylie, *Military Strategy*, p. 85).

64. Watkins et al., *The Maritime Strategy*.

65. *Operations, FM 100-5* (1986); and London, *Military Doctrine and the American Character*.

66. See Weinberger, *Annual Report, 1987*, pp. 128-32; and Robert L. Pfaltzgraff, Jr., and Uri Ra'anan, eds., *The U.S. Defense Mobilization Infrastructure: Problems and Priorities* (Hamden, Conn.: Archon Books, 1983).

67. Weinberger, *Annual Report, 1987*, pp. 230-34; and *Annual Report, 1988*, pp. 223-28.

68. In *A Grand Strategy for the West*, p. 153, Helmut Schmidt recommends strongly that "none of us...undertake major steps in the external security sector without previously consulting our allies." However plausible this sounds, it could translate in practice into policy paralysis for the United States. Schmidt had the SDI very much in mind (see pp. 61-63). Allied consultation, rather than prior notification, would most likely have aborted the SDI.

69. Inevitably, there is some tension among the need to communicate clearly to the NATO allies that the days of nuclear dependency are past; the desirability, for prewar deterrence, of Soviet uncertainty as to the scale of the nuclear risks of an invasion; the undesirability of the Soviet Union's being so fearful of nuclear use by NATO that it deems it prudent to strike first and hard with nuclear weapons; and U.S. unwillingness to deny all operational utility to any kind and scale of nuclear

employment. At the very least, the official U.S. position would be both no early nuclear use and no automatic powder trail from a theater war to a central war.

15. Conclusions

1. Caspar Weinberger has characterized the scale of U.S. military-competitive ambition in the following way: "Whether the United States should be willing to accept a position of parity in military power with the Soviet Union over the longer run can be debated. But about our current defense programs, there should be no illusions. We are not trying to regain the early [1950s] margin of advantage. Rather, we are struggling to win the resources to ensure parity in military power" (*Annual Report, 1987*, p. 73).

2. The Peace of Westphalia in 1648, the Congress of Vienna in 1815, and the Peace of Versailles in 1919 all redistributed power and shuffled the pawns; they set the stage for the next phase of the enduring game of power politics.

3. Kissinger argues that "Public support for defense and for resistance to Soviet challenges can be sustained in the democracies only by demonstrating that the West is not the cause of confrontations" ("Nuclear Weapons and the Peace Movement," p. 36).

4. The character of Soviet tyranny is exposed mercilessly in Heller and Nekrich, *Utopia in Power*.

5. Their distinctive history and culture instruct Soviet leaders to work determinedly to secure a permissive balance of power.

6. Mackinder, "Geographical Pivot of History," p. 261, fig. 5.

7. To understand Mackinder, it is essential to consult both his own writings and Parker, *Mackinder*. Zoppo and Zorgbibe, *On Geopolitics*, is a collection of outstanding essays but is strangely light in its coverage of Halford Mackinder. Paret, *Makers of Modern Strategy*, a recent monumental collection of essays on strategic thought, both omits any contribution on the subject of geopolitics—in contrast to the work to which it is a sequel, Edward Mead Earle, ed., *Makers of Modern Strategy: Military Thought from Machiavelli to Hitler* (Princeton, N.J.: Princeton Univ. Press, 1941)—and does not even contain index entries for Mackinder, Spykman, or geopolitics. This is not a criticism of Paret; unlike the situation in 1941, there is today no rich vein of recent geopolitical theory to be presented and assessed.

8. In 1944-45 the U.S. government essentially abdicated its political responsibilities for the higher direction of the war in Europe to Gen. Dwight D. Eisenhower, who was pursuing strictly military objectives. In large measure, allied military statecraft in 1944-45 could have prevented the geostrategic problems of NATO's Central Front. See Erickson, *The Road to Berlin*, esp. pp. 331-37.

9. For the view that Soviet writers and officials have been uninterested in Mackinder's Heartland thesis, or indeed in any Western geopolitical doctrines, see Vigor, "The Soviet View of Geopolitics."

10. I do not imply that strategic forces have lost, or must lose, *all* extended deterrent value; that a nuclear war for certain cannot be controlled and its conduct *must* be a self-defeating exercise; or that Soviet thinking on the operational use of

strategic nuclear forces is very well understood in the United States. See Gray, *Nuclear Strategy and National Style*.

11. John R. Elting, *The Super-Strategists: Great Captains, Theorists, and Fighting Men Who Have Shaped the History of Warfare* (New York: Scribner, 1985), p. xiii.

12. Weinberger, *Annual Report, 1987*, pp. 78-81.

13. Ibid., pp. 78-79: "If the United States decides that it is necessary to commit its troops to combat in a specific situation, we must commit them in sufficient numbers and with sufficient support to win.... The necessity to win requires a clearly defined, achievable objective—not unlimited objectives."

14. See Stephen Peter Rosen, "Vietnam and the American Theory of Limited War," *International Security* 7 (Fall 1982): 83-113; Bruce Palmer, Jr., *The 25-Year War: America's Military Role in Vietnam* (Lexington: Univ. Press of Kentucky, 1984), pp. 129-93; Cohen, "Why We Should Stop Studying the Cuban Missile Crisis"; and Harry G. Summers, Jr., *Vietnam War Almanac* (New York: Facts on File, 1985), pp. 324-27.

15. Allies in Asia, too, should be required to do much more for the defense of their region. See Edward A. Olsen, "Determinants of Strategic Burdensharing in East Asia: The U.S.-Japan Context," *Naval War College Review* 39 (May-June 1986): 4-21.

Index

Adler, Selig, 89

Afghanistan, 72, 167, 169, 172; and Reagan Doctrine, 165; Soviet invasion of, 24, 63, 81, 101, 102, 166

Africa, 101, 138, 249 n 35; democracy in, 142, 255 n 8; and France, 85; and Reagan Doctrine, 165; and Soviet Union, 24, 26, 109, 132, 137, 145, 167, 171, 178

AirLand Battle doctrine, U.S., 81, 86, 126, 190, 225 nn 17, 18, 227 n 35

air power, 126, 157, 190

Alaska, 104

Alexander (the Great), 31

Alexander I (of Russia), 103

Allaun, Frank, 94

Allende, Salvador, 169

American Revolution, 64, 213 n 14, 219 n 13

Americas, 26, 109, 110, 155, 203 n 21, 249 n 35

Amin, Hafizullah, 102

Angell, Norman, 23

Anglo-Japanese Alliance of 1902, 5

Anglo-Russian Convention (1907), 98, 232 n 16

Angola, 101, 111, 142, 166, 169, 172

anti-communism, 127, 141

arms control, 52, 57, 60, 62, 111, 172, 208 n 47; and arms race, 113, 177; and national security, 24, 29, 73-74, 135; and noncompliance, 135-36; and Soviet Union, 122, 243 n 14

Asia, 98, 122, 142, 145, 177, 251 n 46; allies in, 101, 263 n 15; democracy in, 255 n 8; and Reagan Doctrine, 165; and Soviet Union, 36, 51, 70, 137, 178; U.S. forces in, 150, 151. *See also* Eurasia

Asquith, Herbert, 15

Athens, 27, 31, 33, 37

Atlantic alliance, 11

Australia, 109, 249 n 35

Austria-Hungary, 98, 174

balance of power, 23, 26, 76, 77, 85, 92, 93, 99, 110, 221 n 3; European, 2, 13, 15, 19, 32, 34-35, 58, 69, 73, 98, 104, 117, 121, 203 n 22; global, 197; and national security, 196; in New World, 104; and peace, 206 n 24; and United States, 90, 224 n 4

Baldwin, Stanley, 41

Bay of Pigs, 168

Betts, Richard K., 228 n 39

Blücher, Marshal, 203 n 22

Bolsheviks, 96-97, 103, 108-9, 117, 168, 231 n 14

Booth, Ken, 43, 53, 54-55

Boulding, Kenneth, 222 n 15

Bozeman, Adda, 121

Braudel, Fernand, 208 n 52

Brezhnev, Leonid, 225 n 16, 241 n 2

Bright, John, 23

Brodie, Bernard, 136

Brzezinski, Zbigniew, 82, 224 n 12, 225 n 16

Builder, Carl, 14

Bulgaria, 78, 101

Bundy, McGeorge, 13